GEOGRAPHICAL
PSYCHOLOGY

GEOGRAPHICAL PSYCHOLOGY

Exploring the Interaction of Environment and Behavior

EDITED BY Peter J. Rentfrow

AMERICAN PSYCHOLOGICAL ASSOCIATION

WASHINGTON, DC

Published by
American Psychological Association
750 First Street, NE
Washington, DC 20002
www.apa.org

To order
APA Order Department
P.O. Box 92984
Washington, DC 20090-2984
Tel: (800) 374-2721; Direct: (202) 336-5510
Fax: (202) 336-5502; TDD/TTY: (202) 336-6123
Online: www.apa.org/pubs/books
E-mail: order@apa.org

In the U.K., Europe, Africa, and the Middle East, copies may be ordered from
American Psychological Association
3 Henrietta Street
Covent Garden, London
WC2E 8LU England

Typeset in Goudy by Circle Graphics, Inc., Columbia, MD

Printer: Maple Press, York, PA
Cover Designer: Berg Design, Albany, NY

The opinions and statements published are the responsibility of the authors, and such opinions and statements do not necessarily represent the policies of the American Psychological Association.

Library of Congress Cataloging-in-Publication Data

Geographical psychology : exploring the interaction of environment and behavior / edited by Peter J. Rentfrow. — First edition.
    pages cm
  Includes bibliographical references and index.
  ISBN-13: 978-1-4338-1539-3
  ISBN-10: 1-4338-1539-7
  1. Environmental psychology. 2. Human geography—Psychological aspects. I. Rentfrow, Peter J.
  BF353.G47 2014
  155.9'1—dc23
                                2013013605

British Library Cataloguing-in-Publication Data

A CIP record is available from the British Library.

Printed in the United States of America
First Edition

http://dx.doi.org/10.1037/14272-000

CONTENTS

CONTRIBUTORS

Tomas Brodin, PhD, Department of Ecology and Environmental Science, University of Umeå, Umeå, Sweden

Felix Cheung, BA, Department of Psychology, Michigan State University, East Lansing

Cindy K. Chung, PhD, Department of Psychology, The University of Texas at Austin

Jean Clobert, PhD, Station d'Ecologie Expérimentale du CNRS à Moulis USR, Moulis, France

Agathe Colléony, MSc, Centre for Behaviour & Evolution, Newcastle University, Newcastle, England

Lucian Gideon Conway III, PhD, Department of Psychology, University of Montana, Missoula

Julien Cote, PhD, Laboratoire Evolution et Diversité Biologique, CNRS-Université de Toulouse, Toulouse, France

Richard Florida, PhD, Martin Prosperity Institute, Rotman School of Management, University of Toronto, Toronto, Canada

Sean Fogarty, PhD, Department of Environmental Science and Policy, University of California, Davis

Alyssa S. Fu, MA, Department of Psychology, Stanford University, Stanford, CA

Laura Janelle Gornick, PhD candidate, Department of Psychology, University of Montana, Missoula

Shannon C. Houck, PhD candidate, Department of Psychology, University of Montana, Missoula

Markus Jokela, PhD, Institute of Behavioural Sciences, University of Helsinki; and Population Research Institute, Helsinki, Finland

Nicole M. Lawless, MS, Department of Psychology, University of Oregon, Eugene

Robert V. Levine, PhD, Department of Psychology, California State University, Fresno

Richard E. Lucas, PhD, Department of Psychology, Michigan State University, East Lansing

Hazel Rose Markus, PhD, Department of Psychology, Stanford University, Stanford, CA

Stewart J. H. McCann, PhD, Psychology Department, Cape Breton University, Sydney, Nova Scotia, Canada

Charlotta Mellander, PhD, Department of Economics, Finance and Statistics, Jönköping International Business School, Jönköping, Sweden

Damian R. Murray, PhD candidate, Department of Psychology, University of British Columbia, Vancouver, Canada

Daniel Nettle, PhD, Centre for Behaviour & Evolution, Newcastle University, Newcastle, England

Shigehiro Oishi, PhD, Department of Psychology, University of Virginia, Charlottesville

Nansook Park, PhD, Department of Psychology, University of Michigan, Ann Arbor

James W. Pennebaker, PhD, Department of Psychology, The University of Texas at Austin

Christopher Peterson, PhD, Department of Psychology, University of Michigan, Ann Arbor

Victoria C. Plaut, PhD, Berkeley Law, University of California, Berkeley

Peter J. Rentfrow, PhD, Department of Psychology, University of Cambridge, Cambridge, England

Stephen Reysen, PhD, Department of Psychology, Texas A & M University, Commerce

Mark Schaller, PhD, Department of Psychology, University of British Columbia, Vancouver, Canada

Andrew Sih, PhD, Department of Environmental Science and Policy, University of California, Davis

Thomas Talhelm, PhD candidate, Department of Psychology, University of Virginia, Charlottesville

Jodi R. Treadway, MA, Department of Psychology, University of Georgia, Athens

Evert Van de Vliert, PhD, Department of Psychology, University of Groningen, Groningen, Netherlands, and University of Bergen, Bergen, Norway

Huadong Yang, PhD, School of Business, Economics and Informatics, Birkbeck, University of London, London, England

GEOGRAPHICAL
PSYCHOLOGY

INTRODUCTION

PETER J. RENTFROW

Geography matters. The neighborhoods, cities, and states we live in provide the backdrop against which so many of life's important events occur. They are the places where friendships are formed, lovers meet, families are conceived, and dreams are pursued. They are where we learn about ourselves, explore our identities, and construct our worldviews. These are the places where the psychology of everyday life unfolds. The places in which we live vary so much in terms of their social, economic, political, cultural, climatic, and physical characteristics that one cannot help but wonder how they contribute to our own behavior. Having lived in many cities in the United States and United Kingdom, I am always struck by how differently people in different places behave and interact with each other. For example, a slight nod and smile to a stranger is an acceptable greeting in Austin, Texas, but such behavior would be considered an affront in New York City and possibly perverted in London. How do the places in which

http://dx.doi.org/10.1037/14272-001
Geographical Psychology: Exploring the Interaction of Environment and Behavior, P. J. Rentfrow (Editor)

we live contribute to our psychological development? Is there a place for geography in psychology?

It is well established that geography is necessary for developing a complete understanding of human behavior. Indeed, geography is a cornerstone of several of the social and behavioral sciences. *Economic geography*, for example, examines the ways in which location and spatial factors affect economic prosperity and job growth. *Social epidemiology* focuses on the social determinants of health and its incidence and distribution across geographic regions. And *political geography* investigates the influence of local demography and historical migration patterns on election returns and the quality of representation by elected officials. Although each discipline has a different focus, the key theme to emerge from all of them is that social and physical characteristics of the environment significantly affect health, well-being, attitudes, and identity—constructs at the core of psychology.

This volume attempts to make the case that our understanding of psychological phenomena can be greatly informed by a geographical perspective—one that explores the spatial organization of psychological phenomena and considers how individual characteristics, social entities, and physical features of the environment contribute to their organization. The chapters in the book highlight the ways in which social and physical features of the environment, such as local demography, political and economic institutions, topography, and climate, influence and interact with psychological processes. The perspectives described herein complement and extend theory and research in several areas of psychology, including social, personality, cultural, environmental, evolutionary, and comparative. By bringing together streams of research at the intersection of geographical psychology, I have tried to show how widely studied psychological constructs relate to and are influenced by broad social, ecological, economic, and political forces. At the same time, this research demonstrates the relevance of psychology for understanding macro-level processes. Ultimately, this book is designed to inform researchers about the value of examining psychological phenomena and their spatial components.

Two areas of psychological research that acknowledge the importance of location and spatial factors are cultural and environmental psychology. Cultural psychology has broadened psychology's focus from the effects of the immediate social environment to the impact that chronic macro-level situations have on cognition, emotion, and behavior (Markus & Kitayama, 1991). However, research in cultural psychology typically focuses on the cultural factors that shape cognition and behavior (e.g., intellectual histories, social norms) and gives less attention to the impact of social geography (e.g., population structures, political systems) or physical geography (e.g., climate, ecology) on such processes (Oishi & Graham, 2010; Yamagishi, 2011). Environmental psychology has demonstrated the various ways in which physical features of the environment influence and interact with human behavior (Craik, 1973). However, much of the work in this area concentrates on components of the immediate environment (e.g., offices, homes, public places) and devotes less attention to aspects of the broader environment (e.g., neighborhoods, cities, states, regions).

Geographical psychology attempts to bridge research across areas of psychology and other disciplines by investigating the spatial organization and geographical representation of psychological phenomena and the mechanisms guiding those processes. The research described in this volume considers how ecological, climatic, and psychological factors contribute to the spatial organization of cultural values, personality traits, attitudes, moral beliefs, and political ideology. The work also presents evidence indicating that personality, political ideology, well-being, happiness, human virtues, and personal concerns are related to several important geographic social indicators. In addition, the research in this book shows how aspects of the social and physical environment influence and interact with health, well-being, prosociality, identity, creativity, and community orientation. Collectively, the chapters in this volume provide a foundation for developing theory and research in geographical psychology.

OVERVIEW OF THIS VOLUME

The book is divided into three parts. The first part focuses on the environmental and psychological mechanisms that contribute to the spatial organization of psychological phenomena. Chapter 1 deals with the impact of climate, Chapter 2 with terrain, Chapter 3 with pathogens, Chapter 4 with human migration, and Chapter 5 with migration in nonhuman animals. The second part examines the geographical distribution of psychological characteristics and their associations with individual demographics, social entities, and physical features of the environment. Chapter 6 focuses on personality traits, Chapter 7 on political ideology, Chapter 8 on well-being, Chapter 9 on character strengths, and Chapter 10 on values. The final part of the volume takes an integrative perspective by focusing on the interactions between individuals and the environments in which they live. Chapter 11 focuses on residential mobility and happiness; Chapter 12 on the physical characteristics of places and helping behavior; Chapter 13 on social tolerance, psychological openness, and economic innovation; Chapter 14 on regional cultures and identity; and Chapter 15 on economic deprivation and social behavior.

Mechanisms Underlying Geographical Variation in States, Traits, and Behaviors

Part I of this volume is concerned with the question, How do geographical differences in thoughts, feelings, and behavior come about? Van de Vliert and Yang (Chapter 1) focus on the impact of climate and economic prosperity on geographical differences. The climate–economic theory they propose provides a framework for examining geographical differences in a range of social and psychological phenomena. They challenge single-factor explanations for geographical differences and argue that variation in cultural values is the result of the interaction between the climatic demands and economic conditions of regions. The authors present evidence indicating that individuals residing in countries with demanding climates and economic difficulties display more communal and collectivistic values compared with individuals who live in less harsh environments. They conclude that geographical differences in cultural value systems are the result of long-standing adaptations to environmental demands and pressures.

Conway, Houck, and Gornick (Chapter 2) propose that physical topography contributes to geographical differences in values and personality traits. They argue that frontier terrain, which is treacherous and has limited vegetation, attracts individuals who are independent and capable of surviving such harsh conditions. Over time this results in large proportions of individuals with agentic qualities. The authors present empirical evidence at both national and regional levels of analysis indicating that individualism is higher in areas with frontier terrains than in less demanding and more developed areas. They conclude that studying the physical topography of nations and regions within nations is necessary for developing a complete understanding of geographical variation in cultural value systems.

Murray and Schaller (Chapter 3) propose that geographical differences in psychological characteristics are due, in part, to ecological variation in the prevalence of infectious diseases. They argue that the risk of exposure to parasitic diseases has, over generations, influenced the ways in which individuals interact with each other and their environments. The authors provide empirical evidence indicating that disease-causing pathogens contribute to geographic variation in personality, sexual behavior and sociosexual attitudes, value systems, conformity, family relations, ethnocentrism, moral judgments, and political ideology. They conclude that disease-causing pathogens are influential mechanisms responsible for geographical variation in human psychology.

Jokela (Chapter 4) focuses on the ways in which selective migration contributes to geographical differences in personality and behavior. Drawing on interactionist theories positing that individuals seek out environments that satisfy and reinforce their psychological needs, Jokela argues that individuals' decisions about where to live are based, at least in part, on their personalities. He reviews theory and research on residential mobility and migration and presents evidence indicating that individual differences in personality are directly linked to people's intentions to move and their desires about where to move. He concludes that the study of residential mobility can inform our understanding of why people move from one place to another and can shed light on the impact of migration on geographical differences.

For a broader perspective on the origins of geographical differences, Cote, Clobert, Brodin, Fogarty, and Sih (Chapter 5) focus on the associations between personality traits and spatial ecology in nonhuman animals. Since the field's inception, psychologists have recognized the value of studying nonhuman animals to develop and test hypotheses about human behavior. The authors demonstrate that animal research can yield useful insights into migration and geographical differences. They review theory and research on the links between personality and migration patterns in a number of nonhuman animal species and make comparisons between findings from studies with nonhuman animals and humans.

Geographical Representation of Social Psychological Phenomena

Part II shifts away from the mechanisms that bring about geographic differences and focuses on the manifestation of those differences on social indicators. This section examines the question, How are the psychological characteristics of individuals expressed at a geographic level of analysis? In Chapter 6, I address this question by examining personality differences across the United States. I offer a brief historical overview of theory and research on geographical differences in personality and present a model for conceptualizing the processes through which personality becomes represented on geographic social indicators. I then present evidence showing statewide differences in the Big Five personality domains and provide evidence indicating that state-level personality traits are linked to indicators of health, crime, social capital, political ideology, social tolerance, and economic innovation. I argue that the geographic representation of personality traits results from mutually complementary bottom-up and top-down processes.

McCann (Chapter 7) provides a psychological perspective for understanding regional differences in political, social, and economic conservatism in the United States. He reviews theory and research in political psychology on the links between personality and political orientation, which show robust links between the Big Five personality domains and political conservatism. He then presents data on the relations of state-level personality variables to political, social, economic, and overall conservatism. Consistent with research at the individual level, the evidence indicates that states with large proportions of open and emotionally unstable residents display lower rates of conservatism. This work demonstrates that a macro perspective can help bridge psychological theory with theory and research in political science.

Lucas, Cheung, and Lawless (Chapter 8) provide evidence for geographic differences in subjective well-being. Although typically studied at the individual level, there is increasing interest in assessing regional levels of well-being. Studying regional variation in well-being has the potential to identify broad social, economic, or political factors that might contribute to well-being, which has both theoretical and practical importance. The authors review previous investigations of regional differences in well-being within the United States. They also analyze new data that help to resolve some of the initial discrepancies that have emerged regarding regional differences in well-being. The evidence makes it clear that happiness and satisfaction with life are geographically clustered within the United States and that those regional differences are associated with important social indicators.

Park and Peterson (Chapter 9) focus on regional differences in character strengths and well-being. A dominant theme in this chapter concerns the challenges faced when working with aggregate data. Whereas most of the work covered in other chapters focuses on one geographic level of analysis, the authors examine regional variation at multiple levels of analysis, from Spanish provinces and municipalities to American states and cities. They show that the average level of well-being and the most prominent character strengths in places are associated with aggregate-level social indicators, including suicide rates, entrepreneurial activity, physical fitness, and volunteerism. They conclude by arguing that an accurate understanding of how regions vary psychologically requires careful study of geographical variation at multiple levels of analysis.

Chung, Rentfrow, and Pennebaker (Chapter 10) provide evidence for regional differences in psychological values and personal concerns across the United States. Thus far, most of the work on geographical differences in psychological characteristics has relied on self-report data. In this chapter, the authors examine regional differences in psychological values by analyzing essays written about personal concerns that were submitted to a national radio station. This novel approach revealed regional differences in psychological values and personal concerns. The values that are most central to residents of particular regions are reflected in state-level indicators of health, well-being, crime, economic prosperity, and community involvement. The authors conclude that the places in which people live strongly affect values and beliefs.

Person × Environment Interactions

The theme of Part III is Person × Environment interactions. The central question examined in this section is, How do the psychological characteristics of individuals interact with features of the environments in which they live? Talhelm and Oishi (Chapter 11) address this question by examining the effects of residential mobility on self-concept, group support, and well-being. The theme of the chapter focuses on the causes and consequences of mobility for individuals and for communities. The authors review research indicating that residential mobility influences helping behavior, personality, and happiness in individuals. They also present evidence indicating that individuals who move frequently participate less in their communities than people who do not move residences and that communities with large proportions of transplanted residents display low levels of social capital. This research demonstrates the ways in which individual traits and regional characteristics affect residents and communities alike.

Reysen and Levine (Chapter 12) examine the ways in which individual characteristics, place characteristics, and culture interact to affect helping behavior. Drawing on research concerned with situational determinants of helping behavior, the authors offer a broad reconceptualization of situations that includes local norms and cultural values. They review laboratory-based studies of helping behavior, as well as studies of real-world helping and the relation to environmental factors, which show variations between cities that differ in size and geographic location. They conclude that focusing solely on either person or environmental factors ignores the complexity of human behavior and the unseen influence of prior generations on people today.

Florida and Mellander (Chapter 13) discuss person–environment interactions on creativity and openness. They review research in psychology, geography, and economics to build a theory that explains regional differences in economic innovation and social tolerance. The theory posits that regional innovation and tolerance are due, in part, to the influx of creative and open-minded individuals to particular areas and in response to the social and cultural diversity in those areas. In this way, the characteristics of individuals and place characteristics effectively reinforce one another. The work presented demonstrates how theory and research in psychology, geography, and economics can be integrated to understand geographic variation in important psychological and economic factors.

Fu, Plaut, Treadway, and Markus (Chapter 14) focus on regional identities and discuss the links between place and identity. They review literature on regional cultures and develop the concept of the cultural cycle to explain how the places in which people live shape their self-views. The cultural cycle concept is based on the idea that people's thoughts, feelings, and worldviews and the norms, practices, and products of regions complement each other. The authors develop this concept by exploring the connections among the histories, norms and practices, and psychological tendencies of various regions in the United States. They conclude that analyses of cultural differences in self and well-being should focus on regional variation in addition to national variation.

In the final chapter, Nettle and Colléony (Chapter 15) examine how the economic characteristics of neighborhoods influence the thoughts, feelings, and behaviors of residents. They discuss results from the Tyneside Neighborhoods Project, an ongoing study of how behavior varies geographically within one city in Northeast England. Using direct behavioral observation, surveys, experimental economic games, and field experiments, they show that the economic characteristics of neighborhoods have significant effects on residents' attitudes and behavior. Their results indicate that social behavior in different parts of a city can be as divergent as the differences between populations of different countries observed in many cross-cultural studies. The authors conclude that comparisons of people at multiple geographic levels—within nations, regions, and cities—are necessary for developing a thorough understanding of the various factors that shape social behavior.

CONCLUSION

My aims in putting this volume together are to inform psychologists about the ways in which a geographical perspective can add to theory and research in psychology and to inspire researchers to embark on this new line of investigation. With that in mind, I recruited the leading experts who are mapping this uncharted terrain and identifying important landmarks for future exploration. Their work provides compelling examples of the relevance of geography for psychology. Collectively, the work also demonstrates a wide range of methods for conducting geographical research in psychology.

By bringing together the different perspectives, it is my hope that the field of psychology can broaden its research focus and begin to chart new directions of inquiry that recognize the ways in which geographical factors link to psychological and behavioral processes and vice versa. Indeed, the work presented in this volume shows clearly that our understanding of psychology and behavior can be informed by examining geographical variation in social, political, ecological, and economic factors. The research also shows the relevance of psychology for understanding macro-level processes that are typically beyond the scope of psychological investigations. Taken together, the chapters in this volume provide a solid foundation on which to develop and test hypotheses about the connections between people and the places in which they live.

More generally, this book provides further evidence for psychology's central location within the social and natural sciences (Boyack, Klavans, Börner, 2005) by highlighting its connections with geography, economics, biology, epidemiology, and political science. Indeed, it is only by integrating theory and research across disciplines that psychologists will be able to develop a thorough and complete understanding of human behavior and the social world. Thus, expanding our focus to include a geographical perspective will help situate psychology in a larger context and inform our understanding of the broader social, historical, political, and economic factors that shape human psychology and behavior.

REFERENCES

Boyack, K. W., Klavans, R., & Börner, K. (2005). Mapping the backbone of science. *Scientometrics, 64,* 351–374. doi:10.1007/s11192-005-0255-6

Craik, K. H. (1973). Environmental psychology. *Annual Review of Psychology, 24,* 403–422. doi:10.1146/annurev.ps.24.020173.002155

Markus, H. R., & Kitayama, S. (1991). Culture and the self: Implications for cognition, emotion, and motivation. *Psychological Review, 98,* 224–253. doi:10.1037/0033-295X.98.2.224

Oishi, S., & Graham, J. (2010). Social ecology: Lost and found in psychological science. *Perspectives on Psychological Science, 5,* 356–377. doi:10.1177/1745691610374588

Yamagishi, T. (2011). *Trust: The evolutionary game of mind and society.* London, England: Springer.

I

MECHANISMS UNDERLYING GEOGRAPHICAL VARIATION IN STATES, TRAITS, AND BEHAVIORS

1

WHERE ON EARTH DO COLLECTIVISTS LIVE? CLIMATO–ECONOMIC IMPACTS ON INGROUP LOVE AND OUTGROUP HATE

EVERT VAN de VLIERT AND HUADONG YANG

Humans are small-group animals. Thus, by nature they tend to distinguish between ingroups and outgroups. Intriguingly, some are driven more by the boundaries between their ingroups and outgroups than others. The *some* we have come to call *collectivists*, the *others* we have come to call *individualists*, and the in-betweens we have come to place on a continuum that connects these opposites (e.g., Gelfand, Bhawuk, Nishii, & Bechtold, 2004; Hofstede, 2001; Oyserman, Coon, & Kemmelmeier, 2002; Triandis, 1995). Given that all plants and animals on earth adapt to demands and resources of their habitat, one may wonder to what extent collectivists are likewise reflecting adaptations to demands and resources of the human habitat. Hence, the question, Where do collectivists live?

In previous endeavors to answer this overly general question, scholars have related population-level collectivism to geographic latitude (Hofstede, 2001), climatic demands (Georgas, Van de Vijver, & Berry, 2004), parasitic

http://dx.doi.org/10.1037/14272-002
Geographical Psychology: Exploring the Interaction of Environment and Behavior, P. J. Rentfrow (Editor)

disease burden (Fincher & Thornhill, 2012; Schaller & Murray, 2011; see also Chapter 3, this volume), settlement in frontier regions (Kitayama, Conway, Pietromonaco, Park, & Plaut, 2010; Kitayama, Ishii, Imada, Takemura, & Ramaswamy, 2006), economic resources (Inglehart & Baker, 2000; Inglehart & Welzel, 2005), and the like. All those perspectives have tremendously enriched our understanding of cultural collectivism. However, single-factor clarifications are seldom useful for explaining complex phenomena such as variation in collectivism. In this chapter, we attempt to interrelate and integrate three of these single-factor explanations.

Specifically, we propose that economic prosperity influences the impact of atmospheric climate on collectivist culture in that monetary resources enable people to cope with climatic demands of winters and summers. In addition, we examine whether this interaction effect is dwarfed by the well-documented main effect of parasitic disease burden and whether it is applicable to both ingroup love and outgroup hate as distinct manifestations of collectivism (for links between ingroup love and outgroup hate, see Brewer, 1999). Our chapter consists of five parts. Following this brief introduction, the second part provides an overview of the climato–economic theory of culture with special attention paid to collectivism. The third part on sampling and measuring describes our operationalizations of climato–economic habitat, parasitic disease burden, and collectivist culture across 85 countries. In the fourth part, we report the results of hierarchical regression analyses that attempt to test climato–economic livability and parasitic disease burden as rival explanations of ingroup love and outgroup hate. We end the chapter by highlighting implications and extensions of our observations.

CLIMATO–ECONOMIC THEORY OF CULTURE

Axioms: Needs, Demands, and Resources

The anthropologic *needs axiom* postulates that humans as a warm-blooded species have existential needs for thermal comfort, nutrition, and health, as exemplified by their natural inclination to seek residence in temperate climates away from arctic areas and deserts (Rehdanz & Maddison, 2005; Tavassoli, 2009; Van de Vliert, 2009).

The climatic *demands axiom* postulates that colder-than-temperate winters and hotter-than-temperate summers are more demanding to the extent that they deviate from 22°C (about 72°F) as a reference point for optimal psychophysiological comfort, abundant nutritional circumstances of flora and fauna, and healthy living conditions (Fischer & Van de Vliert, 2011; Parsons, 2003; Van de Vliert, 2009).

The economic *resources axiom* postulates that present-day humans use monetary resources to cope with demanding winters or summers. Liquid cash and illiquid capital can buy a wide variety of climate-compensating goods and services, including clothing, housing, heating and cooling, transportation, meals, and medical cure and care. Illustrating and articulating the way this is visible in modern human beings, families in richer nations spend up to 50% of their household income on climate-compensating goods and services, a figure that rises to over 90% in poorer nations (Parker, 2000).

Demands–Resources Effects

The climato–economic explanation of culture belongs to a family of demands–resources theories (e.g., Ajzen, 1991; Bandura, 1997; Lazarus & Folkman, 1984; Skinner & Brewer, 2002). It is widely believed that demands placed on people are a double-edged sword. Greater demands in interaction with insufficient resources to meet the demands increase closed-mindedness and risk aversion, whereas greater demands in interaction with sufficient resources increase open-mindedness and risk seeking. Climato–economic theorizing (Van de Vliert, 2009, 2011a, 2011b, in press) similarly posits that climatic demands in interaction with poor monetary resources promote avoiding ambiguity through collectivistic seclusion and control, whereas climatic demands in interaction with rich monetary resources promote seeking ambiguity through individualistic exploration and creation. This partial explanation of culture is presented here in points describing appraisals of environmental livability and adaptations in setting group goals and group means.

Appraising Livability

Multiple versions of demands–resources theories state that humans continuously appraise their environmental situation with respect to its significance for well-being (e.g., Drach-Zahavy & Erez, 2002; Lazarus & Folkman, 1984; LePine, LePine, & Jackson, 2004; Skinner & Brewer, 2002). *Primary appraisal* assesses to what extent a situation is stressfully demanding because needs cannot be satisfactorily met; secondary appraisal assesses to what extent a stressfully demanding situation is threatening or challenging given the available resources to meet the demands. In the climato–economic theory, primary appraisal assesses to what extent winters and summers are comforting or stressfully demanding; *secondary appraisal* assesses to what extent stressfully demanding winters or summers are threatening or challenging given monetary resources to cope with cold and heat (Van de Vliert, 2009). Inhabitants of a given area are exposed to the same winters, summers, and standard of living; are assessing and discussing this climato–economic situation frequently;

and are gradually pushing and pulling each other toward a predominantly shared appraisal of environmental livability, which is bound to lead to collective adaptations.

Setting Group Goals and Group Means

The climato–economic theory further proposes that inhabitants of lower income areas appraise more demanding winters and summers as threatening and adapt to them by falling back more on their ingroups for setting and achieving goals (collectivism; Van de Vliert, 2011b, in press). Existential threats appear to set in motion processes of culture building in directions of closed-mindedness, ingroup commitment, and ingroup favoritism (Richter & Kruglanski, 2004). In a similar vein, the parasite–stress theory asserts that avoiding and managing life-threatening infections cultivate ingroup assortative sociality and collectivism (Fincher & Thornhill, 2012; Fincher, Thornhill, Murray, & Schaller, 2008; Schaller & Murray, 2011). Gelfand et al. (2011) come closest to our demands–resources notions by arguing and demonstrating that greater environmental threats and a greater dearth of resources promote cultural tightness with clearer norms and stronger sanctions for nonconformity, which are also highly characteristic of collectivist societies (Triandis, 1995).

The theory finally proposes that inhabitants of higher income areas appraise more demanding winters and summers as challenging and adapt to them by falling back more on their individual selves for setting and achieving goals (individualism; Van de Vliert, 2011b, in press). Only under relatively challenging environmental conditions "can people have a low enough need for closure to venture out on their own into the ambiguous, uncertain, and often risky realm of individualism" (Richter & Kruglanski, 2004, p. 116). This is also the central idea of the theory that voluntary settlement in challenging frontier regions promotes cultural values and practices of independence and self-reliance rather than collectivism (Kitayama et al., 2006, 2010).

Hypotheses

Interactive effects of climatic demands and monetary resources on collectivist culture can be differentially translated into hypotheses. One general formulation is that economic hardships strengthen the positive effect of climatic hardships on collectivism. Another general formulation is that climatic hardships strengthen the positive effect of economic hardships on collectivism. The most specific formulation leading to the strictest test of the theory is that more demanding climates come with stronger collectivism in relatively poor countries but weaker collectivism in relatively rich countries.

This hypothesis was tested twice, for ingroup love or positive ingroup discrimination and for outgroup hate or negative outgroup discrimination as distinct manifestations of collectivist culture (Brewer, 1999; Triandis, 1995):

- Hypothesis 1. Collectivism manifested in ingroup love is (a) stronger among inhabitants of poor countries in more demanding climates but (b) weaker among inhabitants of rich countries in more demanding climates.
- Hypothesis 2. Collectivism manifested in outgroup hate is (a) stronger among inhabitants of poor countries in more demanding climates but (b) weaker among inhabitants of rich countries in more demanding climates.

METHODS

Sample

Country-level data on both ingroup love and outgroup hate were available for 85 countries. Although European countries (37) were overrepresented, Asian countries (19), African countries (13), and South American countries (11) were anything but missing. Most important, the anchor points of variation between poor and rich countries with extremely undemanding climates (e.g., poor Indonesia and rich Singapore) and poor and rich countries with extremely demanding climates (e.g., poor Russia and rich Canada) were not dictated by Europe.

Independent Measures: Ecological Predictors

Climatic Demands

The average temperature in a nation over a 30-year period has typically been used as a predictor of local culture (e.g., Georgas et al., 2004; House, Hanges, Javidan, Dorfman, & Gupta, 2004). However, the use of such averages is inaccurate as they (a) neglect the existence of a thermal optimum (4°C and 40°C both pose existential problems), (b) overlook the impact of year-round variations in temperature (small and large differences between winters and summers may have the same average), and (c) are negatively correlated with year-round variations in temperature (higher latitudes have both lower averages and larger variations). An appropriate indicator of a country's climatic demands should take account of winter and summer deviations from a biologically optimal point of reference.

As has become customary in this burgeoning line of research, 22°C (about 72°F) is adopted as a point of reference for optimal climatic livability, not only because 22°C is the approximate midpoint of the range of comfortable temperatures (Parsons, 2003) but also because existence needs for nutrition and health are met more easily in temperate climates varying around a base range of, say, 17°C to 27°C (Cline, 2007; Fischer & Van de Vliert, 2011; Parker, 2000; Tavassoli, 2009). Climates are more demanding to the extent that their winters are colder than 22°C and their summers hotter than 22°C. Climatic demands are operationalized across each country's major cities, weighted for population size, as the sum of the absolute deviations from 22°C for the average lowest and highest temperatures in the coldest month and in the hottest month (source: Van de Vliert 2009). Belarus, for example, with its cold winters ($|-32°C-22°C| + |5°C-22°C| = 71$), and hot summers ($|2°C-22°C| + |32°C-22°C| = 30$), has a *climatic-demands* score of 101.

Criticisms of this measure denounce the neglect of precipitational climate and 22°C as a questionable point of reference for temperate seasons. However, rainfall and snowfall do not appear to alter the impact of thermal climate on culture, at least not at a worldwide level, and somewhat lower or higher reference points than 22°C always yield almost identical research results (Van de Vliert, 2009). The climatic-demands index has also been criticized because of the inadequacy of a single score for large countries spanning multiple climatic subzones. But adjusting for error-inducing temperature variations within nations, or even excluding large countries, strengthens rather than weakens the effects (Fischer & Van de Vliert, 2011; Van de Vliert, 2009, 2011a, 2011b). Consequently, the empirical results reported here, which refer to both smaller and larger countries, may be interpreted as conservative estimates of support for the climato–economic theory.

Monetary Resources

Income per head is measured with reference to the current capacity of a country's currency to buy a given basket of representative goods and services (purchasing power parity in Geary-Khamis dollars; United Nations Development Programme, 2004; the index was log transformed to reduce its skewed cross-national distribution). Climatic history is one of many determinants of income per head in human habitats, so that multicollinearity could be a problem in the analyses. However, there is a positive instead of negative worldwide association between climatic demands and monetary resources ($r = .37$ across 175 nations; Van de Vliert, 2011a), and this association is so weak that climatic demands and monetary resources are negligibly overlapping predictors of freedom.

Parasitic Disease Burden

Prevalence of parasites as a well-documented predictor of ingroup assortative sociality and collectivism (Fincher & Thornhill, 2012; Fincher et al., 2008; Schaller & Murray, 2011; see also Chapter 3, this volume) was controlled for. The parasite–stress theory states that outgroup members are more threatening to the extent that they may transmit infectious diseases. Consequently, the boundaries between ingroups and outgroups will be emphasized more and guarded better in regions where nonzoonotic parasites rather than zoonotic parasites are more prevalent because only nonzoonotic diseases can be contracted from other humans. This reasoning highlights the crucially important finding that nonzoonotic rather than zoonotic infectious diseases predict cultural collectivism (Fincher & Thornhill, 2012; Van de Vliert & Postmes, 2012). Given this state of the science, we measured parasitic disease burden as the prevalence of nonzoonotic diseases (Fincher & Thornhill, 2012).

Dependent Measures: Collectivist Culture

Ingroup Love

Cross-national indicators of familism, nepotism, and compatriotism have been combined into an overall index of positive ingroup discrimination (for details of index construction, see Van de Vliert, 2011b; Cronbach's α = .89). *Familism*, measured as favoritism shown to one's closest relatives in the nuclear family through mutually beneficial exchanges of accommodation and pride, was initially assessed with four items (initial source: House et al., 2004). *Nepotism*, favoritism shown to relatives by giving them organizational positions because of their relationship rather than on their merits, was initially measured with a single item (initial source: World Economic Forum, 2005). *Compatriotism*, favoritism shown to fellow nationals by giving them easier access to scarce jobs than immigrants, was also assessed with a single item (Inglehart, Basáñez, Díez-Medrano, Halman, & Luijkx, 2004; http://www.worldvaluessurvey.org).

Outgroup Hate

Negative outgroup discrimination is derived from the latest wave of the World Values Surveys (Inglehart et al., 2004; http://www.worldvaluessurvey.org). In face-to-face interviews, at least 1,000 adults per country were asked, "On this list are various groups of people. Could you please sort out any that you would not like to have as neighbors? . . . People of a different race . . . Immigrants/ foreign workers . . . Homosexuals . . . People who have AIDS . . . People with a criminal record" (0 = *not mentioned*, 1 = *mentioned*). This resulted in five proportions of a country's inhabitants who mentioned race, immigrants, homosexuals,

AIDS patients, and criminals, respectively. The five national proportions were cross-nationally standardized (Cronbach's $\alpha = .79$) and then averaged to represent the strength of each country-level tendency toward disliking outgroup members.

RESULTS

It was not surprising that parasitic disease burdens are lower in countries with more demanding climates ($r = -.68$, $p < .001$) and in richer countries with more monetary resources ($r = -.68$, $p < .001$). Other zero-order correlations, reported in the last two rows of Table 1.1, reveal that ingroup love and outgroup hate as overlapping manifestations of collectivist culture ($r = .57$, $p < .001$) tend to be more strongly associated with economic hardships than with parasitic disease burden. Hierarchical regression analysis with standardized predictors and a separately entered interaction term shows that climato–economic hardships predict ingroup love ($\Delta R^2 = .51$) and outgroup hate ($\Delta R^2 = .42$) better than parasitic stress does ($\Delta R^2 = .13$ for ingroup love, $\Delta R^2 = .08$ for outgroup hate). Table 1.2 also shows that parasitic disease burden does not account for any variation in collectivist culture once the interactive impacts of climatic demands and monetary resources have been accounted for.

No matter whether parasitic disease burden and outgroup hate are first controlled for, climatic demands and monetary resources have an interactive impact on ingroup love (see the left part of Table 1.2). In support of Hypothesis 1, ingroup love is stronger among inhabitants of relatively poor countries in more demanding climates (simple slope $b = .60$, $p < .001$) but weaker among inhabitants of relatively rich countries in more demanding climates ($b = -.32$, $p < .01$). This interaction effect can be visualized in

TABLE 1.1

Correlations Among Standardized Climatic Demands, Monetary Resources, Parasitic Disease Burden, Ingroup Love, and Outgroup Hate

Variable	1	2	3	4
1. Climatic demands				
2. Monetary resources	.39***			
3. Parasitic disease burden	−.68***	−.68***		
4. Ingroup love	−.26*	−.59***	.36***	
5. Outgroup hate	−.15	−.60***	.27**	.57***

Note. $N = 85$ countries.
*$p < .05$. **$p < .01$. ***$p < .001$.

TABLE 1.2
Results of Hierarchical Regression Analyses Predicting Ingroup Love and Outgroup Hate as Manifestations of Collectivist Culture

Coefficients	Collectivist culture							
	Ingroup love				Outgroup hate			
	ΔR^2	b	ΔR^2	b	ΔR^2	b	ΔR^2	b
Control variables								
Parasitic disease burden	.13***	.11			.08***	-.12		
Ingroup love								
Outgroup hate	.24***	.29*			.26***	.22*		
Climato–economic habitat								
Climatic demands (CD)	.00	.17	.07*	.17	.00	.05	.02	.05
Monetary resources (MR)	.06**	-.14	.29***	-.14	.12***	-.38***	.35***	-.38***
CD * MR	.11***	-.43***	.15***	-.43***	.00	-.08	.05*	-.08
Control variables								
Parasitic disease burden			.00	.11			.00	-.12
Ingroup love								
Outgroup hate			.03*	.29*			.04*	.22*
R^2 (F)	.54 (18.73)***				.46 (13.91)***			

Note. $N = 85$ countries. Unstandardized beta weights shown in the b columns are from the final step in each prediction model. There was no multi-collinearity (VIFs < 3.56), and there were no outliers (Cook's Ds < .24).
*$p < .05$. **$p < .01$. ***$p < .001$.

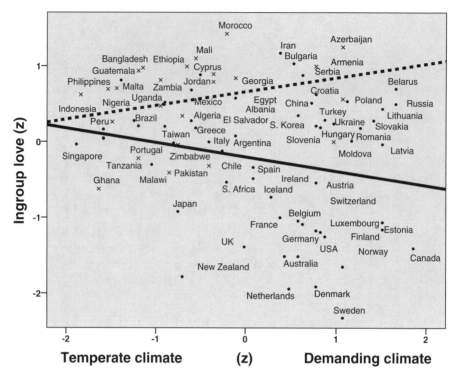

Figure 1.1. Effect of climatic demands on collectivist culture. Broken down for 26 poorer countries (upward slope) and 59 richer countries (downward slope).

slightly different ways depending on the cut-off point between relatively poor and relatively rich countries. In Figure 1.1, 26 poorer countries are contrasted with 59 richer countries because this particular picture also elegantly illustrates that temperate climates on the left nullify the impact of monetary resources ($b = .14$, ns), whereas demanding climates on the right reinforce the intimate link between poorer monetary resources and greater ingroup love ($b = -.78$, $p < .001$).

The right part of Table 1.2 additionally reports that climatic demands and monetary resources also influence each other's impact on outgroup hate but that this interaction effect disappears when ingroup love is first controlled for. Staying on the safe side of the test, this leads one to reject Hypothesis 2 because the evidence indicating that climato–economic hardships promote outgroup hate is not robust. However, given the preceding finding that the climato–economic covariation of ingroup love does not disappear when outgroup hate is first controlled for, one may alternatively conclude that Hypothesis 2 does hold true but that ingroup love mediates the joint impact of climatic demands and monetary resources on outgroup hate.

DISCUSSION

People who emphasize boundaries between ingroups and outgroups are known as *collectivists* (Gelfand et al., 2004; Hofstede, 2001; Triandis, 1995). Here, we demonstrated that collectivists tend to be inhabitants of habitats characterized by colder-than-temperate or hotter-than-temperate climates in conjunction with economic misery. Populations of Armenia, Azerbaijan, Bulgaria, Iran, and Morocco are cases in point. At least, that is what straight-forward cross-sectional reading of our research results suggests. If this climato–economic insight goes beyond sheer description, its explanatory power may gradually unfold as a serious competitor of rival explanations of why humans create collectivism.

Parasitic disease burden as one alternative explanation of sharper psychological boundaries between ingroups and outgroups (Fincher & Thornhill, 2012; Schaller & Murray, 2011; see also Chapter 3, this volume) has already been challenged here and elsewhere (Van de Vliert, in press; Van de Vliert & Postmes, 2012). Although it is clearly the case that parasitic stressors may influence collectivist values and practices, it is also likely that the evolution of culture in humans, just like evolution in other animals, has climatic underpinnings. In comparison with latent concerns over nonzoonotic diseases, it would appear that climato–economic livability is the more powerful predictor of cultural orientations toward ingroup love and outgroup hate.

The novel insight that the interaction of climatic and economic hardships leads humans to create collectivism certainly goes beyond purely economic explanations of collectivist cultures (e.g., Inglehart & Baker, 2000; Inglehart & Welzel, 2005). More to the point, this interactive explanation goes beyond additive main effects of climatic and economic conditions on human functioning advocated by adherents of the ecocultural framework (e.g., Berry, 2011; Georgas et al., 2004). Most important, the support we found for our theory also goes beyond earlier work on the climato–economic origins of collectivist culture (Van de Vliert, 2009, 2011b; Van de Vliert & Postmes, 2012). On the one hand, the covariation of ecological hardships and ingroup love was tested for the first time while controlling for both parasitic disease burden and outgroup hate. On the other hand, the covariation of ecological hardships and outgroup hate was tested for the first time while controlling for both parasitic disease burden and ingroup love.

From these analyses we have learned that climato–economic hardships promote collectivism by leaving imprints on ingroup love rather than outgroup hate. Although the reported cross-sectional associations are in need of longitudinal confirmation, they already start to unfold the dynamics of how ecological factors other than parasitic disease burden might shape cultural ingroup–outgroup differentiation. Breaking away from climatic determinism and economic determinism, climatic demands are expected to influence the course of the economy-drives-collectivism path by making monetary resources more useful. Or put in a complementary way, monetary resources are expected to influence the course of the climate-drives-collectivism path by turning threatening winters or summers into challenging winters or summers. Also breaking away from undifferentiated collectivism, the interaction of climatic demands and insufficient financial resources is expected to produce ingroup love and, only indirectly through it, outgroup hate.

There are three limitations of our cross-national comparisons of collectivism. First, living with the nuclear family, nepotism, compatriotism, and neighbor discrimination are sociological operationalizations rather than psychological manifestations of collectivism. Second, measurement equivalence of ingroup love and outgroup hate across language boundaries and national borders can be questioned. Third, many alternative explanations of the findings cannot be ruled out convincingly because countries differ in numerous characteristics. To address all of these concerns, we (Van de Vliert, Yang, Wang, & Ren, in press) recently downscaled research into the origins of collectivism from the level of relatively poor nations to the lower levels of provinces and individuals within a relatively poor nation.

China was chosen as an appropriate venue to better test the climato–economic covariation of collectivism, not only because China has the climato–economic advantage of large variations in thermal climate and income per head but also especially because China is home to the oldest and largest collectivist civilization on earth. Elegantly replicating and refining the upward slope for poorer countries in Figure 1.1, Chinese collectivism appears to be weakest in provinces with temperate climates, irrespective of income per head (e.g., Guangdong); negligibly stronger in richer provinces with demanding climates (e.g., Hunan); and strongest in poorer provinces with demanding climates (e.g., Heilongjiang). Multilevel analysis consolidates the results by demonstrating that collectivism at the provincial level fully mediates the interactive impact of climato–economic hardships on collectivist orientations at the individual level (for details, see Van de Vliert et al., in press).

Accumulating evidence thus suggests that collectivism is, at least in part, a functional adaptation to the existential problem that atmospheric climate can easily freeze or burn poor humans to death. Most likely, this adaptation is broader than the heightened ingroup–outgroup differentiation highlighted here. According to Triandis (1995), collectivism is a pattern of values, beliefs, and practices that is organized around the shared "notion that groups are the units of analysis and individuals are tightly intertwined parts of these groups" (p. 6) "and that can be found in certain geographic regions during a particular historic period" (p. 43). Although survival values (Inglehart & Baker, 2000; Inglehart & Welzel, 2005), hierarchical relationships (Hofstede, 2001;

Triandis, 1995), and press repression (Van de Vliert, 2011a) have already been exposed as components of collectivist culture, there may still be a promising avenue for further research into the geographic and historic storylines of multiple components of collectivism.

Evolutionary psychologists (e.g., Baumeister, 2005; Buss, 2005; Yamagishi, 2011) may read the empirical results reported here as extra evidence for the validity of models of biotic niche construction within predominantly abiotic habitats. Viewed through an evolutionary lens, cash and capital were gradually constructed as ingenious tools that exist independently of place, time, and items they can buy. In turn, these tools are now intensively used to shape the environment by altering the direct and indirect impacts of adverse winters and summers on meeting existential needs. All of these niche-construction activities lead to new feedback cycles and become the basis for continuous further adaptation, including gradual moves away from collectivist orientations toward individualist orientations. Especially in climates with demanding winters or summers, cash and capital are indispensable tools for continuously turning threatening climato–economic habitats into livable or even challenging climato–economic habitats, with weaker collectivist orientations in the long run. Indeed, the odds are that decreases in climatic threats and decreases in collectivism are in flux together.

REFERENCES

Ajzen, I. (1991). The theory of planned behavior. *Organizational Behavior and Human Decision Processes, 50*, 179–211. doi:10.1111/j.1559-1816.2012.00989.x

Bandura, A. (1997). *Self-efficacy: The exercise of control.* New York, NY: Freeman.

Baumeister, R. F. (2005). *The cultural animal: Human nature, meaning, and social life.* New York, NY: Oxford University Press.

Berry, J. W. (2011). The ecocultural framework: A stocktaking. In F. J. R. Van de Vijver, A. Chasiotis, & S. M. Breugelmans (Eds.), *Fundamental questions in cross-cultural psychology* (pp. 95–114). New York, NY: Cambridge University Press. doi:10.1017/CBO9780511974090.005

Brewer, M. B. (1999). The psychology of prejudice: Ingroup love or outgroup hate? *Journal of Social Issues, 55*, 429–444. doi:10.1111/0022-4537.00126

Buss, D. M. (Ed.). (2005). *The handbook of evolutionary psychology.* New York, NY: Wiley.

Cline, W. R. (2007). *Global warming and agriculture: Impact estimates by country.* Washington, DC: Center for Global Development, Peterson Institute for International Economics.

Drach-Zahavy, A., & Erez, M. (2002). Challenge versus threat effects on the goal-performance relationship. *Organizational Behavior and Decision Processes, 88*, 667–682. doi:10.1016/S0749-5978(02)00004-3

Fincher, C. L., & Thornhill, R. (2012). Parasite–stress promotes in-group assortative sociality: The cases of strong family ties and heightened religiosity. *Behavioral and Brain Sciences, 35*, 61–79. doi:10.1017/S0140525X11000021

Fincher, C. L., Thornhill, R., Murray, D. R., & Schaller, M. (2008). Pathogen prevalence predicts human cross-cultural variability in individualism/collectivism. *Proceedings of the Royal Society: B. Biological Sciences, 275*, 1279–1285. doi:10.1098/rspb.2008.0094

Fischer, R., & Van de Vliert, E. (2011). Does climate undermine subjective well-being? A 58-nation study. *Personality and Social Psychology Bulletin, 37*, 1031–1041. doi:10.1177/0146167211407075

Gelfand, M. J., Bhawuk, D. P. S., Nishii, L. H., & Bechtold, D. J. (2004). Culture and individualism. In R. J. House, P. J. Hanges, M. Javidan, P. W. Dorfman, & V. Gupta (Eds.), *Culture, leadership, and organizations: The GLOBE study of 62 societies* (pp. 437–512). Thousand Oaks, CA: Sage.

Gelfand, M. J., Raver, R. L., Nishii, L., Leslie, L. M., Lun, J., Lim, B. C., . . . Yamaguchi, S. (2011, May 27). Differences between tight and loose cultures: A 33-nation study. *Science, 332*(6033), 1100–1104. doi:10.1126/science.1197754

Georgas, J., Van de Vijver, F. J. R., & Berry, J. W. (2004). The ecocultural framework, ecosocial indices, and psychological variables in cross-cultural research. *Journal of Cross-Cultural Psychology, 35*, 74–96. doi:10.1177/0022022103260459

Hofstede, G. (2001). *Culture's consequences: Comparing values, behaviors, institutions, and organizations across cultures* (2nd ed.). Thousand Oaks, CA: Sage.

House, R. J., Hanges, P. J., Javidan, M., Dorfman, P. W., & Gupta, V. (Eds.). (2004). *Culture, leadership, and organizations: The GLOBE study of 62 societies.* Thousand Oaks, CA: Sage.

Inglehart, R., & Baker, W. E. (2000). Modernization, cultural change, and the persistence of traditional values. *American Sociological Review, 65*, 19–51. doi:10.2307/2657288

Inglehart, R., Basáñez, M., Díez-Medrano, J., Halman, L., & Luijkx, R. (Eds.). (2004). *Human beliefs and values: A cross-cultural sourcebook based on the 1999–2002 values surveys.* Coyoacán, Mexico: Siglo XXI Editores.

Inglehart, R., & Welzel, C. (2005). *Modernization, cultural change, and democracy.* New York, NY: Cambridge University Press.

Kitayama, S., Conway, L. G., Pietromonaco, P. R., Park, H., & Plaut, V. C. (2010). Ethos of independence across regions in the United States: The production–adoption model of cultural change. *American Psychologist, 65*, 559–574. doi:10.1037/a0020277

Kitayama, S., Ishii, K., Imada, T., Takemura, K., & Ramaswamy, J. (2006). Voluntary settlement and the spirit of independence: Evidence from Japan's "northern frontier." *Journal of Personality and Social Psychology, 91*, 369–384. doi:10.1037/0022-3514.91.3.369

Lazarus, R. S., & Folkman, S. (1984). *Stress, appraisal and coping.* New York, NY: Springer.

LePine, J. A., LePine, M. A., & Jackson, C. L. (2004). Challenge and hindrance stress: Relationships with exhaustion, motivation to learn, and learning performance. *Journal of Applied Psychology, 89,* 883–891. doi:10.1037/0021-9010.89.5.883

Oyserman, D., Coon, H. M., & Kemmelmeier, M. (2002). Rethinking individualism and collectivism: Evaluation of theoretical assumptions and meta-analyses. *Psychological Bulletin, 128,* 3–72. doi:10.1037/0033-2909.128.1.3

Parker, P. M. (2000). *Physioeconomics: The basis for long-run economic growth.* Cambridge, MA: MIT Press.

Parsons, K. C. (2003). *Human thermal environments: The effects of hot, moderate and cold environments on human health, comfort and performance* (2nd ed.). London, England: Taylor & Francis.

Rehdanz, K., & Maddison, D. (2005). Climate and happiness. *Ecological Economics, 52,* 111–125. doi:10.1016/j.ecolecon.2004.06.015

Richter, L., & Kruglanski, A. W. (2004). Motivated closed mindedness and the emergence of culture. In M. Schaller & C. S. Crandall (Eds.), *The psychological foundations of culture* (pp. 101–121). Mahwah, NJ: Erlbaum.

Schaller, M., & Murray, D. M. (2011). Infectious disease and the creation of culture. In M. J. Gelfand, C. Chiu, & Y. Hong (Eds.), *Advances in culture and psychology* (Vol. 1, pp. 99–151). New York, NY: Oxford University Press.

Skinner, N., & Brewer, N. (2002). The dynamics of threat and challenge appraisals prior to stressful achievement events. *Journal of Personality and Social Psychology, 83,* 678–692. doi:10.1037/0022-3514.83.3.678

Tavassoli, N. T. (2009). Climate, psychological homeostasis, and individual behaviors across cultures. In R. S. Wyer, C. Chiu, & Y. Hong (Eds.), *Understanding culture: Theory, research, and application* (pp. 211–221). New York, NY: Psychology Press.

Triandis, H. C. (1995). *Individualism and collectivism.* Boulder, CO: Westview.

United Nations Development Programme. (2004). *Human development report 2004.* New York, NY: Oxford University Press.

Van de Vliert, E. (2009). *Climate, affluence, and culture.* New York, NY: Cambridge University Press.

Van de Vliert, E. (2011a). Bullying the media: Cultural and climato–economic readings of press repression versus press freedom. *Applied Psychology, 60,* 354–376. doi:10.1111/j.1464-0597.2010.00439.x

Van de Vliert, E. (2011b). Climato–economic origins of variation in ingroup favoritism. *Journal of Cross-Cultural Psychology, 42,* 494–515. doi:10.1177/0022022110381120

Van de Vliert, E. (in press). Climato–economic habitats support patterns of human needs, stresses, and freedoms. *Behavioral and Brain Sciences.*

Van de Vliert, E., & Postmes, T. (2012). Climato–economic livability predicts societal collectivism and political autocracy better than parasitic stress does. *Behavioral and Brain Sciences, 35*, 94–95. doi:10.1017/S0140525X11001075

Van de Vliert, E., Yang, H., Wang, Y., & Ren, X. (in press). Climato-economic imprints on Chinese collectivism. *Journal of Cross-Cultural Psychology.*

World Economic Forum. (2005). *The global competitiveness report 2004–2005.* New York, NY: Palgrave MacMillan.

Yamagishi, T. (2011). Micro–macro dynamics of the cultural construction of reality: A niche construction approach to culture. In M. J. Gelfand, C. Chiu, & Y. Hong (Eds.), *Advances in culture and psychology* (pp. 251–308). New York, NY: Oxford University Press.

2

REGIONAL DIFFERENCES IN INDIVIDUALISM AND WHY THEY MATTER

LUCIAN GIDEON CONWAY III, SHANNON C. HOUCK,
AND LAURA JANELLE GORNICK

It's easy to curb the freedoms of others when you see no immediate impact on your own.
—Malcolm Forbes (as cited in Scott, 2008, p. 114)

Humans like freedom. All things being equal, they prefer to be able to choose where to eat, how to vote, what brand of peanut butter to buy, who to marry, and whether to take a walk on a fall morning. When people feel like they have no freedom as an individual, they often take steps to reassert that freedom and, if that fails, they frequently become depressed and unhappy. No one wants to feel like they are constrained in a prison.

But individual freedom has some downsides. People must live in proximity to other people, and sometimes individual freedom can clash with the collective good. I may want to walk into a store and take all the peanut butter for myself without paying for it, but my individual freedom to do that would almost certainly hurt a lot of other people. It is hard for any society to function allowing limitless freedom. No one wants to live in a place where their neighbor has the freedom to take their peanut butter or their farm equipment or their cat or their children when they do not want them to.

http://dx.doi.org/10.1037/14272-003
Geographical Psychology: Exploring the Interaction of Environment and Behavior, P. J. Rentfrow (Editor)

One of the most important dilemmas that humans face is this tension between individual freedom and collective good (e.g., Conway, Sexton, & Tweed, 2006). Humans are psychologically motivated to value both things, and humans have a practical investment in both things. Yet often individual freedom and collective good are at odds with each other.

Cultures exist in part to help solve dilemmas such as this (see Van de Vliert, 2011). However, they do not all resolve them in the same way. This fact is directly reflected in an important cross-cultural variable that is the topic of this chapter: individualism/collectivism. In a sense, individualism/collectivism resides at the epicenter of one of the most difficult challenges humanity faces. That is perhaps why it is—by far—the most researched construct in cross-cultural psychology (to illustrate, we performed a PsycINFO search for "individualism" or "collectivism" that yielded a staggering 5,011 citations).

In the present chapter, we discuss this dilemma between individual freedom and the collective good through the lens of regional differences in individualism/collectivism. What we ultimately aim to show is that considering regional differences in individualism/collectivism helps us better understand fundamental aspects of culture, aspects we would not understand as well using traditional "nation-level" units of analysis alone. To do so, we (a) define both individualism/collectivism and regional differences, (b) discuss at a broad level why studying regional differences is important, and then (c) illustrate directly its importance by considering research on two different domains relevant to individualism/collectivism: political structure and physical geography. Along the way, we present some novel research relevant to the effect of frontier topography on individualism. In doing all of this, we hope to accomplish the twin goals of (a) discussing what we know so far about individualism/collectivism at the regional level and (b) illustrating, at a broad level, the general value of regional levels of analyses.

WHAT IS INDIVIDUALISM/COLLECTIVISM?

Individualism means erring on the side of personal freedom in the great human dilemma. It involves a cultural emphasis on personal rights and self-reliance. *Collectivism*, on the other hand, means erring on the side of the collective good. It involves a cultural emphasis on group identity and fitting into the larger fabric of society (see, e.g., Conway, Ryder, Tweed, & Hallett, 2001; Conway et al., 2006; Hofstede, 1980; Kitayama, Conway, Pietromonaco, Park, & Plaut, 2010; Triandis, 1996; Vandello & Cohen, 1999). Although individualism and collectivism do not always operate as opposing forces—consider that it is possible for cultures to encourage collective identity and personal freedom at the same time (e.g., Kagitcibasi, 1997; Singelis, 1994)—the two things are typically inversely related, and that is especially so using aggregate units of analysis such as cultural regions as we do here (see Triandis, 1989; Vandello & Cohen, 1999). Thus, for convenience and ease of discussion, we treat individualism and collectivism as conceptual polar opposites.

The tension between the individual and collective occurs in many far-flung aspects of cultural life. As such, individualism/collectivism is not exactly a singular, easily captured entity but rather a collection of often-discrepant things that are all related by their tie to this central dilemma. This collection of elements has been referred to as a *syndrome* (Triandis, 1996) or an *ethos* (Kitayama et al., 2010). Its pervasive breadth no doubt in part accounts for the popularity of the construct, but it also poses conceptual problems for researchers. Because collectivism can be expressed in so many different aspects of human life, what we call *collectivism* in one part of the world may in fact be quite different from what we call *collectivism* in another part of the world, even though both may legitimately have to do with emphasizing group identity. Similarly, cultures might be highly collectivistic in some aspects of societal life but highly individualistic in others. Japan, for example, is typically considered a highly collectivist culture (e.g., Kitayama, Ishii, Imada, Takemura, & Ramaswamy, 2006), yet it scored low on a generally collectivistic trait ("traditionalism") in the World Values Survey (Inglehart & Baker, 2000).

These different aspects of individualism/collectivism may have different causes and consequences. Consider that collectivism might be represented as an emphasis on group equality ("we're all in this together") or it might be represented as an emphasis on group hierarchy ("to succeed, we must listen to our group leaders"). Researchers refer to this distinction as *horizontal* (equal) versus *vertical* (hierarchical) collectivism (Conway et al., 2006; Triandis & Gelfand, 1998). Although both vertical and horizontal forms of collectivism emphasize collective good over individual rights, they are nonetheless very different. Strong pressure to follow dogmatic authority figures is psychologically quite different from the strong collective identity of equals, and these things surely do not always originate from the same source or have the same consequences.

Consider, too, the common psychological distinction between implicit and explicit processes. Individualism/collectivism can also be represented at both of these levels. New Hampshire's state motto is "Live free or die"; it is thus hard to live in the state without being consciously aware of this explicitly individualistic value. However, norms governing the degree to which persons attribute (and perhaps overattribute) behaviors to the individual traits of the actors are surely rarely discussed out loud, and thus they may exist and be passed on without much—if any—explicit acknowledgment (see Kitayama et al., 2010). As with the vertical/horizontal dimension, implicit and explicit expressions of individualism may have very different causes and consequences:

Quite different processes likely govern the emergence and transmission of things rarely discussed openly in the public sphere than govern those of highly visible values and beliefs (see Kitayama et al., 2010). And yet, in all of these cases—whether vertical or horizontal, implicit or explicit—there exists a clear tie to the tension between the individual and the collective.[1]

WHAT IS A CULTURE? REGIONAL
VERSUS NATIONAL DIFFERENCES

So far, we have loosely bandied about the term *culture* and discussed *cultural differences* in individualism and collectivism without actually pausing to define what a culture is. However, that question turns out to be important in understanding individualism/collectivism itself, so we now pause for our due definitional diligence. A *culture* is a set of beliefs, practices, or symbols that are shared in common by a particular group of people. This set of shared things must distinguish a group from other groups in some way (see Conway & Schaller, 2007). It is not considered a part of U.S. culture, for example, that Americans eat at least once a day—even though this is a clearly shared behavior among Americans—because it does not distinguish people in the United States from the rest of humanity. It is, however, considered a part of U.S. culture that Americans own a lot of guns, because owning guns is more shared among Americans than among a lot of other groups of people.

By far the most common way that culture is operationalized in research is by using national boundaries—comparing one nation's beliefs and practices with another's. Thus, the term *culture* has become almost synonymous at a practical level with the term *nation*. (Consider that when Hofstede, 1980, wrote his famous work about "culture's consequences," he used data that compared nations with each other.) However, there is of course no reason why our study of culture should be constrained to comparing nations with each other. A culture can exist within almost any geographical boundary; it only requires a distinguishing set of shared beliefs among the people within those boundaries. The first author's family opens all their Christmas presents at Thanksgiving, and this set of shared beliefs legitimately constitutes a part of the family's culture because it clearly distinguishes his family from most other families. One can similarly describe cultures of particular businesses, religious groups, chess clubs, bars, cities, parishes, or other small geographical regions.

---

[1]Of course, regardless of the type of collectivism under examination, no nation is wholly individualistic or wholly collectivistic; as such, researchers try to capture cultural differences in degrees of emphasis. "Individualistic" cultures have many collectivistic aspects, and "collectivistic" cultures have many individualistic ones. Part of what cultural researchers do can thus be likened to "caricature" artists, who exaggerate certain features of their subjects to make them clearer (see Tweed & Conway, 2006).

In this chapter, we pursue cultural differences in individualism/ collectivism across such smaller geographical regions, geographical regions that do not always constitute national boundaries. In fact, often they occur within a single nation. For convenience, we here refer to these differences as *regional* differences to distinguish them from differences only on the basis of national boundaries.

WHY DO REGIONAL DIFFERENCES MATTER?

As we have already discussed, individualism/collectivism is one of the most central and heavily researched topics our field has to offer. Much of this work has involved comparing one nation with another, and as a result of this nation-as-culture research, we understand a lot about the construct. Given the immense amount of knowledge generated from the nation-level approach, what is the value of exploring regional differences? Why not just stick to the tried-and-true traditional nation-as-culture approach? Why should we care about regional differences in individualism/collectivism?

The answer is simple: We will not fully understand individualism/ collectivism until we delve deeper into regional differences. Probably some of what we have learned at the nation level is wrong, and probably some of it is right, and studying regions can help us separate the wheat from the proverbial chaff. Many cultural psychologists are aiming to create broad theories about the causes and consequences of individualism/collectivism at a nomothetic level. Other cultural psychologists are aiming to understand each individual culture at an idiographic level. Either way, it is clear that each of these goals requires going beyond national boundaries to understand individualism/ collectivism. This need can be seen in at least two different ways.

Regional Culture Is Often a More Appropriate Unit of Analysis

First, often the national level is simply too clunky as a unit of analysis. A nation is frequently too large to be easily categorized as a culture. If you have a theory that harsh environments create individualism (we actually discuss evidence related to one such theory later in this chapter), to test that theory you might create a score for each nation according to how harsh the environment is and then correlate that score with national scores for individualism. Although that is a reasonable approach, it is not a precise test of the hypothesis and has an incredible amount of unnecessary noise. It is obvious that in each nation there are harsh and less harsh environments; a more honed test would distinguish these regional differences in harshness that occur within each nation. The Australian outback and the Australian coast surely differ in harshness, and thus if one is trying to test the effect of harshness on individualism, it seems wiser to compare these two regions within Australia than to compare Australia itself with, say, Samoa.

In some ways, noise created by using nation-level analyses would only interfere with the ability to find an effect but would be unlikely to produce spurious effects. On the flip side, however, is the potential that other national differences might account for the observed relation. Australia has many things besides its environment that differ from Samoa: They have different shared histories, different religious backgrounds, different languages, and so forth. However, when one looks at regional differences that are smaller and occur within a nation, one de facto controls for a lot of those sorts of variables. In other words, it is easier to isolate the variable of interest by using within-nation regions that differ on the key variable, because the people in that nation (to a greater degree) share the same language, religious background, and so forth.

The Principle of Triangulation

This is not to say the national level is irrelevant (indeed, we have done some of that kind of work ourselves). Nation-level analyses deal with averages across large groups of people, and their results, although clunky, are still meaningful as such. Even so, there is much to be gained by using different levels of analyses because it is more compelling for different levels of analyses to point in the same direction than it is for only one level to point there. This principle has been called *triangulation* (see, e.g., Kitayama et al., 2006, 2010).

To go back to our harsh environments example, in Chapter 1 of this volume, Van de Vliert and Yang compellingly argue that nations with extreme temperatures tend to produce more individualism, but only when they are wealthy. The authors present data at the nation level that are fully consistent with this theory. This is a reasonable approach because nations, writ large, differ in their average temperature and in their average level of individualism.

However, because nations also differ on other things that might overlap with the harshness of environment, there is still a possibility that these results merely represent the work of some other unmeasured confounding variable.[2] That possibility could be reduced by testing regional differences

---

[2] We would also like to point out that the possibility of confounding variables accounting for Van de Vliert and Yang's results is reduced by the presence of a moderating variable—in their case, national wealth. For a "confound" to account for an interaction, it must be more complex than for a simpler main effect relationship because it must in some way "mimic" the interaction. Although this is possible, it is less likely than a straightforward main effect confound (see Conway, Schaller, et al., 2001, for a discussion). We are only using Van de Vliert's work as an example for discussion relevant to the usefulness of including regional levels of analyses, and not actually estimating its overall likelihood of being true. The issue we raise in the text is of course only one of many that should go into estimating this probability, and we think Van de Vliert's work exceptionally good.

within nations. Nations themselves often have harsh and less harsh climates, all within their own borders. Logically speaking, if it is the harshness of the climate that is responsible for the cultural individualism in richer countries, that should be so for harsh (wealthy) regions within a rich country as compared with less harsh (but equally wealthy) regions within the same country. Thus, this sort of test can be particularly useful for providing additional compelling evidence of the climate–individualism relationship.[3]

TWO DEMONSTRATIONS OF WHY
REGIONAL DIFFERENCES MATTER

So far, we have discussed the importance of both understanding individualism/collectivism and considering regional differences in this construct beyond mere national differences. Next, drawing on some of our own work, we illustrate two cases where regional differences may help contribute to our understanding of individualism/collectivism. The first involves the relationship of political structures to individualism; the second examines the role of frontier geography in creating individualism. Along the way, we present some new data on regional differences in frontier geography to illustrate the potential usefulness of triangulating national and regional levels of analysis, adding to a bourgeoning body of work across multiple domains that examines such regional cultural differences (e.g., Kashima et al., 2004; Plaut, Markus, & Lachman, 2002; Rentfrow, 2010; Rentfrow, Gosling, & Potter, 2008).

The Relationship Between Political Structures and Individualism

If culture reflects the aggregate values and beliefs of a population, it would be quite remarkable if these values were not represented in some way in the political system governing that population. But what is the nature of this relationship?

At one level, it is easy to imagine some straightforward examples in which the relation of cultural values to political structures is hardly mysterious or even interesting. In a democracy, where people get to vote (either directly or indirectly) on the laws that govern them, people surely vote in part reflecting their personal values. Thus, it is easy to see, for example, why regions where gun ownership is valued tend to have looser gun control laws. Further, the causal arrow may go the other way: For example, in a pure

---

[3]Indeed, Van de Vliert and his colleagues (Van de Vliert, Matthiesen, Gangsøy, Landro, & Einarsen, 2010) have recently begun to explore within-nation regional differences on a domain related to individualism: democratic versus autocratic leadership. These results, within regions of Norway, provide additional compelling support for the climato–economic theory.

dictatorship, the government controls the flow of information and can thus directly influence the values of its populace. Thus, if the government decides that stricter gun control is good and makes laws in that regard, it is not hard to see how this may influence the populace to agree with those laws and thus change the culture to match the government decree.

However, at a different level, the relationship may not be so clear. Individualism, for example, is not a belief in one specific value; if it exists at all, it is a pervasive ethos or syndrome that permeates not just one thing but also a huge part of life (see Kitayama et al., 2010; Triandis, 1996). Is there evidence that different regions have different political structures that reflect differences in individualism at some large and pervasive level?

A series of studies conducted by Conway et al. (2006) attempted to answer this question. They reasoned that if an individualistic ethos was pervasive, this ought to be reflected in a less restrictive legal structure that allowed citizens more individual freedom across multiple types of legal issues. This effect ought not be limited to just one or two particular domains specific to the values and behaviors used to measure individualism but rather ought to be fairly pervasive across domains that have no direct semantic link to each other, except that they are conceptually related to individualism.

The first investigation considered regional differences within the United States by developing an index of legal restriction for all 50 states that was composed of four separate categories of laws (gun prohibition, gay and lesbian rights, tax laws, and road safety laws). The researchers then correlated states' legal restriction score with a validated measure of collectivism for each state (from Vandello & Cohen, 1999), while controlling for a number of demographic and political ideology measures. Results suggested that legal restriction is negatively correlated with cultural individualism. More individualistic states (e.g., Montana) have more individual freedom built into their legal structure across multiple domains than do more collectivistic states (e.g., Louisiana).

In a second investigation, Conway et al. (2006) applied the triangulation principle by analyzing cross-cultural patterns of individualism and legal restriction across nations. They used multiple measurements of legal and political restriction and national individualism (including Smith, Dugans, & Trompenaars's 1996 indexes and Hofstede's famous 1980 index). This work similarly revealed a negative correlation between political restriction and cultural individualism, and this occurred beyond basic demographic variables.[4] In

---

[4]This relationship occurred for a measurement of political restriction as defined by the overall restrictiveness of government type, but not for a legal restriction measurement analogous to the one for the U.S. states. We gloss over this issue here to focus on the larger storyline (see Conway et al., 2006, for discussion of the complexities and what they might mean). As we demonstrate later in this chapter, both state legal restriction and national legal restriction nonetheless show almost identical patterns of correlations with frontier topography, thus perhaps suggesting that the nation legal restriction index has some validity.

other words, nations with individualistic attitudes tend to have more political freedom for their citizens.

The first two studies suggested that individualistic attitudes and behaviors in the populace of a given region or nation are correlated with more political and legal freedom for those living in that region. But where does that relationship come from? Conway et al. (2006) took a kind of crude "chicken-or-egg" approach to this question. Specifically, they examined whether cultural individualism precedes legal freedom or vice versa. The answer to this question might help paint, in broad brushstrokes, the degree to which cultural attitudes must change prior to political change or whether, as some argue, it is a change in the political system that ultimately translates into future cultural attitudinal change. Using different indicators of cultural individualism and political freedom over a 40-year period, results suggested that cultural individualism was a stronger predictor of future legal freedom than legal freedom was of future individualism. In other words, cultural change preceded political change, not the other way around. It is notable that this trend was observed both at the state and region level and at the national level (though it was stronger at the national level).

Overall, this set of results suggests that cultural individualism may be more than a collection of beliefs—it may be a pervasive ethos or syndrome reflecting a general cultural approach to resolving the tension between individual freedom and collective good. This cultural ethos may not merely follow from the local political structure—it may well create it.

The Psychology of (Physical) Geography: Frontiers and Individualism

If political freedom comes in part from a culturally shared individualistic ethos, where does this individualistic ethos come from? Many researchers and academics have suggested over the years that the physical environment may have an impact on the development of culture (e.g., Berry, 1994, 2011; Murray, Trudeau, & Schaller, 2011; Nisbett & Cohen, 1996; Rentfrow et al., 2008; Schaller & Murray, 2011; Turner, 1920; Vandello & Cohen, 1999; Van de Vliert, 2007, 2009, 2011). Yet, studies directly tying the physical environment to the emergence of cultural traits are relatively rare (see, e.g., Rentfrow et al., 2008). Two prominent examples of this approach are already outlined in this volume. One of those highlights the impact of climate on the emergence of culture (see Chapter 1); the other focuses on the prevalence of pathogens and their influence on culture (see Chapter 3). We focus here on a related aspect of the physical environment, namely, physical topography.

A new line of research has put a fresh face to some theory and speculation as to how the physical environment influences the development of culture. In particular, it has suggested that voluntary settlement to a frontier area tends to produce individualism (Kitayama et al., 2010). There are two reasons for this. The first is self-selection: On average, individualistic people are more likely to voluntarily choose to settle in an unknown frontier. The second involves the harshness of the typical frontier terrain: Frontiers often require independent attitudes to survive and thrive (Kitayama et al., 2006, 2010).

In addition to across-nation work showing that more recently settled nations (e.g., the United States) have more individualism than less recently settled ones (e.g., Japan; e.g., Kitayama, Park, Sevincer, Karasawa, & Uskul, 2009), a growing body of work comparing within-nation regions has shown differences across regional cultures consistent with this thesis. In Japan, frontier Hokkaido shows more implicit individualism than mainland Japanese society (Kitayama, Park, Sevincer, Karasawa, & Uskul, 2006; Takemura & Arimoto 2008), whereas in the United States, frontier states show more explicit individualism (Kitayama et al., 2010) and a greater propensity to choose nonconforming names (Varnum & Kitayama, 2011) than their nonfrontier counterparts.

Next, we present some new data testing an extension of the frontier thesis in a way that attempts to highlight the value of triangulating national and regional levels of analyses. Most prior work on the voluntary settlement/ frontier hypothesis has used a fairly small number of comparison cultures (e.g., four states in Kitayama et al., 2010; two regions in Kitayama et al., 2006). This approach has its advantages but might be complemented by a more large-scale approach. If voluntary settlement to a frontier produces more independence, then on average, places with more frontier topography ought to have more individualism. Although it is possible to have a frontier that no one voluntarily settles, it is impossible to settle a frontier when there is no frontier to settle in the first place. Thus, on average, nations with frontiers ought to have more voluntary settlement of those frontiers and (if the voluntary settlement theory is true) should exhibit higher levels of individualism. Further, places with large populations in a currently existing frontier region would have ostensibly (in a sense) tamed the frontier to survive, and this process of successful survival in a sometimes-harsh environment may facilitate the development of individualism. Following our approach emphasizing the value of both national and regional levels of analyses, we present data both across nations and within one nation (the United States).

Method

Frontier Terrain Estimates: Mountainous Terrain and Inland Population

We focus here on two potential markers of frontier terrain: mountainous and inland terrain. Mountains are often directly associated with frontiers because they are generally forbidding and difficult environments. Similarly, inland (vs. coastal) environments are typically associated with the frontier for two related reasons: (a) They often have less temperate climates than coastal regions, and (b) especially after the advent of large ships, they have typically been settled less recently than coastal areas. Therefore, inland areas are more likely on average to be on a modern frontier (or in a region that was more recently "tamed" as a frontier).

Terrain Measurements Across American States. Raters from our lab (using topographical maps) measured the degree of mountainous terrain for each city in the United States that exceeded 100,000 people. This score was on a 1-to-9 scale, where 1 meant there was no noticeable mountainous terrain anywhere near the city and 9 meant the entire city was surrounded by large mountains. Scores between 1 and 9 represented accompanying degrees of mountainous terrain around the city. Raters scored some overlapping cities, and interrater reliability was satisfactory (average $r = .84$). The same raters similarly measured the distance from each city over 100,000 people to the nearest ocean or great lake. Again, interrater reliability was satisfactory for overlapping scores (average $r = .96$).

These judgments were originally made at the city level. This allowed us to estimate the frontier topography in the parts of each state where people are most likely to actually live. To produce state-level estimates, we averaged the final score for all cities with over 100,000 people in each state. The result was one score representing the mountainous terrain of each state and another score representing the degree to which each state was inland. For the eight states where no city existed with a population of over 100,000, the first author estimated both terrain variables by looking at the scores for comparable surrounding states while using a topographical map. (Results were also computed without these eight estimated variables and they looked virtually identical to those reported, both inferentially and descriptively.)

Terrain Measurements Across Nations. We estimated the mountainous terrain for each nation by using two variables analogous to considerations of our nine-point rating scale for the U.S. states (both obtained from Socioeconomic Data and Applications Center, 2007). First, we used a measurement of the amount of vertical rise within the nation. Second, we used a measurement of the percentage of the nation considered to be geographic lowlands (inverse-scored). These two variables were converted to z scores and averaged to produce a single mountainous terrain score for each nation.

We estimated inland terrain by using the percentage of persons who live in coastal regions (inverse-scored; obtained from Socioeconomic Data and Applications Center, 2007). This gave us an estimate of the number of persons within each nation who live in a terrain that is inland from major bodies of water. (See Table 2.1 for examples of high and low nations and regions for each of the key variables used in this study.)

TABLE 2.1
Examples of High and Low Regions/Nations on Key Variables Used in Present Study

Variable	Across American states		Across nations	
	Low exemplars	High exemplars	Low exemplars	High exemplars
Individualism	Hawaii, Louisiana, Maryland, Mississippi, South Carolina	Colorado, Montana, Nebraska, North Dakota, Wyoming	Ecuador, Fiji, Guatemala, Panama, Venezuela	Australia, Canada, Netherlands, United Kingdom, United States
Legal freedom	Hawaii, Illinois, Minnesota, New Jersey, South Carolina	Colorado, Montana, New Hampshire, South Dakota, Wyoming	Bahamas, Barbados, Fiji, Malta, Sri Lanka	Bolivia, Saudi Arabia, Philippines, Switzerland, Taiwan
Mountains	Delaware, Florida, Georgia, Indiana, Iowa	Alaska, Arizona, Nevada, New Mexico, West Virginia	Bahamas, Barbados, Denmark, Monaco, Singapore	Bhutan, China, Columbia, India, Nepal
Inland	Alaska, Hawaii, New Jersey, New York, Rhode Island	Colorado, Montana, New Mexico, Utah, Wyoming	Kuwait, New Zealand, Panama, Philippines, South Korea	Andorra, Bhutan, Bolivia, Switzerland, Uganda

Mountain and Inland Terrain Correlated With Other Frontier Markers. To provide a brief test of our assumption that mountainous and inland terrains are related to the frontier, we compared them with other types of frontier markers. At the state level, we averaged two measurements based on population-density approaches (where greater frontier means lower population density and miles to a market-service area): (a) the percentage of land in each state designated as frontier and (b) the percentage of population in that state designated as living in frontier areas (both based on U.S. census data and obtained from http://www.frontierus.org/). We converted these to z-scores and averaged them to produce one population-based frontier measurement.

We could find no such population-density-based frontier designation at the nation level. However, we did find a rough marker of whether a given nation had any frontier forest (here dummy coded as 0 or 1) for most nations (Bryant, Nielsen, & Tangley, 1997) as well as several estimates of some North,

TABLE 2.2

Relationship Between Terrain and Other Frontier Measurements

Frontier measure	Mountains	Inland
Across American states		
Population-based frontier	.53***	.31*
Across nations		
Forest frontier	.42***	−.09*
N/S American frontier	.11	.50*

Note. N/S American frontier = North, South, and Central American frontier in the 1850s. For Across American States, $N = 50$. For Across Nations Forest Frontier–Mountains r, $N = 116$. For Across Nations Forest Frontier–Inland r, $N = 103$. For N/S American Frontier, $N = 21$.
*$p < .05$. ***$p < .07$.

South, and Central American nations' percentage of frontier lands during the 1850s (we averaged these together into one summative score for each nation for convenience; all markers taken from Garcia-Jimeno & Robinson, 2009).

Results are presented in Table 2.2. As can be seen there, these results generally show positive correlations between our terrain measurements and other frontier estimates. This pattern was especially robust across U.S. states. Across nations, although the results overall reflect our assumption, the pattern is less consistent. This may be a function of the crudeness of the nation-level frontier variables—one of them is specific to forests and uses an all-or-none categorical approach, and the other only deals with 21 nations (and is composed of data that are over 150 years old). All the same, in the main, these tests are nonetheless consistent with our general assumption about inland and mountainous terrain reflecting the frontier. However, even if it is not representing the frontier, we think it is a useful enterprise to discover relationships between geographical variables and psychological ones that can be demonstrated at both regional and national levels. We return to exactly what these relationships may mean in the discussion.

Individualism and Freedom Measurements

Across American States. We used two measurements related to individualism or personal freedom in the United States. First, we used Vandello and Cohen's (1999) United States Collectivism Index (inverse scored). We refer to this as *individualism.* Second, we used the measurement discussed earlier of legal restriction in each U.S. state (Conway et al., 2006); for ease of presentation, we inverse-scored this variable as well and present it as a measure of *legal freedom* within each state.

Across Nations. We similarly used two parallel measurements across nations. First, we used Hofstede's (1980) famous measurement of individualism. Second, we used Conway et al.'s (2006) measurement of legal restriction in each nation, which captured restriction across three different categories of laws (tax, gun control, and speed limits). We inverse scored this and refer to it as *legal freedom* here.

Control Variable: Gross Domestic Product Per Capita

Any time one uses aggregates in nations or regions, there are many possible confounding variables. Here we include one that has both been at the center of discussion for much theory and research and is somewhat at the practical epicenter of many other potential confounds: gross domestic product (GDP) per capita. Because individualism variables tend to be positively correlated with GDP per capita (e.g., Conway et al., 2006; Hofstede, 1980) and other per capita income variables (e.g., Conway et al., 2006), it may either account for effects we report or suppress such effects. As a result, in all analyses we controlled for GDP per capita. Resulting effects are the predictive power of frontier topography above this basic demographic marker of a nation's wealth.

Results

Primary results are presented in Table 2.3. As can be seen there, across nations and within the U.S. states, inland terrains were fairly consistently positively related to individualism and freedom variables. Indeed, when controlling for GDP per capita, all four correlations (two for nations, two for within the United States) were statistically significant at $p < .05$. The story

TABLE 2.3
Mountain and Inland Environments' Relationship to Measurements
of Individualism and Freedom

Frontier measure	Zero order		Controlling for GDP per capita	
	Mountains	Inland	Mountains	Inland
Across American states				
Individualism	.13	.43**	.12	.41**
Legal freedom	.32*	.47***	.32**	.42**
Across nations				
Individualism	−.18^	−.01	−.01	.26*
Legal freedom	.33**	.29**	.37***	.32**

Note. For Across American States, $N = 50$. For Across Nations Individualism–Mountains *r*, $N = 94$. For Across Nations Individualism–Inland *r*, $N = 87$. For Across Nations Legal Freedom–Mountains *r*, $N = 82$. For Across Nations Legal Freedom–Inland *r*, $N = 72$. For Across Nations Political Freedom–Mountains *r*, $N = 113$. For Across Nations Political Freedom–Inland *r*, $N = 101$.
*$p ≤ .05$. **$p ≤ .01$. ***$p ≤ .001$.
^$p < .12$.

for mountainous terrain was similar but less consistent across individualism-related variables. In particular, all legal freedom variables were statistically significant both across nations and within the United States, but the correlations for individualism were inconsistent and nonsignificant.

A glance at Table 2.3 reveals a vital fact: The patterns for the predictive ability of mountain and inland terrain were similar for both the nation and the state level. Indeed, when controlling for GDP per capita, the patterns were virtually identical; the same three correlations that were significant for the state-level data were also significant in the same direction for the nation-level data, whereas the one nonsignificant state-level correlation was also nonsignificant at the nation level.[5]

Discussion

Can we predict individualism from frontier topography? These results suggest we can. Nations with more mountainous and (especially) inland terrain were more likely to be individualistic and/or have more political freedom, and the same pattern was true for regions within the United States. This demonstration of the individualism–frontier terrain relationship within one of the most individualistic nations in the world is particularly interesting. Why might this relationship exist? It is possible that it reflects the processes outlined in the voluntary settlement hypothesis (e.g., Kitayama et al., 2010): Individualistic people are more likely to move to frontier terrains, and frontier terrains in turn are more likely to produce individualistic people. This dual process could produce more individualism in mountainous and inland terrain.

Of course, individualism has many origins besides mere topography, and it is possible that our terrain measurements merely overlap with some of these other sources, either by chance or for some systematic reason. Therefore, exactly why this relationship emerged in our data is mostly speculation. Consider that although we controlled for one of the most important and pervasive demographic markers that often distinguishes between regions or

---

[5]Inspired by Van de Vliert's excellent work on climate (see Chapter 1, this volume), we tested for interactions between GDP per capita and both terrain variables by computing continuous interaction terms and running a simultaneous regression including the relevant terrain variable, GDP per capita, and the interaction term (for descriptions of this methodology, see, e.g., Conway & Schaller, 2005). We did this separately for each terrain type predicting each of the two dependent measures. Results suggested that there was little in the way of interaction between terrain and GDP per capita. The only interaction that approached significance was the legal freedom inland relation at the state level (interaction $t = 1.93$, $p = .06$). Closer inspection of this interaction suggested that whereas inland terrain predicted individualism in both wealthier and poorer states, a larger effect size was evident for wealthier states. Although the direction of this interaction effect is consistent with Van de Vliert's work on climate, no other interaction terms approached significance at either the state or nation level (all interaction term ts < 1.0, all ps > .45). In the main, then, these results appear to be better described by main effects of the variables than by interactions with GDP per capita.

nations, there are many other potential (and uncontrolled-for) confounds. For example, inland regions are distinguished from coastal areas in many ways beyond mere terrain: Inland areas are less likely engaged in international trade, have less diverse populations, and are generally less cosmopolitan (and more isolated) in nature. Although it could be argued that some of these things are related to the meaning of *frontier*, they nonetheless go beyond the simple story of voluntary settlement of new terrain that we tell here.

Thus, future work would do well to more comprehensively account for these and other demographic variables, as well as test the unique predictive ability of frontier terrain above other environmental factors such as climate and pathogens. Here, we provide these data mostly to illustrate the usefulness of considering both national and regional differences. As such, we hope they represent a starting point for triangulating research on frontier topography and culture; we make no claims that they are a conclusive endpoint.[6]

For whatever reason the relationship between physical geography and individualism emerged in the present data, it is nonetheless potentially quite interesting. The physical terrain presumably preceded the cultures that live on it. People do sometimes remove frontiers by cutting down forests and building cities, but they do not frequently build mountains or create oceans. Thus, we presume that to the degree there is some kind of real and direct causal relationship between physical terrain and individualism, it is likely the terrain causing the individualism and not the other way around. As such, to the degree that this relationship proves to be a central and vital one (as partially remains to be seen), it could provide an important building block in understanding the origins of cultural individualism.

CONCLUDING THOUGHTS

Crucial to understanding federalism in modern day America is the concept of mobility, or "the ability to vote with your feet." If you don't support the death penalty and citizens packing a pistol—don't come to Texas. If you don't like medicinal marijuana and gay marriage, don't move to California.
—Rick Perry, *Fed Up! Our Fight to Save America From Washington*

We cannot understand any culture fully by merely aggregating. To understand a national culture, one must not only aggregate across that nation

---

[6]Indeed, it is further worth noting that the individualism/collectivism measurements used here are largely either focused on horizontal collectivism or are rather ambiguous with respect to the vertical and horizontal dimension (see Conway et al., 2006, for a discussion). If we focused on individualism/collectivism measurements more related to vertical collectivism, the pattern of results may be quite different.

but also understand regional and cultural differences within it. Otherwise, we might fail to see that, although Americans share much in common, Californians and Texans are nevertheless quite different. This has consequences not only for our idiographic understanding of a particular culture but also for our understanding of why cultures exist at all and why they are what they are. If individualism creates political freedom, then that ought to be so whether we consider national or regional political units. If frontiers create individualism, then that ought to apply with even greater force as one narrows in on smaller and smaller geographic areas. If it does not, then we ought to begin to question the validity of the theory. If it does, it becomes harder and harder to explain it away.

REFERENCES

Berry, J. W. (1994). Ecology of individualism and collectivism. In U. Kim, H. C. Triandis, C. Kagitcibasi, S.-C. Choi, & G. Yoon (Eds.), *Individualism and collectivism: Theory, method, and applications* (pp. 77–84). Thousand Oaks, CA: Sage.

Berry, J. W. (2011). The ecocultural framework: A stocktaking. In F. J. R. Van de Vijver, A. Chasiotis, & S. M. Breugelmans (Eds.), *Fundamental questions in cross-cultural psychology* (pp. 95–114). New York, NY: Cambridge University Press. doi:10.1017/CBO9780511974090.005

Bryant, D., Nielsen, D., & Tangley, L. (1997). *The last frontier forests: Ecosystems and economies on the edge*. Washington, DC: World Resources Institute.

Conway, L. G., III, Ryder, A. G., Tweed, R. G., & Hallett, D. (2001). Intra-national cultural variation: Exploring further implications of collectivism in the United States. *Journal of Cross-Cultural Psychology, 32*, 681–697. doi:10.1177/0022022101032006003

Conway, L. G., III, & Schaller, M. (2005). When authority's commands backfire: Attributions about consensus and effects on deviant decision making. *Journal of Personality and Social Psychology, 89*, 311–326. doi:10.1037/0022-3514.89.3.311

Conway, L. G., III, & Schaller, M. (2007). How communication shapes culture. In K. Fiedler (Ed.), *Social communication* (pp. 107–127). New York, NY: Psychology Press.

Conway, L. G., III, Schaller, M., Tweed, R. G., & Hallett, D. (2001). The complexity of thinking across cultures: Interactions between culture and situational context. *Social Cognition, 19*, 228–250. doi:10.1521/soco.19.3.228.21472

Conway, L. G., Sexton, S., & Tweed, R. G. (2006). Collectivism and governmentally initiated restrictions: A cross-sectional and longitudinal analysis across nations and within a nation. *Journal of Cross-Cultural Psychology, 37*, 20–41. doi:10.1177/0022022105282293

Garcia-Jimeno, C., & Robinson, J. A. (2009, March). *The myth of the frontier* (National Bureau of Economic Research Working Paper No. 14774). Paper presented at Understanding Long-Run Economic Growth: A Conference Honoring the Contribution of Kenneth Sokoloff, Cambridge, MA.

Hofstede, G. (1980). *Culture's consequences: International differences in work-related values*. Beverly Hills, CA: Sage.

Inglehart, R., & Baker, W. E. (2000). Modernization, cultural change, and the persistence of traditional values. *American Sociological Review, 65*, 19–51. doi:10.2307/2657288

Kagitcibasi, C. (1997). Individualism and collectivism. In J. W. Berry, M. H. Segall, & C. Kagitcibasi (Eds.), *Handbook of cross-cultural psychology: Vol. 3. Social behavior and applications* (2nd ed., pp. 1–49). Boston, MA: Allyn &Bacon.

Kashima, Y., Kokubo, T., Kashima, E. S., Boxall, D., Yamaguchi, S., & Macrae, K. (2004). Culture and self: Are there within-culture differences in self between metropolitan areas and regional cities? *Personality and Social Psychology Bulletin, 30*, 816–823. doi:10.1177/0146167203261997

Kitayama, S., Conway, L. G., III, Pietromonaco, P. R., Park, H., & Plaut, V. C. (2010). Ethos of independence across regions in the United States: The production–adoption model of cultural change. *American Psychologist, 65*, 559–574. doi:10.1037/a0020277

Kitayama, S., Ishii, K., Imada, T., Takemura, K., & Ramaswamy, J. (2006). Voluntary Settlement and the Spirit of Independence: Evidence from Japan's "Northern Frontier." *Journal of Personality and Social Psychology, 91*, 369–384. doi:10.1037/0022-3514.91.3.369

Kitayama, S., Park, H., Sevincer, A. T., Karasawa, M., & Uskul, A. K. (2009). A cultural task analysis of implicit independence: Comparing North America, Western Europe, and East Asia. *Journal of Personality and Social Psychology, 97*, 236–255. doi:10.1037/a0015999

Murray, D. R., Trudeau, R., & Schaller, M. (2011). On the origins of cultural differences in conformity: Four tests of the pathogen prevalence hypothesis. *Personality and Social Psychology Bulletin, 37*, 318–329. doi:10.1177/0146167210394451

Nisbett, R. E., & Cohen, D. (1996). *Culture of honor*. Boulder, CO: Westview Press.

Perry, R. (2010). *Fed up! Our fight to save America from Washington*. New York, NY: Little, Brown.

Plaut, V. C., Markus, H. R., & Lachman, M. E. (2002). Place matters: Consensual features and regional variation in American well-being and self. *Journal of Personality and Social Psychology, 83*, 160–184. doi:10.1037/0022-3514.83.1.160

Rentfrow, P. J. (2010). Statewide differences in personality: Toward a psychological geography of the United States. *American Psychologist, 65*, 548–558. doi:10.1037/a0018194

Rentfrow, P. J., Gosling, S. D., & Potter, J. (2008). A theory of the emergence, persistence, and expression of geographic variation in personality traits. *Perspectives on Psychological Science, 3,* 339–369. doi:10.1111/j.1745-6924.2008.00084.x

Schaller, M., & Murray, D. R. (2011). Infectious disease and the creation of culture. In M. Gelfand, C.-y. Chiu, & Y.-y. Hong (Eds.), *Advances in culture and psychology* (Vol. 1, pp. 99–151). New York, NY: Oxford University Press.

Scott, M. (2008). *Harley-Davidson motor company (corporations that changed the world).* Westport, CT: Greenwood Reference.

Singelis, T. M. (1994). The measurement of independent and interdependent self-construals. *Personality and Social Psychology Bulletin, 20,* 580–591. doi:10.1177/0146167294205014

Smith, P. B., Dugans, S., & Trompenaars, F. (1996). National culture and the values of organizational employees: A dimensional analysis across 43 nations. *Journal of Cross-Cultural Psychology, 27,* 231–264. doi:10.1177/0022022196272006

Socioeconomic Data and Applications Center. (2007). *SEDAC compendium of environmental sustainability indicator collections, version 1.1.* Retrieved from http://sedac.ciesin.org/

Takemura, K., & Arimoto, H. (2008). Independent self in Japan's "Northern frontier": An experiment of cognitive dissonance in Hokkaido. *Japanese Journal of Experimental Social Psychology, 48,* 40–49. http://dx.doi.org/10.2130/jjesp.48.40

Triandis, H. C. (1989). The self and social behavior in differing cultural contexts. *Psychological Review, 96,* 506–520. doi:10.1037/0033-295X.96.3.506

Triandis, H. C. (1996). The measurement of cultural syndromes. *American Psychologist, 51,* 407–415. doi:10.1037/0003-066X.51.4.407

Triandis, H. C., & Gelfand, M. J. (1998). Converging measurement of horizontal and vertical individualism and collectivism. *Journal of Personality and Social Psychology, 74,* 118–128. doi:10.1037/0022-3514.74.1.118

Turner, F. J. (1920). *The frontier in American history.* New York, NY: Holt.

Tweed, R. G., & Conway, L. G., III. (2006). Coping strategies and culturally influenced beliefs about the world. In P. T. P. Wong & L. C. J. Wong (Eds.), *Handbook of multicultural perspectives on stress and coping: International and cultural psychology series* (pp. 133–153). Dallas, TX: Spring. doi:10.1007/0-387-26238-5_7

Vandello, J. A., & Cohen, D. (1999). Patterns of individualism and collectivism across the United States. *Journal of Personality and Social Psychology, 77,* 279–292. doi:10.1037/0022-3514.77.2.279

Van de Vliert, E. (2007). Climatoeconomic roots of survival versus self-expression cultures. *Journal of Cross-Cultural Psychology, 38,* 156–172. doi:10.1177/0022022106297298

Van de Vliert, E. (2009). *Climate, affluence, and culture.* New York, NY: Cambridge University Press.

Van de Vliert, E. (2011). Climato–economic origins of variation in ingroup favoritism. *Journal of Cross-Cultural Psychology, 42,* 494–515. doi:10.1177/0022022110381120

Van de Vliert, E., Matthiesen, S. B., Gangsøy, R., Landro, A. B., & Einarsen, S. (2010). Winters, summers, and destructive leadership cultures in rich regions. *Cross-Cultural Research, 44,* 315–340. doi:10.1177/1069397110369093

Varnum, M. E. W., & Kitayama, S. (2011). What's in a name? Popular names are less common in frontiers. *Psychological Science, 22,* 176–183. http://dx.doi.org/10.1177/0956797610395396

3

PATHOGEN PREVALENCE AND GEOGRAPHICAL VARIATION IN TRAITS AND BEHAVIOR

DAMIAN R. MURRAY AND MARK SCHALLER

Extensive geographical variation exists in personality traits, value systems, and human behavior. For example, people in Bulgaria report higher levels of Extraversion than people in Botswana (McCrae & Terracciano, 2005), and people in France tend to conform more in laboratory studies than do people in Finland (Bond & Smith, 1996). Why does this geographical variation exist? Might specific features of a local geography foster specific behavioral patterns and personality profiles? Here, we summarize and discuss a growing body of evidence demonstrating that geographical variation in behavior, personality, and values is due, at least in part, to regional variation in the prevalence of infectious diseases (or, as we term it here, *pathogen prevalence*).

Investigating the antecedents of geographical differences in human psychology is an enormous enterprise. These antecedent variables do not operate exclusively and, in addition, can change over time as a result of natural

http://dx.doi.org/10.1037/14272-004
Geographical Psychology: Exploring the Interaction of Environment and Behavior, P. J. Rentfrow (Editor)

circumstances and human intervention. This chapter, therefore, is offered as an introduction to this topic and to some of the broad implications of pathogen prevalence.

PATHOGENS AND PSYCHOLOGY

Disease-causing pathogens have posed a substantial threat to survival and reproduction throughout human history. In fact, infectious diseases have likely accounted for more deaths than all wars, noninfectious diseases, and natural disasters combined (Inhorn & Brown, 1990). Infectious diseases have thus imposed immense selective pressure on human physiology and behavior (e.g., Ridley, 1993). Not surprisingly, humans have evolved elaborate defenses that serve to mitigate the harmful effects of pathogens. One such defense involves the suite of complex physiological mechanisms that compose the immune system, which identifies disease-causing organisms within the body and responds with a set of biochemical and cellular defenses designed to eliminate the parasitic threat. These physiological immune responses are adaptive, but they are costly as well. For example, an inflammatory response produces fever that helps to kill bacterial infections, but to raise body temperature by just 1°C (a very modest fever) requires as much as a 13% increase in metabolic activity (Dantzer, Kent, Bluthe, & Kelley, 1991). Along with these metabolic costs, immunological responses can also invoke behavioral responses (e.g., lethargy) that are temporarily debilitating and that prevent one from performing other adaptive activities such as acquiring resources or caring for kin (Klein & Nelson, 1999). Thus, although activation of the immune system is beneficial when it becomes absolutely necessary, it is even more beneficial to engage this system as infrequently as possible.

For this reason, immunological defenses against pathogens are complemented by behavioral responses that serve to minimize contact with infectious agents in the first place. Evidence of such behavioral defenses against pathogens is rife across the animal kingdom: Chimpanzees react with unusual violence to ingroup members infected with polio (Goodall, 1986), rodents avoid mating with other rodents who produce olfactory cues connoting disease (Kavaliers & Colwell, 1995), and bullfrog tadpoles avoid swimming in the vicinity of other infected tadpoles (Kiesecker, Skelly, Beard, & Preisser, 1999).

Humans too are equipped with a suite of psychological mechanisms that promote behavioral defense against pathogens—a sort of *behavioral immune system* (Schaller, 2011; Schaller & Park, 2011). Broadly, these mechanisms are designed to detect potential pathogen cues within the immediate

environment and trigger specific affective and cognitive responses that promote specific kinds of behavioral reactions that, in turn, reduce the likelihood
of pathogen transmission. Much evidence now implicates these mechanisms
across a gamut of human psychological phenomena, including implications
for attention (Ackerman et al., 2009), emotion (Oaten, Stevenson, & Case,
2009), prejudice and person perception (e.g., Faulkner, Schaller, Park, &
Duncan, 2004; Park, Schaller, & Crandall, 2007), conformity (Murray &
Schaller, 2012), and interpersonal behavior in general (Mortensen, Becker,
Ackerman, Neuberg, & Kenrick, 2010).

PATHOGEN PREVALENCE AND THE EMERGENCE OF
GEOGRAPHIC VARIATION IN HUMAN PSYCHOLOGY

Although disease-causing pathogens have posed a serious threat
throughout history, the magnitude of this threat varies geographically
(see Figure 3.1). Many pathogens thrive in warm, wet conditions; the

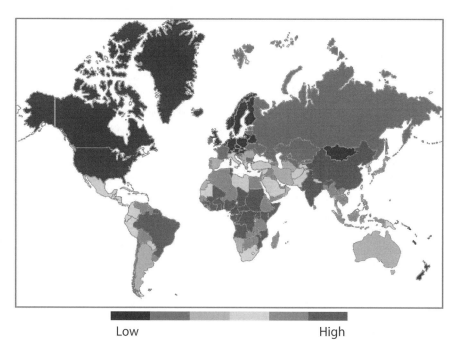

Low   High

Figure 3.1. Global pathogen prevalence, ~1900 A.D. World map of the historical
prevalence of infectious disease (by country).

prevalence and diversity of pathogens are therefore predictable functions of latitude and additional geographical characteristics of a place (Guernier, Hochberg, & Guégan, 2004). The substantial geographical variation that exists in the prevalence of pathogens has obvious implications for regional differences in health outcomes; less obviously, it also predicts regional differences in psychological outcomes.

Exactly why might geographical variation in pathogen prevalence predict variation in psychological outcomes? A cost–benefit framework is useful for addressing this question. The logical analysis proceeds as follows: Any behavioral tendency that inhibits contact with pathogens has the benefit of reducing the likelihood of pathogen-related illness or mortality. However, it may have costs as well. Thus, this behavioral tendency will be functionally adaptive only when its disease-mitigating benefits outweigh its costs. The benefits will be especially high in geographical regions where pathogens are most highly prevalent, and so it is also in these regions that the benefits are more likely to outweigh costs. The logical upshot is that any behavior that serves to reduce the likelihood of pathogen transmission should be most prevalent among populations inhabiting high-disease geographical regions and least prevalent among populations in low-disease regions. Conversely, any behavior that increases exposure to pathogens (but that has unrelated adaptive benefits) should be least prevalent in high-disease regions and most prevalent in low-disease regions.

Geographical variation in mate preferences offers an illustrative example. Although physical attractiveness in a mate is universally valued, regional differences exist in the relative value placed on physical attractiveness relative to other desired traits (Buss, 1989). Interestingly, subjective appraisals of physical attractiveness are influenced by a variety of features—clear skin, bilateral symmetry, morphological typicality—that are associated with health and genetically heritable immunocompetence (Rhodes, 2006; Thornhill & Gangestad, 1999; Weeden & Sabini, 2005). Thus, preferences for physically attractive mates are beneficial insofar as they increase the likelihood of choosing a disease-free mate and the likelihood of producing immunocompetent offspring.

However, a preference for attractive mates is not without some potential costs. Mate preferences often involve trade-offs; by placing a relatively higher priority on physical attractiveness, people may place relatively lower value on other beneficial traits, such as wealth or intelligence (Gangestad & Simpson, 2000). It follows that individuals may be most likely to place a high value on physical attractiveness under conditions in which the benefits associated with physical attractiveness are most pronounced, such as when there is greater threat posed by infectious diseases. Consistent with this logic is experimental evidence showing that when the threat of disease is made temporarily salient, people show an exaggerated tendency to judge symmetrical faces to be more highly attractive (Little, DeBruine, & Jones, 2011). A conceptually similar effect emerges when comparing different geographical regions: In an analysis of data on mate preferences collected from 29 countries worldwide, the historical prevalence of disease-causing pathogens within a country positively predicted the value that people within that country placed on the physical attractiveness of a mate (Gangestad & Buss, 1993; see also Gangestad, Haselton, & Buss, 2006). This effect occurred for both men and women and was robust when controlling for other socioeconomic variables.

This example illustrates a conceptual cost–benefit analysis that has been applied to deduce many additional hypotheses linking pathogen prevalence to geographic variation in psychological phenomena. Before proceeding to summarize these hypotheses and the evidence that supports them, it is useful to identify some of the thorny methodological and inferential issues inherent in these types of investigations.

One obvious inferential problem stems from the fact that empirical studies of this sort are necessarily correlational. Researchers studying the relation between ecological variation in pathogen prevalence and geographic variation in psychological outcomes do not have the luxury of experimental control or random assignment. Thus, although a nonzero relationship between pathogen prevalence and a psychological trait may be consistent with a causal hypothesis, this relationship alone cannot provide convincing evidence that varying pathogen prevalence truly caused geographical variation in the trait.

Several strategies can be used to help address the various alternative causal explanations that might be offered to account for predicted correlations. First, other variables that might create spurious correlations (because they are themselves related both to pathogen prevalence and to the outcome variable) can be measured and statistically controlled for. In their research linking pathogen prevalence to mate preferences, for example, Gangestad and Buss (1993) controlled for a variety of such "third variables." Conclusions about the causal influence of pathogen prevalence require that pathogen prevalence remains a unique predictor of outcome variables when controlling for plausible third variables. Second, in order to logically infer that pathogen prevalence actually caused geographical variation in psychological phenomena (rather than vice versa), it is useful to use a measure of pathogen prevalence that temporally precedes the outcome measures of interest.

In our own research, we have employed methods modeled after those described by Gangestad and Buss (1993), who used old epidemiological atlases to estimate country-level prevalence of seven kinds of pathogens across 29 countries. We expanded on this strategy and computed an index on the basis of the historical prevalence of nine different kinds of pathogens (trypanosomes, schistosomes, leishmanias, typhus, dengue, malaria, tuberculosis, filariae, and leprosy), mostly from data aggregated near the end of the 19th century. These pathogens are characterized by an acute stage of infection, with the possibility of either death, long-term debilitation, or recurrence of acute episodes. This index represents only a small subset of debilitating infectious pathogens; however, it serves as a useful and diagnostic indicator of relative geographical differences in the historical prevalence of disease-causing pathogens (for a detailed discussion of computation and validity of this index, see Murray & Schaller, 2010). This index is available for over 160 geopolitical regions worldwide. It can be especially informative to compare the predictive strength of this measure of historical pathogen prevalence with the predictive strength of indices that assess contemporary pathogen prevalence. If pathogen prevalence is a consequence rather than a cause of the psychological outcome variable, then the outcome variable should be more strongly related to contemporary rather than historical pathogen prevalence. If instead historical prevalence more strongly predicts the outcome variable, the reverse causal explanation is less plausible.

Another inferential issue arises from the fact that many contemporary geographical comparisons of psychological outcomes use countries as units of analysis. Countries cannot be assumed to be statistically independent (ideas, cultural norms, and people flow freely across geopolitical boundaries), and this has important implications for statistical inference based on country-level analyses (Nettle, 2009). Therefore, it can be useful to supplement comparisons between countries with additional comparisons between world regions that, historically, have been more culturally distinct (e.g., Africa, Eastern Eurasia). When individual-level data are available from individuals within countries, multilevel modeling approaches may also be especially informative (e.g., Van Leeuwen, Park, Koenig, & Graham, 2012).

These inferential issues are worth keeping in mind as we summarize results from recent studies identifying a variety of links between pathogen prevalence and geographical differences in human personality, values, and behavioral tendencies.

Sociosexual Attitudes

We begin with an investigation of geographical differences in dispositional tendencies toward restricted versus unrestricted sexual behavior (Schaller & Murray, 2008). Sexual behavior provides much opportunity for disease transmission. This risk exists both for infections spread exclusively through sexual contact and infections spread through nonsexual contact. The implication is simple: The more "unrestricted" (e.g., sexually promiscuous) individuals are, the more they put themselves at risk of contracting diseases and spreading these diseases to others. However, unrestricted sexual attitudes can also have specific kinds of adaptive benefits—providing, for example, the opportunity to produce more offspring. These benefits must be weighed against the disease-related costs, and this cost–benefit ratio varies depending on the prevalence of disease-causing pathogens. Where pathogen prevalence is higher, the costs of unrestricted sociosexuality are more likely to outweigh the benefits, whereas in places characterized by lower pathogen prevalence the benefits are more likely to outweigh the costs. This logic leads to the hypothesis that greater pathogen prevalence predicts more sociosexually restricted attitudes.

To test this hypothesis, we employed the results of a cross-national study (Schmitt, 2005) that assessed responses on a Sociosexual Orientation Inventory (SOI; Simpson & Gangestad, 1991) from over 14,000 people in 48 different countries and reported mean male and female SOI scores for each country. High SOI scores indicate unrestricted sexual attitudes and behavior, whereas low SOI scores indicate more restricted attitudes and behavior. The hypothesis predicts a negative relationship between these SOI scores and historical pathogen prevalence, and that is what we found: In places with a higher level of historical pathogen prevalence, both men and women reported more restricted attitudes toward sexual relations (r's for men and women were $-.27$ and $-.62$, respectively; Schaller & Murray, 2008).

This effect is stronger for female SOI scores, and this sex difference in effect sizes fits with the cost–benefit framework. Men have a lower minimum level of parental investment than do women; thus, the fitness benefits associated with unrestricted sexual behavior are likely to be greater among men than among women. Therefore, for men only, these benefits may outweigh the costs (disease transmission) even at relatively high levels of pathogen prevalence. Among women, however, the benefits of unrestricted sexuality are relatively minimal and so are more likely to be outweighed by disease-related costs as pathogen prevalence increases.

Additional analyses revealed that historical pathogen prevalence predicted these sociosexuality measures better than did a contemporary (and much more precise) measure of pathogen prevalence. Plus, the effect (among women only) persisted even when controlling for a variety of plausible third variables. These results are consistent with the hypothesized causal relationship and are inconsistent with alternative causal explanations.

Extraversion and Openness

An individual's proclivity to engage in restricted versus unrestricted sexual behavior is a type of personality trait. However, it is a very specific trait. Might pathogen prevalence predict variation in more fundamental personality traits as well? Several research projects have gathered data on the Big Five personality traits (Extraversion, Openness, Agreeableness, Conscientiousness, and Neuroticism) from tens of thousands of individuals from dozens of countries worldwide. These studies produced country-level scores on each of the five fundamental dimensions of personality and have revealed cross-national differences in each of the five traits. These scores provide a useful tool for investigating geographic variation in two of these fundamental personality traits—Extraversion and Openness—that, on the basis of cost–benefit analyses, can be predicted to vary in response to pathogen prevalence.

Extraversion

The logic that underlies a potential link between pathogen prevalence and Extraversion is similar to its relationship with sociosexuality. Although being sexually unrestricted is associated with a higher variety and frequency of intimate interpersonal contact, Extraversion too is associated with a higher variety and frequency of (nonintimate) contact with others. These social contacts have the potential to expose individuals to interpersonally transmitted pathogens. (In fact, empirical evidence does suggest that dispositional Extraversion is associated with enhanced risk of disease transmission; Nettle, 2005.) However, Extraversion is also associated with many benefits. More highly extraverted individuals report higher levels of happiness, are more effective leaders, and enjoy more opportunities for sexual reproduction (Berry & Miller, 2001; Silverthorne, 2001). These benefits of Extraversion are more likely to outweigh the disease-related costs under ecological conditions in which these costs are relatively minimal—in places characterized by low levels of interpersonally transmitted pathogens. Conversely, in areas characterized by high pathogen prevalence, the disease-related costs of Extraversion may outweigh its benefits. This cost–benefit analysis suggests that regional variation in pathogen prevalence should be inversely related to population-level variation in Extraversion.

We (Schaller & Murray, 2008) conducted multiple tests of this hypothesis using results from three different cross-national surveys of the Big Five personality traits (McCrae, 2002; McCrae & Terracciano, 2005; Schmitt, Allik, McCrae, & Benet-Martinez, 2007). As predicted, across every measure regional differences in Extraversion were negatively correlated with historical pathogen prevalence. These relationships remained even when controlling for a variety of additional country-level variables (e.g., GDP, individualistic vs. collectivistic values). Further, consistent with the causal relation specified by the hypothesis, Extraversion was more strongly predicted by historical pathogen prevalence than by contemporary pathogen prevalence. Finally (and consistent with our analysis of the specific kinds of costs associated with

Extraversion), a follow-up investigation revealed that geographic variation in Extraversion is especially highly predicted by the prevalence of a specific subset of pathogens—those that are transmitted through human interaction (Thornhill, Fincher, Murray, & Schaller, 2010).

Openness

A similar cost–benefit analysis also suggested that regional variation in pathogen prevalence may help account for geographic differences in Openness to Experience. Dispositional Openness is characterized by creativity, attraction to novelty, and a willingness to try new and unfamiliar things (Larsen & Buss, 2005). These behavioral dispositions can be beneficial in that they encourage innovation and adaptive problem solving. These dispositions can also be costly: Many traditional ways of doing things (particularly in domains such as food preparation, personal hygiene, and public health) serve as buffers against pathogen transmission. (In fact, in many technologically "primitive" small-scale societies of the sort traditionally studied by ethnographers, the majority of social norms may operate as prescriptions to avoid illness in some way [Fabrega, 1997].) To the extent that individuals deviate from these accustomed norms (e.g., experiment with novel or idiosyncratic approaches to hygiene or food preparation), those individuals expose themselves and others in their community to an increased risk of pathogen infection. These particular kinds of costs are greater (and more likely to outweigh benefits associated with Openness) under conditions of greater pathogen prevalence. Thus, regional variation in pathogen prevalence is expected to be inversely related to population-level variation in Openness to Experience.

We conducted multiple tests of this hypothesis using exactly the same source materials as we used in our investigations of Extraversion (Schaller & Murray, 2008). Again, across every measure cross-cultural differences in Openness to Experience were negatively correlated with historical pathogen prevalence. These negative relationships remained even when controlling for additional country-level variables. Again, consistent with the causal hypothesis, Openness to Experience was more strongly predicted by historical pathogen prevalence than by contemporary pathogen prevalence.

We also performed analyses on the three remaining fundamental personality traits (Agreeableness, Conscientiousness, and Neuroticism). Across measures, results revealed no appreciable or consistent relationships between pathogen prevalence and these personality traits. These results, when taken in concert with the consistent significant relationships obtained for Extraversion and Openness, suggest that the significant results for Extraversion and Openness were not due to response biases or other methodological artifacts that often pose issues for cross-national investigations, and increase confidence in a conclusion that the results obtained reflect truly meaningful causal relationships. It is also worth noting that convergent significant results for both Openness and Extraversion (as well as negligible results for the remaining variables) have been documented using world regions as the units of analysis (e.g. Schaller & Murray, 2012).

Individualism and Collectivism

Adaptive logic suggests that the influence of pathogen prevalence should have implications for cultural value systems as well. Although there are many forms of cultural values, the value constructs of individualism and collectivism have been subjected to more rigorous scientific inquiry than any other (Heine, 2008). At least three characteristics of individualism/collectivism suggest that geographic variation along this dimension may have been causally influenced by pathogen prevalence.

First, collectivistic (compared with individualistic) value systems imply a more rigid psychological distinction between ingroup and outgroup (Gelfand, Nishii, & Raver, 2006), which manifests in higher levels of ethnocentrism and xenophobia. Higher levels of xenophobia have costs, including reduced opportunities for trade and coalitional alliances. But xenophobia may also have disease-relevant benefits. Outgroup members are more likely to harbor exotic pathogens, which are especially virulent to individuals with no prior exposure to them. Outgroup members are also more likely to be ignorant of local norms that buffer against pathogen transmission. These disease-specific benefits of xenophobia are likely to be greater in regions of higher pathogen prevalence.

Second, collectivist cultural values are characterized by a higher expectation of prosocial behavior among family members and other individuals within a local social alliance. There are costs associated with the obligatory expenditure of resources. Reciprocal benefits of this obligatory prosociality accrue whenever one (or one's immediate kin) is in need of assistance from others. These benefits are likely to be especially pronounced under conditions characterized by high levels of threat to health and welfare. Thus, because of the emphasis on obligatory prosociality among group members, collectivistic value systems are likely to be relatively more advantageous under conditions of greater pathogen prevalence.

A third relevant feature of collectivistic value systems is *tightness*: A strong premium is placed on conforming to ingroup norms, and a lack of tolerance exists for individuals who deviate from those norms (Gelfand et al., 2006). Individualistic value systems, however, place a premium on individual rights and are more tolerant of deviance. Thus, the cost–benefit implications are similar to those discussed for Openness to Experience: Although there are costs associated with vigilant adherence to established norms (e.g., decreased innovation), the pathogen-mitigating characteristics of many of these norms makes adherence beneficial too. These benefits are more likely to outweigh the costs in geographical regions of high disease prevalence.

Overall, these multiple distinct lines of deduction converge on a hypothesis linking pathogen prevalence to geographic variation in individualistic versus collectivistic values: Pathogen prevalence should negatively predict measures of individualism and positively predict indicators of collectivism.

We conducted four tests of this hypothesis using two different country-level measures of individualism and two country-level measures of collectivism (Fincher, Thornhill, Murray, & Schaller, 2008). The results were clear across all four sets of analyses: Consistent with the hypothesis, geographical variation in historical pathogen prevalence was significantly negatively correlated with individualism (r's = $-.69$ and $-.71$) and significantly positively correlated with collectivism (r's = $.73$ and $.63$, all p's < .001). These results were further corroborated using world regions as the units of analysis (in fact, correlations tended to be even stronger when using these larger units of analysis). Additional analyses revealed that the predictive effect of pathogen prevalence remained even when controlling for a variety of additional variables that might plausibly have a causal influence on individualistic/collectivistic value systems (e.g., GDP, inequality, other threats to health and morality). Consistent with the causal relation specified by the hypothesis, individualism/collectivism was more strongly predicted by historical pathogen prevalence than by contemporary pathogen prevalence. Similar sets of analyses have since been performed using American states as the unit of analysis (Fincher & Thornhill, 2012) and have produced inferentially identical results.

These results provide compelling evidence for a causal relationship between pathogen prevalence and cultural value systems. Individualism and collectivism are, however, multifaceted constructs, comprising several conceptually distinct kinds of values (pertaining to intergroup relations, family dynamics, conformity to norms, etc.). Evidence bearing on this broad construct does not speak to whether pathogen prevalence specifically relates to geographic variation in xenophobia, obligatory prosociality, conformity pressure, or any other specific facet underlying the individual/collectivism dimension. Disentangling which of these relationships contributes to the relationship between pathogen prevalence and individualism/collectivism requires additional analyses on additional measures of geographic variation.

Conformity Pressure

We recently conducted a series of analyses designed to focus specifically on the hypothesis that regional differences in pathogen prevalence predict worldwide geographic differences in conformity pressure (Murray, Trudeau, & Schaller, 2011). In testing this prediction, we used a methodologically diverse set of four country-level measures of conformity pressure. One measure was taken from a meta-analysis of dozens of behavioral conformity experiments performed worldwide (Bond & Smith, 1996), which allowed us to compute mean conformity effect sizes for individual countries. A second measure was obtained from the World Values Survey (http://www.worldvaluessurvey.org/) and pertained to attitudes toward obedience: the percentage of respondents within each country who indicated that obedience was an important trait for children to learn. A third measure follows from the logical implication that, in populations characterized by stronger conformity pressure, there is less tolerance for deviation from established norms. One way to measure this tolerance for deviation is through the mean level of within-population variability on personality traits (reduced tolerance for nonconformity should result in reduced variability). Exactly such a measure of within-country personality variability was reported by McCrae (2002). The fourth measure was the percentage of individuals within a country who are left-handed. The logic underlying this measure arises from the fact that right-handedness is normative, and so, in regions characterized by conformity pressure, it is more likely that naturally left-handed people will be compelled to become right-handed (Porac & Martin, 2007; Triandis, 1995). Thus, the percentage of left-handers serves as an indirect indicator of tolerance for behavioral nonconformity.

Our results revealed that each of these four measures of conformity pressure was predicted by pathogen prevalence. The historical prevalence of pathogens correlated significantly positively with behavioral conformity effect sizes and the value placed on obedience (r's = .49 and .48) and significantly negatively with personality variation and the percentage of left-handers (r's = −.52 and −.73). Additional analyses revealed that pathogen prevalence remained a significant predictor when controlling for additional variables that might be conceptually linked to conformity (e.g., level of agriculture, life expectancy, population density). Analyses performed at the world-region level produced correlations that were even higher in magnitude than those obtained at the country level. Historical pathogen prevalence was a stronger predictor of these conformity variables than was contemporary prevalence. These results all support the proposed causal link between pathogens and conformity.

Strength of Family Ties

The strength of family ties—which is associated with obligatory prosociality toward extended family members—is an integral part of collectivist (vs. individualist) value systems. Recently, Fincher and Thornhill (2012) investigated whether pathogen prevalence predicts this specific facet of collectivism. They created a country-level index of "strength of family ties" on the basis of five responses obtained from the World Values Survey (e.g., the percentage of respondents who indicated that one of their goals in life was to "make their parents proud"; http://www.worldvaluessurvey.org/). Consistent with the hypothesis, geographic variation in strength of family ties was positively predicted by pathogen prevalence at both the country and world-region levels of analysis. This relationship remained after controlling for possible confounds such as economic development and human freedoms. Fincher and Thornhill replicated these findings with independent analyses that used American states as units of analysis. These convergent results support the hypothesized causal link between pathogen prevalence and geographic variation in values pertaining to family ties and obligatory prosociality.

Xenophobia and Ethnocentrism

Several results provide some support for a link between pathogen prevalence and regional variation in ethnocentrism and xenophobia. For instance, pathogen prevalence is positively correlated with the percentage of people in a country who indicate that they would not want "people of a different race" as neighbors (Schaller & Murray, 2010). High pathogen prevalence is also associated with population-level outcomes that indirectly indicate reduced levels of contact between ethnic groups (e.g., Fincher & Thornhill, 2008). The frequency of intrastate conflict and civil war is also positively correlated with pathogen prevalence—a relationship that is conceptually consistent with higher levels of xenophobia and ethnocentrism within pathogen-prevalence regions (Letendre, Fincher, & Thornhill, 2010).

"Binding" Moral Values

The preceding findings all suggest intriguing relations between pathogen prevalence and fundamental cultural value systems. Values are conceptually linked to moral judgments and moral behavior, suggesting that geographic differences in morality might also be predicted by pathogen prevalence. One recent investigation examined the possibility that regional differences in pathogen prevalence may help to explain worldwide geographic variation on a particular subset of moral values (Van Leeuwen et al., 2012). According to moral foundations theory, the many different kinds of moral values can be located within two foundational categories: Some moral values are considered to be *individualizing*, whereas others are considered to be *binding*. Binding moral foundations are relevant to concerns such as group loyalty, respect for authority, and purity. These binding aspects of morality have obvious implications for a variety of attitudes and behaviors (e.g., ethnocentrism, obedience, cleanliness) that, as we have already discussed, may serve as buffers against disease transmission. It follows, therefore, that binding moral values will be endorsed more fervently in places characterized by a greater threat of pathogen infection.

Van Leeuwen and colleagues (2012) tested this hypothesis on data obtained from over 120,000 people in 147 countries. The results showed that historical pathogen prevalence was a significant predictor of binding moral values but not of individualizing moral values. The predictive effect of historical pathogen prevalence was greater than the effect of contemporary pathogen prevalence—a finding that is inconsistent with a reverse causal explanation. These effects emerged even when controlling for a variety of additional variables that can influence moral values, thus eliminating a variety of alternative explanations. Also, importantly, this result emerged not only from analyses that treated countries as units of analysis but also from multilevel analyses on individual responses.

Political Ideology

Just as cultural values have implications for morality, they also have implications for political ideology, and this can have important consequences. Economic and political outcomes within a country are influenced substantially by the political ideologies held by its citizens. A culture that prizes tradition and conformity, for example, may perceive specific kinds of individual rights and freedoms (e.g., freedom of speech) to pose a threat. Consistent with this analysis is evidence that cultural tightness and collectivism are highly associated with the existence of authoritarian governments and legalized repression of civil liberties and individual freedoms (Conway, Sexton, & Tweed, 2006). The overall upshot is that cross-national differences in political systems and style of governance may result, in part, from regional differences in pathogen prevalence.

In support of this hypothesis, Thornhill, Fincher, and Aran (2009) found that a measure of contemporary pathogen prevalence significantly predicted a variety of country-level measures of political ideologies and additional outcomes pertaining to governance—including positive correlations with measures that assess repression of individual rights and freedoms, negative correlations with additional measures of social and political liberalism, and negative correlations with democratization in general. These relations persist even when controlling for a variety of potential confounds. Follow-up analyses revealed that these outcomes pertaining to political ideology and governance are even more strongly predicted by historical pathogen prevalence (Murray & Schaller, 2010).

IMPLICATIONS AND FUTURE DIRECTIONS

Taken together, these findings support a range of conceptual hypotheses that link pathogen prevalence to geographical variation in traits, values, behaviors, and societal outcomes. These findings also provide a more complete understanding of previously documented relationships between psychological outcomes that vary geographically. For example, it has been previously observed that regional differences in Extraversion are linked to regional differences in individualistic value systems, and discussions of this relationship have centered on the possible causal influence of cultural value systems on individual dispositions, or vice versa (e.g., Hofstede & McCrae, 2004). Our analyses reveal, however, that the relationship between Extraversion and individualism disappears when statistically controlling for pathogen prevalence (Fincher et al., 2008; Schaller & Murray, 2008). Therefore, it appears that there is no meaningful causal relationship between Extraversion and individualism; their relation may be a result of both variables being consequences of lower pathogen prevalence.

Another example is latitude, which has been cited as a strong predictor of many cross-cultural differences (e.g., Hofstede, 2001). Of course, a latitude value is an abstract cartographic convention; it has no meaningful causal influence on human psychology. Any correlation between latitude and psychological phenomena requires explanations that focus on additional variables that vary geographically and that actually do have an impact on human experience and psychological functioning. Pathogen prevalence is one such variable, and it may be an integral part of any causal explanation for a relationship between latitude and psychological outcomes.

The prevalence of pathogens within any geographic region is not immutable, however; as mentioned at the outset of this chapter, it can change over time, both as a result of natural circumstances and as a result of human intervention. Consequently, public health initiatives (e.g., vaccination campaigns) may have consequences that extend far beyond epidemiological morbidity and mortality; efforts designed to reduce the prevalence of infectious diseases may also lead to meaningful changes in personality, cultural values, intergroup relations, political practices, and many other aspects of human life. A reduction in pathogen prevalence may, for example, lead to a higher tolerance for nonconformity, thereby facilitating artistic creativity and technological innovation. It is worth noting here, perhaps, that the number of Nobel laureates per capita within a country is strongly negatively predicted by historical pathogen prevalence ($r = -.59$, $p < .0001$), and this relationship remains robust when controlling for variables such as economic development (Murray, 2013). Rigorous longitudinal investigations will be needed to test whether temporal variation in pathogen prevalence does indeed lead to changes in these kinds of psychological and societal outcomes.

If changes in pathogen prevalence do have the downstream effects that we suggest, another question that arises is when these effects might become evident. This "when" question is largely dependent on another scientific factor that requires much more investigation: the mechanism by which pathogen prevalence might produce these geographic differences in the first place. At least four such mechanisms are possible. One possibility is that these differences are created through facultative cognitive mechanisms, wherein individuals detect disease cues within their immediate environment and respond by emitting appropriate disease-mitigating behaviors. Alternatively, these differences may be more genetically based, whereby historical geographical variation in pathogen prevalence has led to differential selection for genes associated with behaviors that have implications for pathogen transmission. A different type of genetic mechanism—an epigenetic mechanism—is also a possibility, wherein genes associated with traits such as collectivism and conformity are more likely to be developmentally expressed in regions of higher disease. Finally, these cultural differences may have arisen through cultural transmission, wherein information about the most locally adaptive sets of traits, behaviors, or practices is selectively communicated across generations.

The time frame whereby changes in disease prevalence lead to cultural change will provide clues as to which of these mechanisms is at play: Any cultural change that transpires within days or weeks of disease outbreak (or disease eradication) would indicate the operation of facultative mechanisms; changes that occur one generation after a disease outbreak are more likely to implicate an epigenetic process; and changes that accumulate across multiple generations would be more indicative of a cultural transmission process or even a genetic process. (For a more substantive discussion of these mechanisms, and the evidence bearing on each of them, see Schaller & Murray, 2011.)

Investigating the antecedents of geographical differences in human psychology is an enormous enterprise. These antecedent variables do not operate exclusively, and only now are we beginning to appreciate the complex interplay between the variables that contribute to the geographical differences we see today. Much work remains to be done in investigating the mechanisms by which these variables operate, the interactions that exist between them, and their implications.

REFERENCES

Ackerman, J. M., Becker, D. V., Mortensen, C. R., Sasaki, T., Neuberg, S. L., & Kenrick, D. T. (2009). A pox on the mind: Disjunction of attention and memory in processing physical disfigurement. *Journal of Experimental Social Psychology*, *45*, 478–485. doi:10.1016/j.jesp.2008.12.008

Berry, D. S., & Miller, K. M. (2001). When boy meets girl: Attractiveness and the Five-Factor Model in opposite-sex interactions. *Journal of Research in Personality, 35*, 62–77. doi:10.1006/jrpe.2000.2304

Bond, R., & Smith, P. B. (1996). Culture and conformity: A meta-analysis of studies using Asch's line judgment task. *Psychological Bulletin, 119*, 111–137. doi:10.1037/0033-2909.119.1.111

Buss, D. M. (1989). Sex differences in human mate preferences: Evolutionary hypotheses tested in 37 cultures. *Behavioral and Brain Sciences, 12*, 1–14. doi:10.1017/S0140525X00023992

Conway, L. G., III, Sexton, S. M., & Tweed, R. G. (2006). Collectivism and governmentally initiated restrictions: A cross-sectional and longitudinal analysis across nations and within a nation. *Journal of Cross-Cultural Psychology, 37*, 20–41. doi:10.1177/0022022105282293

Dantzer, R., Kent, S., Bluthe, R. M., & Kelley, K. W. (1991). Cytokines and sickness behaviour. *European Neuropsychopharmacology, 1*, 377–379. doi:10.1016/0924-977X(91)90576-G

Fabrega, H. (1997). Earliest phases in the evolution of sickness and healing. *Medical Anthropology Quarterly, 11*, 26–55. doi:10.1525/maq.1997.11.1.26

Faulkner, J., Schaller, M., Park, J. H., & Duncan, L. A. (2004). Evolved disease-avoidance mechanisms and contemporary xenophobic attitudes. *Group Processes & Intergroup Relations, 7*, 333–353. doi:10.1177/1368430204046142

Fincher, C. L., & Thornhill, R. (2008). Assortive sociality, limited dispersal, infectious disease and the genesis of the global pattern of religious diversity. *Proceedings of the Royal Society: B. Biological Sciences, 275*, 2587–2594. doi:10.1098/rspb.2008.0688

Fincher, C. L., & Thornhill, R. (2012). Parasite-stress promotes in-group assortative sociality: The cases of strong family ties and heightened religiosity. *Behavioral and Brain Sciences, 35*, 61–79. doi:10.1017/S0140525X11000021

Fincher, C. L., Thornhill, R., Murray, D. R., & Schaller, M. (2008). Pathogen prevalence predicts human cross-cultural variability in individualism/collectivism. *Proceedings of the Royal Society: B. Biological Sciences, 275*, 1279–1285. doi:10.1098/rspb.2008.0094

Gangestad, S. W., & Buss, D. M. (1993). Pathogen prevalence and human mate preferences. *Ethology and Sociobiology, 14*, 89–96. doi:10.1016/0162-3095(93)90009-7

Gangestad, S. W., Haselton, M. G., & Buss, D. M. (2006). Evolutionary foundations of cultural variation: Evoked culture and mate preferences. *Psychological Inquiry, 17*, 75–95. doi:10.1207/s15327965pli1702_1

Gangestad, S. W., & Simpson, J. A. (2000). The evolution of human mating: Trade-offs and strategic pluralism. *Behavioral and Brain Sciences, 23*, 573–644. doi:10.1017/S0140525X0000337X

Gelfand, M. J., Nishii, L. H., & Raver, J. L. (2006). On the nature and importance of cultural tightness-looseness. *Journal of Applied Psychology, 91*, 1225–1244. doi:10.1037/0021-9010.91.6.1225

Goodall, J. (1986). Social rejection, exclusion, and shunning among the Gombe chimpanzees. *Ethology and Sociobiology, 7*, 227–236. doi:10.1016/0162-3095(86)90050-6

Guernier, V., Hochberg, M. E., & Guégan, J.-F. (2004). Ecology drives the worldwide distribution of human diseases. *PLoS Biology, 2*, 740–746. doi:10.1371/journal.pbio.0020141

Heine, S. J. (2008). *Cultural psychology.* New York, NY: Norton.

Hofstede, G. (2001). *Culture's consequences. Comparing values, behaviors, institutions, and organizations across nations* (2nd ed.). Thousand Oaks, CA: Sage.

Hofstede, G., & McCrae, R. R. (2004). Personality and culture revisited: Linking traits and dimensions of culture. *Cross-Cultural Research, 38*, 52–88. doi:10.1177/1069397103259443

Inhorn, M. C., & Brown, P. J. (1990). The anthropology of infectious disease. *Annual Review of Anthropology, 19*, 89–117. doi:10.1146/annurev.an.19.100190.000513

Kavaliers, M., & Colwell, D. D. (1995). Discrimination by female mice between the odours of parasitized and non-parasitized males. *Proceedings of the Royal Society: B. Biological Sciences, 261*, 31–35. doi:10.1098/rspb.1995.0113

Kiesecker, J. M., Skelly, D. K., Beard, K. H., & Preisser, E. (1999). Behavioral reduction of infection risk. *Proceedings of the National Academy of Sciences of the United States of America, 96*, 9165–9168. doi:10.1073/pnas.96.16.9165

Klein, S. L., & Nelson, R. J. (1999). Influence of social factors on immune function and reproduction. *Reviews of Reproduction, 4*, 168–178. doi:10.1530/ror.0.0040168

Larsen, R. J., & Buss, D. M. (2005). *Personality psychology* (2nd ed.). New York, NY: McGraw-Hill.

Letendre, K., Fincher, C. L., & Thornhill, R. (2010). Does infectious disease cause global variation in the frequency of intrastate armed conflict and civil war? *Biological Reviews of the Cambridge Philosophical Society, 85*, 669–683.

Little, A. C., DeBruine, L. M., & Jones, B. C. (2011). Exposure to visual cues of pathogen contagion changes preferences for masculinity and symmetry in opposite-sex faces. *Proceedings of the Royal Society: B. Biological Sciences, 278*, 2032–2039. doi:10.1098/rspb.2010.1925

McCrae, R. R. (2002). NEO-PI-R data from 36 cultures: Further intercultural comparisons. In R. R. McCrae & J. Allik (Eds.), *The Five-Factor model of personality across cultures* (pp. 105–126). New York, NY: Kluwer Academic/Plenum. doi:10.1007/978-1-4615-0763-5_6

McCrae, R. R., & Terracciano, A. (2005). Personality profiles of cultures: Aggregate personality traits. *Journal of Personality and Social Psychology, 89*, 407–425. doi:10.1037/0022-3514.89.3.407

Mortensen, C. R., Becker, D. V., Ackerman, J. M., Neuberg, S. L., & Kenrick, D. T. (2010). Infection breeds reticence: The effects of disease salience on self-perceptions of personality and behavioral tendencies. *Psychological Science, 21*, 440–447. doi:10.1177/0956797610361706

Murray, D. R. (2013). *The implications of pathogen prevalence for scientific and techno-logical innovation*. Manuscript submitted for publication.

Murray, D. R., & Schaller, M. (2010). Historical prevalence of disease within 230 geopolitical regions: A tool for investigating origins of culture. *Journal of Cross-Cultural Psychology, 41*, 99–108. doi:10.1177/0022022109349510

Murray, D. R., & Schaller, M. (2012). Threat(s) and conformity deconstructed: Per-ceived threat of infectious disease and its implications for conformist attitudes and behavior. *European Journal of Social Psychology, 42*, 180–188. doi:10.1002/ejsp.863

Murray, D. R., Trudeau, R., & Schaller, M. (2011). On the origins of cultural differ-ences in conformity: Four tests of the pathogen prevalence hypothesis. *Personal-ity and Social Psychology Bulletin, 37*, 318–329. doi:10.1177/0146167210394451

Nettle, D. (2005). An evolutionary approach to the extraversion continuum. *Evolution and Human Behavior, 26*, 363–373. doi:10.1016/j.evolhumbehav.2004.12.004

Nettle, D. (2009). Ecological influences on human behavioral diversity: A review of recent findings. *Trends in Ecology & Evolution, 24*, 618–624. doi:10.1016/j.tree.2009.05.013

Oaten, M., Stevenson, R, J. & Case, T. I. (2009). Disgust as a disease-avoidance mechanism. *Psychological Bulletin, 135*, 303–321. doi:10.1037/a0014823

Park, J. H., Schaller, M., & Crandall, C. S. (2007). Pathogen-avoidance mecha-nisms and the stigmatization of obese people. *Evolution and Human Behavior, 28*, 410–414. doi:10.1016/j.evolhumbehav.2007.05.008

Porac, C., & Martin, W. L. B. (2007). A cross-cultural comparison of pressures to switch left-handed writing: Brazil versus Canada. *Laterality: Asymmetries of Body, Brain and Cognition, 12*, 273–291. doi:10.1080/13576500701269462

Rhodes, G. (2006). The evolutionary psychology of facial beauty. *Annual Review of Psychology, 57*, 199–226. doi:10.1146/annurev.psych.57.102904.190208

Ridley, M. (1993). *The red queen: Sex and the evolution of human nature*. New York, NY: Penguin Books.

Schaller, M. (2011). The behavioural immune system and the psychology of human sociality. *Philosophical Transactions of the Royal Society: B. Biological Sciences, 366*, 3418–3426. doi:10.1098/rstb.2011.0029

Schaller, M., & Murray, D. R. (2008). Pathogens, personality, and culture: Disease prevalence predicts worldwide variability in sociosexuality, extraversion, and openness to experience. *Journal of Personality and Social Psychology, 95*, 212–221. doi:10.1037/0022-3514.95.1.212

Schaller, M., & Murray, D. R. (2010). Infectious diseases and the evolution of cross-cultural differences. In M. Schaller, A. Norenzayan, S. J. Heine, T. Yamagishi, & T. Kameda (Eds.), *Evolution, culture, and the human mind* (pp. 243–256). New York, NY: Psychology Press.

Schaller, M., & Murray, D. R. (2011). Infectious disease and the creation of culture. In M. Gelfand, C.-y. Chiu, & Y.-y. Hong (Eds.), *Advances in culture and psychology* (Vol. 1, pp. 99–151). New York, NY: Oxford University Press.

Schaller, M., & Park, J. H. (2011). The behavioural immune system (and why it matters). *Current Directions in Psychological Science, 20*, 99–103. doi:10.1177/0963721411402596

Schmitt, D. P. (2005). Sociosexuality from Argentina to Zimbabwe: A 48-nation study of sex, culture, and strategies of human mating. *Behavioral and Brain Sciences, 28*, 247–311. doi:10.1017/S0140525X05000051

Schmitt, D. P., Allik, J., McCrae, R. R., & Benet-Martinez, V. (2007). The geographic distribution of Big Five personality traits: Patterns and profiles of human self-description across 56 nations. *Journal of Cross-Cultural Psychology, 38*, 173–212. doi:10.1177/0022022106297299

Silverthorne, C. (2001). Leadership effectiveness and personality: A cross cultural evaluation. *Personality and Individual Differences, 30*, 303–309. doi:10.1016/S0191-8869(00)00047-7

Simpson, J. A., & Gangestad, S. W. (1991). Individual differences in sociosexuality: Evidence for convergent and discriminant validity. *Journal of Personality and Social Psychology, 60*, 870–883. doi:10.1037/0022-3514.60.6.870

Thornhill, R., Fincher, C. L., & Aran, D. (2009). Parasites, democratization, and the liberalization of values across contemporary countries. *Biological Reviews of the Cambridge Philosophical Society, 84*, 113–131. doi:10.1111/j.1469-185X.2008.00062.x

Thornhill, R., Fincher, C. L., Murray, D. R., & Schaller, M. (2010). Zoonotic and non-zoonotic diseases in relation to human personality and societal values: Support for the parasite-stress model. *Evolutionary Psychology, 8*, 151–169.

Thornhill, R., & Gangestad, S. W. (1999). Facial attractiveness. *Trends in Cognitive Sciences, 3*, 452–460. doi:10.1016/S1364-6613(99)01403-5

Triandis, H. C. (1995). *Individualism & collectivism.* Boulder, CO: Westview Press.

Van Leeuwen, F., Park, J. H., Koenig, B. L., & Graham, J. (2012). Regional variation in pathogen prevalence predicts endorsement of group-focused moral concerns. *Evolution and Human Behavior, 33*, 429–437. doi:10.1016/j.evolhumbehav.2011.12.005

Weeden, J., & Sabini, J. (2005). Physical attractiveness and health in Western societies: A review. *Psychological Bulletin, 131*, 635–653. doi:10.1037/0033-2909.131.5.635

4

PERSONALITY AND THE REALIZATION OF MIGRATION DESIRES

MARKUS JOKELA

Residential mobility and migration patterns are often conceptualized in terms of migration flows between different geographical areas, and the data are aggregated at the level of populations (Greenwood & Hunt, 2003). However, residential mobility is not only a collection of discrete events that take place as people move from one place to another. For the individual who is making the decision, voluntary residential mobility can be seen as a process that transitions through different stages (Kley, 2011). The process initiates with a *desire to move*. Perhaps the person becomes bored with her current neighborhood or would like to live in a bigger house. If the desire is strong enough, it develops into a more committed *intention to move*. The person may start to look for new apartments in the newspapers and begin to evaluate different neighborhoods as potential places to move into. After the person has already made some preparations to move, the intention to move materializes into an *expectation to move*. Finally, the desires, intentions, and expectations of moving are realized as an *actual move* to a new location.

http://dx.doi.org/10.1037/14272-005
Geographical Psychology: Exploring the Interaction of Environment and Behavior, P. J. Rentfrow (Editor)
Copyright © 2014 by the American Psychological Association. All rights reserved.

The psychology of residential mobility thus involves a sequence of preferences, intentions, and decisions. If one is interested in the psychological aspects of migration behavior, it is important to consider all of these steps in detail. The psychological nature of migration behavior was already recognized by Peter H. Rossi (1995) in his classic work on residential mobility titled *Why Families Move: A Study in the Social Psychology of Urban Residential Mobility*. Several demographic studies following the work of Rossi have examined topics such as the influence of housing and neighborhood characteristics on residential satisfaction and how migration desires and intentions predict actual residential mobility (De Groot, Mulder, & Manting, 2011; Lu, 1999). However, the demographic literature has remained largely separated from psychology—or at least the demographic models of migration decisions have not been updated in pace with more recent advances in personality and social psychology (Hobcraft, 2006).

This chapter takes the integration of personality psychology and demographic models one step further by exploring the role of personality in the realization of people's migration desires and expectations. By examining how different stages of migration decisions are related to general personality dispositions, it is possible to better understand the psychological basis of migration behavior and the dynamics of psychological geography. To this end, data from the British Household Panel Survey (BHPS; Research Centre on Micro-Social Change, 2010) are used to examine (a) how personality traits are related to migration desires and expectations and (b) whether personality traits predict residential mobility differently depending on the individual's desire for and expectations of moving in the future. The purpose is to investigate in more detail the potential mechanisms that explain why and how some personality traits are associated with people's propensity to move.

MIGRANT PERSONALITY

Evidence from several countries suggests that personality traits are differently distributed over geographical areas. Large-scale data from the United States have shown consistent differences in personality profiles between regions and individual states (Rentfrow, Gosling, & Potter, 2008). In an Australian study, people residing in remote parts of the country tended to be less open to new experiences and more introverted than those living in more central locations (Murray et al., 2005). In the archipelago of Italy, people living in the islands nearby the mainland were more introverted, conscientious, and emotionally stable, and less open to new experiences than their counterparts living in the mainland (Camperio Ciani & Capiluppi, 2011; Camperio Ciani, Capiluppi, Veronese, & Sartori, 2007).

At least part of the regional personality differences is likely to reflect the consequences of selective migration. Several longitudinal studies have demonstrated associations between personality traits and individual differences in migration patterns. In a prospective study of Finnish twins with a follow-up period spanning from 1975 to 2002, high Extraversion and high Neuroticism at baseline predicted higher probability of emigration from Finland to Sweden, Finland's neighboring country to which many Finns immigrated in the 1970s and 1980s to seek better employment opportunities (Silventoinen et al., 2008). Lower life satisfaction also predicted higher emigration probability. In another prospective Finnish study with a 9-year follow-up (Jokela, Elovainio, Kivimäki, & Keltikangas-Järvinen, 2008), individuals with high sociability were more likely to move from rural to urban areas and more likely to stay put if they were already residing in an urban rather than a rural area. High activity—a tendency to carry out daily activities vigorously and with high tempo—was also associated with higher migration propensity irrespective of urban–rural difference. Negative emotionality, a trait closely related to Neuroticism, was associated with increased migration probability, especially if the person was living in a rural area.

In the representative population-based Midlife in the United States Study (MIDUS), higher Openness to Experience and lower Agreeableness were predictive of residential mobility within and between states over a 7-year follow-up period, whereas higher Extraversion predicted only within-state migration (Jokela, 2009). In a sample of older Americans, symptoms of depression and anxiety and low life satisfaction were associated with higher likelihood of moving to a new location (Colsher & Wallace, 1990). In the Italian study cited earlier, individuals who had left the islands and moved to the mainland were more extroverted and more open to experiences than those who had stayed in the islands (Camperio Ciani et al., 2007; Camperio Ciani & Capiluppi, 2011).

Longitudinal data on the association between personality and residential mobility are still scarce, but the findings reviewed previously suggest some consistent patterns between personality and migration behavior. First, outgoing and sociable dispositions (Extraversion, sociability, activity) and Openness to Experience appear to increase the odds of migration. Perhaps people with these personality characteristics are more spontaneous and active in their decision making, which helps to nudge their migration desires and intentions forward. They may also have a lower threshold for leaving the old neighborhood for new opportunities (Boneva & Frieze, 2001; Camperio Ciani et al., 2007).

Second, Neuroticism and related psychological characteristics, including mental distress and low life satisfaction, also seem to increase migration propensity. This is somewhat surprising given that Neuroticism is associated with avoidant behavior and heightened stress reactivity in many domains of life. One might therefore expect high Neuroticism to decrease rather than to increase migration propensity. One plausible explanation for the positive association between Neuroticism and mobility is that people with high Neuroticism tend to be dissatisfied with many things, including their neighborhood, housing conditions, and other residential qualities (Jokela, 2009). A heightened level of dissatisfaction with residential qualities may drive these individuals to move more often in the hope of improving their residential conditions. In the MIDUS study cited earlier, high Neuroticism was associated with lower neighborhood satisfaction, but this association did not account for the association between Neuroticism (or any other personality traits) and migration probability (Jokela, 2009). Thus, the mechanisms mediating the association between Neuroticism and increased residential mobility have not been empirically established and remain largely hypothetical.

The evidence for other personality dimensions in predicting migration propensity remains limited. In the United States, agreeable people were shown to be less likely to move than their disagreeable peers (Jokela, 2009). Individuals with high Agreeableness are often described as friendly, helpful, and compassionate. The lower migration propensity associated with high agreeableness might be explained by their tendency to build strong ties with their neighborhood and community and by their unwillingness to break those ties by relocating (Boneva & Frieze, 2001; Frieze, Hansen, & Boneva, 2006). However, data addressing the more detailed mechanisms of agreeableness and migration behavior are lacking. Only a few studies of residential mobility have measured personality traits related to Conscientiousness—a disposition characterized by orderliness, achievement striving, and preference to follow rules and norms. These studies have not found associations between Conscientiousness and migration.

MIGRATION DESIRES AND EXPECTATIONS AS PRECURSORS OF RESIDENTIAL MOBILITY

One influential strand of migration theories has emphasized the importance of sociodemographic transitions as the impetuses for residential mobility (Kley, 2011). Considering migration patterns over the life course, residential moves can be seen as a response to social transitions such as marriage, education, parenthood, employment, and aging (Rossi, 1955). These transitions are often accompanied by new requirements for housing and residential location. Young adults need to move to a new city to pursue an education, parents tend to move to a bigger house and child-friendly neighborhoods as their family size grows, starting a new job may require relocation, and people planning their retirement can move to more rural areas if they so prefer. Changes in employment status and household income may constrain how people can follow their housing preferences in different phases over the life course.

Another strand of migration theories has emphasized the role of "housing stress" and "place utility" in driving people's migration patterns. The *stress-threshold model* of residential mobility (Wolpert, 1966) postulates that individuals begin to consider moving when their level of dissatisfaction with their current housing conditions and environment do not meet the newly developed requirements. For example, having children often leads to a need for more space, which forces parents to move to a larger apartment or house. Whereas the stress-threshold model emphasizes the negative sides of current location, the *utility perspective* is based on the assumption that people try to locate themselves in residential areas that provide the best possible opportunities and amenities for their needs (Kley & Mulder, 2010). Individuals move to a specific place because they believe they are more likely to achieve important life goals in that place than in their current location. Such a process is in action, for instance, when highly educated individuals migrate to urban areas where there are better employment opportunities for them than in rural areas. Desires and decisions to migrate are thus influenced by pushes determined by the unattractive features of the current location and by pulls of the attractive features of the destination.

On the basis of the associations between personality and migration probability, it is reasonable to assume that personality differences are also involved in the development and realization of migration desires, intentions, and expectations. The BHPS (Research Centre on Micro-Social Change, 2010) offers an opportunity to explore these issues with a large longitudinal data set. The following section addresses three specific research questions: (a) How are personality traits associated with migration desires, migration expectations, and actualized residential mobility? (b) Are the associations between personality traits and residential mobility different depending on whether the individual has desires or expectations to move? In other words, do migration desires and expectations amplify or attenuate the associations between personality and actualized residential mobility? (c) Are personality traits associated with specific reasons for the desire to leave the current residential location (e.g., dissatisfaction with current accommodation or neighborhood)?

PERSONALITY AND MIGRATION BEHAVIOR IN THE BRITISH HOUSEHOLD PANEL SURVEY

The BHPS (Research Centre on Micro-Social Change, 2010) is a longitudinal survey of a nationally representative sample of over 5,000 British households, with annual follow-ups since 1991. The original cohort included

10,264 individuals ages 16 to 97 at baseline ($M = 44.4$, $SD = 18.3$) and was based on a clustered, stratified sample of addresses throughout Great Britain south of the Caledonian Canal (excluding North of Scotland and Northern Ireland). New participants have been included in the sample over the years if they were born to original sample members, if they moved into a household in the original sample, or if a member of the original sample moved into a new household with one or more new people. In addition, the sample was enriched with additional recruitment of participants at Waves 9 and 11, from Scotland and Wales, and from Northern Ireland, respectively, thus extending the sample to cover the whole United Kingdom. The most recent (18th) follow-up of the BHPS was carried out in 2008–2009, after which the cohort became part of the larger Understanding Society Study (http://www. understandingsociety.org.uk/).

In the 15th study wave in 2005–2006, the participants were administered a 15-item version of the Big Five Inventory (BFI; John, Naumann, & Soto, 2008), with three items assessing each personality trait and rated on a 7-point scale: Extraversion (talkative; outgoing and sociable; reserved [R: reverse coded]), Neuroticism (worries a lot; gets nervous easily; relaxed, handles stress well [R]), Agreeableness (sometimes rude to others [R]; has forgiving nature; considerate and kind), Conscientiousness (does a thorough job; tends to be lazy [R]; does things efficiently), and Openness to Experience (original, comes up with ideas; values artistic and aesthetic experiences; has an active imagination).

In each study wave, the participants were asked about their desires to move ("If you could choose, would you stay here in your present home, or would you prefer to move somewhere else?" $0 = stay$, $1 = move$, $2 = don't know$) and whether they expected to move ("Even though you may not want to move, do you expect you will move in the coming year?"). Because only 1% and 4% of participants, respectively, answered, "don't know" to these two questions, these individuals were excluded from the analyses. In addition to reporting their migration expectations, the participants were also queried about the main reason for their desire to move ("What is the main reason why you would prefer to move?") with a question in free response format (i.e., without giving specific items to select). The participants' answers were coded into 28 different categories related to housing, area, and other aspects. Actual residential mobility was assessed by asking whether the participant's current address was the same as on September 1 the previous year ($0 = same address$, $1 = different address$). Thus, the time interval by which residential mobility was assessed depended on the participant's interview date, and time interval was therefore included as a covariate in models of residential mobility ($M = 12.9$ months, $SD = 1.1$). All the analyses were adjusted for sex, age, study year, race and ethnicity ($0 = White$, $1 = other$), and subsample group coded as a set of dummy variables (0 = *original sample*, 1 = *Wales*, 2 = *Scotland*, 3 = *Northern Ireland*). Educational level at the time of personality assessment was included as an additional categorical covariate (0 = *primary*, 1 = *secondary*, 2 = *tertiary education*) to examine the role of socioeconomic status.

The repeated measurements of migration desires, expectations, and actualized mobility over the four measurement times were pooled into a single data set so that baseline personality traits were used to predict migration desires and expectations at the four measurement times and actualized migration behavior between successive study waves. Random-intercept multilevel logistic regression was used to analyze the associations to take into account the nonindependence of repeated measurements within individuals.

For this analysis, all individuals with personality data were included ($N = 13,283$). The mean age of the participants was 47.3 years ($SD = 18.1$); 54.9% were women, 85.5% were White, and 55.6% were members of the original sample. Averaged across the four study waves, 30.0% of the participants reported that they would prefer to move, 11.8% expected to move during the next year, but only 8.7% moved between two successive study phases. In total, 23.3% of the participants moved at some point of the follow-up.

Personality and Migration Behavior

High Neuroticism, low Agreeableness, and high Openness to Experience were associated with a higher desire and expectation to move (see Table 4.1, Models 1 and 2). In agreement with these associations, individuals

TABLE 4.1
Associations Between Personality Traits and Migration Desires, Expectations, and Actualized Moves Over a 3-Year Follow-up

| | Outcome | | |
Trait	Model 1: Desire to move	Model 2: Expects to move	Model 3: Actualized moves
Extraversion	1.00 (0.94–1.07)	1.11** (1.05–1.17)	1.03 (0.99–1.09)
Neuroticism	1.41** (1.32–1.49)	1.10** (1.04–1.16)	1.09** (1.04–1.14)
Agreeableness	0.86** (0.81–0.92)	0.94* (0.89–1.00)	0.98 (0.94–1.03)
Conscientiousness	1.03 (0.97–1.10)	0.93* (0.88–0.98)	0.95* (0.90–1.00)
Openness to experience	1.19** (1.12–1.27)	1.24** (1.17–1.31)	1.11** (1.06–1.17)
n (persons; person-observations)	13,814 (49,884)	13,773 (48,431)	13,823 (50,412)

Note. Values are odds ratios (and 95% confidence intervals) for mutually adjusted standardized personality traits *(SD = 1)* of random-intercept multilevel logistic regressions. All models are further adjusted for sex, age, study year, subsample, and race or ethnicity. Data from Research Centre on Micro-Social Change (2010). *$p < .05$. **$p < .001$.

with high Neuroticism and high Openness to Experience were more likely to change residential location between two successive study waves, whereas Agreeableness was not associated with actualized mobility (see Table 4.1, Model 3). Conscientiousness was not associated with migration desire, but individuals with high Conscientiousness were less likely to move and expect to move than those with low Conscientiousness. Extraversion was associated only with a higher expectation to move. These associations were largely independent of educational level; adjusting for education amplified the association between Openness to Experience and migration desire from odds ratio $(OR) = 1.19$ to $OR = 1.21$, attenuated the association between Neuroticism and migration expectations from $OR = 1.10$ to $OR = 1.09$, and attenuated the association between Conscientiousness and actual moves from $OR = 0.95$ to $OR = 0.96$. Other changes in odds ratios were even smaller than these (data not shown).

Of the participants who reported no desire to move at a given study wave, 4.8% nevertheless moved during the next year. The probability of moving was much higher (16.8%) among those who did prefer to move, although the majority of individuals (83.2%) expressing such a migration desire stayed in their current location over the next year. Migration expectations were more strongly associated with subsequent mobility, with 41.8% of the individuals who expected to move actually moving within the next year, compared with only 3.4% of those with no migration expectations.

Personality and the Realization of Migration Desires and Expectations

To test whether personality traits were associated with differences in the actualization of migration desires and expectations, the odds of moving between two successive study waves were predicted by the interaction effects between personality traits and reported migration desires (see Table 4.2) and migration expectations (see Table 4.3) in the previous study wave.

The association between Conscientiousness and migration probability was dependent on migration desires and expectations in a logical manner (see Tables 4.2 and 4.3, respectively). High Conscientiousness was associated with lower migration probability among those with no migration desires $(OR = 0.87, p < .001)$ or expectations $(OR = 0.89, p < .001)$ but with higher migration probability among those with migration desires $(OR = 1.08, p = .06)$ or expectations $(OR = 1.16, p < .001)$. Neuroticism showed the opposite interaction effect with migration desire. Compared with individuals with low Neuroticism, individuals with high Neuroticism were more likely to move if they did not have migration desires $(OR = 1.13, p < .001)$ or expectations $(OR = 1.14, p < .001)$ but less likely to move if

TABLE 4.2
Associations Between Personality Traits and Migration Probability Over 3-Year Follow-up by Migration Desires in the Previous Year ($n = 13,815$)

Trait	Desired to move in the previous year		p for difference
	No	Yes	
Extraversion	1.04 (0.96–1.13)	1.01 (0.94–1.10)	.59
Neuroticism	1.13** (1.05–1.22)	0.93*** (0.86–1.01)	< .001
Agreeableness	0.98 (0.90–1.06)	1.01 (0.94–1.09)	.49
Conscientiousness	0.87** (0.8–0.94)	1.08*** (1.00–1.17)	< .001
Openness to experience	1.11* (1.02–1.20)	1.05 (0.97–1.14)	.33
n (persons; person-observations)	11,120 (26,308)	5,431 (9.847)	

Note. Values are odds ratios (and 95% confidence intervals) for standardized personality traits *(SD* = 1) calculated from logistic regression models including an interaction effect between personality trait and preference to move in the previous year (0 = *no,* 1 = *yes*), adjusted for all other personality traits, sex, age, study year, subsample, and race or ethnicity. Data from Research Centre on Micro-Social Change (2010).
*p <.05. **p < .001. ***p < .10.

they did have migration desires ($OR = 0.93$, $p = .08$) or expectations ($OR = 0.94$, $p = .15$). There were no interaction effects between migration desires and other personality traits in predicting subsequent residential mobility, except that high Extraversion predicted lower migration probability among those with no migration expectations but not among those with migration expectations (see Table 4.3).

TABLE 4.3
Associations Between Personality Traits and Migration Probability Over 3-Year Follow-up by Expectations to Move in the Previous Year ($n = 13,772$)

Trait	Expected to move in the previous year		p for difference
	No	Yes	
Extraversion	1.03 (0.96–1.12)	0.89* (0.81–0.97)	.01
Neuroticism	1.14** (1.06–1.23)	0.94 (0.86–1.02)	< .001
Agreeableness	0.96 (0.89–1.04)	1.02 (0.94–1.12)	.27
Conscientiousness	0.89** (0.82–0.96)	1.16** (1.06–1.27)	< .001
Openness to Experience	1.04 (0.96–1.13)	1.00 (0.91–1.09)	.44
n (persons; person-observations)	12,357 (40,984)	2,982 (4,108)	

Note. Values are odds ratios (and 95% confidence intervals) for standardized personality traits *(SD* = 1) calculated from logistic regression models including an interaction effect between personality trait and migration expectations in the previous year (0 = *no,* 1 = *yes*), adjusted for all other personality traits, sex, age, study year, subsample, and race or ethnicity. Data from Research Centre on Micro-Social Change (2010).
*p <.05. **p < .001.

Personality and Reasons to Move

To determine whether personality differences were associated with specific reasons for why the participants desired to move, five random-intercept multilevel linear regression models were examined (see Table 4.4). The models predicted the standardized personality score of one the five traits with the reason for the desire to move, adjusted for all the other four personality traits and other covariates. For this analysis, only individuals who expressed a desire to move were included and the personality scores were standardized within this group of individuals. This approach of investigating the associations between personality and reasons for the desire to move is not confounded by associations between personality and overall desire to migrate reported in Table 4.1, because only those individuals with a desire to migrate were included.

Health reasons and unspecified reasons had strong correlations with personality traits, but these were based on a small number of participants, so these associations cannot be considered reliable. The lack of safety and unfriendliness of residential areas had the broadest associations with different personality traits, with high Neuroticism, low Extraversion, and low Openness to Experience in particular being associated with these reasons. Most of the associations for Neuroticism were related to negative views of the residential area. Differences in Openness to Experience were associated with a variety of different reasons for migration desires. Individuals with high Openness were more likely to consider occupational reasons, children's education, reducing commuting time, and longing for a more rural environment, whereas individuals with low Openness to Experience viewed their residential area in a more negative light than those with high Openness to Experience. In addition to its associations with area considerations, high Extraversion was related to desires for better and own accommodation and with a desire for a specific place. Agreeableness and Conscientiousness had quite similar associations, with dislike of traffic and wanting larger accommodation being associated with high levels, and feelings of isolation and wanting a change being associated with low levels of these traits.

PERSONALITY AND MIGRATION DECISIONS

The data presented here add insight into the previously reported associations between personality traits and residential mobility. People with high Openness to Experience, high Neuroticism, and low Agreeableness were more eager to move than those with low Openness to Experience, low Neuroticism, and high Agreeableness. These associations with migration desires

TABLE 4.4

Associations Between Personality Traits and Reasons for Desiring to Move
($n = 7,697$ persons; 23,370 person-observations)

Reason to move	Personality trait					% (n)
	E	N	A	C	O	
Health reasons	**−35**	—	[−37]	−38	−35	0.4 (91)
Area unsafe	−11	19	—	−9	−20	4.6 (1075)
No reason specified	**54**	—	[−55]	—	—	0.1 (12)
Unfriendly area	−9	10	−8	—	−10	4.8 (1112)
Dislikes traffic	—	—	17	14	—	1.7 (393)
Own accommodation	9	—	7	−8	7	6.2 (1447)
Feels isolated	—	—	−12	−14	—	4.0 (936)
Occupational reasons	—	—	—	—	24	1.1 (248)
For child's education	—	—	—	[27]	23	0.8 (196)
Retirement	—	—	—	22	—	0.2 (49)
Wants a change	—	—	−10	−10	—	3.9 (902)
Dislikes urban environment	—	—	—	—	18	0.5 (111)
Going to rural environment	—	—	—	10	7	6.7 (1574)
Larger accommodation	—	−5	5	6	—	16.2 (3796)
To buy somewhere	—	—	—	16	—	1.9 (435)
Dislikes area	—	6	—	—	−9	8.3 (1945)
Reduce commuting	—	—	—	—	15	1 (236)
No stairs	—	—	—	—	−13	2.4 (556)
Better accommodation	11	—	—	—	—	1.6 (379)
Another type	—	—	—	—	−9	2.9 (687)
Other housing aspects	—	—	—	—	9	4.3 (998)
Other	[8]	—	—	—	8	6.7 (1573)
Wants a specific place	8	—	—	—	—	8.0 (1867)
Dislikes accommodation	—	—	—	—	—	0.7 (172)
Dislikes noise	—	—	—	—	—	2.7 (635)
Family reasons	—	—	—	—	—	4.4 (1037)
More privacy	—	—	—	—	—	0.8 (178)
Smaller/cheaper accommodation	—	—	—	—	—	3.1 (730)

Note. E = extraversion; N = neuroticism; A = agreeableness; C = conscientiousness; O = openness to experience. Values are standardized ($SD = 100$) personality scores associated with different reasons for migration desires calculated from random-intercept multilevel regression models, adjusted for all other personality traits, age, sex, subsample, and race or ethnicity. Only statistically significant scores ($p < .05$) are shown. Scores printed in bold were significant in both prospective and main analysis. Scores in parenthesis were significant only in prospective analysis. The items are presented in the order of largest combined effect sizes with the five personality traits in the main analysis. Data from Research Centre on Micro-Social Change (2010).

and expectations are in agreement with previous studies that have demonstrated corresponding associations between these three personality traits and migration propensity (Camperio Ciani et al., 2007; Jokela, 2009; Jokela et al., 2008; Silventoinen et al., 2008). In this sample, Openness to Experience and Neuroticism, but not Agreeableness, were also associated with higher probability of actually moving.

The main effects of Conscientiousness suggested lower migration expectations and lower overall probability of moving among those with high Conscientiousness. However, more interesting results were revealed by interaction effects of Conscientiousness with migration desires and expectations. Higher Conscientiousness predicted higher migration probability among those who had migration desires or expectations, but lower probability among those with no desires or expectations to move. Thus, migration desires and expectations were more consistently associated with actual mobility among people with high Conscientiousness. These interaction effects fit in well with the research literature of Conscientiousness in other domains of behavior. People with high Conscientiousness are systematic, orderly, planful, and well-organized (John et al., 2008). Conscientious individuals who are planning to move in the near future are more likely to follow that plan through than are those with low Conscientiousness. Conscientious individuals who prefer to stay in their current location, by contrast, are less likely to move spontaneously or unexpectedly than their less conscientious peers. The main effect of higher Conscientiousness being associated with lower probability of moving thus appeared to reflect the fact that most people had no desire to move, in which case high Conscientiousness contributed to lower migration probability.

Interaction effects with migration desires and expectations suggested quite a different role for Neuroticism compared with Conscientiousness. People with high Neuroticism are highly sensitive to negative emotions, and they tend to experience negative feelings more often. Compared to with their emotionally stable counterparts, individuals with high Neuroticism were more likely to have a desire to move. This is in agreement with the hypothesis that Neuroticism increases neighborhood and housing dissatisfaction, which prompts individuals to relocate (Jokela, 2009). However, Neuroticism was associated with higher odds of actualized migration only among those with no desire or expectation to move in the near future, and there was a tendency for high Neuroticism to predict lower odds of moving among those who did have a desire to move. These patterns imply that high Neuroticism interferes with the realization of migration desires and expectations in both directions, increasing the odds of migration among those with no desire or expectation to move and decreasing the odds among those desiring or expecting to move. In other words, Neuroticism appears to contribute to a higher probability of unwanted and unexpected moves.

Many previous studies have demonstrated high Extraversion and sociability to predict more active migration behavior (Jokela, 2009; Jokela et al., 2008; Silventoinen et al., 2008). The lack of associations between Extraversion and migration outcomes in this sample is therefore surprising. The interaction effect with migration expectations was also unexpected and should be interpreted cautiously because of the lack of main effects and interaction with migration desires. Perhaps this measure of Extraversion did not capture the individual variation that is relevant to migration behavior. Different traits related to Extraversion have been shown to have different effects in other domains of demographic behavior. For example, high Extraversion has been associated with higher probability of having children (Jokela, Alvergne, Pollet, & Lummaa, 2011). The temperament trait "novelty seeking" assessed by the Temperament and Character Inventory (Cloninger, Svrakic, & Przybeck, 1993) correlates positively with Extraversion ($r = 0.38$; Jokela & Keltikangas-Järvinen, 2011), but high novelty seeking has been associated with a lower rather than higher likelihood of having children (Jokela, Hintsa, Hintsanen, & Keltikangas-Järvinen, 2010). Whether similar opposing patterns are present in associations with residential mobility needs to be investigated with alternative measures of Extraversion.

The associations between personality traits and reasons for the desire to migrate suggested that personality differences are associated particularly with neighborhood dissatisfaction such as perceiving the current neighborhood to be unsafe and unfriendly. Openness to Experience, Conscientiousness, and Agreeableness had the most associations with different reasons for migration desires, but the data did not suggest any particularly coherent patterns of reasons for different traits. This analysis was limited by the measurement of the reasons for migration desires, which was not optimal, because the participants were asked only about one main reason for their migration desire. The topic needs to be addressed with a more psychometrically adequate measure of reasons to migrate.

FURTHER DIRECTIONS IN PSYCHODEMOGRAPHY

Migration desires, intentions, and expectations are prominent concepts in most individual-level models of residential mobility. However, several studies have demonstrated that self-reported migration desires, intentions, and expectations are surprisingly weak predictors of actual residential mobility (Colsher & Wallace, 1990; Lu, 1999; Tulloch, Fearon, Fahy, & David, 2010). For example, using the same BHPS data set as used in this analysis, Coulter, van Ham, and Feijten (2010) observed that only 55% of persons who desired and expected to move within the coming year actually moved. This indicates that almost half of the migration plans did not materialize, at least not in the short term. These findings have challenged the simple explanatory models that postulate a direct association between migration intentions and actual residential mobility.

Although various sociodemographic factors (Coulter et al., 2010; Kley & Mulder, 2010) and housing conditions (De Groot et al., 2011) have been hypothesized to influence how migration plans are actualized, the psychological aspects of these explanatory models have not been examined in detail. The current findings help to fill in this gap by showing that migration desires and expectations are actualized differently in individuals with different personality characteristics. Personality may contribute to other stages of the migration process as well (e.g., how strongly a desire to move becomes materialized as an intention or expectation to move, how persistent migration desires or intentions are over time). Moreover, the social determinants of migration desires may be sensitive to personality differences. For example, people's residential dissatisfaction may be influenced to different degrees by different neighborhood and housing factors, depending on individual personality traits, and personality traits may also influence how strongly residential dissatisfaction leads to a desire to move.

It is also important to consider potential moderator effects. On the broadest level of analysis, cultural and sociodemographic differences between societies may modify the associations between personality and migration behavior. Countries differ in their average migration rates and in more specific migration patterns, such as the degree of rural-to-urban migration. Among countries of the Organisation for Economic Co-operation and Development, within-country residential mobility is most frequent in the Nordic countries, Australia, and the United States, and least frequent in Southern and Eastern Europe (Caldera Sánchez & Andrews, 2011); these differences are partially related to public policies regulating housing markets. Such structural factors might amplify or attenuate how personality differences become expressed in migration decisions.

Twin studies carried out in Australia and the Netherlands illustrated the possibility of cross-national differences in the individual determinants of residential mobility. In the Australian study (Whitfield, Zhu, Heath, & Martin, 2005), the urbanicity of residential location was partly heritable, especially in older participants ($h^2 = 0.40$), whereas in the Dutch study urban or rural location was determined solely by shared and nonshared environmental factors (Willemsen, Posthuma, & Boomsma, 2005). The authors of the Dutch study suggested that this may reflect the fact that the Netherlands is a smaller and much more densely populated country than Australia, and Dutch public policies of governmental housing allocations tend to favor moving near the parental home. These factors may attenuate heritable influences on urbanicity of residential location. With respect to personality, one could hypothesize that personality differences are stronger predictors of residential mobility in regions and socioeconomic conditions that set few constraints and obstacles for relocating; these are the circumstances in which external factors limit the expression of personal dispositions the least.

The psychological study of migration behavior also needs to consider the life-course patterns of migration behavior (Kley, 2011). The effects of personality on residential mobility may be moderated by lower level contextual factors that characterize people's social roles and life stages. Age, employment, marriage, and parenthood are among the most discussed indicators of important social roles affecting migration decisions (Kley, 2011). It is reasonable to expect that the same personality traits may influence the migration decisions differently in, say, unemployed parents with many children compared with single individuals with high income.

Thus, research focusing on the conditional interaction effects between personality traits and social circumstances can provide important insights on the psychological basis of migration behavior and mechanisms of migration decisions. Viewed as a sequential decision-making process that depends on the interplay between individual psychological dispositions and social circumstances, the psychological study of residential mobility can provide a more comprehensive understanding of why, how, and when different individuals move from one place to another.

REFERENCES

Boneva, B. S., & Frieze, I. H. (2001). Toward a concept of a migrant personality. *Journal of Social Issues*, *57*, 477–491. doi:10.1111/0022-4537.00224

Caldera Sánchez, A., & Andrews, D. (2011). *To move or not to move: What drives residential mobility rates in the OECD?* (OECD Economic Department Working Papers No. 846) Retrieved from the OECD website: doi:10.1787/5kghtc7kzx21-en

Camperio Ciani, A., & Capiluppi, C. (2011). Gene flow by selective emigration as a possible cause for personality differences between small islands and mainland populations. *European Journal of Personality*, *25*(1), 53–64. doi:10.1002/per.774

Camperio Ciani, A. S., Capiluppi, C., Veronese, A., & Sartori, G. (2007). The adaptive value of personality differences revealed by small island population dynamics. *European Journal of Personality*, *21*(1), 3–22. doi:10.1002/per.595

Cloninger, C. R., Svrakic, D. M., & Przybeck, T. R. (1993). A psychobiological model of temperament and character. *Archives of General Psychiatry*, *50*, 975–990. doi:10.1001/archpsyc.1993.01820240059008

Colsher, P. L., & Wallace, R. B. (1990). Health and social antecedents of relocation in rural elderly persons. *The Journal of Gerontology*, *45*(1), S32–S38. doi:10.1093/geronj/45.1.S32

Coulter, R., van Ham, M., & Feijten, P. (2010). A longitudinal analysis of moving desires, expectations and actual moving behaviour. *Environment and Planning*, *43*, 2742–2760. doi:10.1068/a44105

De Groot, C., Mulder, C. H., & Manting, D. (2011). Intentions to move and actual moving behaviour in the Netherlands. *Housing Studies, 26,* 307–328. doi:10.10 80/02673037.2011.542094

Frieze, I. H., Hansen, S. B., & Boneva, B. (2006). The migrant personality and college students' plans for geographic mobility. *Journal of Environmental Psychology, 26,* 170–177. doi:10.1016/j.jenvp.2006.05.001

Greenwood, M. J., & Hunt, G. L. (2003). The early history of migration research. *International Regional Science Review, 26*(1), 3–37. doi:10.1177/0160017602238983

Hobcraft, J. (2006). The ABC of demographic behavior: How the interplays of alleles, brains, and contexts over the life course should shape research aimed at understanding population processes. *Population Studies, 60,* 153–187. doi:10.1080/00324720600646410

John, O. P., Naumann, L. P., & Soto, C. J. (2008). Paradigm shift to the integrative Big-Five trait taxonomy: History, measurement, and conceptual issues. In O. P. John, R. W. Robins, & L. A. Pervin (Eds.), *Handbook of personality: Theory and research* (pp. 114–158). New York, NY: Guilford Press.

Jokela, M. (2009). Personality predicts migration within and between U.S. states. *Journal of Research in Personality, 43*(1), 79–83. doi:10.1016/j.jrp.2008.09.005

Jokela, M., Alvergne, A., Pollet, T. V., & Lummaa, V. (2011). Reproductive behavior and personality traits of the Five Factor Model. *European Journal of Personality, 25,* 487–500. doi:10.1002/per.822

Jokela, M., Elovainio, M., Kivimäki, M., & Keltikangas-Järvinen, L. (2008). Temperament and migration patterns in Finland. *Psychological Science, 19,* 831–837. doi:10.1111/j.1467-9280.2008.02164.x

Jokela, M., Hintsa, T., Hintsanen, M., & Keltikangas-Järvinen, L. (2010). Adult temperament and childbearing over the life course. *European Journal of Personality, 24,* 151–166.

Jokela, M., & Keltikangas-Järvinen, L. (2011). The association between low socioeconomic status and depressive symptoms depends on temperament and personality traits. *Personality and Individual Differences, 51,* 302–308. doi:10.1016/j.paid.2010.05.004

Kley, S. (2011). Explaining the stages of migration within a life-course framework. *European Sociological Review, 27,* 469–486. doi:10.1093/esr/jcq020

Kley, S. A., & Mulder, C. H. (2010). Considering, planning, and realizing migration in early adulthood. The influence of life-course events and perceived opportunities on leaving the city in Germany. *Journal of Housing and the Built Environment, 25*(1), 73–94. doi:10.1007/s10901-009-9167-8

Lu, M. (1999). Do people move when they say they will? Inconsistencies in individual migration behavior. *Population and Environment, 20,* 467–488. doi:10.1023/A:1023365119874

Murray, G., Judd, F., Jackson, H., Fraser, C., Komiti, A., Hodgins, G., . . . Robins, G. (2005). The five factor model and accessibility/remoteness: Novel evidence for person–environment interaction. *Personality and Individual Differences, 39,* 715–725. doi:10.1016/j.paid.2005.02.007

Rentfrow, P. J., Gosling, S. D., & Potter, J. (2008). A theory of the emergence, persistence, and expression of geographic variation in psychological characteristics. *Perspectives on Psychological Science, 3,* 339–369. doi:10.1111/j.1745-6924.2008.00084.x

Research Centre on Micro-Social Change. (2010). *British Household Panel Survey user manual: Vol. A. Introduction, technical report and appendices.* Colchester, England: University of Essex.

Rossi, P. H. (1955). *Why families move: A study in the social psychology of urban residential mobility.* Glencoe, IL: Free Press.

Silventoinen, K., Hammar, N., Hedlund, E., Koskenvuo, M., Ronnemaa, T., & Kaprio, J. (2008). Selective international migration by social position, health behaviour and personality. *European Journal of Public Health, 18,* 150–155. doi:10.1093/eurpub/ckm052

Tulloch, A. D., Fearon, P., Fahy, T., & David, A. (2010). Residential mobility among individuals with severe mental illness: Cohort study of UK700 participants. *Social Psychiatry and Psychiatric Epidemiology, 45,* 767–777. doi:10.1007/s00127-009-0115-4

Whitfield, J. B., Zhu, G., Heath, A. C., & Martin, N. G. (2005). Choice of residential location: Chance, family influences, or genes? *Twin Research and Human Genetics, 8,* 22–26. doi:10.1375/twin.8.1.22

Willemsen, G., Posthuma, D., & Boomsma, D. I. (2005). Environmental factors determine where the Dutch live: Results from the Netherlands twin register. *Twin Research and Human Genetics, 8,* 312–317. doi:10.1375/twin.8.4.312

Wolpert, J. (1966). Migration as an adjustment to environmental stress. *Journal of Social Issues, 22*(4), 92–102. doi:10.1111/j.1540-4560.1966.tb00552.x

5

PERSONALITY TRAITS AND SPATIAL ECOLOGY IN NONHUMAN ANIMALS

JULIEN COTE, JEAN CLOBERT, TOMAS BRODIN,
SEAN FOGARTY, AND ANDREW SIH

Psychologists have long explored the considerable range of human and nonhuman personalities (Gosling & John, 1999). Studies on nonhuman animals mostly examined domestic animals and primates. Recently, behavioral ecologists have taken an interest in personality traits in wild animals, considering this behavioral variation as adaptive rather than noise around the adaptive optimum (Sih, Bell, & Johnson, 2004). Personality and its importance in ecological processes have now been studied in numerous vertebrate and invertebrate taxa (Réale, Reader, Sol, McDougall, & Dingemanse, 2007; Sih, Cote, Evans, Fogarty, & Pruitt, 2012). To retain ecological validity, behavioral ecologists have redefined, from classical personality axes, their own categories of personality traits (Réale et al., 2007; see the final section of this chapter for a discussion on this issue). Following Réale et al. (2007) we divide personality traits into five categories:

- *Shyness–boldness* (risk averse–risk taking) represents individual reaction toward a risky, but nonnovel, situation. The classical

http://dx.doi.org/10.1037/14272-006
Geographical Psychology: Exploring the Interaction of Environment and Behavior, P. J. Rentfrow (Editor)
Copyright © 2014 by the American Psychological Association. All rights reserved.

example is individual reaction toward predation risk. Measuring this behavior often involves exposing the animal to simulated predation risk and, for example, scoring individual latency to return to normal behavior.

- *Exploration tendency* represents individual reaction to novel environments. It is often measured as the latency to explore a novel environment and the amount of area explored in the novel environment.
- *Activity* represents individual differences in activity levels in a nonnovel environment.
- *Aggressiveness* represents the propensity to exhibit aggression toward another individual. It often implies aggression toward conspecifics but could also include interspecific agonistic behaviors.
- *Sociability* is the nonagonistic reaction to conspecific presence. Social individuals actively seek the presence of conspecifics, whereas asocial individuals avoid them.

These five personality axes describe individual reactions to different ecological contexts (social and nonsocial) that often drive the outcomes of intra- and interspecific interactions and therefore individual and species success in the ecosystem (Sih et al., 2012). A classic example is the effect of boldness on the survival–growth rate trade-off (Stamps, 2007). Bold individuals forage more and thus gain more resources but, in turn, take more (sometimes unnecessary) risks. In contrast, shy individuals take fewer risks but may as a consequence get fewer opportunities to acquire resources. Bold and shy types are thus two strategies (on a continuum) with different costs and benefits in safe and unsafe environments. In a system with both environments, the tradeoff can maintain variability in personality traits. Personality traits have also been linked to other important evolutionary and ecological processes such as sexual selection, predation, parasitism, and space use (Réale, Dingemanse, Kazem, & Wright, 2010). Moreover, a given personality trait can be involved in several ecological processes, and several personality traits can jointly affect a given process. These conditions could create, within a population, correlations either between the same personality trait in two ecological contexts or between two personality traits (i.e., behavioral syndrome).

Here, we focus on *spatial ecology*. Environments are spatially variable, and suitable habitats are often distributed in patches. Spatial ecology aims to understand how and why species are distributed in patchy environments and how individuals move within and between patches. Applied issues include the management of threatened or endangered species in fragmented habitats, of landscape connectivity, and of invasive species. We distinguish four types of spatial movements that differ in spatial scale:

- *Within-habitat movements* are short-distance movements within the living area and its close neighborhood. They allow individuals to explore close-by habitats to find resources (e.g., food, mates) and are sometimes thought of as a mechanism allowing long-distance movements.
- *Between-habitat movements*, often called *dispersal*, are short- to long-distance movements that imply the use of a new habitat. Dispersal is usually defined as the movement from the natal or breeding area to a novel breeding area (Clobert, Danchin, Dhondt, & Nichols, 2001). Dispersal involves three stages: departure from a living area, movement between areas (transience), and settlement in a new area (Bowler & Benton, 2005; Clobert, Le Galliard, Cote, Meylan, & Massot, 2009). Dispersal begins with a clear departure decision from an established living area. Transience often involves movement through unsuitable or hostile environments. Settlement areas can be devoid of conspecifics (i.e., colonization of a new site) or already occupied by conspecifics (i.e., population reinforcement).
- *Ecological invasion* occurs when a species is introduced and grows outside the borders of the species initial distribution. It leads to species range expansion and, for an invasive species, can have major and mostly negative ecological (Mack et al., 2000) and economic impacts (Pimentel, Lach, Zuniga, & Morrison, 2000).
- *Migration* is the seasonally synchronized movements of parts of or entire populations (migration) to track seasonally suitable areas (Salewski & Bruderer, 2007). Migration can take several forms and can take place at variable spatial and temporal scales.

In this chapter, on the basis of a literature review and our own experience, we first describe how within-species variation in personality traits can affect these four spatial movements. Behavioral syndromes involved in each category emerge from this review (e.g., invader, disperser, and migrant syndromes). However, although these spatial categories are often clear-cut, there are some situations in which an individual movement can be classified in several categories, as in nomadic species (Clobert et al., 2001). We therefore discuss the overall link between the sets of personality traits and spatial movements, resulting in a general "movers" syndrome. Finally, we draw parallels with human examples to highlight where we believe human geographical psychology can benefit from studies on nonhuman animal species.

WITHIN-HABITAT DISTRIBUTION AND MOVEMENTS

Individual personality type affects the individual's ability to cope with ecological conditions (Smith & Blumstein, 2008), which should, in turn, affect adaptive individual movements in a variable environment. For example, in the common lizard (*Zootoca vivipara*), we can rank individuals along a gradient of sociability from social individuals attracted to conspecific presence to asocial individuals repulsed by others. In this species, asocial individuals have increased survival at low population density, whereas social individuals have increased survival at high population densities (Cote & Clobert, 2007; Cote, Dreiss, & Clobert, 2008). If individuals are heterogeneously distributed within a population, we expect social individuals to be aggregated in good habitats (i.e., supporting high densities) and asocial individuals to occupy low quality habitats (i.e., low-density areas).

In the western mosquitofish (*Gambusia affinis*), a social fish forming shoals, we also found between-individual differences in sociability (Cote, Fogarty, Weinersmith, Brodin, & Sih, 2010). More asocial individuals tend to shoal less and exhibit weaker choosiness about shoal characteristics (Cote, Fogarty, & Sih, 2012; Cote, Fogarty, et al., 2010). More asocial fish thus spend more time out of the shoal but sometimes still associate with shoals (i.e., as satellite individuals) to gain benefits from them (i.e., protection against predators, mates). In turn, social individuals might pay attention to asocial individuals to acquire information about resources or because they will act as sentinels. Within the population, we thus predict social individuals to form large shoals and asocial fish to swim alone but join shoals occasionally.

Similarly, social female yellow-bellied marmots were clumped in harems, whereas asocial females lived in peripheral burrows at colonies or in satellite sites (Svendsen, 1974). In general, we expect social individuals to use information produced by others for their own spatial decisions and asocial individuals to be more independent of others' behavior. Social individuals might thus move in groups to forage and explore their habitats. Similar predictions could be made for aggressiveness. However, it is more difficult to predict whether aggressive individuals would be more asocial because of their aggressive tendency or whether they would be more social because they follow and dominate other individuals in a social group.

As a broad generality, bolder individuals tend to be more active and cover larger areas (e.g., forage further from refuges) than shy individuals. With regard to effects of boldness on movement in response to predators, bolder prey by definition hide less from predators than do shy prey, but the effects of individual differences in boldness on the tendency to leave areas with more predators have rarely been studied. However, there is parallel literature showing how species differences in boldness affect prey movement away from patches with predators. Interestingly, because hiding in response to predators can be incompatible with leaving a site to avoid danger, different patterns are seen depending on the degree of danger posed by predators (Wooster & Sih, 1995). When predators are slightly dangerous, shy prey avoid sites with predators, whereas bold prey ignore the predators and stay in the site. When predators are moderately dangerous, shy prey hide in refuge and thus stay in the site, whereas bold prey remain active and ultimately leave the site. When predators are very dangerous, both shy and bold prey hide and perhaps paradoxically stay rather than leave the dangerous site, particularly if substantial movement is required to leave the site (Englund, 1997).

Space use and aggregation can depend on both boldness and sociability. Although the general expectation is that social individuals aggregate with conspecifics more than asocial ones, prey aggregation can also be changed by the presence of predators because social grouping has a protective role against predation in many species (Krause & Ruxton, 2002). We thus expect shy individuals to aggregate more than bold individuals in the presence of predators. Interestingly, a clear behavioral syndrome emerges from these predictions (but see General Behavioral Syndromes below). Social, shy, less exploratory, and less active individuals should have smaller home ranges, be less willing to leave the core of their territory, and create larger groups. In contrast, asocial, bold, exploratory, and active individuals should have a more flexible territory and travel longer distance to find resources. An extreme example of this strategy would be satellite individuals that are not affiliated with a specific social group and can travel from one group to another to gain benefits from diverse groups despite the cost of being solitary.

PERSONALITY-DEPENDENT DISPERSAL

Through dispersal, individuals move not just within their current habitat but leave their natal or breeding site to settle in another, often distant, breeding site after a transient period (Clobert et al., 2009). In most cases, some animals disperse whereas others stay. It has long been recognized that dispersal is nonrandom with respect to age, sex, size, condition, and other characteristics (Bowler & Benton, 2005; Clobert et al., 2009). Our emphasis is on the recent and exciting recognition that dispersal is often personality dependent. Dispersers often tend to be more active, exploratory, asocial, aggressive, or bold than residents that stay behind. Here, we review examples of personality-dependent dispersal and present a framework for explaining observed patterns and predicting how personality and environmental factors might interact to influence dispersal (Cote, Clobert, Brodin, Fogarty, & Sih, 2010).

Several studies have shown that dispersers tend to be more active and/ or exploratory than residents (nondispersers). In mole rats and in common lizards, dispersers have higher locomotor and different foraging activity than nondispersers (Aragón, Clobert, & Massot, 2006; Meylan, De Fraipont, Aragón, Vercken, & Clobert, 2009; O'Riain, Jarvis, & Faulkes, 1996). In male house mice (*Mus musculus musculus*), dispersal latency decreased with increasing exploratory activity measured before dispersal (Krackow, 2003). Even if behavioral consistency were not clearly demonstrated, these studies suggest that active, more exploratory individuals are more likely to disperse. To emphasize, although the tendency for more active and exploratory animals to disperse more might suggest that dispersal is just an extension of general activity and exploration, dispersal typically involves a fundamentally distinct decision to leave a current habitat and settle in a new one.

Two studies showed that individual differences in activity in novel environments are correlated with dispersal distance in nature (Dingemanse, Both, van Noordwijk, Rutten, & Drent, 2003; Fraser, Gilliam, Daley, Le, & Skalski, 2001). Fraser et al. (2001) found that in Trinidadian killifish (*Rivulus hartii*) dispersal distance in natural streams is positively related to individual exploration of an unfamiliar area. Perhaps the most complete study demonstrating the link between personality traits and dispersal used great tits (*Parus major*) as a model system (Dingemanse et al., 2003). Consistent and heritable individual differences in exploratory behavior were found (Dingemanse et al., 2003; van Oers, Drent, de Goede, & van Noordwijk, 2004), but most important, Dingemanse et al. (2003) also showed that, in nature, natal dispersal distance was correlated with exploratory behavior and that immigrants were faster explorers than local residents. These studies show that exploratory behavior may affect both departure and transience/ settlement decisions.

Other studies showed that more aggressive individuals tend to disperse more. For example, in rhesus macaques (*Macaca mulatta*), aggressive individuals tend to disperse earlier during their adolescence (Mehlman et al., 1995; Trefilov, Berard, Krawczak, & Schmidtke, 2000). Mehlman et al. (1995) showed that the concentration of a serotonin metabolite, which is consistent over time (Howell et al., 2007), is negatively correlated with aggressiveness and positively correlated with age at emigration from the natal group. Thus, aggressive individuals disperse earlier than less aggressive ones prior to or during adolescence, but this relationship is reversed for individuals that dispersed after sexual maturity (Howell et al., 2007).

Individual sociability levels have also been shown to govern dispersal decisions in some species. For example, in western mosquitofish, asocial individuals tend to disperse more readily (Cote, Fogarty, Brodin, Weinersmith, & Sih, 2011; Cote, Fogarty, et al., 2010). In yellow-bellied marmots (*Marmota flaviventris*), females that had affiliative interactions with more individuals were less likely to disperse (Blumstein, Wey, & Tang, 2009). This corroborated the *social cohesion hypothesis* that posits that more socially embedded individuals are less likely to disperse (Bekoff, 1977). If an individual's low social embeddedness reflects its tendency to avoid conspecifics (as opposed to conspecifics avoiding the individual), these findings might reflect individual variation in the tendency and ability to socialize. In general, differences in behavioral types may affect dispersal behavior in social systems that feature a mix of cooperation and conflict (Schürch, Rothenberger, & Heg, 2010). Shy, nonexplorative, and nonaggressive subordinates might be allowed to stay in a group because they are more helpful and less challenging to aggressive dominant individuals (Bergmüller & Taborsky, 2010), whereas bold and aggressive individuals disperse because they both cooperate less and benefit more from attempting to breed independently (Schürch et al., 2010). This overall scenario might explain personality-dependent differences in individual investment in helping, dispersal, and nonrandom association of behavioral types in postsettlement groups.

Although these examples document cases of personality-dependent dispersal, adaptive reasoning suggests that dispersal should depend not just on personality per se but also on an interaction between personality and the social and ecological factors in the current habitat. Animals should generally be more likely to stay in high quality habitat and leave poor quality habitat; however, if personalities differ in their ability to thrive in different social and ecological conditions (Smith & Blumstein 2008), their dispersal tendencies should also depend on those conditions. Factors that might often affect personality-dependent dispersal include intraspecific competition, predation risk, kin interaction, inbreeding risk, and availability of mates (Bowler & Benton, 2005; Clobert et al., 2009). For example, the strength or direction of sociability and aggressiveness-dependent dispersal should depend on the degree of intraspecific interaction, population density, or group size.

In accordance with this, dispersal behavior of common lizards depends on the relationship between individual sociability measured at birth and local population density. Asocial individuals, who have increased survival at low density, tend to disperse when densities get too high, whereas social individuals, who have increased survival at high densities, disperse when densities are too low (Cote & Clobert, 2007; Cote et al., 2008). Large groups provide individuals with benefits such as protection against predators (e.g., through dilution of risk), easier food localization, and numerous sexual partners. However, a large group can increase competition for food and sexual partners, attract more predators, and facilitate disease transmission.

Individuals are not equally subjected to these costs and benefits. Some individuals are better competitors, have better escape abilities, sexual attractiveness, or better immunocompetence. Those individual specificities (i.e., state variables) are believed to create variation in personality traits that in turn drive group-size dependent departure decisions and habitat selection. Similarly, boldness-dependent dispersal may depend on risk presence in the population. Predation risk could either cause bold or shy individuals to disperse more. If shy individuals generally tend to avoid risk, they might disperse to avoid predators and select safer habitats. However, if bold individuals suffer higher predator-induced mortality rates than shy individuals (Smith & Blumstein, 2008), bolder individuals should be more likely to disperse to avoid predators and select safer habitats. In the earlier section on within-habitat movements, we noted that the relative tendency of bold versus shy individuals to leave sites with high risk could depend on the degree of risk. Those ideas could also apply to larger scale dispersal decisions.

In a recent study on mosquitofish, we showed that the link between individual sociability levels and dispersal decisions depends on predation risk in the population (Cote et al., 2012). We simulated predation risk in half of the populations by adding a caged rainbow trout (i.e., *Oncorhynchus mykiss*, a novel predator for those mosquitofish). With no predator present, we found that asocial/shy fish dispersed more from the released pool. This result is in accordance with our previous studies in which asocial individuals dispersed more. However, when there was a predator present in the released pool, social/bold individuals dispersed more. In this study, boldness and sociability were correlated, so we could not clearly separate effects of boldness and sociability, but it is likely that boldness levels are more important than sociability for the decision to disperse to avoid predation risk. Furthermore, we showed that group composition in sociability types also matters for individual dispersal decisions (Cote et al., 2011). Although asocial individuals are more likely to disperse in general, individuals from populations with more asocial individuals or with more bold individuals are more likely to disperse regardless of their own personality type.

Note that the tendency to disperse should not depend solely on fitness in the current habitat but also on expected fitness in other available habitats and on the cost of moving from one habitat to another (Stamps, 2001). Dispersal may be unsuccessful because the environment during transience is too hostile and suitable habitat patches may be too distant. Movement between habitats also imposes opportunity costs in terms of lost time and energy, and settling into a novel habitat also entails costs. If costs of dispersal or ability to thrive (settle) in new sites are personality dependent, this could explain why some personalities are more likely to disperse than others; individuals who are better at successfully dispersing and settling should be more likely to disperse. For example, dispersal costs can be reduced by behavioral specializations, such as differences in activity patterns, aggressiveness, and social behavior, of dispersers in comparison with nondispersers (Bowler & Benton, 2005; Clobert et al., 2009). That is, bold, aggressive, exploratory, or asocial individuals generally might be more likely to disperse not just because their personalities are predisposed to disperse but also because they are better (than shy, unaggressive, nonexploring, or social individuals) at coping with challenges associated with dispersing and settling in new habitats. If dispersal and settlement success depend on an interaction between personality and ecological/social factors, this interaction should explain who disperses. To date, few studies have experimentally varied ecological factors or costs associated with dispersal and settlement to examine their effects on personality-dependent dispersal.

Personality-dependent dispersal is particularly important in the increasingly fragmented habitats associated with habitat deterioration and fragmentation in the modern world. Habitat loss and fragmentation lead to increased isolation of suitable patches, often with patches being separated by increasingly hostile environments. This thus increases the risks and costs of dispersal and prevents individuals from moving from one patch to another. In such landscapes, bold individuals might be more inclined to leave their initial patch and move through unsuitable, hostile environments. More exploratory individuals can also sample more habitats during transience before they decide where to settle. Prospecting (sampling) is a fundamental process in habitat selection (Doligez, Danchin, & Clobert, 2002; Stamps, 2001), allowing individuals to estimate habitat quality. Fast explorers might visit more habitats, improving the selection of a suitable habitat. However, they might not gain as detailed information on visited patches as slow explorers. Further study of personality-dependent dispersal can thus provide great insights for modern conservation and applied ecology.

PERSONALITY-DEPENDENT INVASION AND RANGE EXPANSION

Ecological invasions occur when species introduced to areas beyond their native range (i.e., nonindigenous species) spread from the point of introduction and become abundant (Mack et al., 2000). Invasion is a multistage process: introduction, spread from the place of introduction (dispersal), establishment in empty habitats, population growth to high density, and potentially high impact on the invaded community (Lodge, 1993). Invasions are classically seen as a result of introduction of alien species, intentional or not, beyond their native range. Because processes are similar, here, we also include range expansion in response to environmental changes.

Human activities profoundly change the habitats for a wide range of species. Habitat alteration is one major human-induced environmental change with, for instance, tropical forest being destroyed at annual rates between 1% and 4% of their current areas (Dobson, Bradshaw, & Baker, 1997). Through habitat destruction, human activities force species to invade and to adapt to novel habitats beyond their native range (Tuomainen & Candolin, 2011). Global warming also modifies species habitats by changing climatic conditions. Climate changes can prevent species from persisting in their native range if resulting conditions do not meet biological requirements of native species (i.e., temperature, but also food items; Biro, Post, & Booth, 2007). It can also provide suitable climatic conditions in habitats beyond the native range. These two changes could lead to range expansion or shift if species cannot adapt to novel conditions (Figuerola, 2007).

Moreover, global changes can also facilitate the invasion of introduced species (Stachowicz, Terwin, Whitlatch, & Osman, 2002). Studies showed that behavioral characteristics are essential to the success of invasive species in the different stages (Chapple, Simmonds, & Wong, 2012; Sol, Timmermans, & Lefebvre, 2002). First, on introduction, individuals are caught in their native range for intentional introduction or are accidentally transported to habitats beyond their native distribution. Studies have demonstrated that captured individuals can be biased in terms of personality types (Biro & Dingemanse, 2009; Biro & Post, 2008). For instance, Biro and Post (2008) experimentally demonstrated that fast-growing, bolder, and more active fish are more heavily harvested than slow-growing, shyer, and less active individuals, though this obviously depends on capture methods. For accidental transportation, active, bolder, and more exploratory individuals can be more likely to encounter human-occupied environments. Therefore, they will more often enter potential transport vectors (e.g., freight, cargo) and might be transported between regions (Chapple et al., 2012). The composition of introduced individuals can thus be biased toward specific behavioral types and can affect the success of invasion if the behavioral composition also influences subsequent steps of the invasion.

For example, some personality traits, such as aggressiveness, can help the success of invasive species when coupled with dispersal tendency. High aggressiveness may help invasive species outcompete native species (Duckworth & Badyaev, 2007) or display higher foraging rate in novel environments (Pintor, Sih, & Kerby, 2009). A good example of how average personality of dispersers influences spatial population dynamics comes from studies of western bluebirds (*Sialia mexicana*; Duckworth & Badyaev, 2007; Duckworth & Kruuk, 2009). Duckworth and Badyaev (2007) showed that because colonists to new sites were highly aggressive before and after immigration, the species was able to displace and ultimately exclude an interspecific competitor, the mountain bluebird (*Sialia currucoides*) from invaded sites. The coupling of dispersal and heritable, repeatable individual levels of aggression has led to a wave of range expansion, with highly aggressive types dispersing to the front of the range expansion and displacing the competitor. In the mosquitofish, an invasive pest, we showed that asocial individuals are more likely to disperse further (Cote, Fogarty, et al., 2010) and are also more likely to survive novel predators at low densities (Brodin, Fogarty, Sih, & Cote, 2012). Sociability-dependent dispersal hence increases the probability for this species to successfully invade at lower densities in novel habitats.

However, for both western bluebirds and mosquitofish, the observed personality-biased dispersal would not allow a population increase reaching the high density needed for a successful invasion. Instead, a mix of personality types in the invading populations is needed to allow such a success. It was recently suggested that successive dispersal waves of individuals with different personality types could enhance the success of invasive species (Fogarty, Cote, & Sih, 2011). First, asocial, aggressive individuals leave established patches in small numbers and colonize empty patches (i.e., they are colonizers). They establish populations in newly occupied patches and facilitate colonization by social, unaggressive individuals who would not colonize empty patches (i.e., joiners). The increased population density associated with social, unaggressive individuals joining asocial, aggressive ones then induces dispersal by asocial individuals who colonize new empty patches (Fogarty et al., 2011). Such successive dispersal waves should create spatiotemporal variation in the distribution of personality types in the landscape.

It is difficult to precisely point out the behavioral types driving biological invasion. For example, introduced individuals might be more active and more exploratory, which would speed up the spread of invasive species but decrease the probability of establishment and the impacts on native species. Similarly, aggressive, asocial individuals can successfully invade empty habitats and displace competitors but will not be able to build high densities. It is therefore difficult to identify a single invader behavioral syndrome. A successful invasion might need the variability in personality traits or more flexible behaviors to adopt the best strategy for each step of the invasion. Behavioral flexibility can also be a benefit in heterogeneous environments. A recent review discussed the idea that behavioral flexibility allows invasive species to succeed in novel environments through innovation and social learning of novel behaviors (Wright, Eberhard, Hobson, Avery, & Russello, 2010). Across taxa, comparisons support the idea that more innovative species are more successful invasive species in birds and mammals (Sol, Bacher, Simon, & Lefebvre, 2008; Sol et al., 2002).

PERSONALITY TYPES AND MIGRATION

Migration is a movement enabling individuals to track seasonally favorable habitats (i.e., exploit seasonal peaks of resources or avoid seasonal resource depletion) and occurs in many arthropod, bird, mammal, and fish species. Migration strategies vary greatly among species and populations and are linked to a suite of physiological, morphological, and behavioral specializations called *migration syndromes*. Even if it is impossible to define a general migration syndrome for all migratory species, some characteristics have been identified for long-distance migratory bird species that can apply to other taxa (Piersma, Perez-Tris, Mouritsen, Bauchinger, & Bairlein, 2005). These include, among others, sophisticated endogenous circannual clocks, navigation and orientation skills, good long-term memory, endurance musculature, and general physiological flexibility (e.g., metabolism). Phylogenic comparisons reveal behavioral differences between migratory and sedentary species in birds.

Although it is believed that migratory birds should have greater nutritional flexibility (Bairlein, 2002), some recent studies showed that resident species have more innovative feeding behavior and are less neophobic toward novel food (Mettke-Hofmann, Wink, Winkler, & Leisler, 2005; Sol, Lefebvre, & Rodríguez-Teijeiro, 2005). Sol et al. (2005) suggested that species with lower foraging flexibility are more likely to migrate because they cannot deal with foraging stress during winter (i.e., the behavioral flexibility-migratory precursor hypothesis). They show that, in Palearctic passerine species, resident passerines innovate more often during winter than during other seasons, that long-distance migrants were less innovative concerning food than residents regardless of the season, and that residents have larger brain size (relative to body size) than migrants (Sol et al., 2005).

Furthermore, resident species have been found to be less neophobic in feeding from novel objects in familiar environments and exploring more novel objects than are related migratory species in parrots and warblers (Mettke-Hofmann, Ebert, Schmidt, Steiger, & Stieb, 2005; Mettke-Hofmann, Wink, et al., 2005). Resident species would benefit more than migratory species from exploring changes in familiar environments and being able to use the information later. However, the pattern is reversed for neophobia in entering novel environments. Migrant warbler species are less repelled by entering novel environments than are resident warbler species (Mettke-Hofmann, Lorentzen, Schlicht, Schneider, & Werner, 2009). This allows migrants to maximize migration speed and to decrease apprehension to enter a stopover site. Differences between migratory and resident species can also include differences in social behavior. Indeed, migration often involves a shift in social behavior. Species with territorial behavior before migration can form large social groups to migrate, and individuals of social species may migrate separately. Migratory species might thus have higher plasticity in their social behavior than resident species.

The migration syndrome is assumed to be inherited as a migratory gene package (Liedvogel, Åkesson, & Bensch, 2011), but there remains important genetic variation in migratory traits. In some bird species, although the genetic migratory machinery is still present, it plays a minor role in determining migratory strategies. Instead, selective pressure will induce a migratory strategy to dominate the population (Liedvogel et al., 2011; Pulido, 2007). Genetic variation in migratory traits also allows for the coexistence of different migratory strategies in a single population (i.e., partial migration; Chapman, Brönmark, Nilsson, & Hansson, 2011; Kaitala, Kaitala, & Lundberg, 1993). Ultimate factors for the evolution of migration include avoidance of intra- and interspecific competition, parasitism, and predation (Alerstam, Hedenström, & Åkesson, 2003; Pulido, 2007). Within a species or a population, between-individual differences in physiological and morphological specificities create heterogeneity in individual abilities to deal with competition, to escape predators, or to overcome high parasite load (Barber & Dingemanse, 2010; Wolf & Weissing, 2010). This heterogeneity can explain within-species differences in migratory strategies.

Variation in personality traits was also recently explained as an adaptive behavioral response to differences in physiological and morphological traits (Wolf & Weissing, 2010). Personality traits might thus have coevolved with the abilities to deal with ecological factors to initiate and facilitate migratory and sedentary strategies. Partial migration (interindividual differences in migratory behavior within a population) exists in many taxa, including birds, fish, mammals, and insects (Chapman, Brönmark, et al., 2011; Kaitala et al., 1993), and provides a great opportunity to study migrant behavioral syndromes.

Several explanations have been proposed for partial migration. One major line of investigation is whether migratory and sedentary behaviors are genetically controlled, condition-dependent (age, sex, dominance), and/or evolutionarily stable strategies (Brodersen, Nilsson, Hansson, Skov, & Brönmark, 2008; Kaitala et al., 1993). An interesting mechanism suggested to induce partial migration is the growth rate–predation risk trade-off (Brodersen et al., 2008). Brönmark, Skov, Brodersen, Nilsson, and Hansson (2008) developed a model for how this trade-off could affect partial migration in roach (*Rutilus rutilus*). Predation risk and food availability decrease when temperature drops during fall and winter. However, declines of predation risk and food availability are not identical in lakes and adjoined streams. The resulting ratio of predation risk to food availability (a cost–benefit ratio) is therefore relatively higher in the lake than in streams during winter

(Brönmark et al., 2008). This could explain the winter migration of cyprinids from lakes into streams.

However, all individuals are not equal within a population. Individual vulnerability to predators and foraging rate should depend on individual personality traits—in particular, boldness. It is notable that the trade-off between predation risk and growth rate has also been proposed to explain the existence and maintenance of variation in boldness. Bold individuals are more vulnerable to predation but have higher access to food than shy ones. Individual differences in boldness could therefore explain individual differences in migratory behavior. In accordance with this, a recent study of partial migration in roach showed that bolder individuals were more likely to migrate from lakes to streams during winter (Chapman, Hulthén, et al., 2011).

Differential migration—interindividual differences in migration distance, departure, or arrival timing in populations where all individuals migrate—also reveals consistent individual differences in migratory behavior (Ketterson & Nolan, 1983). Several factors have been proposed to explain the evolution of differential migration, including sex- and size-dependent intraspecific competition, resistance to winter climate, or risk of mortality in transit. No extant studies directly relate differential migration to personality traits. However, it has been shown that common cranes (*Grus grus*) are consistent in choosing and accepting the level of human disturbance in their breeding and wintering sites (Végvári, Barta, Mustakallio, & Székely, 2011). Cranes that hatched in undisturbed sites choose undisturbed migratory stopover sites, suggesting a role of personality traits in migratory decisions.

GENERAL BEHAVIORAL SYNDROMES

Behavioral syndromes—behavioral correlations across time and space or across ecological conditions—can produce correlations between demographic traits (Réale, Garant, et al., 2010). For instance, bolder individuals have a higher foraging rate and are thus expected to grow faster and to reproduce earlier but, in turn, to have lower life expectancy. Réale, Garant, et al. (2010) summarized predicted connections between personality, physiological, and life-history traits. They applied the pace-of-life syndrome hypothesis at the between-species level to the within-species level. To summarize, within a species, individuals can be ranked along a pace-of-life continuum going from slow lifestyle to fast lifestyle. Slow lifestyle individuals are expected to be shy, thorough and slow explorers, less aggressive, and more social, whereas fast lifestyle individuals are expected to be bold, superficial and fast explorers, aggressive, and asocial. The lifestyle is expected to be linked to demographic traits such that slow lifestyle individuals have a low growth rate, delayed reproduction, and long life, whereas fast lifestyle individuals have a high growth rate, precocious reproduction, and a short life.

Réale, Garant, et al. (2010) considered dispersal behavior to be a correlate of an individual's pace of life, with slow lifestyle individuals tending to remain as residents and fast lifestyle individuals dispersing. However, they did not consider other spatial movement behaviors in their pace-of-life hypothesis. On the basis of our review of spatial behaviors, we can predict how other spatial behaviors fit into this general syndrome. For within-habitat distribution, we predict slow lifestyle individuals to have more a clumped distribution and to cover smaller areas in comparison with fast lifestyle individuals because of their higher social and shyness levels and their lower energetic needs. Within invasive species (introduced or not), it is clear that the first individuals to invade are expected to have a fast lifestyle (bold, superficial explorer, aggressive, and asocial), whereas slow lifestyle individuals should be individuals joining habitats invaded by fast lifestyle individuals. This prediction also matches the role of reproductive strategies in biological invasion. Invaders are expected to have a higher reproductive rate to efficiently colonize empty habitats and start a population, whereas joiners (i.e., individuals joining habitats colonized by invaders) should be individuals with lower reproductive rates but who live longer and stabilize new populations. Finally, migrants should also be fast lifestyle individuals and residents low lifestyle individuals.

Thus, a global syndrome for movers seems to emerge. Individuals moving more within habitats, dispersing earlier or more, invading first, or engaging in seasonal migration have a faster lifestyle than more resident individuals. Although we predict these movers' syndromes, it is also clear that they should vary with ecological and social contexts and with species traits. For instance, the lifestyles of asocial versus social individuals can be questioned. The common idea in population biology is that individuals are distributed within a habitat according to the quantity of resources available. Population density therefore reflects resource availability. Because asocial individuals prefer lower population densities, we can expect them to be in habitats with low food availability, to consume less food, and thus to have a low growth rate and a delayed age at maturity. In low-density populations, there are also fewer mating partners, which can also delay age at first reproduction. All of these examples are in opposition to the fast lifestyle predicted for asocial individuals. However, even if the total quantity of resources (food and mating partners) are lower in habitats with low-density populations, lifestyle strategies should depend on resource quantity per individual (resource quantity divided by number of individuals), which might be equal in low and high density populations.

As we previously stated, the relationships between personality types and spatial behaviors should depend on ecological and social contexts. For instance, dispersers will be bolder or shyer depending on the presence of a risk in the environment and will be social or asocial depending on the social context. An extreme example is the social organization of species. The level of social organization is traditionally classified along a sociality scale from *presocial* (subsocial, semisocial, quasisocial) to *eusocial* (Costa & Fitzgerald, 2005). Although we can expect individuals with lower social integration (i.e., nonhelpers) to disperse in eusocial species, the relationship between dispersal and individual sociability can be disrupted or reversed in subsocial species. Syndromes can also depend on the peculiarities of a species' spatial behaviors. For instance, in some species, dispersal or/and migration is carried out in groups of individuals, whereas in other species, individuals travel independently from others. The behavioral syndrome of movers should therefore vary among species.

Finally, it is interesting to understand how such correlations between behavioral syndromes and demographic traits can be produced and can vary with ecological contexts. Lifestyle is expected to be linked to physiological traits such as metabolism, immune response, and various neurochemicals (e.g., stress hormones, other steroid hormones, serotonin, dopamine). For example, individual variation in different neurochemicals has been associated with variation in both personality traits and spatial behavior (see Cote, Clobert, et al., 2010), and their levels can depend on genes, environmental experiences, and Genes × Environment interactions. Therefore, the coordinated expression of spatial behavior and personalities could be due to shared dependence of traits on genetic and environmental factors during ontogeny (Duckworth & Kruuk, 2009). The actual strategy that emerges (e.g., dispersing or not) will then depend on environmental variation in the living habitat. Another possibility is that only personalities are influenced by gene and environment interactions during offspring development (Stamps & Groothuis 2010) and that this subsequently affects individual performance and reaction to different environmental conditions and therefore spatial behavior.

CONCLUSION: PARALLELS WITH HUMAN CASES

Although the specifics should vary among nonhuman animal species, we were able to highlight several components of disperser, invader, and migrant syndromes. Because these syndromes are related to other demographic traits, personality-dependent spatial behaviors have important consequences for the ecology and the evolution of species as well as the adaptability of species to current changing environmental conditions. Even if we agree that such parallels are difficult to infer, we believe that these syndromes and their consequences in nonhuman animals are sometimes similar to those found in humans. For example, in a 9-year study in Finland, high sociability predicted dispersal to urban areas and high activity positively predicted high dispersal propensity in general (Jokela, Elovainio, Kivimäki, & Keltikangas-Järvinen, 2008; see also Chapter 4, this volume). Another study linked the polymorphism in the dopamine D4 receptor (DRD4) to the migration pattern of 39 human populations (Chen, Burton, Greenberger, & Dmitrieva, 1999). Macro- and micro-migration were correlated to the proportion of long alleles for DRD4, a genetic trait linked to the novelty-seeking personality in some studies (though several studies did not find this link; Ebstein 2006). It is notable that polymorphisms in DRD4 have also been linked to novelty-seeking personality and dispersal behavior in great tits (Fidler et al., 2007).

These studies appear as the only striking comparisons between human and nonhuman dispersal syndromes (Chapter 4, this volume). However, we believe that differences in personality metrics between human and nonhuman animals and the complexity of social environments in humans prevent other types of direct comparison. Although studies on laboratory and domesticated animals or nonhuman primates have often used a human personality framework (Gosling, 1998; King & Figueredo, 1997), ecologists have preferred a framework adapted to wild animals (Réale et al., 2007, but see Gosling, 1998, for example). Behavioral ecologists avoid using terms such as *anxiety, emotionality,* or *creativity* because of a hesitance to anthropomorphize and the lack of ecological relevance. This is particularly true for particular dimensions of human personality; Neuroticism, Agreeableness, Extraversion, and Conscientiousness would clearly fall into an anthropomorphic view of nonhuman animals' personality (McCrae & Costa, 1990). However, the Openness dimension and several facets of the five-factor model (sociability, aggression, cooperation, vulnerability to stress, curiosity) create clear bridges between human and nonhuman studies.

It seems important to compare studies of personalities of human and nonhuman animals for two reasons. First, nonhuman animals allow breeding and cross-fostering experiments, which are not feasible in humans, to tease apart the effects of genes and environments on the ontogeny of personalities (Nettle & Penke, 2010). Second, personality-dependent spatial behavior can have similar consequences in human and nonhuman animals. For instance, dispersers are the agents of a widespread dissemination of diseases (Boulinier, McCoy, & Sorci, 2001). Recent studies have also shown that bolder and more social individuals are more likely to be infected by pathogens or carry a more diverse pathogen community (Barber & Dingemanse, 2010). The link between these personality types and dispersal propensity should be a crucial factor in epidemics in both nonhuman and human animals (see Chapter 3, this volume). Another consequence is the building of a novel population or society when colonizers have a biased personality. For example, Whybrow (2005) suggested that the risk-taking and novelty-seeking temperaments of colonial and postcolonial migrants to the United States have created an excessively consumerist and competitive society. Interestingly, it has been shown in nonhuman species that high levels of aggressiveness and foraging activities in invaders are the keys in the success of invasion and its impacts on invaded communities (Duckworth & Badyaev, 2007; Pintor et al., 2009). Although these examples are only hypotheses, we suggest that some processes might be similar between colonization in human and nonhuman species.

REFERENCES

Alerstam, T., Hedenström, A., & Åkesson, S. (2003). Long-distance migration: Evolution and determinants. *Oikos, 103,* 247–260. doi:10.1034/j.1600-0706.2003.12559.x

Aragón, P., Clobert, J., & Massot, M. (2006). Individual dispersal status influences space use of conspecific residents in the common lizard, Lacerta vivipara. *Behavioral Ecology and Sociobiology, 60,* 430–438. doi:10.1007/s00265-006-0183-3

Bairlein, F. (2002). How to get fat: Nutritional mechanisms of seasonal fat accumulation in migratory songbirds. *Naturwissenschaften, 89,* 1–10. doi:10.1007/s00114-001-0279-6

Barber, I., & Dingemanse, N. J. (2010). Parasitism and the evolutionary ecology of animal personality. *Philosophical Transactions of the Royal Society: B. Biological Sciences, 365,* 4077–4088. doi:10.1098/rstb.2010.0182

Bekoff, M. (1977). Mammalian dispersal and the ontogeny of individual behavioral phenotypes. *American Naturalist, 111,* 715–732. doi:10.1086/283201

Bergmüller, R., & Taborsky, M. (2010). Animal personality due to social niche specialisation. *Trends in Ecology & Evolution, 25,* 504–511. doi:10.1016/j.tree.2010.06.012

Biro, P. A., & Dingemanse, N. J. (2009). Sampling bias resulting from animal personality. *Trends in Ecology & Evolution, 24,* 66–67. doi:10.1016/j.tree.2008.11.001

Biro, P. A., & Post, J. R. (2008). Rapid depletion of genotypes with fast growth and bold personality traits from harvested fish populations. *Proceedings of the National Academy of Sciences of the United States of America, 105,* 2919–2922. doi:10.1073/pnas.0708159105

Biro, P. A., Post, J. R., & Booth, D. J. (2007). Mechanisms for climate-induced mortality of fish populations in whole-lake experiments. *Proceedings of the National Academy of Sciences of the United States of America, 104,* 9715–9719. doi:10.1073/pnas.0701638104

Blumstein, D. T., Wey, T. W., & Tang, K. (2009). A test of the social cohesion hypothesis: Interactive female marmots remain at home. *Proceedings of the Royal Society: B. Biological Sciences, 276,* 3007–3012. doi:10.1098/rspb.2009.0703

Boulinier, T., McCoy, K. D., & Sorci, G. (2001). Dispersal and parasitism. In J. Clobert, E. Danchin, A. A. Dhondt, & J. D. Nichols (Eds.), *Dispersal* (pp. 169–179). Oxford, England: Oxford University Press.

Bowler, D. E., & Benton, T. G. (2005). Causes and consequences of animal dispersal strategies: Relating individual behavior to spatial dynamics. *Biological Reviews of the Cambridge Philosophical Society, 80,* 205–225. doi:10.1017/S1464793104006645

Brodersen, J., Nilsson, P. A., Hansson, L.-A., Skov, C., & Brönmark, C. (2008). Condition-dependent individual decision-making determines cyprinid partial migration. *Ecology, 89,* 1195–1200. doi:10.1890/07-1318.1

Brodin, T., Fogarty, S., Sih, A., & Cote, J. (2012). *Personality-dependent survival of the invasive mosquitofish: Being social can be deadly.* Manuscript in preparation.

Brönmark, C., Skov, C., Brodersen, J., Nilsson, P. A., & Hansson, L.-A. (2008). Seasonal migration determined by a trade-off between predator avoidance and growth. *PloS One, 3*(4), e1957. doi:10.1371/journal.pone.0001957

Chapman, B. B., Brönmark, C., Nilsson, J.-Å., & Hansson, L.-A. (2011). The ecology and evolution of partial migration. *Oikos, 120,* 1764–1775. doi:10.1111/j.1600-0706.2011.20131.x

Chapman, B. B., Hulthén, K., Blomqvist, D. R., Hansson, L.-A., Nilsson, J.-Å., Brodersen, J., . . . Brönmark, C. (2011). To boldly go: Individual differences in boldness influence migratory tendency. *Ecology Letters, 14,* 871–876. doi:10.1111/j.1461-0248.2011.01648.x

Chapple, D. G., Simmonds, S. M., & Wong, B. B. M. (2012). Can behavioral and personality traits influence the success of unintentional species introductions? *Trends in Ecology & Evolution, 27,* 57–64. doi:10.1016/j.tree.2011.09.010

Chen, C., Burton, M., Greenberger, E., & Dmitrieva, J. (1999). Population migration and the variation of dopamine D4 receptor (DRD4) allele frequencies around the globe. *Evolution and Human Behavior, 20,* 309–324. doi:10.1016/S1090-5138(99)00015-X

Clobert, J., Danchin, E., Dhondt, A. A., & Nichols, J. D. (2001). *Dispersal.* New York, NY: Oxford University Press.

Clobert, J., Le Galliard, J. F., Cote, J., Meylan, S., & Massot, M. (2009). Informed dispersal, heterogeneity in animal dispersal syndromes and the dynamics of spatially structured populations. *Ecology Letters, 12,* 197–209. doi:10.1111/j.1461-0248.2008.01267.x

Costa, J. T., & Fitzgerald, T. D. (2005). *Social terminology revisited: Where are we ten years later?* (Vol. 42). Helsinki, Finland: Akateeminen kirjakauppa.

Cote, J., & Clobert, J. (2007). Social personalities influence natal dispersal in a lizard. *Proceedings of the Royal Society: B. Biological Sciences, 274,* 383–390. doi:10.1098/rspb.2006.3734

Cote, J., Clobert, J., Brodin, T., Fogarty, S., & Sih, A. (2010). Personality-dependent dispersal: Characterization, ontogeny and consequences for spatially structured populations. *Philosophical Transactions of the Royal Society: B. Biological Sciences*, 365, 4065–4076. doi:10.1098/rstb.2010.0176

Cote, J., Dreiss, A., & Clobert, J. (2008). Social personality trait and fitness. *Proceedings of the Royal Society: B. Biological Sciences*, 275, 2851–2858. doi:10.1098/rspb.2008.0783

Cote, J., Fogarty, S., Brodin, T., Weinersmith, K., & Sih, A. (2011). Personality-dependent dispersal in the invasive mosquitofish: Group composition matters. *Proceedings of the Royal Society: B. Biological Sciences*, 278, 1670-1678. doi:10.1098/rspb.2010.1892

Cote, J., Fogarty, S., & Sih, A. (2012). Individual sociability and choosiness between shoal types. *Animal Behaviour*, 83, 1469–1476. doi:10.1016/j.anbehav.2012.03.019

Cote, J., Fogarty, S., Weinersmith, K., Brodin, T., & Sih, A. (2010). Personality traits and dispersal tendency in the invasive mosquitofish (*Gambusia affinis*). *Proceedings of the Royal Society: B. Biological Sciences*, 277, 1571–1579. doi:10.1098/rspb.2009.2128

Dingemanse, N. J., Both, C., van Noordwijk, A. J., Rutten, A. L., & Drent, P. J. (2003). Natal dispersal and personalities in great tits (*Parus major*). *Proceedings of the Royal Society: B. Biological Sciences*, 270, 741–747. doi:10.1098/rspb.2002.2300

Dobson, A. P., Bradshaw, A. D., & Baker, A. J. M. (1997, July 25). Hopes for the future: Restoration ecology and conservation biology. *Science*, 277(5325), 515–522. doi:10.1126/science.277.5325.515

Doligez, B., Danchin, E., & Clobert, J. (2002, August 16). Public information and breeding habitat in a wild bird population. *Science*, 297(5584), 1168–1170. doi:10.1126/science.1072838

Duckworth, R. A., & Badyaev, A. V. (2007). Coupling of dispersal and aggression facilitates the rapid range expansion of a passerine bird. *Proceedings of the National Academy of Sciences of the United States of America*, 104, 15017–15022. doi:10.1073/pnas.0706174104

Duckworth, R. A., & Kruuk, L. E. B. (2009). Evolution of genetic integration between dispersal and colonization ability in a bird. *Evolution: International Journal of Organic Evolution*, 63, 968–977. doi:10.1111/j.1558-5646.2009.00625.x

Ebstein, R. P. (2006). The molecular genetic architecture of human personality: Beyond self-report questionnaires. *Molecular Psychiatry*, 11, 427–445. doi:10.1038/sj.mp.4001814

Englund, G. (1997). Importance of spatial scale and prey movements in predator caging experiments. *Ecology*, 78, 2316–2325. doi:10.1890/0012-9658(1997)078[2316:IOSSAP]2.0.CO;2

Fidler, A. E., van Oers, K., Drent, P. J., Kuhn, S., Mueller, J. C., & Kempenaers, B. (2007). Drd4 gene polymorphisms are associated with personality variation in a passerine bird. *Proceedings of the Royal Society: B. Biological Sciences*, 274, 1685–1691. doi:10.1098/rspb.2007.0337

Figuerola, J. (2007). Climate and dispersal: Black-winged stilts disperse further in dry springs. *PLoS ONE, 2*(6), e539. doi:10.1371/journal.pone.0000539

Fogarty, S., Cote, J., & Sih, A. (2011). Social personality polymorphism and the spread of invasive species: A model. *American Naturalist, 177,* 273–287. doi:10.1086/658174

Fraser, D. F., Gilliam, J. F., Daley, M. J., Le, A. N., & Skalski, G. T. (2001). Explaining leptokurtic movement distributions: Intrapopulation variation in boldness and exploration. *American Naturalist, 158,* 124–135. doi:10.1086/321307

Gosling, S. D. (1998). Personality dimensions in spotted hyenas (*Crocuta crocuta*). *Journal of Comparative Psychology, 112,* 107–118. doi:10.1037/0735-7036.112.2.107

Gosling, S. D., & John, O. P. (1999). Personality dimensions in nonhuman animals: A cross-species review. *Current Directions in Psychological Science, 8,* 69–75. doi:10.1111/1467-8721.00017

Howell, S., Westergaard, G., Hoos, B., Chavanne, T. J., Shoaf, S. E., Cleveland, A., . . . Higley, J. D. (2007). Serotonergic influences on life-history outcomes in free-ranging male rhesus macaques. *American Journal of Primatology, 69,* 851–865. doi:10.1002/ajp.20369

Jokela, M., Elovainio, M., Kivimäki, M., & Keltikangas-Järvinen, L. (2008). Temperament and migration patterns in Finland. *Psychological Science, 19,* 831–837. doi:10.1111/j.1467-9280.2008.02164.x

Kaitala, A., Kaitala, V., & Lundberg, P. (1993). A theory of partial migration. *American Naturalist, 142,* 59–81. doi:10.1086/285529

Ketterson, E. D., & Nolan, V. A. L. (1983). The evolution of differential bird migration. In R. F. Johnston (Ed.), *Current ornithology* (Vol. 1, pp. 357–402). New York, NY: Plenum Press.

King, J. E., & Figueredo, A. J. (1997). The five-factor model plus dominance in chimpanzee personality. *Journal of Research in Personality, 31,* 257–271. doi:10.1006/jrpe.1997.2179

Krackow, S. (2003). Motivational and heritable determinants of dispersal latency in wild male house mice (*Mus musculus musculus*). *Ethology, 109,* 671–689. doi:10.1046/j.1439-0310.2003.00913.x

Krause, J., & Ruxton, G. D. (2002). *Living in groups.* Oxford, England: Oxford University Press.

Liedvogel, M., Åkesson, S., & Bensch, S. (2011). The genetics of migration on the move. *Trends in Ecology & Evolution, 26,* 561–569. doi:10.1016/j.tree.2011.07.009

Lodge, D. M. (1993). Biological invasions: Lessons for ecology. *Trends in Ecology & Evolution, 8,* 133–137. doi:10.1016/0169-5347(93)90025-K

Mack, R. N., Simberloff, D., Mark Lonsdale, W., Evans, H., Clout, M., & Bazzaz, F. A. (2000). Biotic invasions: causes, epidemiology, global consequences, and control. *Ecological Applications, 10,* 689–710. doi:10.1890/1051-0761(2000)010[0689: BICEGC]2.0.CO;2

McCrae, R. R., & Costa, P. T., Jr. (1990). *Personality in adulthood.* New York, NY: Guilford Press.

Mehlman, P. T., Higley, J. D., Faucher, I., Lilly, A. A., Taub, D. M., Vickers, J., . . . Linnoila, M. (1995). Correlation of CSF 5-HIAA concentration with sociality and the timing of emigration in free-ranging primates. *The American Journal of Psychiatry, 152,* 907–913.

Mettke-Hofmann, C., Ebert, C., Schmidt, T., Steiger, S., & Stieb, S. (2005). Personality traits in resident and migratory warbler species. *Behaviour, 142,* 1357–1375. doi:10.1163/156853905774539427

Mettke-Hofmann, C., Lorentzen, S., Schlicht, E., Schneider, J., & Werner, F. (2009). Spatial neophilia and spatial neophobia in resident and migratory warblers (*Sylvia*). *Ethology, 115,* 482–492. doi:10.1111/j.1439-0310.2009.01632.x

Mettke-Hofmann, C., Wink, M., Winkler, H., & Leisler, B. (2005). Exploration of environmental changes relates to lifestyle. *Behavioral Ecology, 16,* 247–254. doi:10.1093/beheco/arh159

Meylan, S., De Fraipont, M., Aragón, P., Vercken, E., & Clobert, J. (2009). Are dispersal-dependent behavioral traits produced by phenotypic plasticity? *Journal of Experimental Zoology: Part A. Ecological Genetics and Physiology, 311A,* 377–388. doi:10.1002/jez.533

Nettle, D., & Penke, L. (2010). Personality: Bridging the literatures from human psychology and behavioural ecology. *Philosophical Transactions of the Royal Society: B. Biological Sciences, 365,* 4043–4050. doi:10.1098/rstb.2010.0061

O'Riain, M. J., Jarvis, J. U. M., & Faulkes, C. (1996, April 18). A dispersive morph in the naked mole-rat. *Nature, 380,* 619–621. doi:10.1038/380619a0

Piersma, T., Perez-Tris, J., Mouritsen, H., Bauchinger, U., & Bairlein, F. (2005). Is there a "migratory syndrome" common to all migrant birds? *Annals of the New York Academy of Sciences, 1046,* 282–293. doi.org/10.1196/annals.1343.026

Pimentel, D., Lach, L., Zuniga, R., & Morrison, D. (2000). Environmental and economic costs of nonindigenous species in the United States. *Bioscience, 50,* 53–65. doi:10.1641/0006-3568(2000)050[0053:EAECON]2.3.CO;2

Pintor, L. M., Sih, A., & Kerby, J. L. (2009). Behavioral correlations provide a mechanism for explaining high invader densities and increased impacts on native prey. *Ecology, 90,* 581–587. doi:10.1641/B570211

Pulido, F. (2007). The genetics and evolution of avian migration. *Bioscience, 57,* 165–174. doi:10.1641/B570211

Réale, D., Dingemanse, N. J., Kazem, A. J. N., & Wright, J. (2010). Evolutionary and ecological approaches to the study of personality. *Philosophical Transactions of the Royal Society: B. Biological Sciences, 365,* 3937–3946. doi:10.1098/rstb.2010.0222

Réale, D., Garant, D., Humphries, M. M., Bergeron, P., Careau, V., & Montiglio, P.-O. (2010). Personality and the emergence of the pace-of-life syndrome concept at the population level. *Philosophical Transactions of the Royal Society: B. Biological Sciences, 365,* 4051–4063. doi:10.1098/rstb.2010.0208

Réale, D., Reader, S. M., Sol, D., McDougall, P. T., & Dingemanse, N. J. (2007). Integrating animal temperament within ecology and evolution. *Biological*

Reviews of the Cambridge Philosophical Society, 82, 291–318. doi:10.1111/
j.1469-185X.2007.00010.x

Salewski, V., & Bruderer, B. (2007). The evolution of bird migration—A synthesis.
Naturwissenschaften, 94, 268–279. doi:10.1007/s00114-006-0186-y

Schürch, R., Rothenberger, S., & Heg, D. (2010). The building-up of social relationships: Behavioral types, social networks and cooperative breeding in a cichlid.
Philosophical Transactions of the Royal Society: B. Biological Sciences, 365, 4089–
4098. doi:10.1098/rstb.2010.0177

Sih, A., Bell, A., & Johnson, J. C. (2004). Behavioral syndromes: An ecological and
evolutionary overview. *Trends in Ecology & Evolution, 19,* 372–378. doi:10.1016/
j.tree.2004.04.009

Sih, A., Cote, J., Evans, M., Fogarty, S., & Pruitt, J. (2012). Ecological implications
of behavioral syndromes. *Ecology Letters, 15*(3), 278–289. doi:10.1111/j.1461-
0248.2011.01731.x

Smith, B. R., & Blumstein, D. T. (2008). Fitness consequences of personality: A
meta-analysis. *Behavioral Ecology, 19,* 448–455. doi:10.1093/beheco/arm144

Sol, D., Bacher, S., Simon, M. R., & Lefebvre, L. (2008). Brain size predicts the success of mammal species introduced into novel environments. *American Naturalist,
172,* S63–S71.

Sol, D., Lefebvre, L., & Rodríguez-Teijeiro, J. D. (2005). Brain size, innovative
propensity and migratory behavior in temperate Palaearctic birds. *Proceedings of the Royal Society: B. Biological Sciences, 272,* 1433–1441. doi:10.1098/
rspb.2005.3099

Sol, D., Timmermans, S., & Lefebvre, L. (2002). Behavioral flexibility and invasion
success in birds. *Animal Behaviour, 63,* 495–502. doi:10.1006/anbe.2001.1953

Stachowicz, J. J., Terwin, J. R., Whitlatch, R. B., & Osman, R. W. (2002). Linking climate change and biological invasions: Ocean warming facilitates nonindigenous
species invasions. *Proceedings of the National Academy of Sciences of the United
States of America, 99,* 15497–15500. doi:10.1073/pnas.242437499

Stamps, J. A. (2001). Habitat selection by dispersers: Integrating proximate and ultimate approaches. In J. Clobert, E. Danchin, A. A. Dhondt, & J. D. Nichols (Eds.),
Dispersal (pp. 110–122). New York, NY: Oxford University Press.

Stamps, J. A. (2007). Growth-mortality tradeoffs and "personality traits" in animals.
Ecology Letters, 10, 355–363. doi:10.1111/j.1461-0248.2007.01034.x

Stamps, J. A., & Groothuis, T. G. G. (2010). Developmental perspectives on personality: Implications for ecological and evolutionary studies of individual differences. *Philosophical Transactions of the Royal Society: B. Biological Sciences. 365,*
4029–4041. doi:10.1098/rstb.2010.0218

Svendsen, G. E. (1974). Behavioral and environmental factors in the spatial distribution and population dynamics of a yellow-bellied marmot population. *Ecology,
55,* 760–771. doi:10.2307/1934412

Trefilov, A., Berard, J., Krawczak, M., & Schmidtke, J. (2000). Natal dispersal in rhesus macaques is related to serotonin transporter gene promoter variation. *Behavior Genetics, 30*, 295–301. doi:10.1023/A:1026597300525

Tuomainen, U., & Candolin, U. (2011). Behavioral responses to human-induced environmental change. *Biological Reviews of the Cambridge Philosophical Society, 86*, 640–657. doi:10.1111/j.1469-185X.2010.00164.x

van Oers, K., Drent, P. J., de Goede, P., & van Noordwijk, A. J. (2004). Realized heritability and repeatability of risk-taking behavior in relation to avian personalities. *Proceedings of the Royal Society: B. Biological Sciences, 271*, 65–73. doi:10.1098/rspb.2003.2518

Végvári, Z., Barta, Z., Mustakallio, P., & Székely, T. (2011). Consistent avoidance of human disturbance over large geographical distances by a migratory bird. *Biology Letters, 7*, 814–817. doi:10.1098/rsbl.2011.0295

Whybrow, P. C. (2005). *American mania: When more is not enough.* New York, NY: Norton.

Wolf, M., & Weissing, F. J. (2010). An explanatory framework for adaptive personality differences. *Philosophical Transactions of the Royal Society: B. Biological Sciences, 365*, 3959–3968. doi:10.1098/rstb.2010.0215

Wooster, D., & Sih, A. (1995). A review of the drift and activity responses of stream prey to predator presence. *Oikos, 73*, 3–8. doi:10.2307/3545718

Wright, T. F., Eberhard, J. R., Hobson, E. A., Avery, M. L., & Russello, M. A. (2010). Behavioral flexibility and species invasions: The adaptive flexibility hypothesis. *Ethology Ecology and Evolution, 22*, 393–404. doi:10.1080/03949370.2010.505580

II

GEOGRAPHICAL REPRESENTATION OF SOCIAL PSYCHOLOGICAL PHENOMENA

6

GEOGRAPHICAL DIFFERENCES IN PERSONALITY

PETER J. RENTFROW

A key objective of social–personality psychology is to understand the ways in which personality traits interact with environmental forces to shape people's thoughts, feelings, and behaviors. In an effort to uncover such interactions, a considerable amount of attention has been devoted to a rather narrow conceptualization of the environment that focuses mainly on situations. The evidence is clear that situations influence a host of social and psychological phenomena, but such a restricted notion of the environment offers only a distorted and incomplete depiction of Person × Environment interactions. If we are to develop a clear and thorough understanding of the links between people and the environments they are in, it is crucial that we broaden our notion of the environment.

Geography has long been recognized by many disciplines as essential for understanding behavior. Research in economics, for example, investigates the ways in which local resources, infrastructure, and local amenities

http://dx.doi.org/10.1037/14272-007
Geographical Psychology: Exploring the Interaction of Environment and Behavior, P. J. Rentfrow (Editor)

affect residential mobility. Studies in epidemiology examine the impact of unemployment, overcrowding, and access to basic resources on public health. And work in political science investigates the influence of historical migration patterns and local demography on public opinion. The conclusion that emerges from those lines of research is that the regions in which people live affects individuals' life goals, well-being, and worldviews—constructs that are at the core of social–personality psychology. It thus seems reasonable that broadening our conceptualization of the environment to include a geographical perspective could deepen our understanding of the dynamic relations between individuals and the environment.

Over the past decade, a considerable number of articles have been published concerning geographical differences in personality. The results from that work provide compelling evidence for the value that a geographical perspective can bring to social–personality psychology. The purpose of this chapter is to review theory and research concerned with geographical differences in personality and to present new data showing regional differences in personality across the United States.

GEOGRAPHY AND PERSONALITY

Cross-National Differences

The notion that geography is relevant to understanding the psychological characteristics of individuals is not new. Nearly a century ago, social scientists in psychology, anthropology, and sociology began studying the relations between people and the places in which they live. This work was designed to identify the dominant psychological characteristics that defined citizens of different nations. Several investigations were conducted to identify national differences in motives (McClelland, 1961), values (e.g., Buchanan & Cantril, 1953), and personality (Adorno, Frenkel-Brunswik, Levinson, & Sanford, 1950; Inkeles, Hanfmann, & Beier, 1958). The research produced at this time was thought provoking and considered by many as providing insight into the atrocities witnessed during the Second World War. However, its impact on the field of psychology was short-lived because most of it was based on vague conceptual models of personality and unreliable methodologies (Inkeles & Levinson, 1969; LeVine, 2001). For those and other reasons, mainstream psychology's interest in geographical differences faded away.

Recently, however, renewed interest in geographical variation in personality has emerged. The renewed interest is due to the establishment of the Big Five personality framework (i.e., Extraversion, Agreeableness, Conscientiousness, Neuroticism, Openness to Experience; Costa & McCrae,

1992; Goldberg, 1992) as an empirically based model for conceptualizing the structure of personality.

- *Extraversion* reflects individual differences in sociability and energy; people high in Extraversion tend to be assertive and enthusiastic, whereas people low in this trait are more quiet and reserved.
- *Agreeableness* reflects the degree to which an individual is warm and trusting; people high in Agreeableness are empathic and cooperative, whereas people low in this trait are more dominant and competitive.
- *Conscientiousness* reflects the extent to which a person is hardworking and efficient; people high in Conscientiousness tend to be organized and dependable, whereas people low in this trait are less responsible and careful.
- *Neuroticism* reflects individual differences in anxiety and depression; people high in Neuroticism tend to be emotionally unstable and have low self-esteem, whereas people low in this trait are more relaxed and unflappable.
- *Openness to Experience* reflects the degree to which a person is creative and imaginative; people high in Openness are typically artistic and curious, whereas people low in this trait are more practical and less creative.

Numerous studies provide compelling evidence that these personality traits are rooted in biology (Jang, McCrae, Angleitner, Riemann, & Livesley, 1998; Plomin & Caspi, 1999), are relatively stable throughout life (McCrae & Costa, 2003; Roberts, Walton, & Viechtbauer, 2006; Srivastava, John, Gosling, & Potter, 2003), and emerge in several cultures (e.g., Benet-Martínez & John, 2000; McCrae & Costa, 1997).

Given evidence for the robustness of the Big Five model, several investigations have applied it to the study of cross-national personality differences (e.g., Allik & McCrae, 2004; McCrae, 2001; McCrae & Terracciano, 2005, 2008; Schmitt, Allik, McCrae, Benet-Martínez, 2007; Steel & Ones, 2002). Specifically, personality inventories based on the Big Five framework have been administered to participants in different countries, and their responses to the inventories have been aggregated to devise nation-level personality trait scores. National-level personality traits are thus the mean trait scores of a sample of respondents who live in a nation. So to say that the United States is high in Openness means that the average level of Openness taken from a sample of U.S. citizens is high compared with the average level of Openness in other countries. In this way, the personality of an entire nation's population is taken as the mean of its parts.

The results from studies of national personality differences show geographic variation in each of the personality domains (Allik & McCrae, 2004; McCrae, 2001; McCrae & Terracciano, 2005; McCrae & Terracciano, 2008; Schmitt, Allik, McCrae, Benet-Martínez, 2007; Steel & Ones, 2002). For example, there is evidence that members of Asian cultures score low on measures of Extraversion compared with members of other cultures; members of Central and South American cultures score high on measures of Openness; and members of Southern and Eastern European cultures score higher in Neuroticism compared with members of other European cultures. There is also evidence that national personality scores are associated with national indicators of cancer, smoking, obesity, and life expectancy (McCrae & Terracciano, 2008). These results effectively show that aggregate personality profiles of countries provide reliable and valid indicators of the psychological characteristics of nations.

Most of the research on geographic variation in personality has focused on national differences. That work has uncovered several important findings, but just as the prevalence of traits varies across nations, so too might it vary across regions within nations. Thus, a complete understanding of the processes underlying geographic trait variation will require examining variation across a range of geographic levels of analysis.

Regional Differences

Little attention has been given to regional differences within nations. Using data from the national standardization of Cattell's 16PF (Cattell, Eber, & Tatsuoka, 1970), Krug and Kulhavy (1973) aimed to determine what personality differences, if any, exist across U.S. regions. Their analyses revealed a number of significant regional differences. For instance, residents of the Northeast, Midwest, and West Coast scored significantly higher in "creative productivity" (which in Big Five terms would reflect high Openness) compared with respondents from the Southeast, Southwest, and Mountain regions, whereas people from the Mountain and Southwest regions were higher in "isolation" (which in Big Five terms would reflect low Extraversion) compared with respondents from the Midwest.

Three decades after Krug and Kulhavy's (1973) exploratory study, Plaut, Markus, and Lachman (2002) examined regional differences in self-construal, measured in terms of the Big Five model (Lachman & Weaver, 1997). The aim of their project was to examine regional variation in well-being and self-views. Somewhat consistent with Krug and Kulhavy's findings, Plaut and colleagues found that individuals in the Mid- and South-Atlantic regions rated themselves highly on descriptors associated with Neuroticism, and individuals in the New England, Mid-Atlantic, and Pacific regions rated themselves highly on descriptors associated with Openness.

In an effort to provide a more detailed map of regional personality differences, Rentfrow, Gosling, and Potter (2008) examined state-level differences using data from a large Internet-based personality project. The aim of that project was to explore statewide differences in personality and to examine their relations with state-level social indicators. The results from that project replicated previous findings by showing that states in the Northeast and West Coast were comparatively high in Openness, and states in the Northeast and Southeast were higher in Neuroticism compared with states in the West. Rentfrow and colleagues (2008) also extended the findings from earlier work by examining the correlates of state-level personality traits. The results revealed positive relationships between Neuroticism and rates of heart disease and cancer, for instance, as well as positive associations between Openness and liberal public opinion.

Since the publication of Rentfrow et al. (2008), a surprising number of articles on the correlates of state-level personality traits have been published. These investigations have examined the relationships between the state-level personality scores published in Rentfrow et al. (2008) and a wide range of social indictors, including health and morbidity (McCann, 2010a, 2010b, 2011b; Pesta, Bertsch, McDaniel, Mahoney, & Poznanski, 2012; Voracek, 2009), psychological well-being (McCann, 2011a; Pesta, McDaniel, & Bertsch, 2010; Rentfrow, Mellander, & Florida, 2009), social capital (Rentfrow, 2010), creative capital (Florida, 2008), income inequality (de Vries, Gosling, & Potter, 2011), and political values (Rentfrow, Jost, Gosling, & Potter, 2009). Several of the correlations between state-level personality traits and social indicators are consistent with findings at the individual level. For example, states high in Agreeableness had high rates of social capital and long life expectancies; states high in Neuroticism had higher rates of smoking, diabetes, and cholesterol and lower levels of well-being; and states high in Openness cast more votes for liberal politicians and reported smoking more marijuana than states low in Openness. However, some of the links were inconsistent with what some might expect from personality research at the individual level. State-level Conscientiousness, for instance, has been found to relate negatively to income and longevity, which are both positively related to Conscientiousness at the individual level. The effect sizes of these aggregate-level relationships are generally larger in magnitude than what is usually observed at the individual level. These large correlations are the result of aggregating survey responses from hundreds and thousands of individuals, which effectively reduces the error variances in the personality scores, leaving less variance to explain.

In summary, the regional distribution of personality in the United States appears fairly stable, because the patterns observed in three separate studies revealed some degree of convergence. Furthermore, some of the state-level personality traits appear to possess some degree of validity insofar as they are related to conceptually relevant social indicators.

STATEWIDE DIFFERENCES IN PERSONALITY FACETS: DATA STUDY

The Big Five framework provides a valuable model for conceptualizing and measuring personality at the individual and aggregate levels. However, an important limitation of the five domains is their breadth. Each domain consists of more specific personality facets (Costa & McCrae, 1992, 1995; Soto & John, 2009) that offer more nuanced information that is otherwise lost when focusing solely on the five broad domains. The evidence for statewide differences in personality at the domain level raises the question of whether there are meaningful statewide differences at the facet level. Such findings would provide insight into which personality characteristics are responsible for the domain-level relationships.

To examine the links between social indicators and statewide differences in facets of personality, I used data reported in Rentfrow et al. (2008) on state-level personality. In that study, personality was assessed using the Big Five Inventory (BFI; John & Srivastava, 1999), a commonly used measure of the Big Five domains. Soto and John (2009) recently developed 10 personality facet scales for the BFI, with two facets for each personality domain: Assertiveness and Energy (in the Extraversion domain), Altruism and Compliance (Agreeableness), Order and Self-Discipline (Conscientiousness), Anxiety and Depression (Neuroticism), and Aesthetics and Ideas (Openness). Using these state-level facet scores, we can obtain a finer grained analysis of the associations between state-level personality and social indicators.

Methods

The present analyses used data from Rentfrow et al. (2008) on statewide personality differences across the United States. The only difference between the sample used in this study and that used previously is that this investigation did not include personality scores for Alaska or Hawaii. The data were collected between December 1999 and January 2005 as part of the Gosling-Potter Internet Personality Project (for details, see Rentfrow et al., 2008), which hosts a noncommercial, advertisement-free website containing a variety of personality measures. Respondents could learn about the project through several channels, including search engines or links on such websites as http://www.socialpsychology. org. Participants volunteered for the study by clicking on the personality test icon and were then presented with a series of questions about their personality characteristics, demographics, and state of residence. After submitting their responses, participants received feedback about their personalities.

Participants

Data for repeat responders and duplicate entries were eliminated, resulting in a sample of 612,140 respondents (55% female). The mean age of respondents was 24.73 years ($SD = 10.39$ years), with 347,940 (57%) respondents between the ages of 18 and 24, 252,936 (41%) between 25 and 54, and 10,284 (2%) over 55 years old. Of those who indicated, 488,427 (84%) were White, 38,487 (5%) were Asian, 24,479 respondents (4%) were African American, 28,059 (3%) were Hispanic, and 27,279 (4%) indicated "Other."

Measure

The BFI was used to assess personality. The BFI consists of 44 short statements designed to assess the prototypical traits defining each of the Big Five dimensions. Using a 5-point Likert-type rating scale with endpoints at 1 (*disagree strongly*) and 5 (*agree strongly*), respondents indicated the extent to which they agreed with each statement. The BFI scales have shown a robust factor structure, substantial internal and temporal reliability, and considerable convergent and discriminant validity with other measures of the Big Five domains (John & Srivastava, 1999; Soto & John, 2009).

Secondary Data

To examine the relationships between the state personality facet scores and the social indicators, I gathered data from a variety of secondary sources and developed six indexes: state health, violent crime, social capital, political ideology, social tolerance, and innovation.

Health

State-level health was indexed using data obtained from the U.S. Centers for Disease Control and Prevention (CDC; Miniño, Murphy, Xu, & Kochanek, 2011), the Gallup Organization (2008), and the Substance Abuse and Mental Health Services Administration (SAMHSA; 2007, 2008). Mortality statistics were obtained from the CDC for cancer, diabetes, and coronary heart disease, as well as state-level life expectancy. Death rates for cancer and diabetes were for 2008, and heart disease death rate and life expectancy were for 2007. State levels of psychological well-being were obtained from the Gallup-Healthway's 2008 Well-Being Index. I gathered data for the proportion of state residents who experienced serious psychological distress or serious mental illness in 2003–2004 from SAMHSA. The health index was created by first reverse keying the death rate variables and the proportion of residents who experienced serious mental illness problems, and then standardizing them. I next examined the interitem reliability among the variables. The interitem reliability among the standardized variables was high (Cronbach's α = .88). Thus, I computed the mean of the seven standardized variables for the health index.

Violent Crime

Crime statistics were obtained from the Uniform Crime Reporting Program at the Federal Bureau of Investigation. Specifically, the figures used were from the 2007 Uniform Crime Report (Federal Bureau of Investigation, 2008). In this study, I examined three indicators of violent crime: murder, robbery, and aggravated assault per capita. The interitem reliability among the standardized variables was high (Cronbach's α = .90). Thus, I computed the mean of the three standardized variables for the violent crime index.

Social Capital

Social capital reflects the degree to which states value social relations and community (Putnam, 2000) and is measured in terms of rates of volunteerism, civic participation, and social trust. In this study, I supplemented Putnam's (2000) social capital index with additional markers of social relations, including the proportion of state residents who were married, separated, or divorced, according to the 2010 Census (U.S. Census Bureau, 2010), and also the proportion of children living in safe and supportive neighborhoods, according to the 2003 National Survey of Children's Health, conducted by the U.S. Department of Health and Human Services (CDC, 2003). The social capital index was computed by reverse scoring the separation and divorce statistics and then standardizing all four variables. The interitem reliability among the standardized variables was high (Cronbach's α = .79). Thus, I computed the average of the four standardized variables for the social capital index.

Political Conservatism

To assess regional political preferences, I gathered voting data for each of the 48 contiguous states and Washington, DC, from *Dave Leip's Atlas of U.S. Presidential Elections* (Leip, 2009), an online database consisting of presidential election results obtained from publications by official election agencies within each state (i.e., secretary of state offices, state board of election offices, *Congressional Quarterly*, and the U.S. National Archives and Records Administration). In this study, I computed an index of political conservatism by first standardizing the percentages of votes for George W. Bush in 2004 and for John S. McCain in 2008. The correlation between the two standardized variables was high (.98). Thus, I computed the mean of the two standardized variables for the political conservatism index.

Social Tolerance

Social tolerance was conceptualized in terms of social diversity and operationalized using four population statistics. Specifically, I used Florida's (2002) bohemian index, which ranks states by the proportion of working-aged adults that work as professional artists, entertainers, and musicians. Data for the proportion of same-sex residents were also taken from Florida. Additional markers of social tolerance included the proportion of foreign-born residents and the proportion of residents 5 years and older who speak a language other than English at home; both were obtained from the U.S. Census Bureau (2010). All four variables were standardized. The interitem reliability among the standardized variables was high (Cronbach's $\alpha = .93$), so I computed the average of the four standardized variables for the social tolerance index.

Innovation

Innovation reflects the degree to which states invest and contribute to the creation and discovery of new ideas. State-level innovation was measured by the number of patents produced per capita data from 1977 to 2004 from the U.S. Patent and Trademark Office (2012). The proportions of working-aged adults employed in the high-tech industry and also in scientific professions were gathered from the Bureau for Labor Statistics (2008). The interitem reliability among these three standardized variables was high (Cronbach's $\alpha = .84$). An innovation index was computed by taking the average of the three standardized variables.

Results and Discussion

The primary aim of the analyses was to explore the state-level personality facets and their links with the social indicators. As a first step, I analyzed the reliability and discriminant validity for the personality facets. Next, I mapped the statewide distribution of the 10 personality facets. Finally, I examined the correlations between the state-level facet scores and the six social indicator indexes.

Reliability and Discriminant Validity

I examined the interitem consistency of each of the state-level BFI facet scales. Specifically, I computed Cronbach's alpha on the state-level items for each facet. The results from the reliability analyses revealed large reliability coefficients for most of the facets, with coefficients ranging from .43 for Compliance to .95 for Aesthetics, with an average coefficient across the 10 facet scales of .80. Despite the fact that some of the facet scales include only two to three items each, the reliability coefficients were respectable, suggesting that the facets provide reliable indicators of narrow state-level personality characteristics.

I next examined the discriminant validity of the state-level facet scales. If the state-level facet scores are capturing unique personality variance within their domain, we should expect facets from the same personality domain to correlate moderately with one another; very high correlations would indicate low discriminant validity. The within-domain discriminant correlations were moderate in size for Activity and Assertiveness ($r = .39$), Altruism and Compliance (.49), and Order and Self-Discipline (.59). The discriminant correlations were higher for Anxiety and Depression ($r = .68$) and Aesthetics and Ideas (.94). Across domains, the average hetero-trait correlation was comparatively lower, averaging only .08.

Mapping the Geographic Distribution of the Personality Facets

To determine how the state-level personality facets were geographically distributed, I created maps for each facet. As can be seen in Figure 6.1, there was considerable variance in the distributions, with some facets showing more clearly defined clusters than others. Panels A and B show the distribution of the Extraversion facets. Assertiveness is generally high in the Midwest, Great Plains, and South and comparatively lower in the Northeast and West. Activity is comparatively high in the Plains and Mountain states but lower in the South. Maps for the Agreeableness facets are shown in Panels C and D. Altruism was highest in the Midwest and parts of the South and lower in the Mountain and New England states. Compliance was highest in the Deep South and Great Plains and lowest in the Mid-Atlantic and New England. The Conscientiousness facets are shown in Panels E and F. Although there was no obvious geographic clustering for the Order facet, states in the East and New England were generally low on this facet. Self-discipline was comparatively high in the Southern and Central states and lower in the Northeast and West Coast. Panels G and H show the geographic distributions of the Neuroticism facets. A similar pattern emerged for both facets, with states from Maine to Louisiana displaying high levels of Anxiety and Depression, with lower levels in the West. Maps for the Openness facets are provided in Panels I and J. Aesthetics was high in the Mid-Atlantic, New England, and West Coast and lowest in the North Central states. The Ideas facet was highest in the West and parts of the Northeast and lowest in the Midwest and Great Plains.

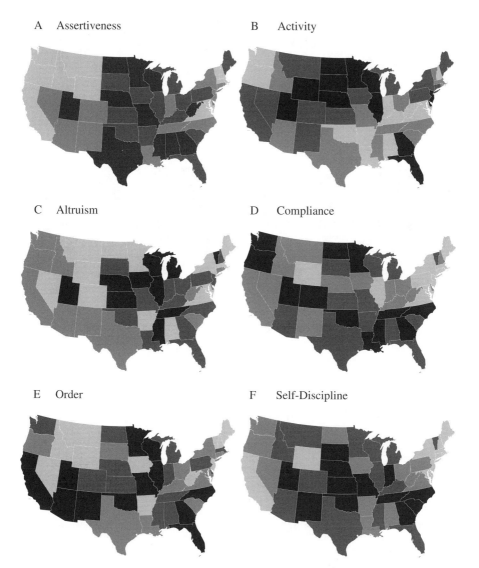

Figure 6.1. Maps of state-level Big Five Inventory facet scores. The maps show the geographical distribution of personality traits across the United States.

(continues)

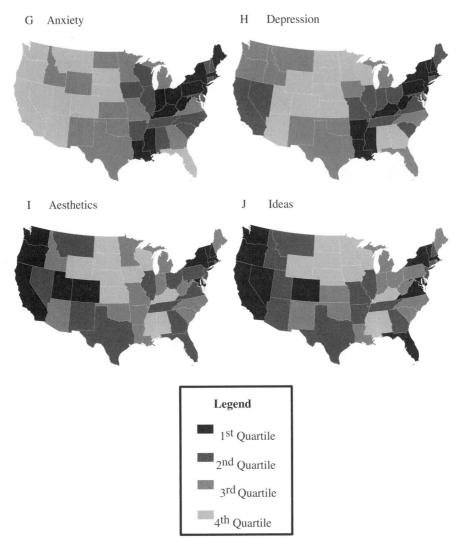

Figure 6.1. (Continued)

Links With Social Indicators

Results from the reliability and discriminant validity analyses indicate that the state-level facet scores provide reliable and unique information. The maps show regional variation across the personality facets. It thus seems reasonable to expect the within-domain facet scores to display slightly different patterns of associations with the social indicator indexes. I examined the patterns of relationships between the state-level personality domains and facets with the social indicators using Pearson's correlations. The results from the analyses are presented in Table 6.1.

TABLE 6.1
Correlations Between State-Level Personality Traits and Social Indicators

			Social indicators			
Traits	Health	Violent crime	Social capital	Political conservatism	Social tolerance	Innovation
Extraversion						
Assertiveness	−.29*	.23	−.03	.10	−.19	−.45*
Activity	.53*	−.15	.35*	−.04	.10	.06
Agreeableness						
Altruism	.04	−.47*	.65*	.37*	−.20	−.09
Compliance	−.12	−.16	.24	.55*	−.23	−.22
Conscientiousness						
Order	.08	.20	−.09	.04	.25	.13
Self-discipline	−.14	.15	−.02	.42*	−.14	−.30*
Neuroticism						
Anxiety	−.49*	−.06	−.07	−.12	−.08	−.13
Depression	−.44*	.17	−.40*	−.34*	.12	−.04
Openness						
Aesthetics	.22	.42*	−.50*	−.65*	.48*	.56*
Ideas	.19	.49*	−.58*	−.60*	.51*	.49*

Note. Cell entries are Pearson correlations between state-level mean personality scores and social indicators. District of Columbia is included but Alaska and Hawaii are not. *N* = 49.
*p < .05.

As can be seen in the first two rows of correlations in Table 6.1, the Extraversion facet scores displayed slightly different patterns of relationships. Specifically, state-level health was negatively associated with Assertiveness and positively associated with Activity, social capital was positively related to state-levels of Activity, and innovation was negatively related to Assertiveness. These divergent patterns of correlations strongly suggest that the facets are capturing different aspects of the Extraversion domain. Indeed, each pair of within-social indicator correlations was different in sign. Overall, these results indicate that states with more sociable and talkative residents have comparatively poor health and less innovation compared with states low in Assertiveness. Moreover, states with more enthusiastic and energetic residents tend to be healthy and rich in social capital compared with states low in Activity.

The second set of correlations in Table 6.1 shows patterns of correlations between the Agreeableness domain facets and the social indicators and provides evidence for the discriminant validity of the facets. Statewide differences in violent crime were negatively associated with Altruism, social capital was positively linked to Altruism, and political conservatism was positively related to both Altruism and Compliance. Thus, it appears that states with large proportions of helpful and trusting residents are safer, more community oriented, and conservative compared with states with fewer altruistic residents. In addition, states with more accepting and forgiving residents appear to be more conservative than states low in Compliance.

The fifth and sixth rows in Table 6.1 present the correlations between the Conscientiousness domain facets and the social indicators. It is notable that Order was not significantly related to any of the social indicators, but Self-Discipline was. Specifically, Self-Discipline was positively related to state-level conservatism and negatively related to innovation. These results suggest that states with large proportions of residents who are responsible and hardworking tend to be more conservative and less innovative compared with states low in Self-Discipline.

The correlations between the Neuroticism facets and the social indicators are shown in Rows 7 and 8 of Table 6.1. Although the discriminant validity of the Anxiety and Depression facet scales was low, these results show some discrimination between the facets. State-level Anxiety and Depression were both negatively related to the health index, and Depression was also negatively related to social capital and political conservatism. These findings suggest that states with large proportions of nervous and unstable residents tend to be less healthy compared with states with fewer anxious residents. Furthermore, states with large numbers of depressed residents are less healthy, less community oriented, and less conservative compared with states low in Depression.

The last set of correlations in Table 6.1 show the relationships between the Openness facets and social indicators. The Openness domain was related to all but one of the social indicators. Specifically, Aesthetics and Ideas were both positively related to rates of violent crime, social tolerance, and innovation, and they were both negatively related to social capital and conservatism. Considering that the Aesthetic and Ideas scales were highly correlated ($r = .94$), it is not surprising that the patterns of correlations were highly similar for the two facets. In general, these results suggest that states where disproportionate numbers of residents are creative, imaginative, and intellectual are violent, culturally diverse, innovative, individualistic, and liberal.

Summary

The results from this investigation indicate that personality facets provide more specific information about the links between state-level personality and social indicators. Extraversion, Agreeableness, Conscientiousness, and Neuroticism showed impressive discriminant validity for five of the six social indicators examined, as evidenced by divergent patterns of within-domain correlations. Indeed, the order of magnitude for many of the within-domain facet correlations was substantially different, and several pairs of correlations had different signs. These findings strongly suggest that relying solely on domain-level personality scores risks masking more nuanced relationships.

MECHANISMS UNDERLYING GEOGRAPHIC PERSONALITY DIFFERENCES

Given evidence for geographical differences in personality and evidence that such differences are associated with a host of important social indicators, it is important to consider how such differences come about and become expressed at the geographical level. What are the mechanisms that cause geographical differences in personality? How do geographical personality traits become linked to social indicators?

What Are the Mechanisms That Cause Geographical Differences in Personality?

Recent research has identified at least three mechanisms responsible for driving geographical differences in personality. One mechanism is *selective migration*. The assumption behind this mechanism is that people choose to live in places that satisfy and reinforce their needs. Research on personality and migration indicates that people high in Openness are likely to move away from their home state to a different state and that people high in Agreeableness are likely to remain within their hometown (Boneva et al., 1998; Jokela, 2009; Jokela, Elovainio, Kivimäki, & Keltikangas-Järvinen, 2008). There is also evidence that people high in Extraversion are likely to migrate and that residential mobility has adverse health consequences for people low in Extraversion (Jokela, 2009; Oishi, 2010; Oishi, Miao, Koo, Kisling, & Ratliff, 2012; Oishi & Schimmack, 2010).

Social influence is another mechanism responsible for geographical personality differences. The assumption underlying this mechanism is that people's thoughts, feelings, and behaviors are influenced by those around them. Most of the research on social influence has focused on contagion within social networks (e.g., Bourgeois & Bowen, 2001; Fowler & Christakis, 2008). No research has directly examined the impact of social influence on regional psychological differences. The relevant research in this area indicates that affect is quite susceptible to social influence. For example, research indicates that the positive affect of friends influences individuals' levels of happiness (Fowler & Christakis, 2008), and the negative affect of intimate partners can increase individuals' levels of Depression (Joiner & Katz, 1999).

Another important mechanism underlying geographical psychological differences is *ecological influence*. This mechanism assumes that features of the environment influence behavior. Climate, terrain, public health, and ethnic diversity can have profound effects on the activities people pursue, their lifestyles, and how they relate to each other. In this way, aspects of the environment can affect the prevalence of certain traits. One line of evidence for ecological influence comes from work by Schaller and colleagues (Schaller, 2006; Schaller & Duncan, 2007; Schaller & Murray, 2008) indicating that national levels of Openness and Extraversion are low in regions where rates of infectious disease are historically high, because limited social contact and exposure to novel stimuli reduce the spread of illnesses.

Although indirect, the available evidence makes it reasonable to hypothesize that geographical differences in personality are a result of selective migration, social influence, and ecological influence. However, it seems reasonable to propose that some traits may be more susceptible to certain mechanisms than to others. For example, current research has suggested that geographical differences in Openness may be driven primarily by selective migration, whereas differences in Neuroticism might be driven by social influence. It is also conceivable that the mechanisms might operate differently at different geographical levels of analysis. Because residential mobility is far more common within nations than between nations, selection migration might have a comparatively weak impact at national levels of analysis compared with the other mechanisms. Furthermore, social influence might have a greater impact at national levels, where citizens are governed by the same institutions and exposed to the same media. Longitudinal research that tracks individuals' migration patterns, values, beliefs, and personalities over extended periods has the potential to shed light on the relative importance of these mechanisms.

How Do Regional Personality Traits Become Expressed Geographically?

Given evidence for the links between geographical personality traits and social indicators, it is necessary to consider the nature of those links. What are the processes through which the personalities of citizens become expressed at the geographical level? Two complementary hypotheses provide clues about how geographical personality traits and social indicators become linked. The first hypothesis adopts a bottom-up perspective by proposing that the prevalence of certain traits in a region (e.g., the number of people who are high in Openness) leads to demonstrative behaviors of those traits (creativity and innovation), which are then represented on social indicators (the proportion of working population with careers in the arts, patent production per capita). Thus, this hypothesis implies that geographical differences in wealth, health, crime, and well-being are an additive effect of the psychological characteristics of residents. The evidence for this hypothesis comes from theory and research concerned with personality (Bogg

& Roberts, 2004; Ozer & Benet-Martínez, 2006; Roberts, Kuncel, Shiner, Caspi, & Goldberg, 2007), cultural psychology (Hofstede & McCrae, 2004), and macroeconomics (Florida, 2002, 2008).

The second hypothesis adopts a top-down perspective by proposing that social structural and institutional variables could influence the prevalence of psychological and behavioral tendencies within regions by shaping the experiences and opportunities available to residents. For example, if a region has a disproportionate number of universities, high-tech companies, museums, and cultural centers, the presence of such institutions should affect the prevalence of psychological and behavioral tendencies associated with Openness by shaping individuals' educational and career aspirations, leisure pursuits, and contact with individuals from diverse cultural backgrounds. This hypothesis implies that regional psychological differences are a result of social and institutional differences. Support for this hypothesis comes from studies in social and cultural psychology that indicate that social structure, institutions, and cultural norms affect the attitudes, opinions, and behaviors of individuals within regions (e.g., Cohen, 1996; Hofstede, 2001; Inkeles & Smith, 1974; Triandis & Suh, 2002).

The hypotheses proposed here are intended to provide clues about the ways in which regional personality traits become represented on social indicators. The processes described are not mutually exclusive, but complementary. Indeed, it is conceivable that the additive effects of personality create an ethos that encourages the development of certain institutions and social practices that, in turn, reinforce the thoughts, feelings, and behaviors that are prevalent in the region. Nonetheless, certain traits might be more susceptible to particular processes than to others. For example, the geographical expression of Openness might be driven by bottom-up processes, given evidence that people high in Openness are likely to selectively migrate (Jokela, 2009; Jokela et al., 2008), whereas the expression of Agreeableness might be driven by top-down processes because there is some evidence to suggest that Agreeableness is affected more by the social environment than by genetics (e.g., Bergeman, Chlpuer, Plomin, Pedersen, McClearn, et al., 1993; but see Jang, Livesley, & Vernon, 1996).

CONCLUSION

Renewed interest in geographical personality differences provides the opportunity to broaden our understanding of Person × Environment interactions. The research evidence accumulated over the past decade provides firm evidence that there are meaningful and robust personality differences between and within nations. Furthermore, the psychological differences observed are associated with important social indicators that have significant real-world consequences. Although we do not yet know precisely how these psychological differences emerge or manifest, we have clear hypotheses on the basis of compelling data. Systematic research concerned with the emergence and expression of geographical personality differences will no doubt shed valuable light on this area.

Broadening our conceptualization of the environment to include a geographical perspective requires recognizing that the dynamic interactions between persons and the environments they occupy extend beyond the immediate situation. Indeed, the thoughts, feelings, and behaviors that emerge in everyday life do so in relation to the contexts in which we live. Thus, revising our notion of the environment to include place can only add to our understanding of human social behavior.

REFERENCES

Adorno, T. W., Frenkel-Brunswik, E., Levinson, D. J., & Sanford, R. N. (1950). *The authoritarian personality*. New York, NY: Harper.

Allik, J., & McCrae, R. R. (2004). Toward a geography of personality traits: Patterns of profiles across 36 cultures. *Journal of Cross-Cultural Psychology, 35*, 13–28. doi:10.1177/0022022103260382

Benet-Martínez, V., & John, O. P. (2000). Toward the development of quasi-indigenous personality constructs. *American Behavioral Scientist, 44*, 141–157.

Bergeman, C. S., Chlpuer, H. M., Plomin, R., Pedersen, N. L., McClearn, G. E., Nesselroade, J. R., . . . McCrae, R. R. (1993). Genetic and environmental effects on openness to experience, agreeableness, and conscientiousness: An adoption/ twin study. *Journal of Personality, 61*, 159–179. doi:10.1111/j.1467-6494.1993. tb01030.x

Bogg, T., & Roberts, B. W. (2004). Conscientiousness and health behaviors: A meta-analysis. *Psychological Bulletin, 130*, 887–919. doi:10.1037/0033-2909.130.6.887

Boneva, B. S., Frieze, I. H., Ferligoj, A., Jarošová, E., Pauknerová, D., & Orgocka, A. (1998). Achievement, power, and affiliation motives as clues to (e)migration desires: A four-countries comparison. *European Psychologist, 3*, 247–254. doi:10.1027/1016-9040.3.4.247

Bourgeois, M. J., & Bowen, A. (2001). Self-organization of alcohol related attitudes and beliefs in a campus housing complex: An initial investigation. *Health Psychology, 20*, 434–437. doi:10.1037/0278-6133.20.6.434

Buchanan, W., & Cantril, H. (1953). *How nations see each other: A study in public opinion*. Urbana, IL: University of Illinois Press.

Cattell, R. B., Eber, H. W., & Tatsuoka, M. M. (1970). *Handbook for the sixteen personality factor questionnaire*. Champaign, IL: Institute for Personality and Ability.

Centers for Disease Control and Prevention (2003). *National Survey of Children's Health*. Washington, DC: U.S. Department of Health and Human Services.

Cohen, D. (1996). Law, social policy, and violence: The impact of regional cultures. *Journal of Personality and Social Psychology, 70,* 961–978. doi:10.1037/0022-3514.70.5.961

Costa, P. T., Jr., & McCrae, R. R. (1992). *Revised NEO Personality Inventory (NEO-PI-R) and NEO Five-Factor Inventory (NEO-FFI) professional manual*. Odessa, FL: Psychological Assessment Resources.

Costa, P. T., Jr., & McCrae, R. R. (1995). Domains and facets: Hierarchical personality assessment using the Revised NEO Personality Inventory. *Journal of Personality Assessment, 64,* 21–50. doi:10.1207/s15327752jpa6401_2

de Vries, R., Gosling, S. D., & Potter, J. (2011). Income inequality and personality: Are less equal U.S. states less agreeable? *Social Science & Medicine, 72,* 1978–1985. doi:10.1016/j.socscimed.2011.03.046

Federal Bureau of Investigation. (2008). *Uniform crime reports*. Washington, DC: Department of Justice.

Florida, R. (2002). *The rise of the creative class*. New York, NY: Perseus Books.

Florida, R. (2008). *Who's your city? How the creative economy is making where to live the most important decision of your life*. New York, NY: Basic Books.

Fowler, J. H., & Christakis, N. A. (2008). Dynamic spread of happiness in a large social network: Longitudinal analysis over 20 years in the Framingham Heart Study. *British Medical Journal, 337,* a2338. doi:10.1136/bmj.a2338

Gallup-Healthways Well-Being Index. (2008). Retrieved from http://www.well-beingindex.com

Goldberg, L. R. (1992). The development of markers for the Big-Five factor structure. *Psychological Assessment, 4,* 26–42. doi:10.1037/1040-3590.4.1.26

Hofstede, G. (2001). *Culture's consequences: Comparing values, behaviors, institutions, and organizations across nations* (2nd ed.). Thousand Oaks, CA: Sage.

Hofstede, G., & McCrae, R. R. (2004). Personality and culture revisited: Linking traits and dimensions of culture. *Cross-Cultural Research, 38,* 52–88. doi:10.1177/1069397103259443

Inkeles, A., Hanfmann, E., & Beier, H. (1958). Modal personality and the adjustment to the Soviet socio-political system. *Human Relations, 11,* 3–22. doi:10.1177/001872675801100101

Inkeles, A., & Levinson, D. J. (1969). National character: The study of modal personality and sociocultural systems. In G. Lindzey & E. Aronson (Eds.), *The handbook of social psychology IV* (pp. 418–506). New York, NY: McGraw-Hill. (Original work published 1954)

Inkeles, A., & Smith, D. H. (1974). *Becoming modern*. Cambridge, MA: Harvard University Press.

Jang, K. L., Livesley, W. J., & Vernon, P. A. (1996). Heritability of the Big Five personality dimensions and their facets: A twin study. *Journal of Personality, 64*, 577–592. doi:10.1111/j.1467-6494.1996.tb00522.x

Jang, K. L., McCrae, R. R., Angleitner, A., Riemann, R., & Livesley, W. J. (1998). Heritability of facet-level traits in a cross-cultural twin sample: Support for a hierarchical model of personality. *Journal of Personality and Social Psychology, 74*, 1556–1565. doi:10.1037/0022-3514.74.6.1556

John, O. P., & Srivastava, S. (1999). The Big Five trait taxonomy: History, measurement, and theoretical perspectives. In L. A. Pervin & O. P. John (Eds.), *Handbook of personality: Theory and research* (2nd ed.; pp. 102–139). New York, NY: Guilford Press.

Joiner, T. E., Jr., & Katz, J. (1999). Contagion of depressive symptoms and mood: Meta-analytic review and explanations from cognitive, behavioral, and interpersonal viewpoints. *Clinical Psychology: Science and Practice, 6*, 149–164. doi:10.1093/clipsy.6.2.149

Jokela, M. (2009). Personality predicts migration within and between U.S. states. *Journal of Research in Personality, 43*, 79–83. doi:10.1016/j.jrp.2008.09.005

Jokela, M., Elovainio, M., Kivimäki, M., & Keltikangas-Järvinen, L. (2008). Temperament and migration patterns in Finland. *Psychological Science, 19*, 831–837. doi:10.1111/j.1467-9280.2008.02164.x

Krug, S. E., & Kulhavy, R. W. (1973). Personality differences across regions of the United States. *The Journal of Social Psychology, 91*, 73–79. doi:10.1080/00224545.1973.9922648

Lachman, M. E., & Weaver, S. L. (1997). The Midlife Development Inventory (MIDI) personality scales [Technical report]. Unpublished manuscript, Brandeis University, Waltham, MA.

Leip, D. (2009). *Dave Leip's atlas of U.S. presidential elections.* Retrieved from http://www.uselectionatlas.org

LeVine, R. A. (2001). Culture and personality studies, 1918–1960: Myth and history. *Journal of Personality, 69*, 803–818. doi:10.1111/1467-6494.696165

McCann, S. J. H. (2010a). Subjective well-being, personality, demographic variables, and American state differences in smoking prevalence. *Nicotine & Tobacco Research, 12*, 895–904. doi:10.1093/ntr/ntq113

McCann, S. J. H. (2010b). Suicide, Big Five personality factors, and depression at the American state level. *Archives of Suicide Research, 14*, 368–374. doi:10.1080/13811118.2010.524070

McCann, S. J. H. (2011a). Emotional health and the Big Five personality factors at the American state level. *Journal of Happiness Studies, 12*, 547–560. doi:10.1007/s10902-010-9215-9

McCann, S. J. H. (2011b). Personality and American state differences in obesity prevalence. *The Journal of Psychology, 145*, 419–433. doi:10.1080/00223980.2011.584081

McClelland, D. C. (1961). *The achieving society*. Princeton, NJ: Van Nostrand.

McCrae, R. R. (2001). Trait psychology and culture: Exploring intercultural comparisons. *Journal of Personality, 69*, 819–846. doi:10.1111/1467-6494.696166

McCrae, R. R., & Costa, P. T., Jr. (1997). Personality trait structure as a human universal. *American Psychologist, 52*, 509–516. doi:10.1037/0003-066X.52.5.509

McCrae, R. R., & Costa, P. T., Jr. (2003). *Personality in adulthood: A five-factor theory perspective* (2nd ed.). New York, NY: Guilford Press. doi:10.4324/9780203428412

McCrae, R. R., & Terracciano, A. (2005). Personality profiles of cultures: Aggregate personality traits. *Journal of Personality and Social Psychology, 89*, 407–425. doi:10.1037/0022-3514.89.3.407

McCrae, R. R., & Terracciano, A. (2008). The five-factor model and its correlates in individuals and cultures. In F. J. R. van de Vijver, D. A. van Hemert, & Y. Poortinga (Eds.), *Individuals and cultures in multi-level analysis* (pp. 249–283). Mahwah, NJ: Erlbaum.

Miniño, A. M., Murphy, S. L., Xu, J., & Kochanek, K. D. (2011). Deaths: Final data for 2008. *National Vital Statistics Reports, 59*. Retrieved from http://www.cdc.gov/nchs/data/nvsr/nvsr59/nvsr59_10.pdf

Oishi, S. (2010). The psychology of residential mobility: Implications for the self, social relationships, and well-being. *Perspectives on Psychological Science, 5*, 5–21. doi:10.1177/1745691609356781

Oishi, S., Miao, F. F., Koo, M., Kisling, J., & Ratliff, K. A. (2012). Residential mobility breeds familiarity seeking. *Journal of Personality and Social Psychology, 102*, 149–162. doi:10.1037/a0024949

Oishi, S., & Schimmack, U. (2010). Residential mobility, well-being, and mortality. *Journal of Personality and Social Psychology, 98*, 980–994. doi:10.1037/a0019389

Ozer, D. J., & Benet-Martínez, V. (2006). Personality and the prediction of consequential outcomes. *Annual Review of Psychology, 57*, 401–421. doi:10.1146/annurev.psych.57.102904.190127

Pesta, B. J., Bertsch, S., McDaniel, M. A., Mahoney, C. B., & Poznanski, P. J. (2012). Differential epidemiology: IQ, neuroticism, and chronic disease by the 50 U.S. states. *Intelligence, 40*, 107–114. doi:10.1016/j.intell.2012.01.011

Pesta, B. J., McDaniel, M. A., & Bertsch, S. (2010). Toward an index of well-being for the fifty U.S. states. *Intelligence, 38*, 160–168. doi:10.1016/j.intell.2009.09.006

Plaut, V. C., Markus, H. R., & Lachman, M. E. (2002). Place matters: Consensual features and regional variation in American well-being and self. *Journal of Personality and Social Psychology, 83*, 160–184. doi:10.1037/0022-3514.83.1.160

Plomin, R., & Caspi, A. (1999). Behavioral genetics and personality. In L. A. Pervin & O. P. John (Eds.), *Handbook of personality theory and research* (Vol. 2, pp. 251–276). New York, NY: Guilford Press.

Putnam, R. D. (2000). *Bowling alone: The collapse and revival of American community*. New York, NY: Simon & Schuster. doi:10.1145/358916.361990

Rentfrow, P. J. (2010). Statewide differences in personality: Toward a psychological geography of the United States. *American Psychologist, 65*, 548–558. doi:10.1037/a0018194

Rentfrow, P. J., Gosling, S. D., & Potter, J. (2008). A theory of the emergence, persistence, and expression of regional variation in basic traits. *Perspectives on Psychological Science, 3*, 339–369. doi:10.1111/j.1745-6924.2008.00084.x

Rentfrow, P. J., Jost, J. T., Gosling, S. D., & Potter, J. (2009). Statewide differences in personality predict voting patterns in 1996–2004 U.S. presidential elections. In J. T. Jost, A. C. Kay, & H. Thorisdottir (Eds.), *Social and psychological bases of ideology and system justification* (pp. 314–348). Oxford, England: Oxford University Press. doi:10.1093/acprof:oso/9780195320916.003.013

Rentfrow, P. J., Mellander, C., & Florida, R. (2009). Happy States of America: A state-level analysis of psychological, economic, and social well-being. *Journal of Research in Personality, 43*, 1073–1082. doi:10.1016/j.jrp.2009.08.005

Roberts, B. W., Kuncel, N. R., Shiner, R., Caspi, A., & Goldberg, L. R. (2007). The power of personality: The comparative predictive validity of personality traits, SES, and cognitive ability for important life outcomes. *Perspectives on Psychological Science, 2*, 313–345. doi:10.1111/j.1745-6916.2007.00047.x

Roberts, B. W., Walton, K., & Viechtbauer, W. (2006). Patterns of mean-level change in personality traits across the life course: A meta-analysis of longitudinal studies. *Psychological Bulletin, 132*, 1–25. doi:10.1037/0033-2909.132.1.1

Schaller, M. (2006). Parasites, behavioral defenses, and the social psychological mechanisms through which cultures are evoked. *Psychological Inquiry, 17*, 96–137.

Schaller, M., & Duncan, L. A. (2007). The behavioral immune system: Its evolution and social psychological implications. In J. P. Forgas, M. G. Haselton, & W. von Hippel (Eds.), *Evolution and the social mind: Evolutionary psychology and social cognition* (pp. 293–307). New York, NY: Psychology Press.

Schaller, M., & Murray, D. R. (2008). Pathogens, personality and culture: Disease prevalence predicts worldwide variability in sociosexuality, extraversion, and openness to experience. *Journal of Personality and Social Psychology, 95*, 212–221. doi:10.1037/0022-3514.95.1.212

Schmitt, D. P., Allik, J. A., McCrae, R. R., & Benet-Martínez, V. (2007). The geographic distribution of Big Five personality traits: Patterns and profiles of human self-description across 56 nations. *Journal of Cross-Cultural Psychology, 38*, 173–212. doi:10.1177/0022022106297299

Soto, C. J., & John, O. P. (2009). Ten facets for the Big Five Inventory: Convergence with NEO PI-R facets, self-peer agreement, and discriminant validity. *Journal of Research in Personality, 43*, 84–90. doi:10.1016/j.jrp.2008.10.002

Srivastava, S., John, O. P., Gosling, S. D., & Potter, J. (2003). Development of personality in early and middle adulthood: Set like plaster or persistent change? *Journal of Personality and Social Psychology, 84*, 1041–1053. doi:10.1037/0022-3514.84.5.1041

Steel, P., & Ones, D. S. (2002). Personality and happiness: A national-level analysis. *Journal of Personality and Social Psychology, 83,* 767–781. doi:10.1037/0022-3514.83.3.767

Substance Abuse and Mental Health Services Administration. (2007). *Results from the 2006 National Survey on Drug Use and Health: National findings.* Retrieved from http://www.samhsa.gov/data/nsduh/2k6nsduh/2k6results.pdf

Substance Abuse and Mental Health Services Administration. (2008). *Results from the 2007 National Survey on Drug Use and Health: National findings.* Retrieved from http://www.samhsa.gov/data/nsduh/2k7nsduh/2k7Results.htm

Triandis, H. C., & Suh, E. M. (2002). Cultural influences on personality. *Annual Review of Psychology, 53,* 133–160. doi:10.1146/annurev.psych.53.100901.135200

U.S. Bureau of Labor Statistics (2008). *Geographic profile of employment and unemployment.* Retrieved from http://www.bls.gov/gps/

U.S. Census Bureau. (2010). *Statistical abstract of the United States.* Washington, DC: U.S. Government Printing Office.

U.S. Patent and Trademark Office. (2012). *Patents by country, state, and year— Utility patents.* Washington, DC: U.S. Department of Labor. Retrieved from http://www.uspto.gov/web/offices/ac/ido/oeip/taf/cst_utl.htm

Voracek, M. (2009). Big Five personality factors and suicide rates in the United States: A state-level analysis. *Perceptual and Motor Skills, 109,* 208–212. doi:10.2466/pms.109.1.208-212

7

BIG FIVE PERSONALITY DIFFERENCES AND POLITICAL, SOCIAL, AND ECONOMIC CONSERVATISM: AN AMERICAN STATE-LEVEL ANALYSIS

STEWART J. H. McCANN

The contemporary American political divide persists and shows no signs of abating. For example, the election of President Obama in 2008 did not indicate a massive shift in partisanship or underlying ideological convictions. The results of the 2008 presidential election showed that Republican or Democratic status remained the same as in 2004 in 41 of the 50 states. All nine states that did change parties in 2008 moved from the Republicans to the Democrats, but even in these states Republican support in 2004 dropped an average of only 6.8 percentage points.

American state and regional differences in political orientation are quite stable and long-standing (e.g., Erikson, Wright, & McIver, 2007; Rentfrow, Jost, Gosling, & Potter, 2009). In a democracy with the freedom to choose, why is there such a degree of stability in the relative position of the states on measures of political preference? Political scientists, sociologists, and pundits tend to attribute these geographical differences to situational factors such as historical settlement patterns, ethnic cultural variation, racial composition,

http://dx.doi.org/10.1037/14272-008
Geographical Psychology: Exploring the Interaction of Environment and Behavior, P. J. Rentfrow (Editor)

local economic conditions, the influence of elite political figures, biased media coverage, political promotion and advertising, and other institutional variables (e.g., Jost, West, & Gosling, 2009; Rentfrow, Jost, et al., 2009).

The present study takes a different tack. Building on recent progress in understanding the psychological foundations of ideological preference at the individual level (e.g., Jost, Glaser, Kruglanski, & Sulloway, 2003; Mondak, 2010), the research focus here is on potential relations between personality and ideology at the American state level. Such an examination of state aggregates holds the possibility of partially explaining stable state differences in ideological orientation through the impacts of dispositional factors.

THE NATURE OF POLITICAL IDEOLOGY

An *ideology* is an interwoven complex of political and moral attitudes with affective, cognitive, and motivational components (Jost, 2006), which is largely shared with a population segment that holds such characteristics in common. An ideology serves both to interpret societal information and to prescribe acceptable societal structure (Denzau & North, 1994) and both affects and is affected by an individual's particular psychological needs, motives, and world orientation (Carney, Jost, Gosling, & Potter, 2008). It can be viewed as deeply rooted in personality characteristics (e.g., Jost, West, et al., 2009) and as a characteristic adaptation produced by personality–environment interactions (Gerber, Huber, Doherty, & Dowling, 2010).

Conservative and liberal differences anchor the most conspicuous ideological dimension. Jost (2006) put forth ample evidence for the functional existence of such a conservative–liberal ideological continuum in the processing of contemporary American political, social, and economic matters. Common citizens may not be highly sophisticated ideologically but "most people can and do use ideological constructs such as liberalism and conservatism meaningfully and appropriately and . . . they are indeed motivated by ideological commitments that guide (or constrain) both attitudes and behaviors" (Carney et al., 2008, p. 808).

It is vitally important to recognize that the foundation for such a conservative–liberal ideological dimension ultimately is psychological rather than political, economic, or sociological (e.g., McCrae, 1996). Mondak (2010) articulated a profound implication of this fact:

> Liberals and conservatives both might believe that, given the opportunity, they could persuade all of their fellow citizens of the wisdom and virtue of their respective ways of thinking. But this is not so. The reason people are not all on the same political page is not that some have seen the light and others have not, but instead because people exhibit fundamental and

persistent psychological differences, differences that are largely rooted in biology. These differences are not *about* politics, yet they matter *for* politics. By their nature, some people are psychologically predisposed to be liberals and others to be conservatives. (p. 131)

Jost et al. (2003) proposed that a person's relative position on the abstract conservative–liberal dimension reflects two underlying correlated components: (a) the degree of acceptance or rejection of inequality and (b) the degree of preference for societal status quo preservation or social change. Furthermore, they assumed that differential stances toward inequality and the status quo among conservatives and liberals emanate from respective motivational concerns particularly related to the psychological management of fear and uncertainty (Carney et al., 2008). This view is compatible with other portrayals of conservatism and liberalism (Jost, 2006).

There also are distinctions between political, social, and economic conservatism. Self-placement on a conservative–liberal or Republican–Democratic partisan dimension provides the most direct assessment of political conservatism in the current American context. *Social conservatism* refers to less progressive stances taken on a variety of social issues such as gay rights, same-sex marriage, abortion, marijuana use, the death penalty, church authority, and atheism (e.g., Henningham, 1996; Jost, Nosek, & Gosling, 2008). *Economic conservatism* refers to positive positions taken toward a number of economic issues such as promotion of a free market and minimal governmental economic intervention (e.g., Cornelis & Van Hiel, 2006).

Social and economic conservatism are conceptually distinct but often positively correlated (e.g., Jost, Krochik, Gaucher, & Hennes, 2009; Zumbrunnen & Gangl, 2008). They appear to be "distinct paths to ideological self-identification" (Zumbrunnen & Gangl, 2008, p. 213), but the magnitude of their correlation remains in some dispute (e.g., Feldman & Johnston, 2009; Jost, Krochik, et al., 2009). As well, both social and economic conservatism are associated with political conservatism (e.g., Jost, Krochik, et al., 2009; Zumbrunnen & Gangl, 2008).

Although the work of Jost and his colleagues (e.g., Jost, 2006; Jost et al., 2003) has primarily focused on political conservatism, they assume that the dynamics involved also pertain to social and economic conservatism. Rejection of equality and status quo preservation can play out within the social or economic sphere. Psychologically, the same dispositional tendencies have the capacity to resonate with issues in both domains. However, as Feldman and Johnston (2009) pointed out,

> We know that certain psychological variables are associated with over-
> all orientations, and we know that different dimensions of ideology are
> interrelated, but little work has systematically examined the empirical

patterns of association between these variables and the different domains separately. (p. 7)

The present study is a step in this direction.

THE BIG FIVE PERSONALITY VARIABLES

Weiten and McCann (2010) defined *personality* as "an individual's unique constellation of consistent behavioural traits" (p. 520) and a *trait* as "a durable disposition to behave in a particular way in a variety of situations" (p. 520). The *Big Five* refers to the most widely accepted contemporary personality trait model (e.g., Goldberg, 1990; John & Srivastava, 1999). It involves five relatively independent overarching trait dimensions: Openness to Experience (O), Conscientiousness (C), Extraversion (E), Agreeableness (A), and Neuroticism (N). High O is associated with greater tolerance for diversity, willingness to experiment, intellectual curiosity, imagination, depth of emotions, and aesthetic interest; high C with a stronger propensity for order, dutifulness, self-discipline, deliberation, competence, and achievement striving; high E with heightened activity, assertiveness, gregariousness, positive emotions, warmth, and excitement seeking; high A with elevated trust, compliance, straight-forwardness, modesty, altruism, and tender-mindedness; and high N with elevated vulnerability, anxiety, self-consciousness, impulsiveness, depression, and angry hostility (Costa & McCrae, 1995).

RELATIONS OF THE BIG FIVE TO CONSERVATISM AT THE INDIVIDUAL LEVEL OF ANALYSIS

A review of the empirical literature revealed that 14 studies with the individual as the unit of analysis are most pertinent to the present project. To be included, works had to have assessments of some or all of the Big Five personality variables, use only American participants, and use conservatism measures rather than related dimensions such as authoritarianism or social dominance. All but one (i.e., Barbaranelli et al., 2007) included a general political conservatism measure (e.g., ideological self-placement item, multi-item instrument). Three studies included separate social and economic conservatism assessments (i.e., Carney et al., 2008; Gerber et al., 2010; Jost, West et al., 2009). Five tapped Republican voting preference (i.e., Barbaranelli et al., 2007; Jost, West et al., 2009; Mondak, 2010; Mondak & Halperin, 2008; Peterson & Maiden, 1993). Table 7.1 displays the direction of the significant relations between the Big Five and the 24 conservatism measures found in the 14 studies.

TABLE 7.1
Studies Reporting American Evidence for Correlations Between
Conservatism and the Big Five

Research	Conservatism	O	C	E	A	N
Gerber et al. (2010)	Political	–	+	+	no	–
	Social	–	+	+	–	–
	Economic	–	+	+	+	–
Carney et al. (2008)	Political	–	+	+	+	–
	Social	–	+[a]	+	no	no
	Economic	no	no	no	no	no
Jost, West, et al. (2009)	Political	–	+	no	no	+
	Social	–	+	no	no	no
	Economic	–	+	no	no	no
	Republican	–	+	+	no	no
Peterson & Maiden (1993)	Political	–	+	no		
	Republican	–	+	–		
Barbaranelli et al. (2007)	Republican	–	+	+	–	–
Mondak & Halperin (2008)	Political	–	+	no	no	–
	Republican	–	+	no	–	–
Mondak (2010)[b]	Political	–	+	no	–	–
	Republican	–	+	no	–	no
Gosling et al. (2003)	Political	–	+	no	no	–
Hirsh et al. (2010)	Political	–	+	no	+[c]	no
Mehrabian (1996)	Political	–	+	no	no	no
Alford & Hibbing (2007)	Political	–	no	no	–	no
Butler (2000)	Political	–	no	no	–	no
Stenner (2005)	Political	–	+			
Trapnell (1994)	Political	–				

Note. A = Agreeableness; C = Conscientiousness; E = Extraversion; N = Neuroticism; O = Openness to Experience.
[a]The relation was at the .06 level of significance.
[b]These relations were based on a data set not already reported in Mondak and Halperin (2008).
[c]Conservatism was positively associated with the politeness aspects of Agreeableness but negatively associated with the compassion features of Agreeableness.

Overall, there was evidence that lower O was associated with higher conservatism for 95.8% of the conservatism criteria and was never associated with lower conservatism. Higher C related to higher conservatism for 85.7% of the criteria (with one occurrence in Carney et al., 2008, at the .06 level) and was never associated with lower conservatism. Higher E linked to higher conservatism for 40.9% of the criteria, but E did not relate to conservatism for the other 59.1%. Lower A was associated with higher conservatism 35.0% of the time, with lower conservatism 11.1% of the time, and was not related 50.0% of the time, whereas Hirsh et al. (2010) found conservatism positively associated with politeness aspects of A but negatively associated with compassion features of A. Finally, lower N was associated with higher conservatism 45.5% of the time, with lower conservatism 4.5% of the time, and was unrelated 50.0% of the time.

A THEORY OF GEOGRAPHIC VARIATION
IN PSYCHOLOGICAL CHARACTERISTICS

In their pioneering work on the relations of personality to social indicators at the American state level of aggregation, Rentfrow, Gosling, and Potter (2008) put forth elements of a theory for the emergence and persistence of geographic differences in psychological characteristics. A foundational assumption of the theory is that a geographic area's aggregate position on a dispositional variable reflects the central tendency of the area's individuals on that variable and is associated with the pervasiveness in that area of the psychological and behavioral tendencies related to that variable. Of course, Rentfrow et al. (2008) recognized that aggregate-level findings may be logically independent of individual-level findings (Pettigrew, 1997; Robinson, 1950), that cross-level generalization cannot be assumed even though relations often are consistent across levels, and that valid cross-level generalization depends on empirical verification at each level.

Rentfrow et al. (2008) also computed mean levels of each of the Big Five in each of the American states on the basis of data from 619,397 respondents to the full Big Five Inventory (John & Srivastava, 1999). Ensuing empirical research has established Big Five relations to various state-level variables including religiosity, crime, liberal values, social involvement, social and enterprising occupations, artistic and investigative occupations, health-promoting behavior, mortality, voting choice in presidential elections, social capital, creativity, patent production, well-being, suicide, smoking, asthma prevalence, obesity, and emotional health (McCann, 2010a, 2010b, 2011a, 2011b, 2011c, 2011d, 2011e; Rentfrow, 2010; Rentfrow et al., 2008; Rentfrow, Jost, et al., 2009; Rentfrow, Mellander, & Florida, 2009; Voracek, 2009).

RELATIONS OF THE BIG FIVE TO CONSERVATISM
AT THE STATE LEVEL OF ANALYSIS

Rentfrow, Jost, et al. (2009) conducted the only study to examine relations between the Big Five and voting preferences, with American states as the units of analysis. They used the state scores of Rentfrow et al. (2008) as predictors and the percentage in each state casting ballots for Republican and Democratic presidential candidates in 1996, 2000, and 2004 as the criteria. Simultaneous regression without statistical control for demographic variables showed that in each of the elections O was negatively related to voting Republican and positively related to voting Democratic, whereas C and E were positively related to voting Democratic and negatively related to voting Republican. Party choice did not relate to A in any of the elections. N related positively to voting Democratic and negatively to voting Republican in 2004. The authors emphasized the importance of relations involving O and C. They did not predict relations involving E and N, which were somewhat contrary to earlier individual-level research results.

Rentfrow, Jost, et al. (2009) also found that the Big Five as a set of predictors still accounted for significant proportions of variance in Republican and Democratic state voting percentages in the three elections when they controlled several demographic and political variables in a multiple regression analysis. However, it cannot be discerned from the data presented whether the same relations between the criteria and O, C, E, A, and N remained with such controls. Therefore, we do not know definitively whether O, C, E, and N retained the same relations to the two criteria in the three elections that were found without the controls.

THE PRESENT STUDY

I conducted the present research to determine the relations of the Big Five personality variables to political, social, and economic conservatism, with the American states as the units of analysis. For this work, I constructed a composite measure of political conservatism on the basis of state ideological self-placement data and the percentage in each state voting Republican in the presidential elections of 2000, 2004, and 2008. I developed a new composite measure of social conservatism that used state data regarding death sentences, religious fundamentalism, evangelical Protestantism, abortion, laws limiting homosexual behavior, same-sex partnerships, firearms, and marijuana use. I also created a composite economic conservatism measure from the 2004 and 2008 versions of the U.S. Economic Freedom Index (Huang, McCormick, & McQuillan, 2004; McQuillan, Maloney, Daniels, & Eastwood, 2008). Also, I formed a composite general conservatism variable from the resulting political, social, and economic conservatism variables. I examined all relations between personality and conservatism with and without statistical control for a number of common state demographic variables including income and educational indicators, White population percentage, and urban population percentage.

The findings in the 14 studies at the individual level of analysis and the lone study at the state level suggested expectations for the results in the present work. For example, the previous individual-level and state-level research showed quite consistently that conservatism correlates negatively with O and positively with C. In addition, conservatism correlated positively with E in almost half of the individual-level studies and never correlated negatively, although the state-level study did produce a negative correlation. The results for A showed no evident trend. N correlated with conservatism in almost half of the individual-level studies: it correlated positively only once, and the state-level study did show a negative correlation for the 2004 election. Recognizing that aggregate-level and individual-level findings may be contrary and independent, I expected that conservatism would relate negatively to O and positively to C. Expectations regarding E, A, and N were more tentative. However, some research suggested that conservatism might correlate positively with E, be unrelated to A, and correlate negatively with N.

Method

Measures

Big Five Personality Variables. Rentfrow et al. (2008) provided z scores for each of the 50 states and the District of Columbia on O, C, E, A, and N on the basis of responses of 619,397 residents to an Internet survey between December 1999 and January 2005 that included the 44-item Big Five Inventory (BFI). Presented data showed that the sample generally was representative of the American population and drew respondents from each state in direct proportion to the 2000 census figures. The authors also reported that the Big Five variables had high reliabilities with mean Cronbach alphas of .81 at the individual level and .89 at the state level.

Political Conservatism. CONSERVATIVE SELF-PLACEMENT. State degree of conservative ideological self-placement was based on state aggregates of 141,798 respondents to 122 1976–1988 CBS News/New York Times national telephone surveys (Erikson, Wright, & McIver, 1993). Key questions were "How would you describe your views on most political matters? Generally, do you think of yourself as liberal, moderate, or conservative?" (p. 14). Alaska and Hawaii were not polled, and Erikson et al. (1993) excluded Nevada because of validity issues. Erikson et al. provided ample reliability, validity, and temporal stability evidence. For this study, I subtracted the liberal percentage from the conservative percentage in each state and converted the results to z scores to indicate political conservatism.

PRESIDENTIAL ELECTION RESULTS. Excluding Alaska, Hawaii, and Nevada, state popular vote percentages for Republican presidential candidates were taken from the Statistical Abstract of the United States (U.S. Census Bureau, 2009) for 2000 and 2004 and from Leip (2009) for 2008. The three variables formed a simple additive election composite with a Cronbach alpha of .98.

CONSTRUCTION OF THE POLITICAL CONSERVATISM COMPOSITE. The ideological self-placement variable and the presidential election composite correlated, $r(45) = .85, p < .001$. I created the political conservatism composite by computing z scores for each of the 47 states on each of the two political conservatism components and computing the mean for each state.

Social Conservatism. DEATH SENTENCES. The number of death sentences in each state was provided by Shepherd (2005) for 1977–1996 and the Death Penalty Information Center (2006) for 1997–2004. The mean of the state resident populations in 1980, 1990, and 2000 (U.S. Census Bureau, 2001) served as state population estimates for 1977–2004. For each state, I divided the total 1977–2004 death sentences by the population estimate to produce state death sentence per population values.

NUMBER OF YEARS WITH A DEATH PENALTY. The Death Penalty Information Center (2006) provided the years from 1977–2004 that each state had a death penalty, ranging from 0 to 28.

RELIGIOUS FUNDAMENTALISM. From state data reported by Johnson, Picard, and Quinn (1974, as cited in Erikson et al., 1993, p. 65), Erikson et al. (1993) provided the percentage of each state's population (excluding Alaska, Hawaii, and Nevada) that was fundamentalist.

EVANGELICAL PROTESTANTISM. The Data Archive (n.d.) provided the number of evangelical Protestants per 1,000 population in each state in 2000. With Arizona, Hawaii, and Nevada excluded, this indicator correlated positively with the previous fundamentalism measure, $r(45) = .56, p < .001$. Excluding Utah, with its large Mormon population, raised the correlation to $r(44) = .89, p < .001$.

ABORTION ACCESS. Page (2006) analyzed states to determine what they would likely do regarding restrictions on abortion if the U.S. Supreme Court overturned the 1973 Roe v. Wade decision granting abortion access. On the basis of multiple criteria, Page concluded that Alaska, California, Colorado, Connecticut, Hawaii, Maine, Maryland, Massachusetts, Montana, New Hampshire, New Jersey, New Mexico, New York, Oregon, Vermont, and Washington would protect abortion access and that Alabama, Arkansas, Florida, Georgia, Idaho, Indiana, Kentucky, Louisiana, Mississippi, Missouri, North Dakota, Ohio, Oklahoma, Pennsylvania, South Carolina, South Dakota, Tennessee, Texas, Utah, Virginia, and Wisconsin would significantly restrict abortion access. The other states formed a middle category. For this study, states protecting access were coded "1," states in the middle "2," and states restricting access "3." Therefore, higher scores reflect greater conservatism.

LAWS RESTRICTING HOMOSEXUAL BEHAVIORS. The *Southern Voice* in Atlanta conducted a study (Keen, 2001) in which each state and the District of Columbia was rated on a 100 to −100 point system based on progay and antigay laws, court rulings, executive orders, and local ordinances. Scores ranged from 97 in Vermont to −92 in Oklahoma. I multiplied state scores by −1, so higher scores are more conservative.

LEGAL POSITIONS CONCERNING SAME-SEX PARTNERSHIPS. Legal stance data for each state on same sex marriage were obtained from Wikipedia (2008). I assigned values from 1 to 7 to each state: (1) allows same-sex marriage,

(2) allows same-sex civil unions, (3) allows same-sex domestic partnerships, (4) recognizes foreign same-sex marriages, (5) statute bans same-sex marriage, (6) constitution bans same-sex marriage, and (7) constitution bans same-sex marriage and other kinds of same-sex unions. States with dual classifications (i.e., Connecticut, New Hampshire, New York, Oregon, and Washington) received the mean of their two classifications. Higher scores indicate greater conservatism.

FIREARMS DEATH RATE. Statemaster.com (2010) provided state firearms death rates per 100,000 persons in 2002, the most recent year available. Rates ranged from 2.8 in Hawaii to 20.0 in Arkansas ($M = 11.10$, $SD = 4.35$). On the basis of Azrael, Cook, and Miller (2004) and Williams and McGrath (1976), I assumed higher rates indicate greater gun availability and conservatism.

PERCENTAGE OF THE POPULATION WHO USE MARIJUANA. The U.S. Census Bureau (2010) provided the marijuana user percentage in each state in 2006–2007. Rates ranged from 3.8 in Iowa to 10.3 in Rhode Island ($M = 6.17$, $SD = 1.44$). I multiplied rates by -1. Higher scores indicate greater conservatism.

CONSTRUCTION OF THE SOCIAL CONSERVATISM COMPOSITE. With Alaska, Hawaii, and Nevada excluded, I converted state scores on each of the preceding nine components to z scores and calculated the mean for each state. The resulting social conservatism composite had a Cronbach alpha of .91.

Economic Conservatism. U.S. ECONOMIC FREEDOM INDEX: 2004. The Pacific Research Institute constructed the 2004 U.S. Economic Freedom Index from 1995–2003 state data on 143 fiscal, judicial, regulatory, welfare spending, and government size variables (Huang et al., 2004). Scores ranged from 18.18 in Kansas to 39.50 in New York ($M = 26.98$, $SD = 4.91$). Lower scores indicate higher conservatism.

U.S. ECONOMIC FREEDOM INDEX: 2008. The 2008 U.S. Economic Freedom Index was similar to the 2004 version but used updated data on the 143 variables (McQuillan et al., 2008). Scores ranged from a highly conservative 14.54 in South Dakota to 27.43 in Delaware ($M = 20.42$, $SD = 3.02$).

CONSTRUCTION OF THE ECONOMIC CONSERVATISM COMPOSITE. The 2004 and 2008 versions, excluding Alaska, Hawaii, and Nevada, were highly correlated, $r(45) = .72$, $p < .001$. I converted the two to z scores and computed the mean to create composite economic conservatism values for each of the 47 states. I then multiplied the values by -1. Higher scores reflect higher economic conservatism.

Political, Social, and Economic Conservatism Composite. With Alaska, Hawaii, and Nevada excluded, I formed a general conservatism composite by computing state z scores on the political, social, and economic conservatism composites and calculating their means to serve as composite conservatism values. Cronbach's alpha was .85.

Socioeconomic Status. For each state in 2000 and 2005, the U.S. Census Bureau (2001, 2002, 2007, 2008) provided information on the percentage of population 25 and over with at least high school graduation, percentage 25 and over with at least an undergraduate degree, personal income per capita in constant dollars, unemployment rate, and percentage of individuals below the poverty line. Excluding Alaska, Hawaii, and Nevada, correlations between 2000 and 2005 values were .88 for high school education, .91 for undergraduate education, .97 for personal income, .50 for unemployment, and .94 for below the poverty line. On the basis of the 2000 and 2005 data, I calculated the mean for each state on each of the five variables with the sign reversed for the unemployment and poverty line variables. Then I converted the five resulting variables to z scores, added them together, and divided by 5 to produce a socioeconomic status (SES) value for each state. The SES composite had a Cronbach's alpha of .88.

White Population Percentage. For each state in 2000, the U.S. Census Bureau (2002) provided the White population percentage. For 2005, the U.S. Census Bureau (2007) displayed only White population figures, so I calculated the percentage using state population figures (U.S. Census Bureau, 2007). Percentages for 2000 and 2005 with Alaska, Hawaii, and Nevada excluded correlated highly, $r(45) = .92$, $p < .001$. The mean of the 2000 and 2005 percentages served as the White percentage of the population values for each state.

Urban Population Percentage. I also obtained from the U.S. Census Bureau (2007) the percentage of each state's population that was urban in the 2000 census. Comparable data for 2005 were not available.

Results

Table 7.2 shows the means, standard deviations, minimums, and maximums for the four conservatism variables, Big Five, and three demographic variables for the 12 American state variables included in the following analyses. All computations excluded Alaska, Hawaii, and Nevada.

Table 7.3 presents Pearson correlations computed between the Big Five personality variables and the four conservatism composites. O correlated negatively with three of the four conservatism measures, and the negative correlation for the fourth closely approached significance ($p = .055$). C correlated positively with each conservatism measure. E only significantly correlated positively with political conservatism. A correlated positively and N correlated negatively with three of the four criteria. Therefore, preliminary evidence showed that state levels of conservatism—whether social, political, economic, or composite—are associated in a fairly consistent way with state modal personality estimates using the Big Five framework.

TABLE 7.2
Variable Means, Standard Deviations, Minimums, and Maximums for the 47 States

Variable	M	SD	Minimum	Maximum
Political conservatism	.00	.96	−1.86	1.86
Social conservatism	.00	.75	−1.51	1.38
Economic conservatism	.00	.93	−2.49	1.65
Composite conservatism	.00	.88	−1.86	1.59
Openness to Experience	−.03	.87	−3.12	1.32
Conscientiousness	.11	.90	−1.64	2.40
Extraversion	.02	.97	−1.99	3.08
Agreeableness	.16	.71	−1.44	1.60
Neuroticism	.07	1.01	−2.52	2.36
Socioeconomic status	−.01	.82	−1.92	1.58
White percentage	82.40	9.75	61.31	96.90
Urban percentage	70.98	14.77	38.20	94.40

To adjust for relations of the three demographic variables to personality and conservatism, I computed partial correlations between personality and conservatism variables with the three demographic variables serving as controls. Table 7.3 also shows these results. O still correlated negatively with three of the four measures of conservatism and C still correlated positively with each of the four conservatism criteria. For E, only the positive partial correlation with political conservatism closely approached significance ($p = .061$). Now, only two of the four conservatism variables correlated positively with A, but the

TABLE 7.3
Correlations and Partial Correlations Between Big Five Personality Variables and Conservatism

Personality variable	Correlation	Conservatism			
		Political	Social	Economic	Composite
Openness to Experience	Pearson	−.53***	−.32*	−.28	−.43**
	Partial	−.44**	−.35*	−.18	−.34*
Conscientiousness	Pearson	.46***	.53***	.32*	.50***
	Partial	.48***	.47***	.46**	.50***
Extraversion	Pearson	.29*	.18	.04	.19
	Partial	.29	.21	.01	.18
Agreeableness	Pearson	.37*	.32*	.20	.34*
	Partial	.32*	.30*	.19	.29
Neuroticism	Pearson	−.35*	−.16	−.54***	−.40**
	Partial	−.61***	−.54***	−.60***	−.63***

Note. State socioeconomic status, White percentage, and urban percentage served as controls in the partial correlations.
*$p < .05$. **$p < .01$. ***$p < .001$.

correlation with the general conservatism composite also narrowly missed the significance threshold ($p = .059$). However, correlations between N and the four conservatism criteria now all were larger and ranged from $-.54$ to $-.63$. Although the overall pattern of partial correlation results is quite similar to the preceding Pearson correlations, the most striking change is that the correlations between N and the four conservatism measures became much more pronounced with demographic controls.

Hierarchical multiple regression equations were then computed for each of the four conservatism criteria by entering the three demographic variables as a block on the first step and entering the five personality variables in stepwise mode on the second step. Table 7.4 contains the results. N surfaced as the prime predictor of each of the four conservatism variables and was the sole predictor significant at the .05 level for three of the four measures. N accounted for between 15.8% and 31.3% of the variance in the conservatism criteria, and lower N was invariably associated with higher conservatism. For political conservatism, O also accounted for an additional 7.7% of the variance, with lower O being associated with greater conservatism.

Given the relatively small sample size, I determined whether additional Big Five variables would enter the regression equation with a somewhat more relaxed significance level for entry. For each criterion, I entered the predictors already in the preceding equations as a block and then allowed the remaining

TABLE 7.4
Results of Hierarchical Multiple Regression Equations Formed
by Entering the Three Demographic Variables as a Block and
Then Selecting the Big Five Stepwise

Criterion	Predictor(s)	df	R^2 Change	F Change
Political	Demographic variables	3, 43	.272	5.34**
conservatism	Neuroticism	1, 42	.270	24.71***
	Openness to Experience	1, 41	.077	8.31**
Social	Demographic variables	3, 43	.461	12.27***
conservatism	Neuroticism	1, 42	.158	17.45***
	(Openness to Experience	1, 41	.034	4.03)[a]
Economic	Demographic variables	3, 43	.137	2.27
conservatism	Neuroticism	1, 42	.313	23.87***
Composite	Demographic variables	3, 43	.207	3.73*
conservatism	Neuroticism	1, 42	.313	27.35***
	(Openness to Experience	1, 41	.039	3.61)[b]

[a]With Neuroticism already in the equation, Openness to Experience entered from a supplementary .10-for-entry stepwise selection from Openness to Experience, Conscientiousness, Extraversion, and Agreeableness at the .051 level of significance.
[b]With Neuroticism already in the equation, Openness to Experience entered from a supplementary .10-for-entry stepwise selection from Openness to Experience, Conscientiousness, Extraversion, and Agreeableness at the .065 level of significance.
*$p < .05$. **$p < .01$. ***$p < .001$.

Big Five variables to enter stepwise at the $p < .10$ level. As Table 7.4 shows, none entered the equation for political or economic conservatism. However, for social conservatism, O accounted for an additional 3.4% of the variance, $F(1, 41) = 4.03$, $p = .051$, and for the general conservatism composite, O accounted for a further increment of 3.9%, $F(1, 41) = 3.61$, $p = .065$. For each criterion, lower O was associated with higher conservatism.

Discussion

This study has shown that Big Five personality variables aggregated at the state level relate to state measures of political, social, economic, and composite conservatism. Furthermore, these relations persist even with statistical control of state differences in SES, race, and urbanism. From the results, three conclusions stand out: (a) The Big Five variables related quite consistently to political, social, economic, and composite conservatism; (b) N related most highly to each of the four indices of conservatism; and (c) N had the capacity to displace C and diminish O as predictors of conservatism in hierarchical multiple regression analyses.

The relatively consistent nature of the relation of the Big Five to conservatism criteria was evident using both partial correlation and multiple regression strategies. Partial correlation revealed that lower N was associated with political, social, economic, and composite conservatism. In multiple regression equations with demographics controlled, N was also the primary predictor of each of the four conservatism criteria and the sole predictor of each of the four except political conservatism. Partial correlation also showed that higher C was associated with political, social, economic, and composite conservatism. As well, in the partial correlation analysis, lower O related to higher conservatism on each of the four criteria, although at the .055 level for economic conservatism. In the regression analyses, O was a significant secondary predictor of political conservatism and was a secondary predictor of social conservatism and composite conservatism at the .051 and .065 levels, respectively. The relations for E and A were more tenuous but also relatively consistent across the four conservatism criteria. However, the dominant state-level relations of lower N to higher conservatism here was somewhat unexpected.

The magnitude of the relation of N to conservatism was rather impressive. Partial correlations ranged from −.54 for social conservatism to −.63 for composite conservatism. The regression analyses, with demographics controlled, showed N could account for another 27.0% of the variance in political conservatism, 15.8% in social conservatism, 31.3% in economic conservatism, and 31.3% in composite conservatism. With both analytic approaches, N produced the largest relation of any Big Five variable across all four conservatism criteria.

Why may those higher on N tend to be less conservative? On the basis of the BFI, a high N person is one who worries a lot, is easily upset, is not relaxed, is not emotionally stable, can be tense, can be moody, is depressed or blue, gets nervous easily, does not remain calm in tense situations, and does not handle stress well (John & Srivastava, 1999). Do any of these dispositional characteristics individually or collectively relate to conservatism at the individual level? Indeed, there is some affirmative evidence, though it is rather sparse. For example, according to an analysis reported by Iyer (2011), conservatives scored lower than liberals did on all BFI N items. Breakwell, Fife-Schaw, and Devereux (1988) found that British teenagers who worried more about external issues and events tended to show lower levels of political conservatism. Peterson and Maiden (1993) found that those lower on N were more supportive of the status quo. Vigil (2010) found that Democrats showed higher emotional distress, lower relationship and life satisfaction, and greater experiential hardships than did Republicans. In fact, despite the paucity of research to support a link between emotional stability and conservatism, the notion of its existence has persisted for a long time (e.g., Moore, 1925).

How do traits such as N, C, and O gain expression on dimensions of conservatism with states as the geographical units? Applying the theory of Rentfrow et al. (2008), this can come about in five different ways. First, if those in a state are disproportionately lower or higher on a trait, there should be corresponding psychological and behavioral manifestations of that trait in that state. Second, if psychological and behavioral manifestations of a trait are prominent in a state, then those proclivities should eventually lead to the building of institutions that support those proclivities. Third, prevalent psychological and behavioral manifestations can form a state psychosocial climate that socially influences even others of contrary disposition to adhere to state norms. Fourth, state institutional and social structure variables can influence psychological and behavioral tendencies by enhancing or limiting personal opportunities. Fifth, the state social norms influence trait prevalence because socialization processes help to foster the acquisition of relevant traits, because that state attracts people with traits similar to the inhabitants of that state, and because people with dissimilar traits may choose to leave that state. All five pathways may promote relations between certain Big Five variables and state levels of conservatism.

The present study has several measurement strengths. State-aggregated Big Five personality scores were based on the responses of 619,397 persons to the full 44-item BFI. State political conservatism was gauged by ideological self-placement polls involving 141,798 respondents combined with the state percentage voting Republican in the presidential races of 2000, 2004, and 2008. Social conservatism was tapped with a composite that included nine indicators based on death sentence, religious fundamentalism, abortion access, homosexual behavior, same-sex partnership, firearms death rate, and marijuana use data. State economic conservatism was based on a comprehensive study by a leading conservative think tank of 143 fiscal, judicial, regulatory, welfare spending, and government size variables. An additive composite of the three types of state conservatism was also used. In addition, variables based on state high school and undergraduate education, personal income, unemployment, poverty line, White population percentage, and urban percentage data served as statistical controls.

Another strong point is that all of the state-aggregated data were based on sufficiently large and representative state samples. Furthermore, not having the same persons in all samples was not detrimental because the goal was to obtain state-aggregated estimates for state-level analysis. Such a lack of sample congruence was only likely to reduce the chances of finding significant relations if individual-level relations indeed are the foundation of the state-level relations. That significant state-level relations were found with variables based on somewhat different segments of the state populations further attests to the robustness of the assumed underlying associations.

Of course, the study also has inherent limitations. One stems from the intrinsic constraint that sample size in state-level research obviously can never exceed 50 and was limited to 47 here. Whenever the ratio of cases to predictors is somewhat less than optimal for multiple regression analysis, some degree of instability in the predictors and coefficients that emerge may occur. However, such small-sample analytics in which the sample includes almost all of the population have succeeded in the past (e.g., McCann, 1992, 1997, 2008). Another limitation is the restriction that the nonexperimental nature of the study precludes causal inference from an empirical perspective. We also cannot know definitively whether the state-level results found here emanate from corresponding individual-level psychological dynamics involving the Big Five and conservatism. As well, some readers might be concerned that one religion measure, some death penalty information, and the ideology scores date back prior to 1995. However, the religion and death penalty variables proved to be worthy contributors to the highly reliable social conservatism composite, and there is strong evidence that state-level ideology is "overwhelmingly stable over time, at least in recent decades" (Erikson et al., 2007, p. 141).

The results also are important from an applied perspective. They have yielded empirical verification at the state level of similar associations between Big Five personality variables and political, social, and economic conservatism and have specified where such links may be different. Therefore, the results provide opportunities to develop tools and strategies to make more informed decisions about which states have the three interrelated varieties of conservatism more deeply embedded in psychological dispositions and, consequently, which states are likely to be more resistant to change in ideological orientation or more resistant to softening in their ideological stance. Perhaps appeals for change tailored to differences in modal personality profiles in different states would be more effective than persuasive attempts that ignore such personality differences. The results also suggest that political persuasion to change conservative–liberal orientation for a host of political, social, and economic issues may be exceedingly difficult in many states given the profound long-term core integration of major dispositional characteristics into the state socio–cultural–political fabric.

Several questions for further research arise from the current work. For example, are there other state-level variables that potentially could account for the relations found in the present study? Does the pattern of relations of the Big Five to ideology found here extend to contemporary American partisanship across a variety of state-level political contexts? Can individual-level research with adequately large samples, suitable participant selection, and sound personality and ideological measures provide valid evidence that N relates negatively to conservatism? Can further individual-level research clarify when and why N, C, and O are likely to surface as primary and secondary predictors of conservatism? What are the particular facets of N, C, and O that are critical to understanding the dynamics of the personality connections to conservatism? Answers to such questions may hold important implications for basic and applied research.

Generally, the present research should encourage the investigation of state-aggregated traits as potential predictors of other phenomena for which state-level measures are available. Perhaps state-level dispositional dimensions also should serve as additional demographic controls in many state-level studies. Rentfrow et al. (2008) suggested that a psychological macro-level research perspective may forge elaborations of our understanding of behavior and lead to greater integration of individual-level and aggregate-level inquiry. Such an approach has the potential to foster further synthesis of certain aspects of psychological, sociological, and political science knowledge. This certainly pertains to the context of the various promoters, concomitants, and consequences of differences in conservative–liberal ideology.

REFERENCES

Alford, J. R., & Hibbing, J. R. (2007). Personal, interpersonal, and political temperaments. *The Annals of the American Academy of Political and Social Science, 614,* 196–212. doi:10.1177/0002716207305621

American Religion Data Archive. (n.d.). *Religious congregations and membership study, 2000 (State File).* Retrieved from http://www.thearda.com/Archive/Files/Descriptions/RCMSST.asp

Azrael, D., Cook, P. J., & Miller, M. (2004). State and local prevalence of firearms ownership: Measurement, structure, and trends. *Journal of Quantitative Criminology, 20*, 43–62. doi:10.1023/B:JOQC.0000016699.11995.c7

Barbaranelli, C., Caprara, G. V., Vecchione, M., & Fraley, C. R. (2007). Voters' personality traits in presidential elections. *Personality and Individual Differences, 42*, 1199–1208. doi:10.1016/j.paid.2006.09.029

Breakwell, G. M., Fife-Schaw, C., & Devereux, J. D. (1988). The relationship of self-esteem and attributional style to young peoples' worries. *The Journal of Psychology: Interdisciplinary and Applied, 122*, 207–215. doi:10.1080/00223980.1988.9915508

Butler, J. C. (2000). Personality and emotional correlates of right-wing authoritarianism. *Social Behavior and Personality, 28*, 1–14. doi:10.2224/sbp.2000.28.1.1

Carney, D. R., Jost, J. T., Gosling, S. D., & Potter, J. (2008). The secret lives of liberals and conservatives: Personality profiles, interaction styles, and the things they leave behind. *Political Psychology, 29*, 807–840.

Cornelis, I., & Van Hiel, A. (2006). The impact of cognitive styles on authoritarianism based conservatism and racism. *Basic and Applied Social Psychology, 28*, 37–50. doi:10.1207/s15324834basp2801_4

Costa, P. T., & McCrae, R. R. (1995). Domains and facets: Hierarchical personality assessment using the Revised NEO Personality Inventory. *Journal of Personality Assessment, 64*, 21–50. doi:10.1207/s15327752jpa6401_2

Death Penalty Information Center. (2006). *Facts about the death penalty.* Retrieved from http://www.deathpenaltyinfo.org

Denzau, A. T., & North, D. C. (1994). Shared mental models: Ideologies and institutions. *Kyklos, 47*, 3–31. doi:10.1111/j.1467-6435.1994.tb02246.x

Erikson, R. S., Wright, G. C., & McIver, J. P. (1993). *Statehouse democracy: Public opinion and policy in the American states.* New York, NY: Cambridge University Press.

Erikson, R. S., Wright, G. C., & McIver, J. P. (2007). Measuring the public's ideological preferences in the 50 states: Survey responses versus roll call data. *State Politics & Policy Quarterly, 7*, 141–151. doi:10.1177/153244000700700203

Feldman, S., & Johnston, C. D. (2009, September). *Understanding political ideology: The necessity of a multi-dimensional conceptualization.* Paper presented at the meeting of the American Political Science Association, Toronto, Canada. Retrieved from http://papers.ssrn.com/sol3/papers.cfm?abstract_id=1451328

Gerber, A. S., Huber, G. A., Doherty, D., & Dowling, C. M. (2010). Personality and political attitudes: Relationships across issue domains and political contexts. *The American Political Science Review, 104*, 111–133. doi:10.1017/S0003055410000031

Goldberg, L. R. (1990). An alternative "description of personality": The Big-Five factor structure. *Journal of Personality and Social Psychology, 59*, 1216–1229. doi:10.1037/0022-3514.59.6.1216

Gosling, S. D., Rentfrow, P. J., & Swann, W. B., Jr. (2003). A very brief measure of the Big-Five personality domains. *Journal of Research in Personality, 37*, 504–528. doi:10.1016/S0092-6566(03)00046-1

Henningham, J. P. (1996). A 12-item scale of social conservatism. *Personality and Individual Differences, 20*, 517–519. doi:10.1016/0191-8869(95)00192-1

Hirsh, J. B., DeYoung, C. G., Xu, X., & Peterson, J. B. (2010). Compassionate liberals and polite conservatives: Associations of agreeableness with political ideology and moral values. *Personality and Social Psychology Bulletin, 36*, 655–664. doi:10.1177/0146167210366854

Huang, Y., McCormick, R. E., & McQuillan, L. J. (2004). *Economic Freedom Index: 2004 Report.* Retrieved from special.pacificresearch.org/pub/sab/entrep/2004/econ_freedom/index.html

Iyer, R. (2011). *Are liberals more neurotic than conservatives?* Retrieved from http://www.polipsych.com/2011/02/11/liberals-conservatives-neuroticism-happiness/

John, O. P., & Srivastava, S. (1999). The Big Five trait taxonomy: History, measurement, and theoretical perspectives. In L. A. Pervin & O. P. John (Eds.), *Handbook of personality: Theory and research* (2nd ed., pp. 102–138). New York, NY: Guilford Press.

Jost, J. T. (2006). The end of the end of ideology. *American Psychologist, 61*, 651–670. doi:10.1037/0003-066X.61.7.651

Jost, J. T., Glaser, J., Kruglanski, A. W., & Sulloway, F. J. (2003). Political conservatism as motivated social cognition. *Psychological Bulletin, 129*, 339–375. doi:10.1037/0033-2909.129.3.339

Jost, J. T., Krochik, M., Gaucher, D., & Hennes, E. P. (2009). Can a psychological theory of ideological differences explain contextual variability in the contents of political attitudes? *Psychological Inquiry, 20*, 183–188. doi:10.1080/10478400903088908

Jost, J. T., Nosek, B. A., & Gosling, S. D. (2008). Ideology: Its resurgence in social, personality, and political psychology. *Perspectives on Psychological Science, 3*, 126–136. doi:10.1111/j.1745-6916.2008.00070.x

Jost, J. T., West, T. V., & Gosling, S. D. (2009). Personality and ideology as determinants of candidate preferences and "Obama conversion" in the 2008 U.S. presidential election. *Du Bois Review, 6*, 103–124. doi:10.1017/S1742058X09090109

Keen, L. (2001). *Who's the best, legally speaking?* Retrieved from http://www.glapn.org/sodomylaws/usa/usnews37.htm

Leip, D. (2009). *Dave Leip's atlas of U.S. presidential elections.* Retrieved from http://www.uselectionatlas.org/RESULTS/

McCann, S. J. H. (1992). Alternative formulas to predict the greatness of U.S. presidents: Personological, situational, and zeitgeist factors. *Journal of Personality and Social Psychology, 62*, 469–479. doi:10.1037/0022-3514.62.3.469

McCann, S. J. H. (1997). Threatening times, "strong" presidential popular vote winners, and the margin of victory (1824–1964). *Journal of Personality and Social Psychology, 73*, 160–170. doi:10.1037/0022-3514.73.1.160

McCann, S. J. H. (2008). Societal threat, authoritarianism, conservatism, and U.S. state death penalty sentencing (1977–2004). *Journal of Personality and Social Psychology, 94*, 913–923. doi:10.1037/0022-3514.94.5.913

McCann, S. J. H. (2010a). Subjective well-being, personality, demographic variables, and American state differences in smoking prevalence. *Nicotine & Tobacco Research, 12*, 895–904. doi:10.1093/ntr/ntq113

McCann, S. J. H. (2010b). Suicide, Big Five personality factors, and depression at the American state level. *Archives of Suicide Research, 14*, 368–374. doi:10.1080/13811118.2010.524070

McCann, S. J. H. (2011a). Conservatism, openness, and creativity: Patents granted to residents of American states. *Creativity Research Journal, 23*, 339–345. doi:10.1080/10400419.2011.621831

McCann, S. J. H. (2011b). Emotional health and the Big Five personality factors at the American state level. *Journal of Happiness Studies, 12*, 547–560. doi:10.1007/s10902-010-9215-9

McCann, S. J. H. (2011c). Florida Creativity Index scores, conservatism, and openness in 268 U.S. regions. *Psychological Reports, 108*, 104–108. doi:10.2466/04.07.PRO.108.1.104-108

McCann, S. J. H. (2011d). Personality and American state differences in obesity prevalence. *The Journal of Psychology: Interdisciplinary and Applied, 145*, 419–433. doi:10.1080/00223980.2011.584081

McCann, S. J. H. (2011e). Relation of asthma prevalence to the Big Five personality factors at the American state level. *Individual Differences Research, 9*, 61–72.

McCrae, R. R. (1996). Social consequences of experiential openness. *Psychological Bulletin, 120*, 323–337. doi:10.1037/0033-2909.120.3.323

McQuillan, L. J., Maloney, M. T., Daniels, E., & Eastwood, B. M. (2008). *U.S. Economic Freedom Index: 2008 report*. Retrieved from special.pacificresearch.org/pub/sab/entrep/2008/Economic_Freedom/authors.html

Mehrabian, A. (1996). Relations among political attitudes, personality, and psychopathology assessed with new measures of libertarianism and conservatism. *Basic and Applied Social Psychology, 18*, 469–491. doi:10.1207/s15324834basp1804_7

Miller, A. S. (1994). Dynamic indicators of self-perceived conservatism. *The Sociological Quarterly, 35*, 175–182. doi:10.1111/j.1533-8525.1994.tb00405.x

Mondak, J. J. (2010). *Personality and the foundations of political behavior*. New York, NY: Cambridge University Press. doi:10.1017/CBO9780511761515

Mondak, J. J., & Halperin, K. D. (2008). A framework for the study of personality and political behavior. *British Journal of Political Science, 38*, 335–362. doi:10.1017/S0007123408000173

Moore, H. T. (1925). Innate factors in radicalism and conservatism. *The Journal of Abnormal and Social Psychology, 20*, 234–244. doi:10.1037/h0075749

Page, S. (2006, April 17). "Roe v. Wade": The divided states of America. *USA Today*. Retrieved from http://www.usatoday.com/news/washington/2006-04-16-abortion-states_x.htm

Peterson, S. A., & Maiden, R. (1993). Personality and politics among older Americans: A rural case study. *The International Journal of Aging & Human Development, 36*, 157–169. doi:10.2190/F01D-XTXD-5TXL-V4KQ

Pettigrew, T. F. (1997). Personality and social structure: Social psychological contributions. In R. Hogan, J. A. Johnson, & S. R. Briggs (Eds.), *Handbook of personality psychology* (pp. 417–438). San Diego, CA: Academic Press. doi:10.1016/B978-012134645-4/50018-4

Rentfrow, P. J. (2010). Statewide differences in personality: Toward a psychological geography of the United States. *American Psychologist, 65*, 548–558. doi:10.1037/a0018194

Rentfrow, P. J., Gosling, S. D., & Potter, J. (2008). A theory of the emergence, persistence, and expression of geographic variation in psychological characteristics. *Perspectives on Psychological Science, 3*, 339–369. doi:10.1111/j.1745-6924.2008.00084.x

Rentfrow, P. J., Jost, J. T., Gosling, S. D., & Potter, J. D. (2009). Statewide differences in personality predict voting patterns in 1996–2004 U.S. presidential elections. In J. T. Jost, A. C. Kay, & H. Thorisdottir (Eds.), *Social and psychological bases of ideology and system justification* (pp. 314–348). New York, NY: Oxford University Press. doi:10.1093/acprof:oso/9780195320916.003.013

Rentfrow, P. J., Mellander, C., & Florida, R. (2009). Happy states of America: A state-level analysis of psychological, economic, and social well-being. *Journal of Research in Personality, 43*, 1073–1082. doi:10.1016/j.jrp.2009.08.005

Robinson, W. S. (1950). Ecological correlations and the behavior of individuals. *American Sociological Review, 15*, 351–357. doi:10.2307/2087176

Shepherd, J. M. (2005). Deterrence versus brutalization: Capital punishment's differing impacts among states. *Michigan Law Review, 104*, 203–255.

Statemaster.com. (2010). *Most trigger happy*. Retrieved from http://www.statemaster.com/graph/cri_mur_wit_fir-death-rate-per-100-000

Stenner, K. (2005). *The authoritarian dynamic*. New York, NY: Cambridge University Press. doi:10.1017/CBO9780511614712

Trapnell, P. D. (1994). Openness versus intellect: A lexical left turn. *European Journal of Personality, 8*, 273–290. doi:10.1002/per.2410080405

U.S. Census Bureau. (2001). *Statistical abstract of the United States*. Washington, DC: U.S. Government Printing Office.

U.S. Census Bureau. (2002). *Statistical abstract of the United States*. Washington, DC: U.S. Government Printing Office.

U.S. Census Bureau. (2007). *Statistical abstract of the United States*. Washington, DC: U.S. Government Printing Office.

U.S. Census Bureau. (2008). *Statistical abstract of the United States*. Washington, DC: U.S. Government Printing Office.

U.S. Census Bureau. (2009). *Statistical abstract of the United States*. Washington, DC: U.S. Government Printing Office.

U.S. Census Bureau. (2010). *Statistical abstract of the United States*. Washington, DC: U.S. Government Printing Office.

Vigil, J. M. (2010). Political leanings vary with facial expression processing and psychosocial functioning. *Group Processes & Intergroup Relations, 13*, 547–558. doi:10.1177/1368430209356930

Voracek, M. (2009). Big Five personality factors and suicide rates in the United States: A state-level analysis. *Perceptual and Motor Skills, 109*, 208–212. doi:10.2466/pms.109.1.208-212

Weiten, W., & McCann, D. (2010). *Psychology: Themes and variations* (2nd Canadian ed.). Toronto, Canada: Nelson.

Wikipedia. (2008). *Laws regarding same-sex partnerships in the United States*. Retrieved from http://en.wikipedia.org/wiki/Image:Samesex_marriage_in_USA.svg

Williams, J. S., & McGrath, J. H. (1976). Why people own guns. *Journal of Communication, 26*, 22–30. doi:10.1111/j.1460-2466.1976.tb01931.x

Zumbrunnen, J., & Gangl, A. (2008). Conflict, fusion, or coexistence? The complexity of contemporary conservatism. *Political Behavior, 30*, 199–221. doi:10.1007/s11109-007-9047-4

8

INVESTIGATING THE SUBJECTIVE WELL-BEING OF UNITED STATES REGIONS

RICHARD E. LUCAS, FELIX CHEUNG, AND NICOLE M. LAWLESS

Subjective well-being (SWB) is a broad construct that is thought to reflect the quality of a person's life from his or her own perspective (Diener, Lucas, Schimmack, & Helliwell, 2009; Diener, Suh, Lucas, & Smith, 1999). This construct can be assessed in a variety of ways, including through self-reports of affective experiences, through more explicit judgments about the conditions in a person's life (including judgments of life satisfaction), and even through non-self-report measures such as reports made by close informants (Schneider & Schimmack, 2009). The overarching goal of such assessment strategies is to determine whether the person finds life to be enjoyable, rewarding, and positive overall.

Researchers assess well-being for a number of reasons. For instance, initial investigations into the construct were conducted with the goal of identifying basic human needs (Wilson, 1967). If certain characteristics are reliably correlated with well-being, then these characteristics might reflect

http://dx.doi.org/10.1037/14272-009
Geographical Psychology: Exploring the Interaction of Environment and Behavior, P. J. Rentfrow (Editor)

the fulfillment of basic needs shared by all people. Thus, research on SWB plays an important theoretical role because it can reveal information about basic human functioning. Much of the ongoing research on the topic is geared toward accomplishing this goal.

However, SWB research can also play an important applied role as well. Specifically, SWB can serve as an important outcome measure that can help determine whether an intervention has been successful. For instance, although many health interventions target specific conditions, the primary goal of treatment is often to improve the overall quality of life of a patient. In many cases, the treatments also have strong side effects, and an important question is whether the net effect is positive or negative. By supplementing outcome measures with measures of life satisfaction or overall affect, researchers can get a broader (and potentially better) sense of how well the intervention worked. Indeed, SWB measures have played an increasingly important role in applied research in a wide variety of domains.

Although well-being research has typically been conducted at the individual level, researchers are beginning to look at broader units of analysis, such as cities, states, or even nations (Diener, Helliwell, & Kahneman, 2010; Lawless & Lucas, 2011; Oswald & Wu, 2010; Rentfrow, Mellander, & Florida, 2009). This new development has occurred for a number of reasons. First, technological advances have made collecting data from large samples of participants much easier than in the past, so it is now feasible to conduct research at this aggregate level. More important, however, is the increasing interest in what such regional analyses can tell us, both among social scientists and among policymakers who might use this research to inform their decisions. Economists and psychologists alike have begun to recognize that economic indicators—the measures, such as median income, that are most often relied on as the basis for policy decisions—cannot tell the whole story about the overall well-being of a population (Diener & Seligman, 2004). Subjective indicators may provide a more nuanced picture of quality of life, and thus they could be useful in providing an additional criterion for success (Diener et al., 2009; Kahneman, Krueger, Schkade, Schwarz, & Stone, 2004). This is not to say that economic indicators should be replaced with well-being-based measures; the well-being measures are instead thought to be complementary to those measures already in place. Of course, for these measures to play a role, it will be important to determine whether meaningful regional differences in well-being exist and whether these differences can be predicted from regional characteristics (especially those that are amenable to policy intervention).

The goal of this chapter is to provide an introduction to some recent research that addresses these questions about well-being. Specifically, we review and attempt to resolve some discrepancies that have emerged in the literature regarding the regional differences that do exist, and we reanalyze county-level data on the correlates of well-being to investigate the robustness of previously identified regional associations. Because these investigations are relatively recent, there is still much to learn about how regions differ in their well-being. However, the evidence suggests that meaningful differences do exist, and thus, there is great potential to learn about the causes of well-being through the analysis of large-scale regional data.

WHICH U.S. STATES ARE REALLY THE HAPPIEST?

Although research examining the SWB of regions is relatively new, the idea of identifying regions where quality of life is highest is not. It is not uncommon to see media outlets report on various strategies for ranking which areas are the "happiest" or "best places to live." These reports typically use existing measures of objective criteria, which are weighted and combined to create a single index that can be used for ranking. Of course, these rankings can be controversial because the results depend heavily on the criterion variables that are selected and the weighting schemes that are used. An alternative approach that becomes available when well-being measures are widespread is to assess the average self-reported SWB of residents of a region. SWB-based rankings simply rely on the responses that representative samples within the regions provide—no controversial weighting schemes are required.

Two recent papers attempted to do just this (though the main focus of both papers was not on the rankings per se but on the correlates of the state-level means). The problem, however, was that these two reports—published within months of each other—provided two very different pictures of which states were the happiest. One of these, a paper by Oswald and Wu (2010), examined data from over one million respondents assessed over a 4-year period from all 50 states of the United States. Specifically, as part of a broader health-tracking project sponsored by the Centers for Disease Control and Prevention (CDC; 2005–2009), respondents provided answers to a single-item life satisfaction question (i.e., "In general, how satisfied are you with your life?"; the responses were "Very Satisfied," "Satisfied," "Dissatisfied," and "Very Dissatisfied"). The primary goal of Oswald and Wu's paper was to determine whether aggregated subjective judgments correlated with rankings of quality of life that were based on more objective characteristics of the regions (see Gabriel, Mattey, & Wascher, 2003; we discuss the nature of these rankings in more detail later). Although the authors emphasized that the subjective ratings agreed with more objective information (which supports the validity of the subjective measures), many media reports focused on which states were ranked as most and least happy. It was somewhat surprising that Louisiana—a state that is not typically high in characteristics that are intuitively linked with high well-being—was ranked as the happiest state in Oswald and Wu's analysis.

The more disturbing aspect was how different the full distribution of scores was when compared with the scores presented in a paper published just a month earlier. Rentfrow et al. (2009) used data from the Gallup-Healthways Well-Being Index to examine the associations between subjective reports of well-being and objective characteristics of those states. Like Oswald and Wu (2010), Rentfrow et al. emphasized the associations with these objective characteristics rather than the rankings per se. However, as with the Oswald and Wu paper, the media picked up on the rankings, and observant readers noticed that the rankings were almost completely different across the two studies. Indeed, Figure 8.1 shows a scatterplot of Oswald and Wu's state scores against those published in Rentfrow et al.; the correlation between the two indexes is just $r = .11$. Such disagreement in the results does not allow for a great deal of confidence in the reliability or validity of regional measures of well-being.

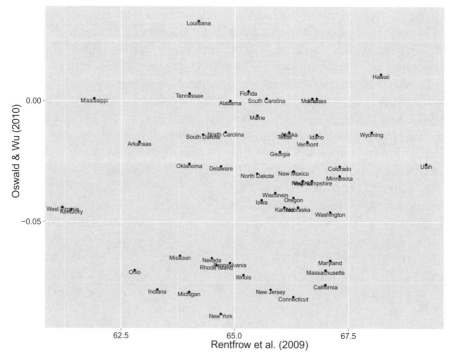

Figure 8.1. Two attempts to quantify state happiness. Units reflect the original units of the scales as presented in the original publications. Data from Oswald and Wu (2010) and Rentfrow et al. (2009).

Although the two studies differed in a number of ways (including the precise measure that was used), one important difference is the method used to construct the indexes. Rentfrow et al. (2009) used the simple mean, adjusted only for the sampling design. In contrast, Oswald and Wu (2010) used the individual-level data to estimate a regression equation predicting life satisfaction from a set of state-level dummy variables. The coefficients from these dummies were then used as estimates of the states' well-being. It is notable that this regression equation controlled for a variety of individual-level characteristics that are theoretically linked with well-being, including household income, marital status, and unemployment. The goal of such an analysis is to determine the extent to which states differ on well-being, controlling for the factors that are already known to be associated with well-being at the individual level. However, this changes the question from "Which states are happiest?" to "Which states are happiest once known correlates of happiness are controlled?" Because the resulting index is qualified by the specific set of controls that were included, it is difficult to interpret (Meehl, 1970). This is particularly true if—as one might expect—the variables being controlled were actually influenced by the state in which one resides (Gelman & Hill, 2007).

One might argue that Oswald and Wu's (2010) second major finding—that their life satisfaction index correlates .60 with an objective measure of quality of life—addresses this issue because it could be interpreted as providing evidence for the validity of the index and, hence, the strategy. But this particular objective criterion is far from a gold standard for quality of life. It is a composite index derived from regression equations predicting housing prices and wages in different regions. The links between this criterion and alternate measures of quality of life are not clear (as we describe later).

An alternative approach is to examine more specific criteria that might help validate the index and that could simultaneously provide information about why states differ. Such an approach would also allow for a comparison of various measures of well-being to determine which match more closely to theoretical expectations and past research. Table 8.1 provides the correlations between separate well-being indexes and other, more objective markers of quality of life, including economic, demographic, and health factors. Four different well-being indexes are compared: the unadjusted state-level means calculated from the same data used by Oswald and Wu (2010; Column 1); the unadjusted state-level means reported by Rentfrow et al. (2009; Column 2); Oswald and Wu's regression-based adjusted measure (Column 3); and their objective quality-of-life ranking, based on Gabriel et al. (2003; Column 4). As this table shows, the pattern of correlations for Oswald and Wu's adjusted indexes would lead to surprising conclusions about the characteristics of the happiest states. According to these indexes, the happiest states are those with

TABLE 8.1
A Comparison of the Correlates for Four State-Level Well-Being Indexes

Measure	Unadjusted means[a]	Rentfrow et al. (2009)[b]	Oswald & Wu (2010)[c]	QoL rank[d]
		Economic factors		
Median household income	0.08	0.56*	−0.48*	−0.71*
Poverty rate	−0.27*	−0.53*	0.38*	0.43*
% Unemployed	−0.36*	−0.25	0.13	0.08
		Demographics		
% High school graduate	0.43*	0.65*	−0.13	−0.14
% College graduate	0.28*	0.71*	−0.32*	−0.45*
% Divorced	−0.04	−0.20	0.27*	0.28*
% Married	0.37*	0.09	0.23	0.30*
		Health		
Physically unhealthy days	−0.39*	−0.67*	0.27*	0.32*
% Obese	−0.28*	−0.70*	0.24	0.20
% Disabled (age 21–64)	−0.43*	−0.63*	0.22	0.23
		Rates of death		
All causes	−0.30*	−0.73*	0.17	0.19
Heart disease	−0.56*	−0.81*	−0.11	0.03
Cancer	−0.34*	−0.79*	−0.07	0.10
Cerebrovascular	−0.04	−0.33*	0.36*	0.18
Lower respiratory	−0.11	−0.36*	0.13	0.41*
Accident	0.14	−0.32*	0.63*	0.60*

Note. The quality of life ranking was reverse scored so that higher scores mean higher quality of life. Physically unhealthy days is a self-report measure from the Behavioral Risk Factor Surveillance System (BRFSS). [a]BRFSS life satisfaction means. [b]Means from the Gallup-Healthways Index. [c]Regression-based life satisfaction estimates. [d]Objective index based on Gabriel et al. (2003).
*$p < .05$.

low incomes, high poverty rates, low percentages of high school and college graduates, high rates of divorce, and slightly higher rates of death.

In contrast, the results from the unadjusted life satisfaction measures (which use the same underlying data as Oswald and Wu, 2010, and the Gallup well-being means shown in Columns 1 and 2) more closely match the CDC's own state estimates of health-related quality of life and past research at the individual level (Strine, Chapman, Balluz, Moriarty, & Mokdad, 2008). According to these indexes (which correlate .57 with one another, even though they are worded differently and come from different respondents), the happiest states are those with good health, low levels of disability and unemployment, high levels of education, high rates of marriage, and low rates of death (especially death from heart disease). These results are much more in line with theoretical expectations regarding the factors that lead to high SWB.

Given the discrepancies in results, it is useful to ask how the regression-based approach that Oswald and Wu (2010) used affected the rankings they obtained and why these values correlated so strongly with the objective indicator created by Gabriel et al. (2003). We believe that the answer comes from the specific covariates that were used as controls in Oswald and Wu's regression equation. Specifically, the inclusion of personal income in the model is likely to have a substantial effect on the state-dummy coefficients that are estimated. To see why this is the case, it is useful to examine how income and life satisfaction are associated both within and between states.

Figure 8.2 plots the results of a multilevel model predicting life satisfaction from the log of both within- and between-state income. The parallel lines reflect estimated within-state associations for five states ranging from

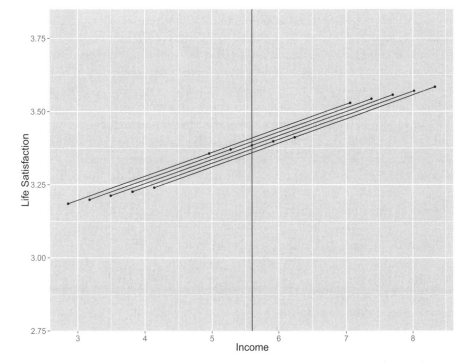

Figure 8.2. Within- and between-state associations between income and life satisfaction. The parallel lines reflect estimated within-state associations for five hypothetical states ranging from the very poor (two *SD*s below the mean) to the very rich (two *SD*s above the mean). The line reflecting a very poor state is the top line, which is shifted to the left on the income distribution; the line reflecting the very rich state is the bottom line, which is shifted to the right.

the very poor (the top line, which is shifted to the left on the income distribution) to the very rich (the bottom line, which is shifted to the right). The points in the middle of each line reflect the average income for the state. This figure demonstrates several important facts about the association between income and life satisfaction. First, the within-state association is positive—as income increases within a state, life satisfaction increases as well. Second, the between-state association is positive but weak. This can be seen by looking at the average life satisfaction at each of the average incomes (represented by the dot at the midpoint of each line) for the five different states—as average income increases, average life satisfaction increases slowly. Finally, the within- and between-state associations are not equivalent, and at any given level of absolute income, people report being more satisfied with life when they live in poor states than they do when they live in rich states. This fact is responsible for the somewhat counterintuitive feature of the graph: The states with the lowest income have lines that are above those for states with higher incomes.

The effect of controlling for personal income when calculating state-level estimates of life satisfaction becomes clear when we consider the vertical line superimposed over the data in Figure 8.2. When controlling for personal income, Oswald and Wu (2010) essentially shifted the meaning of the state-dummy estimates to reflect the average life satisfaction of residents from different states who make the same amount of money. In other words, rather than comparing the means for the individual states (the midpoint dots in Figure 8.2), this analysis compares state values along the vertical line, which means that it compares the richest people in poor states with the poorest people in rich states. It becomes clear that once personal income is controlled, the estimated average life satisfaction will decline with state income—and all of the characteristics that state income correlates with. In support of this interpretation, Oswald and Wu's index correlates −.48 with median household income of the states. Furthermore, this negative correlation with income is the likely explanation for why their index (which is supposed to reflect high quality of life) actually correlates negatively with positive characteristics, such as levels of education, and positively with negative characteristics, such as poverty rates, levels of disability, and rates of death.

But why does the objective quality of life index that Oswald and Wu (2010) use as a criterion correlate so strongly with their own index if their own index is flawed? This index is based on the assumption (see Gabriel et al., 2003, for a discussion) that people will demand higher incomes as compensation for living in regions with fewer amenities. If this assumption is correct, then one can use econometric methods to determine the monetary value of specific amenities. It is then possible to rank regions based on these amenities. However, a basic assumption underlying this analysis is that low wages occur where quality of life is high. Indeed, the quality-of-life index that results reproduces state-level income values quite well—the two values correlate −.71. Thus, it is no surprise that this quality-of-life index will correlate positively with any other measure that correlates negatively with household income.

Oswald and Wu (2010) suggested that the primary contribution of their work is to "measure the pattern of people's feelings of well-being . . . across the geography of the USA" and that their index "offers information about how much Americans enjoy their lives" (p. 2). But the interpretation of their regression-based index is not as straightforward. We agree that regression models such as those tested by Oswald and Wu can be useful for addressing many questions of interest to social scientists, including questions about the factors that influence well-being. However, the decision to control individual-level factors before estimating state-level well-being is a complicated one that must be considered carefully in light of the specific processes that are thought to link the predictor with the outcome (Macintyre, Ellaway, & Cummins, 2002). Oswald and Wu's coefficients for the state-level dummies do not provide the simple descriptive account of the well-being of states that is suggested in the paper and has been portrayed to the media (e.g., http:// www2.warwick.ac.uk/fac/soc/economics/staff/academic/oswald/pressoswu. pdf). We believe that raw means accomplish the desired goal of describing the well-being of states in a much more straightforward and meaningful way.

A CLOSER LOOK AT REGIONAL WELL-BEING IN THE UNITED STATES

Investigations into regional differences in well-being have the potential to increase knowledge about the predictors of well-being. As we have argued elsewhere (Lawless & Lucas, 2011), looking at broader units has a number of advantages over focusing solely on individual-level results. First, because personality is linked with SWB (Lucas & Diener, 2008), much of the between-person variance might result from personality characteristics rather than external circumstances. By aggregating across regions, the effect of personality traits will, to a large extent, be averaged out, and the effects of external circumstances might become clearer. Second, to look across regions, researchers will often be forced to include broader and more representative samples—samples that might include more variance in the relevant predictors. Thus, this strategy might allow researchers to identify associations that had not been noticed when more limited groups of participants were included. Finally, if well-being research is to be used to influence policy decisions, then researchers should conduct analyses that are at the appropriate level of analysis for this question. Because policy decisions affect groups of people (typically within well-defined regions), it can be helpful to use these regions as the level of analysis in policy-focused research.

Typically, research on regional differences has been conducted at the national level (Diener et al., 2010; Diener, Diener, & Diener, 1995; Stevenson & Wolfers, 2008). Although such analyses are informative (primarily because there is considerable variance in predictors when diverse nations are included), there are also limitations. For instance, cross-national studies often involve large numbers of researchers who may not collect data in standardized ways. In addition, language issues become important when administering questionnaires in different countries. Similarly, differences in response styles may influence responses to questionnaires when the underlying variables really do not differ. Although these issues are important for all research that uses self-report methods, they become particularly salient when conducting research across samples from diverse cultures. Looking at regional differences within nations (where geographic regions are not so closely linked with cultural differences) may help address some of these concerns while also maintaining some of the advantages of looking at the aggregate well-being of regions.

In a recent analysis, we used the same data as those included in Oswald and Wu (2010), but with a focus on smaller regions, to examine cross-region differences in SWB (Lawless & Lucas, 2011). These data, from the Behavioral Risk Factor Surveillance System (BRFSS; CDC, 2005–2009), include enough participants and appropriate geographic identifiers to allow for analysis at the county level. Data are available from approximately 2,400 of the more than 3,300 counties in the United States. These counties are diverse in size, demographics, and typical occupations. Thus, looking at the predictors of regional differences in well-being using these data allows for an important new look at potential factors that might underlie regional differences. In our initial investigation, we used a variety of variables assessed by the U.S. Census Bureau as part of the census that takes place once per decade (only data from 2000 were available for these analyses and the additional analyses included later). We also supplemented the census data with health data from the CDC.

When conducting our initial analyses, we were faced with a decision about which counties we should include in our analyses. Although the full BRFSS (from 2005–2008, the years available at the time we conducted our original analyses) includes over one million respondents from over 2,400 counties, many counties had relatively small numbers of respondents, which can lead to concerns about the reliability of the estimates one obtains from them. As a solution to this problem, we conducted analyses only on a subset of 363 counties that were large enough for the CDC to provide separate weights that could be used to get accurate estimates for those counties. Although this decision allows us to be relatively confident about the results that emerged within this subset of counties, there are questions about generalizability because the counties that were included tended to be much larger than those that were excluded.

An alternative strategy—and the one we use in the current analyses—is to use data from all respondents and to estimate county-level differences in the context of a multilevel model, where county estimates are weighted by the number of respondents available for that county (Gelman & Hill, 2007). Specifically, we fit an intercept-only model with a random intercept and respondents nested within county. The county-level estimates of average life satisfaction reflect a balance between the overall average and the individual county average. For counties with large numbers of respondents, the county-specific average is weighted heavily; for counties with smaller numbers of respondents, the overall average across all participants in the sample is weighted more heavily in the estimate. The model-based estimates are then used as outcome variables in our correlational analyses. We should also note that two additional waves of BRFSS data (2009 and 2010) were included in the current analyses. Together, these analyses help clarify the robustness of previous results identified in the state-based analyses reported earlier, along with those identified by Lawless and Lucas (2011). A map of these estimates is presented in Figure 8.3.

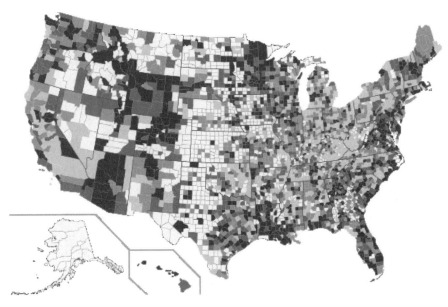

Figure 8.3. County-level life satisfaction *across the United States.* White means no data available; other shades of gray reflect the satisfaction quartile of the county, with darker colors reflecting higher satisfaction.

The predictors we chose to examine were selected on the basis of three criteria. First, although it is possible that between-person effects may not replicate at the aggregate level, we used previous research on individual-level effects as a guide for our variable selection. Second, to the extent that previous regional investigations had identified important predictors, we also included these variables in our analyses. Finally, information had to be available at the appropriate unit of analysis (U.S. county). This criterion limited the pool of candidates considerably. Ultimately, we focused on 61 variables from seven content areas: economic factors; education and occupation or industry; marital status; inclusiveness factors; health variables; death rates from specific causes; and a set of variables related to the size of the community, including population, population density, and length of commute. For space reasons, we highlight important findings instead of presenting details for all 61 variables. However, full tables of results are available from the first author.

Previous research has consistently shown that at both the individual and national level, income is associated with life satisfaction (Deaton, 2008; Diener et al., 1995; Lucas & Schimmack, 2009; Stevenson & Wolfers, 2008). As noted earlier, Table 8.1 shows that at the state level in the United States, some of these effects are replicated: Income correlated strongly with Rentfrow et al.'s (2009) index from the Gallup data but only weakly with the unadjusted index derived from the CDC data. Our county-level analyses show that economic health is associated with high SWB across these different regions, and this finding is robust across the two subsets of counties. Median income ($r = .41$), rates of poverty ($r = -.34$), and the unemployment rate ($r = -.28$) are all moderately correlated with aggregate life satisfaction.

In the initial Lawless and Lucas (2011) paper, we found a more complex association with home values. Although the associations between life satisfaction and indicators of property value (including median home value, median mortgage payment, and median rent payment) were positive but weak, this association depended on the relative value of the typical home in relation to the typical income. For instance, although the median mortgage payment was weakly positively correlated with aggregate life satisfaction, the percentage of people who had to spend more than 35% of their income on their mortgage was negatively correlated with life satisfaction. In the broader sample of counties analyzed here, this pattern is still apparent (at least for mortgages), but it is not as strong. In this broader sample, property values ($r = .37$), mortgage payments ($r = .34$), and rents ($r = .35$) are all moderately correlated with aggregate life satisfaction. Finally, consistent with recent research on income inequality (Oishi, Kesebir, & Diener, 2011), variance in the county-level gini-coefficient (a standard measure of inequality) was significantly (but weakly) correlated with aggregate life satisfaction ($r = -.16$).

Overall, these results show that regions that are doing well economically tend to have residents who report being relatively satisfied with their lives.

Rentfrow et al. (2009) found that some of the strongest associations emerged for variables related to education and occupation. Specifically, their measure of "human capital" (which reflected education levels) correlated .79 with the broadest well-being index they included, and indexes in participation in the creative class and super-creative class were both positively associated with well-being (r's of .49 and .63). In contrast, an index of working class status was negatively correlated with well-being. Our earlier analyses replicated the basic finding for education, but less so for occupations. Education (a variable that is typically downplayed in individual-level research on well-being) correlated moderately to strongly with aggregated life satisfaction ($r = .47$ for percentage with college degree; $r = .40$ for percentage with high school diploma). In terms of occupations and industries, the percentage of people who work in professional occupations ($r = .39$), along with the participation in finance ($r = .30$), the information industry ($r = .20$), and professional industries ($r = .31$) were all correlated with life satisfaction. The correlation with participation in the arts industry was .00 in the select sample of counties included in our earlier analyses, but the .20 correlation found in the broader range of counties analyzed here is somewhat more supportive of the results presented in Rentfrow et al.. The only substantial negative correlation found in the broader set of counties was that for manufacturing, which was small to moderate in size ($r = -.26$).

Marital status is argued to be one of the stronger and more robust correlates of well-being at the individual level (Argyle, 1999; Myers, 1999; but see Lucas, Clark, Georgellis, & Diener, 2003; Lucas & Dyrenforth, 2005). Some associations were found at the state level (see Table 8.1), though these tended to be quite inconsistent across variables and data sets. More consistent results were initially seen in our earlier analysis at the county level, with medium-sized associations between aggregate life satisfaction and marriage rates, rates of separation, rates of single status, and rates of widowhood. However, among the larger sample of counties analyzed here, most of these associations shrink in size. For instance, the correlations with percentage married and percentage divorced were just .19 and −.17 (both significant at $p < .05$). These results inform questions about the broader role of regional differences in social cohesion (e.g., Helliwell, Barrington-Leigh, Harris, & Huang, 2010), though it is unclear whether rates of legal marital status necessarily reflect broader trends in social cohesion.

In addition to showing that participation in the arts predicted well-being, Rentfrow et al. (2009) also found that measures of inclusiveness, such as a gay index (on the basis of the American Community Survey) and the number of immigrants living in a state also positively predicted well-being.

These results were not replicated in our original county-level analyses, and in fact, they were the opposite direction. For instance, the percentage of households with same-sex cohabitating partners correlated −.15 with average life satisfaction, the percentage of foreign-born residents correlated −.28 with life satisfaction, and the percentage of residents who speak English as a first language correlated .27 with life satisfaction. It is notable that these associations from Lawless and Lucas (2011) did not replicate in the broader sample of counties because all associations were weaker than .06. Given the theoretical and practical importance of Rentfrow et al.'s initial findings, a closer look at the reasons for these cross-study discrepancies would be fruitful.

We also examined the associations between aggregate life satisfaction and a variety of health and disease data. Although there is some debate about the extent to which broad indexes of health status correlate with SWB at the individual level (see Diener et al., 1999), more recent evidence has suggested that some severe health conditions are in fact associated with life satisfaction, both in cross-sectional studies and in longitudinal studies that assess the onset of a condition (Lucas, 2007). Consistent with this idea, analyses at the state level, along with those among both sets of counties, show that health is consistently a medium-sized predictor of aggregate life satisfaction. Those counties that are low in physical health ($r = .20$), high in obesity ($r = −.41$), and high in rates of disability ($r = −.42$ for disability among those ages 21–64) consistently report lower levels of life satisfaction. Similarly, counties with high rates of death ($r = −.40$), especially high rates of death due to heart disease ($r = −.43$) or cancer ($r = −.34$), report lower levels of life satisfaction. Thus, health variables—variables that, like education, are also often downplayed in individual-level research—appear to be consistent predictors of well-being at the regional level.

The final set of variables we investigated included some that have typically not been considered in individual-level research. Unlike personal health or demographic variables, these predictors only make sense at a contextual level—they are features of the community that may influence how satisfied people feel. Specifically, we examined whether the size and density of the county (along with the related variable of average commute) predicted the life satisfaction of regions. In our earlier study (Lawless & Lucas, 2011), population ($r = −.20$), population density ($r = −.27$), and length of commute ($r = −.14$) were all significantly associated with life satisfaction, with effects for population density being moderate in size. However, in the new analyses with the larger set of counties, these effects shrink in size considerably, with all correlations smaller in size than .08. Again, as with the inclusiveness variables that Rentfrow et al. (2009) identified, the fact that these variables sometimes predict well-being means that future research should examine the reasons for these discrepancies more closely.

CONCLUSION

Regional differences in SWB provide a promising avenue for future theoretical developments. As shown in this and other studies, robust and moderately strong associations can be found across many levels of analysis and across distinct data sets. Often, the variables that emerge as the strongest predictors are different from those that typically emerge at the individual level. When considered in the context of the strengths of research on regional differences, these new findings can make important new theoretical contributions. For instance, as we noted earlier, health and education variables are typically downplayed in individual-level research as being relatively unimportant (e.g., Diener et al., 1999). However, these emerged as some of the strongest predictors at the aggregate level, and these generalize across state and more local levels. Thus, research into the processes that underlie these effects might be fruitful.

Of course, research at the aggregate level is not without difficulties and limitations. For instance, although more and more data are available for this type of analysis, the work is still quite data intensive, and much of the existing research is based on a small number of data sets. In addition, once individual differences are averaged out, the variance across regions is relatively small. Although the correlations with objective predictors suggest that the variance is meaningful, there are still questions about how we should evaluate the size of the differences that are identified. Finally, it is not always clear what level of analysis is best. As the analyses reported here show, different results may emerge at the state and county levels (and even across different samples of counties). Some of these discrepancies might be due to fluctuations in state-level associations, given the relatively small number of states as compared with counties. In addition, differences in the amount of variance that exist at the different levels might be responsible for differences in effects. Thus, when working at the regional level, it will be important not to generalize past the level that is actually being analyzed—factors that predict weakly at one level may play an important role at another. Despite these difficulties, regional differences in SWB are a promising avenue for future research.

REFERENCES

Argyle, M. (1999). Causes and correlates of happiness. In D. Kahneman, E. Diener, & N. Schwarz (Eds.), *Well-being: The foundations of hedonic psychology* (pp. 353–373). New York, NY: Russell Sage Foundation.

Centers for Disease Control and Prevention. (2005–2009). *Behavioral risk factor surveillance system survey data.* Atlanta, GA: U.S. Department of Health and Human Services, Centers for Disease Control and Prevention.

Deaton, A. (2008). Income, health, and wellbeing around the world: Evidence from the Gallup world poll. *The Journal of Economic Perspectives, 22,* 53–72. doi:10.1257/jep.22.2.53

Diener, E., Diener, M., & Diener, C. (1995). Factors predicting the subjective well-being of nations. *Journal of Personality and Social Psychology, 69,* 851–864. doi:10.1037/0022-3514.69.5.851

Diener, E., Helliwell, J. F., & Kahneman, D. (Eds.). (2010). *International differences in well-being.* New York, NY: Oxford University Press. doi:10.1093/acprof:oso/9780199732739.001.0001

Diener, E., Lucas, R. E., Schimmack, U., & Helliwell, J. (2009). *Well-being for public policy.* New York, NY: Oxford University Press. doi:10.1093/acprof:oso/9780195334074.001.0001

Diener, E., & Seligman, M. E. P. (2004). Beyond money: Toward an economy of well-being. *Psychological Science in the Public Interest, 5,* 1–31. doi:10.1111/j.0963-7214.2004.00501001.x

Diener, E., Suh, E. M., Lucas, R. E., & Smith, H. L. (1999). Subjective well-being: Three decades of progress. *Psychological Bulletin, 125,* 276–302. doi:10.1037/0033-2909.125.2.276

Gabriel, S., Mattey, J., & Wascher, W. (2003). Compensating differentials and evolution in the quality-of-life among us states. *Regional Science and Urban Economics, 33,* 619–649. doi:10.1016/S0166-0462(02)00007-8

Gelman, A., & Hill, J. (2007). *Data analysis using regression and multilevel/hierarchical models.* Cambridge, England: Cambridge University Press.

Helliwell, J. F., Barrington-Leigh, C., Harris, A., & Huang, H. (2010). International evidence on the social context of well-being. In E. Diener, J. F. Helliwell, & D. Kahneman (Eds.), *International differences in well-being* (pp. 291–326). New York, NY: Oxford University Press. doi:10.1093/acprof:oso/9780199732739.003.0010

Kahneman, D., Krueger, A., Schkade, D., Schwarz, N., & Stone, A. (2004). Toward national well-being accounts. *The American Economic Review, 94,* 429–434. doi:10.1257/0002828041301713

Lawless, N. M., & Lucas, R. E. (2011). Predictors of regional well-being: A county level analysis. *Social Indicators Research, 101,* 341–357. doi:10.1007/s11205-010-9667-7

Lucas, R. E. (2007). Long-term disability is associated with lasting changes in subjective well-being: Evidence from two nationally representative longitudinal studies. *Journal of Personality and Social Psychology, 92,* 717–730. doi:10.1037/0022-3514.92.4.717

Lucas, R. E., Clark, A., Georgellis, Y., & Diener, E. (2003). Reexamining adaptation and the set point model of happiness: Reactions to changes in marital status. *Journal of Personality and Social Psychology, 84,* 527–539. doi:10.1037/0022-3514.84.3.527

Lucas, R. E., & Diener, E. (2008). Personality and subjective well-being. In O. John, R. Robins, & L. Pervin (Eds.), *Handbook of personality: Theory and research* (pp. 171–194). New York, NY: Guilford Press.

Lucas, R. E., & Dyrenforth, P. (2005). The myth of marital bliss? *Psychological Inquiry, 16,* 111–115.

Lucas, R. E., & Schimmack, U. (2009). Income and well-being: How big is the gap between the rich and the poor? *Journal of Research in Personality, 43*(1), 75–78. doi:10.1016/j.jrp.2008.09.004

Macintyre, S., Ellaway, A., & Cummins, S. (2002). Place effects on health: How can we conceptualise, operationalise and measure them? *Social Science & Medicine, 55*(1), 125–139. doi:10.1016/S0277-9536(01)00214-3

Meehl, P. E. (1970). Nuisance variables and the ex post facto design. In M. Radner & S. Winokur, *Minnesota studies in the philosophy of science: Vol. IV. Analyses of theories and methods of physics and psychology* (pp. 373–402). Minneapolis, MN: University of Minnesota Press.

Myers, D. G. (1999). Close relationships and quality of life. In D. Kahneman, E. Diener, & N. Schwarz (Eds.), *Well-being: The foundations of hedonic psychology* (pp. 374–391). New York, NY: Russell Sage Foundation.

Oishi, S., Kesebir, S., & Diener, E. (2011). Income inequality and happiness. *Psychological Science, 22,* 1095–1100. doi:10.1177/0956797611417262

Oswald, A. J., & Wu, S. (2010, January 29). Objective confirmation of subjective measures of human well-being: Evidence from the USA. *Science, 327*(5965), 576–579. doi:10.1126/science.1180606

Rentfrow, P., Mellander, C., & Florida, R. (2009). Happy states of America: A state-level analysis of psychological, economic, and social well-being. *Journal of Research in Personality, 43,* 1073–1082. doi:10.1016/j.jrp.2009.08.005

Schneider, L., & Schimmack, U. (2009). Self-informant agreement in well-being ratings: A meta-analysis. *Social Indicators Research, 94,* 363–376. doi:10.1007/s11205-009-9440-y

Stevenson, B., & Wolfers, J. (2008, Spring). Economic growth and happiness: Reassessing the easterlin paradox. *Brookings Papers on Economic Activity,* 1–87. doi:10.1353/eca.0.0001

Strine, T. W., Chapman, D., Balluz, L., Moriarty, D., & Mokdad, A. (2008). The associations between life satisfaction and health-related quality of life, chronic illness, and health behaviors among us community-dwelling adults. *Journal of Community Health, 33*(1), 40–50. doi:10.1007/s10900-007-9066-4

Wilson, W. (1967). Correlates of avowed happiness. *Psychological Bulletin, 67,* 294–306. doi:10.1037/h0024431

9

THE CITY WHERE WE LIVE M̶
THE PSYCHOLOGY OF CITIES

NANSOOK PARK AND CHRISTOPHER PETERSON

When psychology research first began, investigators were indifferent to the sources and identities of research participants. Indeed, psychophysicists like Wilhelm Wundt typically studied themselves in carefully controlled laboratory experiments, a strategy that could be defended given their focus on basic processes of sensation and perception (Boring, 1950). But as psychology grew and became a social science, not only did researchers continue to privilege experimentation but they also used as research participants individuals at conveniently close proximity to themselves. Often these individuals were college students drawn from psychology classes at the schools of the researchers. To judge from contemporary journal articles, one might think that research participants "live" in introductory psychology participant pools. Of course they do not. They live in neighborhoods, cities, states, and nations.

As explained by Danziger (2000), these trends limited not only the generality of findings but also the focus on certain sorts of findings. Thus,

http://dx.doi.org/10.1037/14272-010
Geographical Psychology: Exploring the Interaction of Environment and Behavior, P. J. Rentfrow (Editor)

179

...ological experimentation became limited to the investigation of effects that were (a) *proximal*, meaning that they were the result of an immediate cause (a stimulus) and not a distal one; (b) *local*, meaning that they were observed at a particular time and place, with no explicit attention to whether they generalized, despite hopes that they would; (c) *short-term*, meaning that they lasted no longer than the presence of the stimulus; and (d) *decomposable*, meaning that they could be analyzed into simple components that could be investigated one at a time in isolation from one another. Perhaps these sorts of effects can be studied with arbitrary research participants who bring nothing of importance to an experiment except a willingness to follow directions.

In recent years, demographic characteristics of participants, such as age, gender, and ethnicity, are increasingly mentioned in research reports. However, these are often treated as nuisance variables to be controlled and not studied in their own right. That said, this is an incomplete list of what participants bring to research. What about education, income, and family background? And what about where they happen to live? We therefore applaud the recent interest of research psychologists in what can be termed *psychological geography*. Where someone lives—city, state, and nation—of course matters if we want to understand people, although psychologists have been slow to follow the lead of other social sciences and take seriously one's geographical place of origin or residence as an important human characteristic (cf. Kitchin, 1997).

CITIES AS A PSYCHOLOGIST VIEWS THEM

Here is our thesis. Where one lives matters, and one's city of residence is a powerful unit of analysis, sometimes more than state, region, or nation (Park & Peterson, 2010). When we meet people, we usually ask where they are from. Of the many ways to answer this question, the city where they grew up or now live is often mentioned (Garreau, 1981). Cities have nicknames, sports teams, and cuisines. Think Sin City, the Bronx Bombers, and Philadelphia cheesesteaks. Cities have their own popular songs. Chicago may be your kind of town, unless you left your heart in San Francisco or ever went walking in Memphis.

Cities provide unique challenges and affordances. They have their own histories. They provide identities. They have considerable psychological depth, complexity, and structure and have an impact on their residents that goes beyond the proximal, local, short-term, and decomposable effects often studied in the laboratory. In short, cities have their own personalities (Florida, 2008;

Jacobs, 1961), and how could these not influence, sometimes profoundly, the personalities of those who grew up in them or currently reside in them?

Why have psychology researchers neglected the study of variation across cities? As mentioned, one reason may be the concern with immediate influences on behavior that can be studied in the laboratory. However, the immediate "stimuli" that influence behavior are embedded in larger contexts, including the family, neighborhood, community, and, of course, city (Bronfenbrenner, 1979). Psychologists have occasionally investigated the role of larger social context in terms of neighborhood and community influences on behavior, but this work has usually studied differences within given cities (Pinderhughes & Hurley, 2008).

Psychologists have studied the nation where one lives under the rubric of cross-cultural psychology. However, cross-cultural psychology is often cross-national psychology, meaning that investigators group together research participants from given nations and then compare them with one another (Smith, 2004). To the degree that the nations studied by cross-cultural psychologists are culturally homogeneous, the strategy of comparing people from different nations is a good way to understand cultural differences. Otherwise, even when national differences are found, they may reflect the specific geographical sources of the particular samples and their prevailing local cultures.

We suspect that the most frequent comparison in cross-cultural psychology research is between college students in the United States and China. Two more heterogeneous nations would be hard to find. Studies of variations within a nation provide a more rigorous way of testing the hypotheses of interest to cross-cultural psychologists. Such studies would necessarily do a better job of minimizing potential confounds such as language, mode of government, affluence, and educational opportunities than comparative studies across nations.

The world today has 50,000 settlements of at least 50,000 people, and the number of people living in cities will increase in the decades ahead given global trends toward industrialization and modernization (Dye, 2008). The majority of the world's population now reside in cities, and so too do the majority of Americans (Batty, 2008).

Most scientific approaches to cities have focused on topics such as housing, health, jobs, population growth, and environmental deterioration. Scientific interest in urbanization and cities has grown in recent years, but psychologists have been conspicuously missing. Beyond the inherent interest in knowing whether people from different cities within a nation are psychologically the same or different, documentation of such differences would better characterize the database of psychology and the applications based on it.

STUDIES OF CITIES

We now turn to three lines of research that illustrate our thesis that cities matter psychologically and sometimes more so than states and regions.

Quality of Life in Spanish Regions, Provinces, and Municipalities

Quality-of-life researchers are fond of comparing different nations, using both objective and subjective measures of well-being. Exact details of such rankings differ across studies, but Scandinavian countries usually have the highest quality of life, whereas former Soviet bloc nations and those in sub-Saharan Africa usually have the lowest. Some researchers take an additional step and try to explain these differences in terms of national-level characteristics, finding, for example, that nations whose citizens are doing well psychologically are more affluent and have more freedom (Inglehart, Foa, Peterson, & Weizel, 2008). Per these sorts of analyses, East Asian nations report less well-being than one might expect given their relative affluence, whereas Spanish-speaking nations in South America report greater well-being than one might expect given their relative poverty.

Be that as it may, this entire line of research is guilty of overlooking variations within a given nation. A recent study by González, Cárcaba, and Ventura (2011) is therefore of interest because it simultaneously looked at different geographical units within Spain and asked which unit best explained the psychological well-being of residents. Spain is divided into 17 regions called *Comunidades Autónomas*. These regions are responsible for the administration of schools, universities, health and social services and, in some cases, policing. Regions in turn are divided into provinces. Within the provinces are municipalities (cities); González and colleagues focused on 643 of these cities and created a composite quality-of-life measure for residents of these cities, using such indicators as high-quality housing, transportation, employment, culture, education, and security. The question of interest was which geographical region—region, province, or municipality—accounted for the most variation in quality of life. Municipalities were by far the most important, explaining 52% of the variance. Regions accounted for 38% of the variance and provinces a modest 10%. Said another way, if one wants to know the quality of life of someone in Spain, the most information is provided by knowing the city where he or she resides.

These results seem obvious, but they underscore the importance of taking into account the city where one lives. The contributors to quality of life studied by González et al. (2011) need to be accessible and available to people, and they are concentrated in some cities (and not others). They are not randomly distributed across provinces and regions. The practical importance of these findings is that policy decisions in Spain are often implemented at the level of larger geographical units. If the goal of these decisions is to improve quality of life, they overlook the unit that may matter most: the city.

Suicides in U.S. States Versus Cities

An intriguing study has recently received a great deal of media attention. By looking at the suicide rates across the 50 U.S. states as a function of the average happiness in these states, Daly, Oswald, Wilson, and Wu (2011) followed up an apparent global trend that the happiest countries (judged by the average self-report of their residents) often have the highest suicide rates.

The hypothesized relationship was found: The highest suicide rates in the United States occurred in states that were the most happy (e.g., Utah), whereas the lowest suicide rates occurred in states that were the least happy (e.g., New York). The correlation was not high ($r = .25$, $p < .10$), but it was positive. Perhaps being surrounded by happy people can take a toll on some. Happiness has demonstrable benefits for the individual (Lyubomirsky, King, & Diener, 2005), but in the aggregate it may result in collateral damage. Judgments of happiness are necessarily relative ones, and the vulnerable person surrounded by too many happy folks may be nudged down, with suicide as the extreme response to the insidious comparisons that are made.

We find this argument interesting but implausible. Researchers from Durkheim to the present have linked suicide to individual unhappiness and depression and to societal disarray (Harwitz & Ravizza, 2000). Happiness and unhappiness spread through social networks; so too—by implication—does suicide risk (Fowler & Christakis, 2008). If those who commit suicide do so because they are surrounded by happy people, then the more immediate these other people are, the stronger the link should be between the happiness of most and the suicide of some. It is not obvious that those in one's state provide a typical reference group (Park & Peterson, 2010). Rather, most compare and contrast themselves with family members, friends, colleagues, and neighbors. Accordingly, we investigated the association between happiness and suicide rates in large U.S. cities (Park & Peterson, 2012).

We focused on the 50 largest U.S. cities, those with populations in excess of 362,800. Suicide rates (per 100,000) in 2004 were available from the fifth edition of the *Big Cities Health Inventory* (Benbow, 2007) for most of these cities ($M = 12.5$, $SD = 5.7$). The highest suicide rates were for Tucson (25.0), Colorado Springs (26.1), and Las Vegas (34.5), and the lowest were for Boston (4.2), Baltimore (5.6), and Washington, DC (5.6).

Happiness scores in 2010 were available from the *Gallup-Healthways Well-Being Index* (2011) for most of these cities. These scores were obtained by telephone interviews of adults from nationally representative samples of

1,000 U.S. respondents per day throughout the year (excluding major holidays). Happiness ("life evaluation") was assessed with two questions asking respondents to use a self-anchoring scale (from 0, *the worst possible life*, to 10, *the best possible life*) to indicate where they saw themselves at present and where they expected to be 5 years in the future. Composite happiness scores were averaged within respondents from a city, weighted by demographic characteristics such as gender, age, and race to match census figures. These scores were reported as the rank order of a given U.S. city (out of 188). The happiest cities in the sample were Honolulu (#1), Washington, DC (#6), and Austin (#8), and the least happy were Tulsa (#134), Detroit (#142), and Cleveland (#149). The correlation between the happiness of a city and its suicide rate was significant: Spearman's rho = .37 ($p < .014$). Because the least happy cities had the highest ranks, these positive correlations mean that happy cities had low suicide rates and that unhappy cities had high suicide rates.

The Gallup-Healthways assessment of happiness, based on representative sampling, is laudable, but suicide rates, based on coroner or medical examiner judgments, are notoriously fickle (Phillips & Ruth, 1993). In the data available, happiness and suicide were measured 6 years apart: 2010 versus 2004, respectively. Nonetheless, we found that happy U.S. cities had low suicide rates. These findings are at odds with the Daly et al. (2011) study showing that happy U.S. states had high suicide rates, and the findings are also more robust. The present results should be taken seriously in terms of placing suicide in its more immediate social context.

That happy cities had low suicide rates is worth reporting in view of the Daly et al. (2011) study and the attention it has garnered. At the aggregate level, high levels of reported happiness and low levels of suicide indicate overall social and societal well-being. The correlation may reflect a number of underlying factors—such as the stress associated with unemployment or crime or alcohol abuse—that differ across cities. In light of research showing that happiness is contagious within social networks, there may even be a direct link between happiness and reduced risk of suicide (Fowler & Christakis, 2008). Conversely, suicide reduces the well-being of survivors in cascading ways, so again there may be a direct link (Schneidman, 1973).

Why Daly et al. (2011) found what they did is not clear, but we repeat our argument that states may not always be the appropriate unit of analysis for psychological studies (Park & Peterson, 2010). Grouping together all research participants within a given state obscures distinctions across cities within that state. Furthermore, studies that collapse within states mix together urban and rural residents, and these people, of course, may differ (e.g., Middleton, Gunnell, Frankel, Whitley, & Dorling, 2003). In the United States, states reflect important political distinctions but not always psychological ones (Seyle & Newman, 2006).

Character Strengths in U.S. Regions, States, and Cities

Good character is the foundation of a happy, healthy, and moral life. Regardless of how we define character, its importance for individual and societal well-being has been emphasized through the ages from East to West (Park, 2004). Good character is not singular but plural (Dahlsgaard, Peterson, & Seligman, 2005). *Character* is a family of positive traits reflected in how people think, feel, and behave. For the past several years, we have been involved in a project identifying important strengths of character and devising ways to measure them (Park & Peterson, 2006a; Peterson & Seligman, 2004; Seligman, Steen, Park, & Peterson, 2005). We have focused on 24 widely valued character strengths, and the associated assessment strategies provide a starting point for the systematic and comparative investigation of character.

Do people who reside in different cities in the United States have different strengths of character? This question is a good one if our interest is psychological geography. Character strengths pertain to a variety of important outcomes (e.g., achievement, health, leadership, law-abidingness, social relationships, psychological well-being) that in turn show considerable variation within the United States. Indeed, several recent studies have documented differences across regions of the United States in basic personality traits and self-conceptions, some of which overlap with the character strengths of interest to us (e.g., agreeableness, conscientiousness, and curiosity; Plaut, Markus, & Lachman, 2002; Rentfrow, Gosling, & Potter, 2008). However, these studies did not examine traits at the level of cities but rather at the level of states or larger regions (e.g., New England).

In a previous study, we compared character strengths across research participants from the 50 U.S. states and found no differences of note across states or census regions—except for religiousness, which was marginally higher in southern and midwestern states (Park, Peterson, & Seligman, 2006). We now believe that "state" and "region" were the wrong units of analysis to show differences in the positive traits of interest to us. As emphasized, grouping together all respondents within a given state or region obscures distinctions, treating as equivalent residents from what may be very different cities.

Our inventory measures 24 character strengths, with items rated on 5-point scales according to how well respondents believe they describe how they typically think, feel, and act. For example, the character strength of curiosity is measured with items such as "I am always asking questions," and the character strength of kindness is measured with items such as "I really enjoy doing small favors for friends." These scales are internally consistent and stable, and they have broad construct validity, including good convergence with informant reports (Park & Peterson, 2006b; Park, Peterson, & Seligman, 2004).

This questionnaire was completed on an Internet site by 203,303 adults from the United States between September 2002 and December 2005. Respondents registered freely on the website and provided demographic information, including their postal zip code. They then completed a measure of character strengths. Respondents received immediate feedback about their scores on completion of the survey, and this feature apparently motivated participants.

Although our convenience sample was tilted toward women (70%) and more educated individuals (60% with college degrees), the size of the sample indicates that substantial sociodemographic diversity exists that can be taken into account in statistical analyses. In our research, we weighted our data by respondent age, gender, and education to match the cities in which respondents lived, and we further controlled for these demographic characteristics in our analyses. The exact same results were found with and without weighting and with and without controlling for these demographic characteristics, which suggests that the demographic characteristics did not account for what we found.

Zip codes were used to identify the city in which respondents lived. We paid special attention to respondents who resided in the 50 largest cities in the United States. There were small but reliable differences across these cities with respect to each of the 24 character strengths, about one third to one half a standard deviation difference in each case between a city whose residents scored highest and a city where they scored lowest ($p < .001$).

Here we focus on two composite scales that have emerged from our previous research. Factor analyses we have done with individual-level data have varied somewhat across samples (e.g., Park & Peterson, 2006b; Peterson, Park, Pole, D'Andrea, & Seligman, 2008), but always evident are two important dimensions: (a) strengths that are intellectual and self-oriented (e.g., creativity) and (b) strengths that are emotional and interpersonal (e.g., gratitude). We identify these two dimensions as *head strengths* and *heart strengths*, respectively (Park & Peterson, 2006a, 2010; Peterson, 2006; Peterson & Park, 2009).

We replicated this structure at the level of cities by computing the average-strengths scores for respondents from each city and then doing a factor analysis with varimax rotation using these average scores (excluding bravery, perspective, self-regulation, and social intelligence, which according to individual-level analyses could not be assigned to just a head factor or a heart factor). Two factors emerged, accounting for 74% of the variance. One factor reflected strengths of the head (appreciation of beauty and excellence, creativity, curiosity, judgment, love of learning) and the other strengths of the heart (e.g., forgiveness, gratitude, hope, kindness, love). We formed composites by averaging component strength scores (at the level of cities,

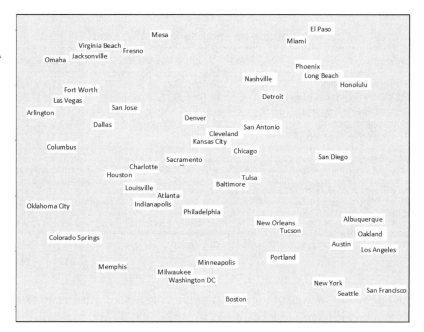

HEAD STRENGTH COMPOSITE ⇨

Figure 9.1. Large U.S. cities: head and heart scores.

head strengths α = .91, and heart strengths α = .90). At the level of cities, weighted and unweighted scores correlated .99 for both head strengths and heart strengths. This strong convergence reflects the typically modest associations of demographic variables with character strengths (Peterson & Seligman, 2004) as well as the substantial demographic similarities of the city subsamples.

As shown in Figure 9.1, the cities with the highest head strengths scores were Los Angeles, San Francisco, and Oakland, and those with the lowest were Arlington, Oklahoma City, and Omaha. The cities with the highest heart strengths scores were El Paso, Mesa, and Miami, and those with the lowest were Seattle, San Francisco, and Boston. Across the 50 cities, the two composites were negatively associated ($r = -.34$, $p < .02$). Please note that although we use shorthand in the remainder of this section to describe head cities and heart cities, the head and heart composites are dimensions, and a city can be higher or lower on each, with many clustered in the middles of both.

We went on to investigate, at the level of cities, the associations between the two strengths composites and important outcomes. Given the

TABLE 9.1
Character Strengths and City-Level Outcomes ($N = 50$)

Outcome	Head strength composite	Heart strength composite
Entrepreneurship	.38 ($p < .02$)	−.59 ($p < .001$)
2008 Presidential voting (for Barack Obama)	.44 ($p < .001$)	−.46 ($p < .001$)
Physical fitness	.34 ($p < .02$)	−.43 ($p < .003$)
Formal volunteer work	−.08 (ns)	−.47 ($p < .001$)

Note. Entrepreneurship was assessed by an equally weighted composite of (a) the proportion of a city's workforce in the creative class, (b) patents per capita, (c) presence of high-tech industries, and (d) diversity and tolerance (Florida, 2002). 2008 Presidential voting was assessed from information on media websites as the percentage of voters in the county in which a city was located voting for Barack Obama (vs. John McCain). Physical fitness was assessed with 2009 ratings from Men's Fitness (2009) magazine based on a composite of the number of fitness centers, parks, and open spaces in a city; city health and fitness initiatives; junk food consumption (reverse-scored); sports participation; obesity prevalence (reverse-scored); and the like. Formal volunteer work was assessed by city-level rates of volunteer activity "through and for an organization" between 2005 and 2007, using statistics compiled by the Corporation for National and Community Service (2012).

hierarchical structure of the data (respondents nested within cities), we used hierarchical linear modeling to analyze the data (Park & Peterson, 2010). The exact same results were found when we did simpler analyses, correlating the aggregate strengths scores for cities with city-level outcomes, and we report these here (see Table 9.1).

Head cities were more entrepreneurial, and their residents were more liberal in their voting and more physically fit. Heart cities were less entrepreneurial, and their residents were more conservative in their voting, less physically fit, and less likely to do formal volunteer work. We have previously discussed our findings with respect to entrepreneurship and voting (Park & Peterson, 2010), so let us comment on the newly reported results about fitness and formal volunteer work across different U.S. cities.

Perhaps residents of head cities approach fitness as one more way to achieve and to enhance the self. Fitness, at least as reflected in the ratings available to us, may be an individual pursuit and an activity with which residents of head cities feel comfortable. A poll of Americans who regularly exercise found that 59% preferred to work out alone (Waehner, 2007). There are many reasons for exercise, but among the motives that people cite are weight management and personal appearance (Gill, Williams, Dowd, Beaudoin, & Martin, 1996). Along these lines, "personal enjoyment" sustains workout adherence (Ingledew, Markland, & Medley, 1998).

In contrast, the more socially oriented residents of heart cities may be drawn to group activities with friends and family (e.g., watching sports rather than playing them, having people over for dinner) that end up making them less fit. Perhaps fitness initiatives in heart cities would be more compelling to residents if they emphasized working out with others and for the sake of others (Putnam, 2000). Among people who do not work out, many cite the lack of an "exercise partner" as a reason—an intriguing finding given that those who exercise regularly prefer doing so alone (Ebben & Brudzynski, 2008). Perhaps cities should incorporate different strategies to promote fitness based on characteristics of their residents.

We expected that cities with heart strengths would show the highest rates of volunteerism, but we found the opposite. Caution is needed in interpreting this finding because heart strengths such as love and kindness may show themselves more in how we treat family members and peers than in how we treat strangers (Park et al., 2006). Further research is needed that looks at other forms of caring and giving, because associations with strengths of character may differ according to the measures used. "Unpaid volunteer work through a formal organization" is not the same thing as caring for an elderly relative or watching a neighbor's children after school. It is not the same thing as doing church-related charity work or making donations. Formal volunteer rates are greater in cities with higher home ownership and educational attainment but lower in cities in with longer commutes and lower average income. Perhaps heart cities do not afford organization-based volunteerism, but other forms of caring may be more possible. For the time being, our results add to a growing literature showing that "those who care" may not always be the usual suspects (Brooks, 2006).

As Cohen (2009) noted, cross-cultural psychology treats individualism versus collectivism as the contrast of interest. As important as this feature may be, other ways in which cultures differ also warrant theoretical and empirical attention. Perhaps the head versus heart distinction we have studied should be among them.

CONCLUSION

We have described three lines of research showing that the city where one lives predicts quality of life, suicide, entrepreneurship, voting, physical fitness, and formal volunteer work. None of these outcomes is proximal, local, short-term, or decomposable. All are important, however, and we think we have made good sense of the findings. We highlighted research that shows cities to be more important than states or larger regions. We acknowledge that states and regions can be important, but the message of this chapter is to urge researchers, theorists, policymakers, and citizens not to lose sight of cities as attention turns to psychological geography.

The lines of research we have described can be criticized. Only relatively large cities were studied, leaving unknown how smaller cities or towns influence the behavior of those who live in them. We suspect that small towns have unique features just as large cities do. The present data and their interpretation may run afoul of the *ecological fallacy* (Robinson, 1950), which involves making inferences about individuals on the basis of aggregated data for a group. For instance, we could not ascertain who our respondents actually voted for in the 2008 presidential election—held several years after character strengths were measured. It is conceivable that the respondents to our survey in a given city were not the ones who voted for the candidate favored by the majority of other residents in that city. This possibility does not seem likely, but more generally, investigators need to be cautious about moving glibly between individual-level data and group-level data.

In most cases, the research programs described here leave unanswered questions about the directions of effects. Do features of cities influence individual-level psychological characteristics, or do the aggregated characteristics of individuals influence the features of cities? Questions like these deserve further study with more fine-grained longitudinal designs.

Finally, we do not know from this research why residents in different cities vary in their psychological makeup. Rentfrow et al. (2008) discussed possible reasons for geographical variation in personality, including selective migration, social influence, and environmental influence. All may play a role in accounting for the differences across U.S. cities, and some further U.S. city research by us implicates factors such as city affluence, number of nearby colleges, average cost of living, proportion of families with children, population size, population density, and even average temperature—heart cities are warmer, literally as well as metaphorically (Park & Peterson, 2010).

In sum, geographically based differences within a nation deserve the attention of psychologists. Studies of different cities show that such differences exist and that they have important individual and societal consequences. Where we live matters.

REFERENCES

Batty, M. (2008, February 8). The size, scale, and shape of cities. *Science, 319*(5864), 769–771. doi:10.1126/science.1151419

Benbow, N. (Ed.). (2007). *Big cities health inventory: The health of urban America* (5th ed.). Washington, DC: National Association of County and City Health Officials.

Boring, E. G. (1950). *A history of experimental psychology* (2nd ed.). New York, NY: Appleton-Century-Crofts.

Bronfenbrenner, U. (1979). *The ecology of human development: Experiments by nature and design.* Cambridge, MA: Harvard University Press.

Brooks, A. C. (2006). *Who really cares: The surprising truth about compassionate conservatism*. New York, NY: Basic Books.

Cohen, A. B. (2009). Many forms of culture. *American Psychologist, 64*, 194–204. doi:10.1037/a0015308

Corporation for National and Community Service. (2012). *Volunteering in America*. Retrieved from http://www.volunteeringinamerica.gov

Dahlsgaard, K., Peterson, C., & Seligman, M. E. P. (2005). Shared virtue: The convergence of valued human strengths across culture and history. *Review of General Psychology, 9*, 203–213. doi:10.1037/1089-2680.9.3.203

Daly, M. C., Oswald, A. J., Wilson, D., & Wu, S. (2011). Dark contrasts: The paradox of high rates of suicide in happy places. *Journal of Economic Behavior & Organization, 80*, 435–442. doi:10.1016/j.jebo.2011.04.007

Danziger, K. (2000). Making social psychology experimental: A conceptual analysis, 1920–1970. *Journal of the History of the Behavioral Sciences, 36*, 329–347. doi:10.1002/1520-6696(200023)36:4<329::AID-JHBS3>3.0.CO;2-5

Dye, C. (2008, February 8). Health and urban living. *Science, 319*(5864), 766–769. doi:10.1126/science.1150198

Ebben, W., & Brudzynski, L. (2008, October). Motivations and barriers to exercise among college students. *Journal of Exercise Physiology Online, 11*(5). Retrieved from http://faculty.css.edu/tboone2/asep/EbbenJEPonlineOctober 2008.pdf

Florida, R. (2002). *The rise of the creative class*. New York, NY: Perseus Books.

Florida, R. (2008). *Who's your city?* New York, NY: Basic Books.

Fowler, J. H., & Christakis, N. A. (2008). Dynamic spread of happiness in a large social network: Longitudinal analysis over 20 years in the Framingham Heart Study. *British Medical Journal, 337*, a2338.

Gallup-Healthways Well-Being Index. (2011). *City, state, and congressional well-being reports*. Retrieved from http://www.well-beingindex.com/stateCongres Districtrank.asp

Garreau, J. (1981). *The nine nations of North America*. New York, NY: Avon Books.

Gill, D. L., Williams, L., Dowd, D. A., Beaudoin, C. M., & Martin, J. J. (1996). Competitive orientations and motives of adult sport and exercise participants. *Journal of Sport Behavior, 19*, 307–318.

González, E., Cárcaba, A., & Ventura, J. (2011). The importance of the geographic level of analysis in the assessment of the quality of life: The case of Spain. *Social Indicators Research, 102*, 209–228. doi:10.1007/s11205-010-9674-8

Harwitz, D., & Ravizza, L. (2000). Suicide and depression. *Emergency Medicine Clinics of North America, 18*, 263–271. doi:10.1016/S0733-8627(05)70123-1

Ingledew, D. K., Markland, D., & Medley, A. R. (1998). Exercise motives and stages of change. *Journal of Health Psychology, 3*, 477–489. doi:10.1177/135910539800300403

Inglehart, R., Foa, R., Peterson, C., & Weizel, C. (2008). Development, freedom, and rising happiness: A global perspective, 1981-2007. *Perspectives on Psychological Science, 3*, 264–285. doi:10.1111/j.1745-6924.2008.00078.x

Jacobs, J. (1961). *The death and life of great American cities.* New York, NY: Random House.

Kitchin, R. M. (1997). Relations between psychology and geography. *Environment and Behavior, 29*, 554–573. doi:10.1177/001391659702900406

Lyubomirsky, S., King, L. A., & Diener, E. (2005). The benefits of frequent positive affect: Does happiness lead to success? *Psychological Bulletin, 131*, 803–855. doi:10.1037/0033-2909.131.6.803

Middleton, N., Gunnell, D., Frankel, S., Whitley, E., & Dorling, D. (2003). Urban–rural differences in suicide trends in young adults: England and Wales, 1981–1998. *Social Science & Medicine, 57*, 1183–1194. doi:10.1016/S0277-9536(02)00496-3

Park, N. (2004). Character strengths and positive youth development. *Annals of the American Academy of Political and Social Science, 591*, 40–54. doi:10.1177/0002716203260079

Park, N., & Peterson, C. (2006a). Methodological issues in positive psychology and the assessment of character strengths. In A. D. Ong & M. van Dulmen (Eds.), *Handbook of methods in positive psychology* (pp. 292–305). New York, NY: Oxford University Press.

Park, N., & Peterson, C. (2006b). Moral competence and character strengths among adolescents: The development and validation of the Values in Action Inventory of Strengths for Youth. *Journal of Adolescence, 29*, 891–909. doi:10.1016/j.adolescence.2006.04.011

Park, N., & Peterson, C. (2010). Does it matter where we live? The urban psychology of character strengths. *American Psychologist, 65*, 535–547. doi:10.1037/a0019621

Park, N., & Peterson, C. (2012). *Happiness and suicide in large U.S. cities.* Unpublished manuscript, University of Michigan, Ann Arbor, MI.

Park, N., Peterson, C., & Seligman, M. E. P. (2004). Strengths of character and well-being. *Journal of Social and Clinical Psychology, 23*, 603–619. doi:10.1521/jscp.23.5.603.50748

Park, N., Peterson, C., & Seligman, M. E. P. (2006). Character strengths in fifty-four nations and the fifty US states. *The Journal of Positive Psychology, 1*, 118–129. doi:10.1080/17439760600619567

Peterson, C. (2006). *A primer in positive psychology.* New York, NY: Oxford University Press.

Peterson, C., & Park, N. (2009). Classifying and measuring strengths of character. In C. R. Snyder & S. J. Lopez (Eds.), *Handbook of positive psychology* (2nd ed., pp. 25–33). New York, NY: Oxford University Press.

Peterson, C., Park, N., Pole, N., D'Andrea, W., & Seligman, M. E. P. (2008). Strengths of character and posttraumatic growth. *Journal of Traumatic Stress, 21*, 214–217. doi:10.1002/jts.20332

Peterson, C., & Seligman, M. E. P. (2004). *Character strengths and virtues: A handbook and classification*. Washington, DC: American Psychological Association.

Phillips, D. P., & Ruth, T. E. (1993). Adequacy of official suicide statistics for scientific research and public policy. *Suicide & Life-Threatening Behavior, 23*, 307–319.

Pinderhughes, E. E., & Hurley, S. (2008). Disentangling ethnic and contextual influences among parents raising youth in high-risk communities. *Applied Developmental Science, 12*, 211–219. doi:10.1080/10888690802388151

Plaut, V. C., Markus, H. R., & Lachman, M. E. (2002). Place matters: Consensual features and regional variation in American well-being and self. *Journal of Personality and Social Psychology, 83*, 160–184. doi:10.1037/0022-3514.83.1.160

Putnam, R. D. (2000). *Bowling alone: The collapse and revival of American community*. New York, NY: Simon & Schuster. doi:10.1145/358916.361990

Rentfrow, P. J., Gosling, S. D., & Potter, J. (2008). The geography of personality: A theory of the emergence, persistence, and expression of regional variation in basic traits. *Perspectives on Psychological Science, 3*, 339–369. doi:10.1111/j.1745-6924.2008.00084.x

Robinson, W. S. (1950). Ecological correlations and the behavior of individuals. *American Sociological Review, 15*, 351–357. doi:10.2307/2087176

Schneidman, E. S. (1973). *On the nature of suicide*. San Francisco, CA: Jossey-Bass.

Seligman, M. E. P., Steen, T. A., Park, N., & Peterson, C. (2005). Positive psychology progress: Empirical validation of interventions. *American Psychologist, 60*, 410–421. doi:10.1037/0003-066X.60.5.410

Seyle, D. C., & Newman, M. L. (2006). A house divided? The psychology of red and blue America. *American Psychologist, 61*, 571–580. doi:10.1037/0003-066X.61.6.571

Smith, P. B. (2004). Nations, cultures, and individuals. *Journal of Cross-Cultural Psychology, 35*, 6–12. doi:10.1177/0022022103260460

Waehner, P. (2007). Do you prefer to exercise alone or with other people? *About.com*. Retrieved from http://exercise.about.com/b/2007/03/19/vote-in-this-weeks-poll-do-you-prefer-to-exercise-alone-or-with-someone-else.htm

10

FINDING VALUES IN WORDS: USING NATURAL LANGUAGE TO DETECT REGIONAL VARIATIONS IN PERSONAL CONCERNS

CINDY K. CHUNG, PETER J. RENTFROW, AND JAMES W. PENNEBAKER

Personal concerns include our values, life goals, and evaluations of ourselves and others. McAdams (1995) suggested that personal concerns reflect the core of our personalities. Personal concerns do not emerge in isolation. Rather, they are discussed among people in shared social networks and, in a sense, help to define groups at a particular time and place, including entire cultures (Hofstede, 2001; Lehman, Chiu, & Schaller, 2004). Indeed, by studying values and personal concerns, it is possible to begin to understand the relationships between a culture and the people within it.

Although many studies have shown national differences in values and personal concerns, only recently have regional differences been explored. Using large-scale surveys, several authors have found regional and community

We are grateful to Jay Allison and Dan Gediman for providing the "This I Believe" corpus. Preparation of this manuscript was aided by funding from the Army Research Institute (W91WAW-07-C-0029) and National Science Foundation (NSCC-0904913).

http://dx.doi.org/10.1037/14272-011
Geographical Psychology: Exploring the Interaction of Environment and Behavior, P. J. Rentfrow (Editor)

differences in standardized questionnaires such as the Big Five Inventory, which assesses personality traits (BFI; John & Srivastava, 1999; see also Rentfrow, Gosling, & Potter, 2008), and the Midlife Development Inventory, which assesses well-being (see Plaut, Markus, & Lachman, 2002). Although an important first step, many approaches to personality suggest that an idiographic methodology would be more appropriate for personal concerns. Rather than forcing participants to rate different personal concerns, an alternative approach is to have them describe their values in an open-ended fashion. Such a strategy can reveal those issues that people are naturally thinking about (Claeys, de Boeck, van den Bosch, Biesmans, & Bohrer, 1985; McGuire & Padawer-Singer, 1976). However, it has been impractical to study regional differences, in which large samples are required for comparison, in idiographic responses because of the time and effort required to code open-ended text—that is, until the development of efficient computerized text analysis.

In this chapter, we present ways in which regional variations in personal concerns can be efficiently assessed in natural language—both in open-ended surveys and in cultural products, the published words of a culture. We begin by describing why personal concerns are best elicited in natural language. Next, we review recent studies that have assessed personal concerns in natural language within open-ended surveys and in unprecedentedly large numbers of cultural products. Finally, we illustrate the assessment of personal concerns expressed in open-ended essays across the United States from "This I Believe," an archival project on the values of Americans. This chapter, then, provides an introduction to the advances in methodological toolkits that are enabling psychologists to elicit and to efficiently study personal concerns in time and place.

THE NARRATIVE OF PERSONAL CONCERNS

Personal concerns include the ongoing and salient motivational, emotional, and cognitive structures of the self. They are influenced by the challenges and affordances that a context provides (Kitayama, Conway, Pietromonaco, Park, & Plaut, 2010). Researchers have studied a variety of personal concerns, including dominant interests (Allport & Vernon, 1931), personal constructs (e.g., Kelly, 1955), values (Rokeach, 1973), motives (McClelland, 1985), personal strivings (Emmons, 1992), characteristic adaptations (McAdams & Pals, 2006), and many others.

Reliable and valid rating questionnaires have been used to compare values and personal concerns of individuals, groups, regions, and nations (e.g., Rokeach Values Survey; Rokeach, 1973). However, because they are unique to individuals, researchers have aimed to elicit personal concerns using more idiographic methods. Structured interviews (e.g., The Repertory Grid interview for personal constructs; Fransella, Bell, & Bannister, 2004) or fill-in-the-blank stems on surveys (e.g., Personal Concerns Inventory; see Cox & Klinger, 2004) are much richer in capturing unique personal concerns. However, with either restricted responses or researcher-imposed coding schemes, they fall short of providing an efficient means of summarizing how individuals commonly construe their personal concerns across large samples.

Another strategy is to take advantage of the ways people naturally describe their personal concerns with others: letting them write or talk about them. We see this phenomenon frequently when people are in a new emotional situation. People may go to talk therapy; write an e-mail, love letter, blog, or text message; or simply talk to another person about it. Putting thoughts and feelings into words allows people to process and to communicate their experiences to others. Indeed, it is an age-old idea with empirical support that storytelling (Bruner, 1992), talk therapy (Freud, 1914), or even writing therapy (Pennebaker, 1997) can place an experience into context.

Putting personal constructs into words allows people to integrate them into their sense of well-being (Little & Chambers, 2004), their life story (McAdams, 2006), or cultural context (Mead, 1934). In verbalizing personal constructs, we come to know the person. On a larger scale, putting thoughts into words as cultural products—for example in books, newspapers, lyrics, laws, and more recently, in blogs, tweets, and status updates—is how we come to know the shared values and personal concerns of a particular time and place; it is how we come to know a culture (McClelland, 1961; Morling & Lamoreaux, 2008).

FINDING VALUES IN WORDS

Because personal concerns are conveyed using natural language, social scientists have historically been stymied because of the inherent difficulties of analyzing large data sets efficiently. For example, Thematic Apperception Tests (Murray, 1943) and narrative therapy techniques (e.g., White, 2007) allow for less restricted responses, but their administration, coding, and scoring are labor intensive, and they are difficult to compare across large groups of individuals. Most analytic strategies have relied on the careful reading and ratings of multiple human judges, each of whom reads texts with their own personal concerns that can add additional noise to the rating process.

More recently, advances in natural language processing (a field merging computer science with linguistics and cognitive science) in quantitative studies of cultural products have enabled larger samples of written or spoken words—the kinds of samples that are amenable to comparisons across time and place. One way to approach the computational analysis of large corpora (i.e., collections of text) is to use a deductive approach in which the researcher searches for predefined terms of interest. Alternatively, an exploratory inductive approach can be used to determine the words and higher order values participants express within and across groups and cultures.

Deductive Approaches

One of the most impressive deductive projects of cultural products has been the analysis of single word search terms in Google's digitized collection of 4% of all books ever published (Michel et al., 2011). The relative frequency of use of particular terms indicates the degree to which specific word-level concepts have been prevalent over the last several centuries. For example, the authors examined the appearance of words indicating particular widespread diseases (e.g., *Spanish flu*), cuisines (e.g., *sushi*), political regimes (e.g., *Nazis*), or religious terms (e.g., *God*) over time. Each of the terms peaked when the culture was experiencing change specific to the term. The authors termed this method of investigation *culturomics*, which is a natural language processing method for highlighting cultural change (the concepts discussed) and linguistic change (the words used for a concept) in large corpora.

Michel et al. (2011) did not have the specific goal of assessing personal concerns, but with the right search terms, it is possible to assess previously defined values or personal concerns over time. For example, Campbell and Gentile (2012) examined the use of first person singular pronouns (e.g., *I, me, my*) and first person plural pronouns (e.g., *we, us, our*) using Google books Ngram Viewer (http://books.google.com/ngrams/), which is an application that reports on the relative use of search terms in the Google Books Project over time. Presuming that *I* represents individualism and *we* represents collectivism, the authors found that there was a trend for increasing individualism and a decreasing trend for collectivism in English-language books in the past half century. Note that this pronoun-use pattern was also found in American popular song lyrics from 1980 to 2007 (DeWall, Pond, Campbell, & Twenge, 2011) using the questionable assumption that I-word use reflected narcissism. (Note that across dozens of laboratory and field studies, I-word use has been found to reflect anxiety, depression, insecurity, honesty, low status, and being self-focused; Pennebaker, 2011.)

In another study, Bardi, Calogero, and Mullen (2008) derived a lexicon of three words that typically tend to co-occur with each of Schwartz's Value Survey's 10 categories of values (see Schwartz, 1992). The lexicon was shown to be valid, with increases in their use in American newspapers during expected times across history (e.g., the words *power, strength,* and *control* to represent the Power value peaked in their collective occurrence in American newspapers during World War II and were highly correlated with times of high military participation). Their study showed that lexicons of personal concerns can be used to examine the context in which those concerns are likely to be expressed—for example, during challenge or prosperity.

Kramer (2010) used a dictionary-based system to assess gross national happiness across America in 100 million Facebook users. Kramer used a previously validated set of emotion dictionary terms from Linguistic Inquiry and Word Count (Pennebaker, Booth, & Francis, 2007). By graphing a standardized metric of the difference in positive and negative emotion word use in status updates across time, he found that Americans were more positive on national holidays (e.g., Christmas, Thanksgiving) and on the culturally most celebrated day of the week, Friday. Kramer further found that Americans were the least positive on days of national tragedy (e.g., the day Michael Jackson died) and on Mondays. In other words, the dictionary-based metric was found to be a valid indicator of happiness as a function of the cultural context.

Inductive Approaches

The approaches discussed earlier allow for known constructs or researcher-defined search terms to be assessed in a deductive manner. However, to assess participant-defined search terms, one can use an inductive approach. For example, Chung and Pennebaker (2008) used a factor analytic strategy called the *meaning extraction method* (MEM) to determine how groups of words commonly clustered in self-descriptions without predefined or potentially biased coding schemes or dictionaries. They analyzed 1,165 writing assignments from introductory psychology students at a large American university who were asked to describe their personality. A principal components analysis on the use of the most frequently occurring content words (i.e., nouns, regular verbs, adjectives, and some adverbs) in the self-descriptions produced a nine-component solution. Some dimensions were unipolar (e.g., negativity, wherein loaded items were mostly negatively valenced adjectives such as *mad, hurt, bad, sad*); others were dimensional in that semantically opposite words clustered together (e.g., sociability, wherein terms such as *shy, outgoing, reserved,* and *loud* all loaded in the same direction).

The components exhibited modest reliability across different types of writing samples and were correlated with self-reports and behaviors consistent with the dimensions. For example, the sociability component was mentioned more by introverts than by extraverts. It may be that extraverts assumed a level of sociability and thus focused on ways of relating rather than on socializing itself. Indeed, extraverts tended to score higher on the fitting-in component (e.g., *interesting, funny, crazy, cool*). Introverts, however, were more focused on whether or not they socialized. The MEM captured the shared dimensions along which people think; the MEM was able to capture how people were commonly construing their personal concerns.

Several studies have shown the MEM to be a promising approach in examining personal concerns across cultures. Ramírez-Esparza, Chung, Sierra-Otero, and Pennebaker (2012) extended the MEM to compare Mexicans' self-descriptions in Spanish with Americans' self-descriptions in English. They found comparable components in the Mexican sample as in the American sample. Furthermore, they found culture-specific components in how people construed their personal concerns. For example, a component termed *sympatia* (*affectionate, honest, noble, tolerant*) was unique to the Mexican sample.

Kramer and Chung (2011) used the MEM to compare personal concerns in status updates of four million Facebook users across America, Australia, Canada, and the United Kingdom. They found large similarities in how users in the various countries construed positive events, informal speech, and updates about school. In another analysis, they found a MEM component that indicated that when a person used words such as *arse, mate, pub,* and *England,* they tended not to use the words *mom, laundry, vacation,* and *Halloween.* Facebook users from the United States and Canada scored differently on this component than did users from Australia and the United Kingdom. Indeed, the latter tend not to use the words *mom, laundry,* or *vacation;* they would likely use the words *mum, wash,* or *holiday* in their place. Furthermore, Halloween is not as widely celebrated in Australia and the United Kingdom as in North America. In sum, the MEM was able to capture meaningful dimensions along which English-speaking cultures vary.

When applied to narrative texts, the MEM overcomes many problems in manual content analysis. Interrater reliability is not a concern because the themes are not based on subjective ratings; they are based on the co-occurrence of frequently used words in a corpus. This allows respondents to generate and define the categories or dimensions most salient to them for any given topic without the use of potentially biased researcher-defined schemes. For example, Pennebaker and Chung (2008) used the MEM to assess topics of concern in al-Qaeda's leaders over time. They found that particular topics peaked during times that reflected various regions, targets, or motivations in al-Qaeda's missions without having imposed a researcher-defined coding scheme.

From a personality perspective, the MEM assesses personal concerns, which is the level of personality at which one begins to know a person's motivations, interests, and values (McAdams, 1995). The word-based components reflect how people are structuring their worlds—how they are thinking about themselves and other salient topics of self-relevance. What distinguishes this approach from traditional self-report measures is that it is purely inductive; participants write whatever they think is relevant to their self and the computer simply calculates the degree to which their words form semantic clusters.

REGIONAL VARIATIONS IN PERSONAL CONCERNS: MEANING EXTRACTION METHOD APPLIED TO "THIS I BELIEVE"

In this section, we apply the MEM to the "This I Believe" (TIB) corpus to illustrate the extraction of personal concerns in open-ended text. The TIB project is based on a popular 1950s radio series originally hosted by Edward R. Murrow and was later associated with a National Public Radio program broadcast from 2005 to 2009 during which listeners were encouraged to write essays describing the personal beliefs that guide their lives. The TIB project (http://thisibelieve.org) continues to attract submissions from people around the world, some of which are selected to be read and broadcast through podcasts or individual public radio stations (Allison & Gediman, 2008). The essays are typically around 500 words in length and are open-ended and vary widely in topic and style.

We applied the MEM to semiautomatically extract belief topics from the TIB corpus. Next, we averaged the topic scores by state to describe patterns in belief topics across America. Finally, we assessed the validity of the belief topics by correlating topic scores averaged by state to statistics from national surveys and experimental psychology surveys. From this analysis, we were able to more closely examine patterns in belief topics across America as a function of geographical variations in diversity, health, personality, performance, politics, wealth, social orientation, and well-being.

The TIB producers provided us with the entire TIB corpus as of November 2008, which comprised 37,592 anonymous essays, along with demographic information on the respondents. To be included in our final sample, essays had to be written in English, consist of more than 100 words, and be written by authors who identified themselves as living in the United States. The final sample was based on 36,986 essays.

Over 17 million words were written, with an average of 473 words per essay ($SD = 143$). Thirty-four percent of the respondents in the sample were male, 48.5% were female, and 17.5% did not indicate their sex. The TIB project did not collect information on exact age. Instead, 98.9% of the respondents indicated their age from a drop-down menu. Over half of the sample was 30 years or younger. The proportion of respondents per state reflected the actual proportion of the American population in 2008 (United States Census Bureau, 2010).

State-level statistics were acquired from a variety of sources, largely from the United States Census Bureau's American Community Survey 1-year estimates for 2004. The state-level statistics reflected a wide range of demographic information (Florida, 2002; United States Census Bureau, 2004, 2010), health and economic data (Centers for Disease Control and Prevention, 2003; Putnam, 2000; United States Census Bureau, 2004), and other cultural and behavioral measures (Cinema Treasures, 2006; National Restaurant Association, 2004; United States Census Bureau, 2004; United States Patent and Trademark Office, 2003; see also http://www.uselectionatlas.org). In addition, state-level psychological traits (e.g., BFI) that had been included in previous studies of regional variations in psychology (Rentfrow et al., 2008) were analyzed along with other survey information from http://www.statemaster.com, a repository of state-level statistics from national surveys.

For the extraction of belief topics, the MEM was applied to the essays. First, we determined the most commonly used content words (used in at least 3% of all texts) and any variant of the root form of those words—for example, *happy* included *happiness, happier, happiest,* and so forth—resulting in a total of 519 content words. Next, the occurrence of each of the most common words in each essay was assessed, resulting in a 519 word × 36,986 essay matrix. A principal components analysis with varimax rotation was then computed on the matrix. Our analyses were limited to the extraction of 20 components, accounting for a total of 11.6% of the total variance.

The regression-based component scores of the MEM were correlated with state-level indices, controlling for the sex ratio of the sample. Partial correlations with *p* values less than or equal to .01 were considered significant.

Dimensions of Personal Concerns

The MEM results produced coherent clusters of words. For example, the first component included words such as *car, drive, road, walk, head, window, pull, door, street,* and *air.* This component was labeled *travel* because the terms, when considered together, all related to sensory experiences and objects associated with travel, possibly short walks, local commutes, or road trips rather than foreign holidays. All words were loaded positively on the component, meaning that the words tended to be used together within and across texts. The marriage component indicated that words such as *husband, marriage, daughter, wife, woman, month, son,* and *baby* tended to co-occur within and across texts. With one minor exception, all words within a component tended to load in the same direction.

From a qualitative glance at Table 10.1, it is apparent that there were several broad, overlapping themes when people wrote about their beliefs:

TABLE 10.1
Meaning Extraction Method–Derived Components and Words With Large Loadings on Each Component

Component	Words with large component loadings
Travel	car, drive, road, walk, head, window, pull, door, street, air
Individual in society	individual, society, personal, action, social, result
Decision	think, bad, happen, want, people, make, wrong, know, tell, friend
America	America, country, united, nation, government, war, state, political
Existential	universe, earth, human, planet, science, create, exist, natural, space
Family of origin	child, parent, dad, grow, old, mom, young, family, sister, brother
Education	school, class, student, high, college, grade, education, teach, study
Emotions	pain, tears, heart, cry, fear, hurt, love, trust, feel, emotional
Achievement	goal, achieve, succeed, accomplish, dream, hard, work, reach
Blessings	smile, joy, moment, gift, laugh, day, love, memory, happy, mom
Daily events	sleep, bed, night, dinner, morning, eat, wake, hour, room
Religion	god, church, Christmas, Jesus, religion, faith, Sunday, heaven, spirit
Health concerns	hospital, doctor, cancer, disease, dead, health, sick, pain, suffering
Narrative	read, write, ask, word, book, question, speak, answer, tell
Sports	team, game, sports, play, win, field, feet, practice, running
Money	money, pay, job, work, food, buy, need, care, help
Race	color, skin, white, black, wear, hair, clothes, blue, look
Music	music, song, listen, dance, express, sound, emotional, play, hear
Community	friend, families, meet, share, relationship, visit, group
Marriage and family	husband, marriage, daughter, wife, woman, month, son, baby, learn

Note. Words listed have loadings greater than .20.

experiences and assumptions about beliefs, cognitive and affective evaluations, and belief topics. When people expressed their beliefs, they tended to mention experiences or assumptions about how beliefs are formed, such as travel, decisions, family of origin, emotions, blessings, daily events, and narrative. Some of these components could also be characterized as cognitive and affective evaluations—for example, as decisions, emotions, achievement, blessings, and narrative.

Other components resembled values in self-report questionnaires and in MEM-derived self-schemas from narrative corpora. Several of the components could reasonably be categorized in at least one or more categories regarding relationships (i.e., family of origin, marriage and family), achievement (i.e., education, achievement, money), spirituality (i.e., existential, religion), community (i.e., America, race, community), politics (i.e., individual in society, America), self-direction (i.e., individual in society, decision, achievement), leisure (i.e., sports, music), and health concerns (i.e., health, emotion).

Regional Variations in Personal Concerns and State-Level Indicators

To assess the content validity of the extracted themes, regression-based component scores were computed for each essay, averaged by state, and correlated with secondary state-level statistics, controlling for the sex ratio of the sample (see Table 10.2). Recall that there were no hypotheses about the direction of relationships between MEM-derived belief topics and state-level indicators. Instead, it was expected that belief topics would be mentioned in an essay if that state presented a context in which particular beliefs were challenged or if the state provided other affordances for that belief to become salient. So, for example, there were no predictions about whether health concerns would be mentioned in a particularly healthy or particularly diseased state—we simply expected mentions of health in the essays to have a significant correlation with health indicators.

Individuals can each hold multiple personal concerns, but some personal concerns may be more salient given the conditions of a particular time and place. For example, it is known that there are strong regional differences in political ideology, religion, health, and social capital. Thus, similarly themed MEM-derived personal concerns such as individual in society, religion, health concerns, emotions, and community might also show regional differences. It is less clear that there would be regional differences in state-level indicators for those concerns that may be more common across states, such as travel, decision, narrative, and so forth. Thus, although 20 MEM components were extracted, for the sake of clarity and brevity the presentation of the results focuses on several value-oriented concerns (individual in society, health, emotions, religion, and community), as opposed to the MEM-derived themes that resemble assumptions, experiences, or evaluations in how beliefs might be formed. Overall, the emergent patterns revealed content validity for the MEM themes.

To develop a sense of how the themes were distributed geographically across states, we mapped the mean state-level theme scores. As can be seen in Figure 10.1, there was considerable variation for each theme, with some showing clearer patterns of geographic clustering than others. For example, the map in Panel A shows that personal concerns relating to individualism were more pronounced in states on the East Coast and

TABLE 10.2
Partial Correlations Between State-Level Personal Concerns
and Social Indicators Controlling for Sex Ratio

| Social indicators | State-level personal concerns | | | | | |
	Individual in society	Health concerns	America	Emotions	Religion	Community
Demographics						
White[a]	.04	−.26	−.22	−.12	−.10	.07
Separated[b]	.07	.33†	.37*	.18	.25	.01
Widowed[b]	.08	.40*	.18	−.16	.29†	.01
Divorced[b]	−.23	.21	.27	.21	.10	−.33†
Married household[b]	−.06	−.54**	−.46**	−.06	−.17	.05
% Foreign born[b]	.27	.05	.28	.19	−.28	−.03
% Gay[c]	.24	.21	.50**	.45**	−.21	−.12
Human capital						
Poverty[b]	−.42*	.27	.18	−.02	.27	−.15
Bachelor's degree[b]	.52**	−.18	.06	.28	−.23	.28
Patents[d]	.39*	−.13	.02	.23	−.25	.13
Health and well–being						
Excellent health[e]	.31†	−.30†	.03	.34†	−.21	.26*
Well–being[f]	.27	−.32†	−.15	.26	−.30†	.31†
Life expectancy[g]	.31†	−.43*	−.19	.06	−.46**	.11
Political orientation						
Voted for McCain[h]	−.49**	−.08	−.31†	−.23	.34†	.03
Voted for Obama[h]	.49**	.11	.31†	.23	−.30†	−.04
Social involvement						
Commute alone[b]	−.22	.18	−.10	−.06	.42*	−.24
Commute by bus or train[b]	.25	.08	.19	.06	−.28	.20
Bars & restaurants[i]	.46**	−.05	.09	.06	−.18	.43*
Church attendance[b]	−.50**	−.05	−.38*	−.39*	.42*	−.03
Social capital[j]	.21	−.45**	−.36*	−.15	−.23	.20
Personality						
Extraversion[k]	−.23	−.05	−.56**	−.50**	−.07	.08
Agreeableness[k]	−.31†	−.22	−.53**	−.29†	.26	.00
Conscientiousness[k]	−.26	−.16	−.42*	−.18	.34†	−.25
Neuroticism[k]	.16	.46**	.44*	.14	.06	.10
Openness[k]	.29†	−.02	.37*	.40*	−.09	−.12

Note. Cells indicated partial correlations (controlling for sex ratio of the sample).
[a]United States Census Bureau (2010) reports on year 2008. [b]United States Census Bureau (2004) American Community Survey, 1-year estimate. [c]Florida (2002). [d]United States Patent and Trademark Office (2003). [e]Centers for Disease Control and Prevention (2002). [f]Gallup-Healthways Well-Being Index (2000). [g]United States Census Bureau (2000). [h]http://www.uselectionatlas.org. [i]National Restaurant Association (2004). [j]Putnam (2000). [k]Rentfrow, Gosling, and Potter (2008)
†$p \leq .05$. *$p \leq .01$. **$p \leq .001$.

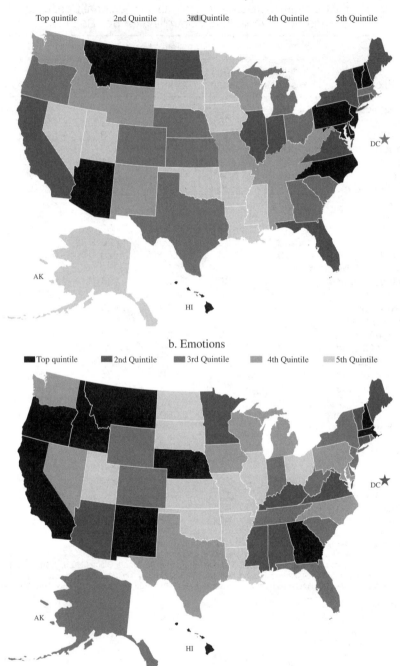

Figure 10.1. Use of the components across the United States. For each component, mean regression-based component scores were computed for each state. The state maps were colored according to the mean regression-based component scores, with darker colors representing greater use of the component in essays from that state.

(*continues*)

c. Religion

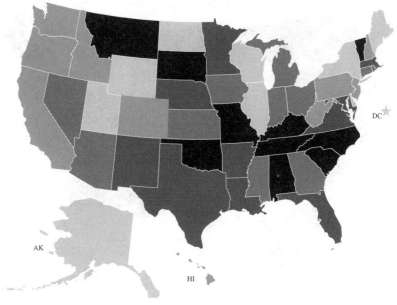

d. Health concerns

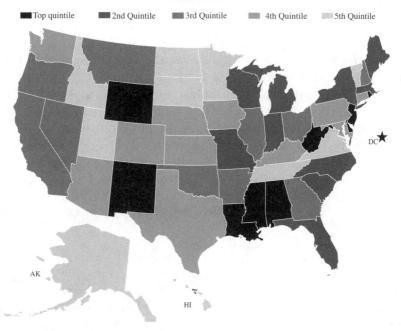

Figure 10.1. (Continued)

e. Community

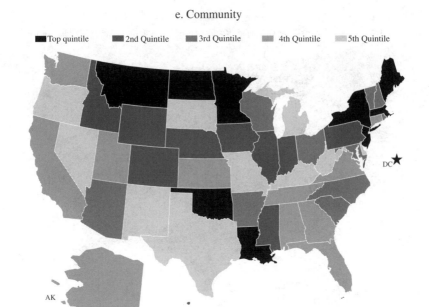

Figure 10.1. (Continued)

parts of the West compared with the central states. The map in Panel B indicates that themes relating to Emotion were more prominent in the West and Southeast than in the middle states. The map in Panel C shows more prominence for the Religions theme in the Bible Belt region than in the Northeast and West. Health Concerns, shown in Panel D, appear to be greater in the Deep South and Midwest compared with the Great Plains. And the map displayed in Panel E indicates that the Community theme was generally more prominent in the North Central and Northeastern states than it was in the South.

Individual in Society

Writing about individual in society (*individual, society, personal, action, positive, social, result, negative, view, effect*) was correlated with state-level behaviors and outcomes characteristic of *self-direction*, defined as "independent thought and action-choosing, creating, exploring" in Bardi and Schwartz (2003, p. 1208). For example, states whose inhabitants tended to write about Individual in Society had more patents per capita, a higher proportion of residents with a bachelor's degree, less poverty, and more bars and restaurants per capita. Furthermore, there were trends suggesting that states with inhabitants who wrote about this component had lower state levels of Agreeableness ($p = .03$) and higher state levels of Openness ($p = .05$).

This component was significantly more likely to be mentioned in essays from states with more votes for Obama than for McCain in the 2008 presidential elections. Indeed, liberals generally have a personality profile that is characterized by self-direction more than do conservatives, who are generally more concerned with order and convention (Carney, Jost, Gosling, & Potter, 2008; see also Rentfrow, Jost, Gosling, & Potter, 2009). Note also that this component was negatively associated with the proportion of residents who reported taking their children to religious services weekly.

Health Concerns

Writing about health (*hospital, doctor, cancer, disease, dead, health, sick, pain, suffering*) was a bidirectional construct along which health and illness were considered together. Indeed, health is typically taken for granted until people experience a major illness diagnosis or other health threat to themselves or those around them (Petrie & Weinman, 1997). Thus, the relationships with state-level indicators suggest that when health is challenged, this construct is more likely to be called to one's attention; life expectancy and social capital were significantly lower in states where residents wrote about health.

Consistent with research showing that neurotic people tend to perceive and experience greater physical symptoms and illness (Ebert, Tucker, & Roth, 2002), this component was significantly associated with higher state levels of Neuroticism. Consistent with research showing that married people enjoy greater health benefits and that widowed people experience greater distress (Cramer, 1993; Graham, Christian, & Kiecolt-Glaser, 2006), this component was significantly negatively associated with the proportion of residents in married couple households and positively associated with the proportion of widowed residents.

Emotions

Consistent with emotions as inner experiences that are generally healthy to express and to talk about (Pennebaker, 1997), the emotions component (*pain, tears, heart, cry, fear, hurt, love, trust, feel, emotional*) was significantly more likely to be mentioned in states with higher state levels of introversion and higher Openness. A trend for self-reported health ($p = .02$) was in the expected direction. Emotions were also mentioned significantly more in essays from states that had a higher proportion of gays and lower church attendance.

Religion

States whose inhabitants wrote about religion (*god, church, Christmas, Jesus, religion, faith, Sunday, heaven, spirit*) tended to be concentrated in the southern United States in a region informally called the Bible Belt for its high proportion of devout socially conservative evangelical Protestants (Mencken, 1947; see Figure 10.1c). The religion component was significantly associated with a greater proportion of parents reporting taking their children to religious services weekly. Recall that the significance level was set at $p < .01$. Given this, the relationships between this component and state levels of Agreeableness ($p = .08$) and Conscientiousness ($p = .02$) were not significant, although the pattern of effects is of interest because most religions preach virtues such as courage, justice, humanity, temperance, wisdom, and transcendence (Dahlsgaard, Peterson, & Seligman, 2005). Also consistent with the relationship between religion and cultural conservatism (Duriez, 2003) is the trend for religion to be mentioned more in essays from states that voted for McCain ($p = .02$) and less in states that voted for Obama ($p = .04$).

Interestingly, religion tended to be mentioned in essays from states that were not faring well on a number of measures. For example, the religion component was higher in states that had a lower life expectancy and in states with more people who commuted alone. There were also nonsignificant effects for more widows and widowers ($p = .05$) and lower well-being ($p = .04$).

Community

Writing about community (*friend, families, meet, share, relationship, visit, group*) was more common in states with the availability of meeting venues (i.e., more eating and drinking venues per capita) and the type of health status conducive to getting out more frequently (more residents reporting excellent health and a trend for greater well-being, $p = .03$).

Conclusions and Future Directions

The MEM-derived values from "This I Believe" narrative essays were shown to be associated with state-level social indicators in expected ways. The taxonomy of values in the current study could be used to develop questionnaires of values (for an example, see Stankov, Higgins, Saucier, & Knezevic, 2010) or to develop a dictionary to assess values in other texts, such as newspapers and blogs, or in speeches and documents by political, religious, or other social or cultural groups. Another strategy would be to conduct a new MEM analysis on other communications or cultural products to assess regional differences in personal concerns for a more specialized topic or forum. Yet another strategy would be to use the MEM to make comparisons of cultural products across countries and languages. The MEM requires translation only at the end of all analyses and so does not involve the translation of questionnaire items (see Pennebaker, 2011; Ramírez-Esparza et al., 2012; Wolf, Chung, & Kordy, 2010a; 2010b).

The current project indicates that personal concerns tend to be salient when in a context where they may be challenged. Thus, future research might apply text analytic techniques to text produced in contexts during social or political strife, uprisings, or cultural movements—for example, in the social media surrounding shared upheavals, during elections for a given region, or in the aftermath of widespread disasters. The findings from the current study support the notion that the MEM captures how people in particular contexts are thinking, perceiving, or behaving as a function of what is going on in the culture.

Today, there are many reliable methods for deductively and inductively exploring thematic and stylistic content in natural language texts (see McCarthy & Boonthum, 2012). Topic modeling methods, including the MEM, latent semantic analysis (Foltz, 1996), and latent Dirichlet allocation (Blei, Ng, & Jordan, 2003) have many applications, including indexing text themes, building search engines, disambiguating word meaning, identifying authorship, and classifying documents by topic (Griffiths, Steyvers, & Tenenbaum, 2007). Recent topic modeling applications such as the MEM have been applied to understand personality, clinical, cultural, and forensic constructs using a series of simple, user-friendly, Windows-based programs.

Overall, the regional clustering of TIB themes observed in this project can serve as a barometer that captures the concerns and values of people in certain parts of the country. Instead of relying solely on public opinion surveys and political polls, which assess people's views about a defined subject, open-ended natural language sources such as the TIB essays provide valuable information about what is on the minds of people throughout the country. The fact that people who live in the same region share the same values and concerns offers strong evidence for the notion that place matters—where we live affects our lives and what is important to us. Given the promise of new language-analysis technologies—together with large geographically dispersed text sources from Internet-based data collection methods and digitized cultural products—we encourage our colleagues to find values in words in exploring the geography of psychology.

REFERENCES

Allison, J., & Gediman, D. (2008). *This I believe II*. Baltimore, MD: Holt.

Allport, G. W., & Vernon, P. E. (1931). *A study of values*. Oxford, England: Houghton Mifflin.

Bardi, A., Calogero, R. M., & Mullen, B. (2008). A new archival approach to the study of values and value–behavior relations: Validation of the value lexicon. *Journal of Applied Psychology, 93*, 483–497. doi:10.1037/0021-9010.93.3.483

Bardi, A., & Schwartz, S. H. (2003). Values and behavior: Strength and structure of relations. *Personality and Social Psychology Bulletin, 29*, 1207–1220. doi:10.1177/0146167203254602

Blei, D. M., Ng, A. Y., & Jordan, M. I. (2003). Latent Dirichlet allocation. *Journal of Machine Learning Research, 3*, 993–1022. doi:10.1162/jmlr.2003.3.4-5.993

Bruner, J. (1992). The narrative construction of reality. In H. Beilin & P. B. Pufall (Eds.), *Piaget's theory: Prospects and possibilities* (pp. 229–248). Hillsdale, NJ: Erlbaum.

Campbell, W. K., & Gentile, W. (2012, January). *Cultural changes in pronoun usage and individualistic phrases: A culturomic analysis*. Paper presented at the meeting of the Society for Personality and Social Psychology, San Diego, CA.

Carney, D. R., Jost, J. T., Gosling, S. D., & Potter, J. (2008). The secret lives of liberals and conservatives: Personality profiles, interaction styles, and the things they leave behind. *Political Psychology, 29*, 807–840. doi:10.1111/j.1467-9221.2008.00668.x

Centers for Disease Control and Prevention. (2002). *National Health Interview Survey (NHIS) Public Use Data Release NHIS Survey Description, 2002*. Retrieved from http://www.cdc.gov/nchs/nhis.htm

Centers for Disease Control and Prevention. (2003). *National Survey of Children's Health*. Retrieved from http://www.cdc.gov/nchs/slaits/nsch.htm#2003nsch

Chung, C. K., & Pennebaker, J. W. (2008). Revealing dimensions of thinking in open-ended self-descriptions: An automated meaning extraction method for natural language. *Journal of Research in Personality, 42*(1), 96–132. doi:10.1016/j.jrp.2007.04.006

Cinema Treasures. (2006). *Classic movie theaters and drive-ins (per capita) by state*. Retrieved from http://www.StateMaster.com/graph/lif_cla_mov_the_and_dri_percap-theaters-drive-ins-per-capita

Claeys, B., de Boeck, P., van den Bosch, W., Biesmans, R., & Bohrer, A. (1985). A comparison of one free-format and two fixed-format self-report personality assessment methods. *Journal of Personality and Social Psychology, 49*, 1028–1039. doi:10.1037/0022-3514.49.4.1028

Cox, W., & Klinger, E. (2004). Measuring motivation: The Motivational Structure Questionnaire and Personal Concerns Inventory. In W. Cox & E. Klinger

(Eds.), *Handbook of motivational counseling: Concepts, approaches, and assessment* (pp. 141–174). New York, NY: Wiley.

Cramer, D. (1993). Living alone, marital status, gender and health. *Journal of Community & Applied Social Psychology, 3*(1), 1–15. doi:10.1002/casp.2450030102

Dahlsgaard, K., Peterson, C., & Seligman, M. P. (2005). Shared virtue: The convergence of valued human strengths across culture and history. *Review of General Psychology, 9*, 203–213. doi:10.1037/1089-2680.9.3.203

DeWall, C., Pond, R. R., Campbell, W., & Twenge, J. M. (2011). Tuning in to psychological change: Linguistic markers of psychological traits and emotions over time in popular U.S. song lyrics. *Psychology of Aesthetics, Creativity, and the Arts, 5*, 200–207. doi:10.1037/a0023195

Duriez, B. (2003). Religiosity and conservatism revisited: Relating a new religiosity measure to the two main conservative political ideologies. *Psychological Reports, 92*, 533–539. doi:10.2466/pr0.2003.92.2.533

Ebert, S. A., Tucker, D. C., & Roth, D. L. (2002). Psychological resistance factors as predictors of general health status and physical symptom reporting. *Psychology, Health & Medicine, 7*, 363–375. doi:10.1080/13548500220139449

Emmons, R. A. (1992). The personal striving approach to personality. In L. A. Pervin (Ed.), *Goal concepts in personality and social psychology* (pp. 98–126). Hillsdale, NJ: Erlbaum.

Florida, R. (2002). *The rise of the creative class: And how it's transforming work, leisure, community and everyday life.* New York, NY: Perseus.

Foltz, P. W. (1996). Latent semantic analysis for text-based research. *Behavior Research Methods, Instruments & Computers, 28*, 197–202. doi:10.3758/BF03204765

Fransella, F., Bell, R., & Bannister, D. (2004). *A manual for Repertory Grid Technique* (2nd ed.). Chichester, England: Wiley.

Freud, S. (1914). Errinern, Wiederholen und Durcharbeiten (Weitere Ratschläge zur Technik der Psychoanalyse, II) [Remembering, repeating and working-through]. *Psychoanalyse: Klinik und Kulturkritik, 2*, 485–491.

Gallup-Healthways Well-Being Index. (2008). Retrieved from http://www.well-being index.com

Graham, J. E., Christian, L. M., & Kiecolt-Glaser, J. K. (2006). Marriage, health, and immune function. In S. H. Beach, M. Z. Wamboldt, N. J. Kaslow, R. E. Heyman, M. B. First, L. G. Underwood, & D. Reiss (Eds.), *Relational processes and DSM–V: Neuroscience, assessment, prevention, and treatment* (pp. 61–76). Washington, DC: American Psychiatric Association.

Griffiths, T. L., Steyvers, M., & Tenenbaum, J. B. (2007). Topics in semantic representation. *Psychological Review, 114*, 211–244. doi:10.1037/0033-295X.114.2.211

Hofstede, G. H. (2001). *Culture's consequences: Comparing values, behaviors, institutions and organizations across nations* (2nd ed.). Thousand Oaks, CA: Sage.

John, O. P., & Srivastava, S. (1999). The Big Five trait taxonomy: History, measurement, and theoretical perspectives. In L. A. Pervin & O. P. John (Eds.), *Handbook of personality: Theory and research* (2nd ed., pp. 102–138). New York, NY: Guilford Press.

Kelly, G. A. (1955). *A theory of personality: The psychology of personal constructs*. New York, NY: Norton.

Kitayama, S., Conway, L., Pietromonaco, P. R., Park, H., & Plaut, V. C. (2010). Ethos of independence across regions in the United States: The production–adoption model of cultural change. *American Psychologist, 65*, 559–574. doi:10.1037/a0020277

Kramer, A. D. I. (2010). An unobtrusive behavioral model of "gross national happiness." *Proceedings of the 28th International Conference on Human Factors in Computing Systems*, 287–290. doi:10.1145/1753326.1753369

Kramer, A. D. I., & Chung, C. K. (2011). Dimensions of self-expression in Facebook status updates. *Proceedings of the Fifth International AAAI Conference on Weblogs and Social Media*, 169–176.

Lehman, D. R., Chiu, C., & Schaller, M. (2004). Psychology and culture. *Annual Review of Psychology, 55*, 689–714. doi:10.1146/annurev.psych.55.090902.141927

Little, B. R., & Chambers, N. C. (2004). Personal project pursuit: On human doings and well-beings. In W. Cox and E. Klinger (Eds.), *Handbook of motivational counseling: Concepts, approaches, and assessment* (pp. 65–82). New York, NY: Wiley.

McAdams, D. P. (1995). What do we know when we know a person? *Journal of Personality, 63*, 365–396. doi:10.1111/j.1467-6494.1995.tb00500.x

McAdams, D. P. (2006). *The redemptive self: Stories Americans live by*. New York, NY: Oxford University Press. doi:10.1093/acprof:oso/9780195176933.001.0001

McAdams, D. P., & Pals, J. L. (2006). A new Big Five: Fundamental principles for an integrative science of personality. *American Psychologist, 61*, 204–217. doi:10.1037/0003-066X.61.3.204

McCarthy, P. M., & Boonthum, C. (Eds.). (2012). *Applied natural language processing: Identification, investigation and resolution*. Hershey, PA: IGI Global. doi:10.4018/978-1-60960-741-8

McClelland, D. C. (1961). *The achieving society*. Princeton, NJ: Van Nostrand.

McClelland, D. C. (1985). *Human motivation*. Glenview, IL: Scott, Foresman.

McGuire, W. J., & Padawer-Singer, A. (1976). Trait salience in the spontaneous self-concept. *Journal of Personality and Social Psychology, 33*, 743–754. doi:10.1037/0022-3514.33.6.743

Mead, G. H. (1934). *Mind, self, and society from the standpoint of a social behaviorist*. Chicago, IL: University of Chicago Press.

Mencken, H. L. (1947). *The American language: An inquiry into the development of English in the United States*. New York, NY: Knopf.

Michel, J.-B., Shen, Y. K., Aiden, A. P., Veres, A., Gray, M. K., The Google Books Team, . . . Aiden, E. L. (2011, January 14). Quantitative analysis of culture using millions of digitized books. *Science, 331*(6014), 176–182. doi:10.1126/science.1199644

Morling, B., & Lamoreaux, M. (2008). Measuring culture outside the head: A meta-analysis of individualism-collectivism in cultural products. *Personality and Social Psychology Review, 12*, 199–221. doi:10.1177/1088868308318260

Murray, H. A. (1943). *Thematic Apperception Test.* Cambridge, MA: Harvard University Press.

National Restaurant Association. (2004). *Number of eating and drinking venues.* Retrieved from http://www.statemaster.com/graph/lif_res_percap-lifestyle-resturants-per-capita

Pennebaker, J. W. (1997). *Opening up: The healing power of expressing emotion.* New York, NY: Guilford Press.

Pennebaker, J. W. (2011). *The secret life of pronouns: What our words say about us.* New York, NY: Bloomsbury.

Pennebaker, J. W., Booth, R. J., & Francis, M. E. (2007). *Linguistic Inquiry and Word Count.* Retrieved from http://www.liwc.net

Pennebaker, J. W., & Chung, C. K. (2008). Computerized text analysis of al-Qaeda statements. In K. Krippendorff & M. Bock (Eds.), *A content analysis reader* (pp. 453–466). Thousand Oaks, CA: Sage.

Petrie, K. J., & Weinman, J. (Eds.). (1997). *Perceptions of health and illness: Current research and applications.* Amsterdam, Netherlands: Harwood Academic Publishers.

Plaut, V. C., Markus, H., & Lachman, M. E. (2002). Place matters: Consensual features and regional variation in American well-being and self. *Journal of Personality and Social Psychology, 83*, 160–184. doi:10.1037/0022-3514.83.1.160

Putnam, R. D. (2000). *Bowling alone: The collapse and revival of American community.* New York, NY: Touchstone Books/Simon & Schuster. doi:10.1145/358916.361990

Ramírez-Esparza, N., Chung, C. K., Sierra-Otero, G., & Pennebaker, J. W. (2012). Cross-cultural constructions of self-schemas: American and Mexican college students. *Journal of Cross-Cultural Psychology, 43*, 233–250. doi:10.1177/0022022110385231

Rentfrow, P. J., Gosling, S. D., & Potter, J. (2008). A theory of the emergence, persistence, and expression of geographic variation in psychological characteristics. *Perspectives on Psychological Science, 3*(5), 339–369. doi:10.1111/j.1745-6924.2008.00084.x

Rentfrow, P. J., Jost, J. T., Gosling, S. D., & Potter, J. (2009). Statewide differences in personality predict voting patterns in 1996–2004 U.S. Presidential elections. In J. T. Jost, A. C. Kay, & H. Thorisdottir (Eds.), *Social and psychological bases of ideology and system justification* (pp. 314–347). New York, NY: Oxford University Press. doi:10.1093/acprof:oso/9780195320916.003.013

Rokeach, M. (1973). *The nature of human values*. New York, NY: Free Press.

Schwartz, S. H. (1992). Universals in the content and structure of values: Theoretical advances and empirical tests in 20 countries. *Advances in Experimental Social Psychology, 25*, 1–65. doi:10.1016/S0065-2601(08)60281-6

Stankov, L., Higgins, D., Saucier, G., & Knezevic, G. (2010). Contemporary militant extremism: A linguistic approach to scale development. *Psychological Assessment, 22*, 246–258. doi:10.1037/a0017372

United States Census Bureau (2000). *Statistical abstracts of the United States*. Washington, DC: U.S. Department of Commerce.

United States Census Bureau. (2004). *American Community Survey 1-year estimates*. Retrieved from http://www.census.gov/acs/www/

United States Census Bureau. (2010). Population. In *Statistical abstracts of the United States* (pp. 1–77). Washington, DC: U.S. Department of Commerce.

United States Patent and Trademark Office. (2003). *2003 performance and accountability report*. Washington, DC: U.S. Department of Labor

White, M. (2007). *Maps of narrative practice*. New York, NY: Norton.

Wolf, M., Chung, C. K., & Kordy, H. (2010a). Inpatient treatment to online aftercare: E-mailing themes as a function of therapeutic outcomes. *Psychotherapy Research, 20*(1), 71–85. doi:10.1080/10503300903179799

Wolf, M., Chung, C. K., & Kordy, H. (2010b). MEM's search for meaning: A rejoinder. *Psychotherapy Research, 20*(1), 93–99. doi:10.1080/10503300903527393

III

PERSON × ENVIRONMENT INTERACTIONS

11

RESIDENTIAL MOBILITY AFFECTS SELF-CONCEPT, GROUP SUPPORT, AND HAPPINESS OF INDIVIDUALS AND COMMUNITIES

THOMAS TALHELM AND SHIGEHIRO OISHI

It is surprising that for the first century of the discipline of psychology, personality and social psychologists paid virtually no attention to how moving affects people (Oishi, 2010). Every country in the world has people who are moving, and almost everyone who has moved will tell you that it affected them. But until recently, personality and social psychology were silent on what should have been a rich research topic.[1]

In this chapter, we review evidence from the past 10 years showing that moving affects important and widely studied constructs, including altruism, self-concept, and well-being. We also show that moving can, paradoxically, affect people who have never moved in their life. That is because moving affects the mover and because living in a mobile community affects the people in that community, even the people who have not moved.

---

[1]Developmental and community psychologists have studied mobility for decades, but the questions they asked were different from those of social psychologists (see Adam, 2004, for a review).

http://dx.doi.org/10.1037/14272-012
Geographical Psychology: Exploring the Interaction of Environment and Behavior, P. J. Rentfrow (Editor)

TYPES OF EVIDENCE

Before reviewing the evidence, we need to understand how we can infer that moving is actually causal rather than a selection effect. There is a question at the heart of all mobility research: Does moving change people, or is it just a certain type of person who moves? Is it a cause or a selection effect? Without true experiments or forcing people to move, we are left with three different basic types of evidence.

Correlational Evidence

The simplest form of evidence is to ask whether movers are different from nonmovers and whether mobile communities are different from stable communities.[2] For example, we show later that movers have more individualistic self-concepts and that mobile communities donate less to local charities. The drawbacks of correlational research are clear. For example, maybe individualistic people are the ones who decide to move, so it is not moving that is causing them to be more individualistic.

There is already good evidence that adult moves have a selection effect. Adult movers tend to have different personalities. For instance, in a Finnish longitudinal study, Jokela, Elovainio, Kivimäki, and Keltikangas-Järvinen (2008) found that sociability at Year 0 of the study (Time 1) predicted whether adults moved between Year 0 and Year 9 of the study (10 years later), the number of times they moved between Year 0 and Year 9, and the distance they moved. Highly sociable participants who had been living in rural areas were much more likely to move elsewhere than highly sociable participants who had been living in urban areas in Year 0. Jokela (2009) also found that Extraversion and Openness to Experience predicted whether Americans moved within U.S. states (see also Silventoinen et al., 2008). Thus, there is evidence that adults who choose to move are more extraverted and open to experience on average than people who choose not to move—a selection effect. Therefore, readers should take the correlational findings we report here with a grain of caution.

Evidence From Natural Experiments

One way to try to get better evidence is to look for natural experiments. Psychologists have criticized the use of college student samples (e.g.,

---

[2]*Mobile communities* are communities that have higher rates of moving. Most of our studies are in the United States, so we use U.S. Census statistics, which report the percentage of households that have moved houses in the last 5 years. We use this to compare neighborhoods (census tracts), cities, and entire states. The U.S. Census reports percentages of residents who moved (a) states, (b) counties, and (c) houses. We used the percentage that moved houses as the broadest category.

Henrich, Heine, & Norenzayan, 2010), but college students are useful to study the effect of mobility because most of their childhood moves were not self-chosen (with some exceptions, such as the choice to go to boarding school). Instead, their parents or their parents' jobs often determined whether they moved.

There is some evidence that childhood moves are largely free from the Extraversion confound. In the Midlife in the U.S. (MIDUS) data set, Openness to Experience and Extraversion predicted future moves in adulthood—a straightforward selection effect (within-state moves between Time 1 and Time 2; Jokela, 2009). But in the same data set, neither Openness to Experience nor Extraversion was associated with the number of moves during childhood ($r = .02$ and $-.02$, respectively; Oishi & Schimmack, 2010).

Of course, parents probably give their children the experience of moving and genes for traits such as Extraversion. But the research suggests that genes are not a crucial confound either. Parent–children similarity in personality is small (e.g., $r = .07$ between father and offspring in Extraversion, $r = -.02$ between mother and offspring; Bratko & Marusic, 1997; see also Loehlin, 1992; Plomin, Coon, Carey, DeFries, & Fulker, 1991, for a similar result). Children of moving parents do not appear to differ substantially from children of nonmovers in terms of inherited personality. Thus, differences between college students who moved a lot as children and students who stayed put do not appear to be due to inherited personality.

However, other elements of family background (e.g., parents' occupation, marital status, and socioeconomic status [SES]) might still account for these differences. Future studies should look into this question. Childhood moves get around the selection effect, but there is also the possibility that moves in childhood are different from moves in adulthood. For example, perhaps children are worse at adjusting to moves because they have not fully developed self-regulation or socialization skills.

Research on whether adult moves raise or lower well-being has been mixed (Oishi, 2010). Some studies have found increases in well-being after adult moves (Kling, Seltzer, & Ryff, 1997; Smider, Essex, & Ryff, 1996), but another study found a decrease (Larson, Bell, & Young, 2004). One study looked at adults whose employers asked them to transfer and found that movers reported leading more interesting lives and having greater satisfaction with their family and marriage (Brett, 1982). However, they were less satisfied with their friendships, and they reported more shortness of breath and stomach upset. Although moving may make some American adults happier, there is evidence that Americans overestimate the importance of novelty and underestimate the social relationship consequences (Oishi, Whitchurch, Miao, Kurtz, & Park, 2009).

Evidence From Simulated Mobility Studies

Perhaps the only way to get around using correlations is to try to simulate moving in the laboratory. We cannot make people move, but we can try to create situations that are similar to moving. For example, we describe later an experiment where we had people simulate mobility and stability by creating (a) stable groups that worked together for three rounds of group decision-making tasks with the same members and (b) mobile groups that got shuffled between every round (Oishi, Rothman, et al., 2007). In other experiments, we had participants mentally simulate mobility and stability by asking them to imagine and write about a life of moving around a lot or staying put or about a typical day as a control (Lun, Oishi, & Tenney, 2012; Oishi, Miao, Koo, Kisling, & Ratliff, 2012). Of course, changing work groups is not the complete experience of moving—far from it. But it does mimic the most basic part of stable and mobile communities, and it allows for random assignment.

MOBILITY'S PARADOXICAL EFFECT: HAVING MOVED VERSUS LIVING IN A MOBILE COMMUNITY

There is also an important difference between individual mobility and community mobility. To understand this, take the example of SARS. If you get SARS individually, it will obviously affect your health, making you feverish, making you cough, and making you generally miserable. Now imagine you are SARS free, but half the people in your city have SARS. You will not get a fever, but you might get "cabin fever" from staying in your home and avoiding public places for weeks. At that point, SARS is affecting you at the community level, even though you as an individual are SARS free.

The same is true for mobility. Moving as a child can disrupt relationships and decrease well-being. But moving can make people suffer even if they have never moved. If the people around you are constantly moving, it becomes hard to hold onto stable relationships, decreasing your happiness. This could explain why mental illness is higher in mobile neighborhoods, even controlling for SES (Silver, Mulvey, & Swanson, 2002). Therefore, in this chapter, we distinguish between individual mobility and community mobility.

MOVERS HAVE MORE INDIVIDUALISTIC SELF-CONCEPTS

Early mobility researchers asked whether moving shapes the self-concept. In one study, participants listed personality traits (e.g., hardworking), groups they belonged to (e.g., Catholic church), and how central each was to their identity (Oishi, Lun, & Sherman, 2007). Movers were less likely to name a group identity, and those movers who did said it was less central to their identity. Movers were more likely than nonmovers to say that personality traits were central to their identity.

In sum, movers had more individualized self-concepts and fewer group identities. The most intuitive explanation is that people who move around constantly have a hard time getting deeply involved with church groups, schools, or sports teams. The most stable part of the self for movers is probably the thing that moves with them: their personality.

MOVERS IDENTIFY WITH GROUPS CONDITIONALLY

When movers do identify with groups, they identify more conditionally. In other words, they are more willing to disassociate themselves with unsuccessful groups or groups that fail to serve their needs. In one study, students at the University of Virginia read an article that ranked the school as the #1 public university in the nation (Oishi, Ishii, & Lun, 2009). Other students read an article saying that Virginia was no longer #1. Students who had not moved identified with the university regardless of the ranking. But mobile students identified with the university much less if it was no longer #1.

MOBILITY CAN EXPLAIN CULTURAL AND REGIONAL DIFFERENCES IN INDIVIDUALISM

Cultural Differences

Mobility has the potential to explain where some cultural differences come from (although it still raises the question of why some cultures are more mobile than others). To begin with, mobility could explain some East–West differences. It could explain why Americans have more individualistic identities, because the United States is one of the most mobile nations on the planet. The logic works like this: It is hard for movers to base their identities on groups because their constant moving severs their ties with those groups. Nonmovers face a different situation. They are a part of a single community for a long time, sometimes even their entire life. That means they can establish deep ties with groups and form their identities around those groups.

To test that idea, researchers took the previous finding that mobile individuals identify less with the group (Oishi, Lun, & Sherman, 2007) and applied it to cultures. They looked at one of the most mobile countries (the United States) and a much more stable but highly modernized country (Japan). They had college students read about a successful alum who went on to develop new AIDS drugs or an alum who went on to steal clients' money as a bank executive (Oishi, Ishii, & Lun, 2009). The American college students said the story was more relevant to their identity when the alum was successful than when the alum was a criminal. In effect, the American college students identified with the alum who reflected positively on them but not with the alum who reflected poorly on them. The Japanese students identified much less conditionally. To the Japanese participants, identifying with members of a group depended much less on whether that person was successful.

Regional Differences

There are so many differences between Japan and the United States that other variables—such as religion, income equality, or demographics—could explain why Americans identify with groups more conditionally. Finding regional differences explained by mobility within cultures that keep third variables more constant would be much more convincing.

A study in Minnesota looked at Minneapolis–St. Paul area residents who decided to buy "critical habitat" license plates (Oishi, Rothman, et al., 2007, Study 1). The license plates cost an extra $30, with the extra money going to support natural habitat in the state. Thus, buying the license plate is a way for people to pay to support the community. Of course, supporting the environment tends to be a liberal cause and wealthy people have more money to buy the plates, so the researchers controlled for politics and income (although liberals actually turned out to be less likely to buy the plate). In the end, people in mobile communities were less likely to buy the plate ($r = -.34$).

The same researchers also looked at whether mobile communities were more likely to be "fair weather fans" and stop supporting the home baseball team after it lost (Oishi, Rothman, et al., 2007, Study 2). By analyzing the win–loss record of U.S. and Japanese baseball teams going into home games, they found that mobile communities were less likely to show up to games when the team had a losing record (U.S.: Oishi, Rothman, et al., 2007; Japan: Oishi, Ishii, & Lun, 2009). The most mobile cities—such as Atlanta, Phoenix, and Miami—had attendance that correlated as highly as .48 with win–loss records. It is notable that a few of the most stable cities actually increased their attendance when the team had a losing record. These stable cities may have actually supported their team more when they most needed it. (That was the case with the "lovable losers," the Chicago Cubs, one of the longest running baseball teams in a relatively stable city. They are also the longest without a championship: 103 years.)

Experimental Evidence

Even though these correlational studies all provide corroborating evidence, they still fall short of true experimental evidence. Thus, researchers set up mobile and stable "communities" in the lab (Oishi, Rothman, et al., 2007, Study 3). Participants were assigned to groups of three to five and worked on four different tasks together. Some people were assigned to "mobile communities" that split up after each task and started working with a new group. Other people were assigned to "stable communities" and worked with the same group for all four tasks.

The first three tasks were filler tasks designed to let the stable community members get to know each other. After the filler tasks, everyone came to the final task, a game of Trivial Pursuit. To create a purely altruistic situation (i.e., to make helping others costly), the experimenters told everyone that whoever answered the most questions would win a gift certificate. In other words, although people were allowed to help each other, doing so would lower the helper's chances of winning the prize.

During the contest, a trained confederate sighed and wondered aloud about their questions. Would team members offer help? Fewer people in the mobile communities helped the clueless confederate than in the stable communities. People in the stable communities were more likely to help, even though it meant they were less likely to win themselves. This simulation gives us the only experimental evidence that mobility makes people less likely to help their community members.

These studies suggest that mobility causes regional differences. And it is notable that the studies show that mobility can explain regional differences between nearby neighborhoods (the license plate study), cities (the baseball studies), and cultures (the alum study). The evidence says that mobility can be toxic to community identity and support. Economists tend to like mobility because it helps the economy when people move to where the jobs are (Greenwood, 1985; Ritchey, 1976). But considering how harmful mobility can be to the community, policymakers might want to reconsider tax policies that subsidize Americans' moves and adjust policies so that they encourage people to stay in the same community.[3]

---

[3]The interest on a mortgage can be deducted from income in the United States. Because most people pay only the interest on their mortgage for the first 5 years or so (this depends in part on the structure of mortgage payment; conventional mortgages are structured such that payments go mostly toward the interest), staying in the same house over 5 years does not have much tax benefit. Thus, some people move to a new house to maximize tax benefits. In this sense, the current U.S. tax system favors movers.

CHILDHOOD MOVERS HAVE LOWER WELL-BEING—
UNLESS THEY ARE EXTRAVERTED

There is evidence that mobility affects another pillar of social psychology: happiness. Using data from over 7,000 participants from the MIDUS study, researchers found that people who had moved more when they were young were less happy when they were adults ($r = -.07$; Oishi & Schimmack, 2010). Considering that people typically move to pursue a better life (sometimes for a better life for the family, including their own children), the negative correlation is surprising.

Of course, a correlation of .07 is quite small. But a stronger correlation was obscured by Extraversion. To understand why Extraversion is central to how moves affect movers, it helps to start with *The Organization Man* (Whyte, 1956), a book that followed one of the most mobile groups of Americans in the 1950s. In 1950s America, big companies such as GE were sending their "organization men" from city to city, wherever the company needed them. Of course, it was hard for the families to deal with moving to a new city every couple of years. In his field study, Whyte (1956) observed that families that adjusted well to the moves tended to be outgoing enough to build a new social network in every new town they landed in. Whyte speculated that Extraversion was a buffer, allowing movers to adjust and thrive after the disruption of the moves (see Chapters 21–26, particularly Chapter 26, "The Outgoing Life").

Whyte's (1956) observation of organization men leads to an interesting prediction: Moving should only hurt introverts. Extraverts should be able to cope better with moving. And that is just what the MIDUS data showed (Oishi & Schimmack, 2010). With each successive move, introverts had lower well-being ($b = -.04$, $\beta = -.10$, $z = -6.16$, $p < .001$), but extraverts' well-being hardly budged ($b = -.01$, $\beta = -.02$, $z = -.86$, ns; see Figure 11.1). It is notable that introverted movers were actually more likely to die over the 10 years of the study. The most mobile introverts were about twice as likely to die during the study as the introverts who never moved in childhood. Extraverts were unaffected by childhood moves.

Another study supported the theory that childhood movers have lower well-being, except when they are extraverted (Oishi, Krochik, Roth, & Sherman, 2012). Introverted European American students who moved a lot as children had elevated cortisol (a stress hormone) in the afternoon and evening, compared with equally introverted students who had not moved in childhood. It is notable that mobility actually seemed to make European American extraverts slightly happier (Oishi, Krochik, et al., 2012).[4] The

---

[4] The Mobility × Extraversion interaction was not present among African American and Asian American students. That could be due to small sample sizes, or it could be that cultures differ in how they express Extraversion.

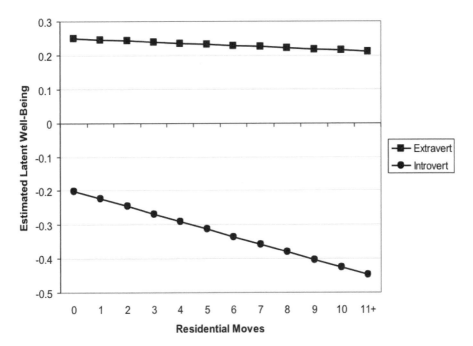

Figure 11.1. Childhood mobility and adulthood subjective well-being. The well-being measure is a latent score based on life satisfaction, psychological well-being, and affect balance. Adapted from "Residential Mobility, Well-Being, and Mortality," by S. Oishi and U. Schimmack, 2010, *Journal of Personality and Social Psychology, 98,* p. 986, Figure 2. Copyright 2010 by the American Psychological Association.

positive effect on extraverts was smaller than the negative effect on introverts, but the possibility that moving actually makes extraverts happier is intriguing. Being an extravert around the same old group of friends forever might make extraverts feel stifled and bored. If extraverts crave the stimulation of meeting new people, forcing them to stay in the same place might make them feel confined (see Jokela et al., 2008, for evidence in support of this).

Importantly, these two studies (Oishi & Schimmack, 2010; Oishi, Krochik, et al., 2012) looked at nonchosen moves in childhood and adolescence. To the extent that these participants did not have a say over the moves, childhood moves seem to have an undeniable effect on well-being in adulthood for introverted people, who have difficulty creating new social networks in new places. Adulthood moves are a different story. Adults often choose to move, so chances are they like the idea of moving and can cope with moving. There is already good longitudinal evidence that people who choose to move tend to be extraverts (Jokela et al., 2008), so it is not surprising that adulthood moves do not seem to decrease well-being (e.g., Kling et al., 1997). In short, adulthood moves do not make people unhappy, probably because they are often self-chosen. Childhood moves do seem to harm well-being, probably because they are not self-chosen.

DO MOBILE NEIGHBORHOODS MAKE PEOPLE UNHAPPY?

As we have argued, people do not have to move to be affected by moving. It is possible that living in a mobile community brings down residents' happiness, even for people who have not moved. Unfortunately, well-being researchers have not investigated this issue. Community psychologists and sociologists have looked at neighborhood mobility, but they have looked mostly at social relationships and mental disorders rather than positive types of well-being. For instance, Sampson (1988) studied local friendship ties and found that people living in a residentially stable neighborhood had more close friends in the neighborhood, controlling for several individual-level (e.g., SES, sex, marital status, having children) and neighborhood-level (e.g., crime rate, urbanization, and population density) variables. In other words, even if you are new to a neighborhood, you are more likely to create closer local friendships if the neighborhood is residentially stable. To the extent that close social ties are important predictors of subjective well-being (Diener & Seligman, 2002), there is an advantage to living in a stable neighborhood rather than in a mobile one.

As with the research on social ties, most of the evidence on mental health has shown that mobile communities have higher rates of psychological disorders. For example, a National Institute of Mental Health survey of more than 11,000 people in four U.S. cities found that people in mobile neighborhoods had higher rates of major depression, schizophrenia, and substance abuse (Silver et al., 2002). This was true even after controlling for individual age, sex, race, education, and income, as well as neighborhood-level disadvantage factors, such as unemployment rate and poverty rate. A study of neighborhoods in Winnipeg, Canada, found that people in stable neighborhoods had higher overall health (Farrell, Aubry, & Coulombe, 2004), although another Canadian study found no relationship (Randall, Kitchen, & Williams, 2008).

Other researchers have argued that stability is only good for people in good neighborhoods. A representative sample of Illinois residents found that stability was helpful in most neighborhoods but actually harmful in poor neighborhoods (Ross, Reynolds, & Geis, 2000). People in nonpoor, stable neighborhoods had lower depression and anxiety, and they felt less powerless and felt they had less fear and less neighborhood disorder. But people in poor, stable neighborhoods actually felt worse on those measures. The authors argued that stability in poor neighborhoods makes people feel "powerless to leave a dangerous place" (Ross et al., 2000, p. 581). Similarly, a study of neighborhoods in Detroit found that people in stable neighborhoods had lower rates of depression only if those neighborhoods had a decent proportion of middle-income families (Coombe, 2008). Thus, stability may actually be a bad thing if the neighborhood is struggling.

However, what this research is missing is that physical health and even mental health are not the same as happiness. As Seligman (2003) argued, measuring mental disorder is not the same as measuring happiness. Just because people lack mental disorders does not necessarily mean they are happy. Thus, it is still an open question as to whether mobility is related to happiness.

Most studies have looked at neighborhoods in the same city or state, which means we still do not have good large-scale data, and we do not know whether mobility over larger areas matters. Studies have shown that living in a mobile neighborhood or city matters, but what about living in a mobile state or even a mobile country? We present a new study here to fill two gaps in the prior research. First, it uses data from larger areas, U.S. states. Second, it uses a measure of positive psychological well-being, rather than negative well-being, such as mental illness.

STUDY: MOBILE STATES ARE HAPPIER— UNLESS THEY ARE INTROVERTED

On the basis of the mental health studies discussed previously, we would expect that mobile states should be less happy than stable states. The research comparing poor neighborhoods with nonpoor neighborhoods adds another condition: wealth (Ross et al., 2000). Social psychology studies add an important "if": Mobility hurts if states are introverted. To test these theories, we analyzed data from U.S. states on well-being, personality, mobility, and control demographics.

Well-Being Data

The well-being data came from a Gallup survey of 353,039 U.S. residents interviewed in 2008 (reported in Rentfrow, Mellander, & Florida, 2009). The data are weighted to be representative of the overall American population. We used the life evaluation score, which is made up of two items that asked people to evaluate their life from 0 (*the worst possible life*) to 10 (*the best possible life*), one for their current life and one for 5 years in the future. Gallup converted the scores so that they ranged from 0 to 100. We chose life evaluation rather than the health and work measures from that study because health and mobility has already been studied in depth and because we have no reason to suspect that work satisfaction would be related to our theory.

Personality Data

The personality data came from over 600,000 U.S. visitors to a personality website from December 1999 to January 2005 (data from Rentfrow, Gosling, & Potter, 2008; sample details described in Gosling, Vazire, Srivastava, & John, 2004). The sample was 80% White, which is about 8% higher than the national average. But, in general, the data are representative of the United States. For example, the percentage of respondents from each state correlated .98 with census percentages (for details on the sample, see Rentfrow et al., 2008).

Census Statistics

For demographics, we used data from the 2000 census. We chose 2000 because most of the participants took the personality test around that year. Also, our main 5-year measure of mobility was not yet available in the 2010 census at the time of this writing. For mobility, we used the percentage of residents who had changed residences in the previous 5 years (see Figure 11.2). The census also provided data on percentage of residents who had moved between counties and between states, but the results are virtually identical using any one of the measures. For demographic variables, we used median family income, percentage White, and percentage with a bachelor's degree or higher. All of the data in this study are state-level means. The District of Columbia could not be included because it did not have well-being data.

Results

Previous studies of individual childhood moves found a negative correlation between mobility and well-being (Oishi & Schimmack, 2010; Oishi, Krochik, et al., 2012). At the state level, however, mobile states were happier than stable states, $r(50) = .33, p = .02$ (Figure 11.3). This could be because state-level moves are mostly adult moves, and adult moves are mostly self-chosen. Of course, mobility could be confounded with income, education, and percentage of White residents. Indeed, states with higher income were happier ($r = .38$, $p = .007$), and states with more education were happier ($r = .53, p < .001$). Also, states with a lower percentage of White residents were happier ($r = -.53$, $p < .001$). Thus, if mobile states were also richer, more educated, and less White, then the correlation between the mobility and happiness of states could be

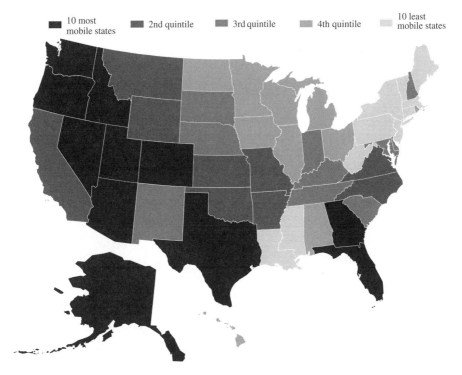

Figure 11.2. Residential mobility rates by state. Rates are U.S. 2000 census statistics for percentage of households that moved in the previous 5 years. This included long and short moves—within the same city to moves across the country. Rates ranged from 35% (Pennsylvania) to 57% (Nevada).

due to these third factors. However, mobility itself did not correlate significantly with income ($r = -.22, p = .13$), percentage White ($r = .01, p = .93$), or education ($r = -.07, p = .64$). Furthermore, the partial correlation controlling for income, percentage White, and education was actually stronger than the simple correlation $r(45) = .56, p < .001$. Thus, mobile states seem to be happier than stable states, and secondary variables (in particular, income and education) seemed to act as suppressor variables, slightly dampening the relationship between happiness and mobility.

Next we ran a regression with all Big Five personality traits and mobility as simultaneous predictors of the mean life evaluation of states. Neuroticism, $b = -3.32$ ($SE = 0.72$), $\beta = -.81$, $t(49) = -4.60$, $p < .001$, and Extraversion, $b = -1.62$ ($SE = 0.75$), $\beta = -.38$, $t(49) = -2.15$, $p = .04$, were the only significant predictors of state well-being. It is interesting that Extraversion correlated negatively with life satisfaction at the state level; this is the opposite of the common individual-level finding. We ran another multiple regression

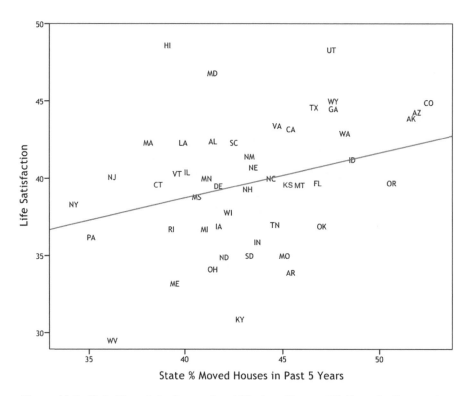

Figure 11.3. State life satisfaction and mobility ($r = .33$, $p = .02$). To make the graph easier to interpret, one outlier (Nevada) is not shown. It is included in all statistical results. The y-axis is a composite of two items that ask people to evaluate their life from 0 (*the worst possible life*) to 10 (*the best possible life*), one for their current life and one for 5 years in the future. Gallup converted the scores so that they range from 0 to 100.

predicting state well-being from Extraversion, Neuroticism, residential mobility, and two interaction terms (Extraversion × Mobility and Neuroticism × Mobility). Extraversion, Neuroticism, and residential mobility were standardized before forming the interaction terms.

Consistent with the individual-level findings (Oishi, Krochik, et al., 2012; Oishi & Schimmack, 2010), we found a significant interaction between Extraversion and residential mobility, $b = 1.58$ ($SE = .66$), $\beta = .28$, $t(44) = 2.41$, $p < .05$. In contrast, there was no interaction between Neuroticism and residential mobility, $b = -0.22$, ($SE = .47$), $\beta = -.06$, $t(44) = -0.46$, $p = .65$. Simple slope analyses revealed that mobility was marginally positively associated with life evaluation in extraverted states (1 *SD* above mean Extraversion), $b = 1.40$, $t = 1.61$, $p = .12$, whereas mobility was negatively associated with life evaluation among introverted states (1 *SD* below mean in Extraversion), $b = -1.76$, $t = -2.20$, $p < .05$.

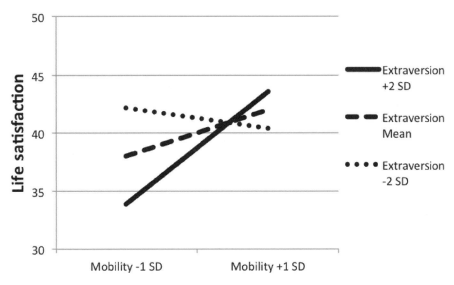

Figure 11.4. Interaction between state-level mobility and Extraversion. Extraverted states (solid line) seem to be happier with mobility. Introverted states (dotted line) seem to be less happy with mobility.

In other words, mobile states were less happy if they were introverted, and they were happier if they were extraverted (Figure 11.4). Extraversion moderated the association between residential mobility and subjective well-being (all at the state level). Just as residential mobility means different things for the well-being of extraverted and introverted individuals, mobility means different things for the well-being of extraverted and introverted U.S. states.

Because state-level Extraversion and Neuroticism could be associated with other factors such as median income, population size, education (percentage with a bachelor's degree), and racial composition (percentage White), we entered these state-level variables as controls in the multiple regression described earlier. The key interaction between Extraversion and residential mobility remained significant, $b = 0.96$ ($SE = 0.48$), $\beta = .17$, $t(40) = 1.99$, $p = .05$. Thus, the finding seems robust against typical confounding variables.

Some sociologists have shown that the effect of neighborhood mobility depends on whether the neighborhood is poor. The argument is that people living in impoverished neighborhoods are better off moving to new neighborhoods. There is some evidence in support of this idea (Ross et al., 2000). Our analysis, however, did not support the idea: There was no interaction between mobility and income, $b = -0.42$ ($SE = 0.60$), $\beta = -.10$, $t(49) = -0.70$, $p = .49$.

That is, the association between residential mobility and state well-being did not differ depending on the median income of the states. The discrepancy between our findings and those of Ross and colleagues (2000) could be because our study looked at life satisfaction rather than the negative indicators (anxiety and depression) that Ross and colleagues studied. This could also be because past studies looked at neighborhoods, whereas our study looked at entire states. It is possible that stability only makes people feel trapped by poverty at the smaller, neighborhood level. States are much larger, heterogeneous entities than neighborhoods. For example, even poor states should have wealthy pockets that ambitious movers can move to. That is not true at the neighborhood level. However, this is speculation; our data cannot tease apart the difference between the effects of neighborhoods and states.

SUMMARY

In less than 10 years, researchers have shown that movers are different from stable people and that mobile places are different from stable places on several of the most commonly studied variables in social psychology. Movers have more individualistic self-concepts, support the local community less, identify more conditionally with groups, and have lower well-being (if those moves are in their childhood, unless they are extraverted). Of course, as with any theory of culture, it is hard to pin down causality. The data gathered so far has suggested that mobility could in part cause the many behaviors it is associated with. For example, studies with college students are mostly based on moves that the students did not choose, which minimizes the self-selection confound (although it does not eliminate it). The few truly experimental studies showed that simulated mobility can cause people to behave differently (Lun et al., 2012; Oishi, Miao, et al., 2012; Oishi, Rothman, et al., 2007). More longitudinal studies could provide more insight on whether mobility precedes these effects.

Culture Bound?

Researchers have criticized psychologists for building universal theories of human nature on the basis of studies of Westerners (Henrich et al., 2010). Most of the studies here are from North America, but there is also preliminary evidence that the effects of mobility are not just a Western phenomenon. One study has replicated a Western finding in Japan, which psychologists often use to represent a culture at the opposite end of the individualism–collectivism spectrum from the United States (Oishi, Ishii, et al., 2009, Study 2). There is also recent evidence that movers think more analytically than nonmovers and that this is true in the United States, Japan, and China (Talhelm, Oishi, & Miao, 2013). Of course, it would be helpful to have studies in more diverse and understudied places—Africa and South America, for example.

Unanswered Questions

Because research on mobility is so new, researchers still have not tackled several important questions. For example, people move for very different reasons—divorce, a change of scenery, the military, seasonal farm work, for example. Do these different types of moves affect people's well-being differently? We do not know (but see Magdol & Bessel, 2003, for the effect of various moves on social support).

The geography of the country could also be important. Moves in a small country such as Switzerland would probably affect people's social ties less than would moves in the vast country of Russia. The same could be true for islands such as Japan and New Zealand. Whether mobility disrupts your family and friendships probably also depends on whether your country has a convenient transportation network. With new technology such as cell phones, it is now possible to maintain relationships beyond the physical boundaries of where we live (see Shklovski, 2007). These topics remain for researchers to consider as we start to examine questions about mobility.

Finally, the most fundamental unanswered questions are why the United States is such a mobile nation to begin with and why some American states are so much more mobile than other states. Only 38% of New Yorkers moved between 1995 and 2000, but that number reaches 63% in Nevada. Why? Historically, population growth in American states has been driven by economic opportunities and migration (Greenwood, 1985; Ritchey, 1976). States such as Nevada and Colorado attracted many newcomers because of the booming economy in the 1990s. States such as Arizona and Florida have attracted many retirees because of their pleasant climates and recreational opportunities.

The housing market is yet another factor that increased residential mobility in many U.S. states (e.g., Chan, 2001). Rising house prices made it a good idea for Americans to sell their old house and buy a more expensive house, sometimes several times in a row. But as the housing market declined over the past 5 years, residential mobility decreased. These recent changes in residential mobility suggest that economic opportunities and housing markets are two critical factors that drive residential mobility at the level of neighborhood, city, state, and nation. Thus, future work on mobility should take into account economic opportunities and housing markets.

Another possibility is that long-term economic and housing conditions shaped the American ethos (Oishi, 2010). The fact that the United States has mostly had abundant economic growth and improving housing markets for hundreds of years may have encouraged Americans to believe in the benefit of moving when opportunity knocks. Then, over time, this cultural ethos of high mobility might have become a collective reality, which Durkheim (1897/1951) said has "an existence of [its] own, *sui generis*" (p. 309). At this point, the mobility ethos could start exerting its influence by itself, independent of objective economic and housing markets. As with most socio–ecological factors, it is likely that objective economic and housing conditions have both direct and indirect effects (mediated through cultural norms and beliefs) on our feelings, thoughts, and behaviors (see Oishi & Graham, 2010, Figure 1).

In the world's emergent markets, such as Brazil, India, Turkey, and China, it is now possible to trace whether a bubbling economy and housing market increases residential mobility and whether the increased mobility will cause people to form a more individualistic conception of the self, conditional group identification, and a weaker desire to contribute to the community. Important questions such as these remain because social psychologists have only begun to investigate residential mobility. It is exciting to find this psychological stone unturned and figure out how the age-old act molds our minds—and how our minds mold our moves.

REFERENCES

Adam, E. K. (2004). Beyond quality: Parental and residential stability and children's adjustment. *Current Directions in Psychological Science, 13*, 210–213. doi:10.1111/j.0963-7214.2004.00310.x

Bratko, D., & Marusic, I. (1997). Family study of the big five personality dimensions. *Personality and Individual Differences, 23*, 365–369.

Brett, J. M. (1982). Job transfer and well-being. *Journal of Applied Psychology, 67*, 450–463. doi:10.1037/0021-9010.67.4.450

Chan, S. (2001). Spatial lock-in: Do falling house prices constrain residential mobility? *Journal of Urban Economics, 49*, 567–586. doi:10.1006/juec.2000.2205

Coombe, C. M. (2008). The effects of urban residential environments on mental well-being: A multilevel analysis of neighborhood stability, middle income composition and depression in Detroit. *Dissertation Abstracts International: Section B. Sciences and Engineering, 68*(10-B), 6613.

Diener, E., & Seligman, M. E. P. (2002). Very happy people. *Psychological Science, 13*, 81–84. doi:10.1111/1467-9280.00415

Durkheim, E. (1951). *Suicide: A study in sociology* (J. A. Spaulding & G. Simpson, Trans.). New York, NY: Free Press. (Original work published 1897)

Farrell, S. J., Aubry, T., & Coulombe, D. (2004). Neighborhoods and neighbors: Do they contribute to personal well-being? *Journal of Community Psychology, 32*(1), 9–25. doi:10.1002/jcop.10082

Gosling, S. D., Vazire, S., Srivastava, S., & John, O. P. (2004). Should we trust web-based studies? A comparative analysis of six preconceptions about Internet questionnaires. *American Psychologist, 59,* 93–104. doi:10.1037/0003-066X.59.2.93

Greenwood, M. J. (1985). Human migration: Theory, models, and empirical studies. *Journal of Regional Science, 25,* 521–544. doi:10.1111/j.1467-9787.1985.tb00321.x

Henrich, J., Heine, S. J., & Norenzayan, A. (2010). The weirdest people in the world? *Behavioral and Brain Sciences, 33,* 61–83. doi:10.1017/S0140525X0999152X

Jokela, M. (2009). Personality predicts migration within and between U.S. states. *Journal of Research in Personality, 43,* 79–83. doi:10.1016/ j.jrp.2008.09.005

Jokela, M., Elovainio, M., Kivimäki, M., & Keltikangas-Järvinen, L. (2008). Temperament and migration patterns in Finland. *Psychological Science, 19,* 831–837. doi:10.1111/j.1467-9280.2008.02164.x

Kling, K. C., Seltzer, M. M., & Ryff, C. D. (1997). Distinctive late-life challenges: Implications for coping and well-being. *Psychology and Aging, 12,* 288–295. doi:10.1037/0882-7974.12.2.288

Larson, A., Bell, M., & Young, A. F. (2004). Clarifying the relationships between health and residential mobility. *Social Science & Medicine, 59,* 2149–2160. doi:10.1016/j.socscimed.2004.03.015

Loehlin, J. C. (1992). *Genes and environment in personality development.* Newbury Park, CA: Sage.

Lun, J., Oishi, S., & Tenney, E. R. (2012). Residential mobility moderates preference for egalitarian versus loyal helpers. *Journal of Experimental Social Psychology, 48,* 291–297. doi:10.1016/j.jesp.2011.09.002

Magdol, L., & Bessel, D. R. (2003). Social capital, social currency, and portable assets: The impact of residential mobility on exchanges of social support. *Personal Relationships, 10,* 149–170. doi:10.1111/1475-6811.00043

Oishi, S. (2010). The psychology of residential mobility: Implications for the self, social relationships, and well-being. *Perspectives on Psychological Science, 5,* 5–21. doi:10.1177/1745691609356781

Oishi, S., & Graham, J. (2010). Social ecology: Lost and found in psychological science. *Perspectives on Psychological Science, 5,* 356–377. doi:10.1177/1745691610374588

Oishi, S., Ishii, K., & Lun, J. (2009). Residential mobility and conditionality of group identification. *Journal of Experimental Social Psychology, 45,* 913–919. doi:10.1016/j.jesp.2009.04.028

Oishi, S., Krochik, M., Roth, D., & Sherman, G. D. (2012). Residential mobility, personality, and well-being: An analysis of cortisol secretion. *Social Psychological and Personality Science, 3,* 153–161. doi:10.1177/1948550611412395

Oishi, S., Lun, J., & Sherman, G. D. (2007). Residential mobility, self-concept, and positive affect in social interactions. *Journal of Personality and Social Psychology, 93,* 131–141. doi:10.1037/0022-3514.93.1.131

Oishi, S., Miao, F., Koo, M., Kisling, J., & Ratliff, K. A. (2012). Residential mobility breeds familiarity-seeking. *Journal of Personality and Social Psychology, 102,* 149–162. doi:10.1037/a0024949

Oishi, S., Rothman, A. J., Snyder, M., Su, J., Zehm, K., Hertel, A. W., . . . Sherman, G. D. (2007). The socio-ecological model of pro-community action: The benefits of residential stability. *Journal of Personality and Social Psychology, 93,* 831–844. doi:10.1037/0022-3514.93.5.831

Oishi, S., & Schimmack, U. (2010). Residential mobility, well-being, and mortality. *Journal of Personality and Social Psychology, 98,* 980–994. doi:10.1037/a0019389

Oishi, S., Whitchurch, E., Miao, F. M., Kurtz, J., & Park, J. (2009). 'Would I be happier if I moved?' Retirement status and cultural variations in the anticipated and actual levels of happiness. *The Journal of Positive Psychology, 4,* 437–446. doi:10.1080/17439760903271033

Plomin, R., Coon, H., Carey, G., DeFries, J. C., & Fulker, D. W. (1991). Parent-offspring and sibling adoption analyses of parental ratings of temperament in infancy and childhood. *Journal of Personality, 59,* 705–732. doi:10.1111/j.1467-6494.1991.tb00928.x

Randall, J., Kitchen, P., & Williams, A. (2008). Mobility, perceptions of quality of life and neighbourhood stability in Saskatoon. *Social Indicators Research, 85,* 23–37. doi:10.1007/s11205-007-9126-2

Rentfrow, P. J., Gosling, S. D., & Potter, J. (2008). A theory of the emergence, persistence, and expression of geographic variation in psychological characteristics. *Perspectives on Psychological Science, 3,* 339–369. doi:10.1111/j.1745-6924.2008.00084.x

Rentfrow, P. J., Mellander, C., & Florida, R. (2009). Happy States of America: A state-level analysis of psychological, economic, and social well-being. *Journal of Research in Personality, 43,* 1073–1082. doi:10.1016/j.jrp.2009.08.005

Ritchey, P. N. (1976). Explanations of migration. *Annual Review of Sociology, 2,* 363–404. doi:10.1146/annurev.so.02.080176.002051

Ross, C. E., Reynolds, J. R., & Geis, K. J. (2000). The contingent meaning of neighborhood stability for residents' psychological well-being. *American Sociological Review, 65,* 581–597. doi:10.2307/2657384

Sampson, R. J. (1988). Local friendship ties and community attachment. *American Sociological Review, 53,* 766–779. doi:10.2307/2095822

Seligman, M. E. P. (2003). Positive psychology: Fundamental assumptions. *The Psychologist, 16*(3), 126–127.

Shklovski, I. (2007). *Residential mobility, technology, and social ties* (Unpublished doctoral dissertation). Carnegie Mellon University, Pittsburgh, PA.

Silventoinen, K., Hammar, N., Hedlund, E., Koskenvuo, M., Ronnemaa, T., & Kaprio, J. (2008). Selective international migration by social position, health behavior and personality. *European Journal of Public Health, 18,* 150–155. doi:10.1093/eurpub/ckm052

Silver, E., Mulvey, E. P., & Swanson, J. W. (2002). Neighborhood structural characteristics and mental disorder: Faris and Dunham revisited. *Social Science & Medicine, 55,* 1457–1470. doi:10.1016/S0277-9536(01)00266-0

Smider, N. A., Essex, M. J., & Ryff, C. D. (1996). Adaptation to community relocation: The interactive influence of psychological resources and contextual factors. *Psychology and Aging, 11*(2), 362–372. doi:10.1037/0882-7974.11.2.362

Talhelm, T., Oishi, S., & Miao, F. (2013). *Movers think more analytically than nonmovers.* Manuscript in preparation.

Whyte, W. H., Jr. (1956). *The organization man.* New York, NY: Simon & Schuster.

12

PEOPLE, CULTURE, AND PLACE: HOW PLACE PREDICTS HELPING TOWARD STRANGERS

STEPHEN REYSEN AND ROBERT V. LEVINE

The guiding mantra of modern academic social psychology is *the power of the situation*—the belief that features of the situation exert considerably more influence on our behavior than people generally think they do. In this chapter, we take a broad view of what this means by exploring aspects of the situation at multiple levels, including not only the particulars of the immediate situation but also the aspects of the culture that create the environment in which it occurs, and we attempt to demonstrate how these factors are reflected in social psychological differences at the geographic level. Specifically, our analysis focuses on differences between cities in helpfulness toward strangers. We include discussions of studies of these differences across cities around the world and within the United States.

The topic of helpfulness taps into the analysis of altruism, which has been a central concern of modern evolutionary theory. The psychology of

http://dx.doi.org/10.1037/14272-013
Geographical Psychology: Exploring the Interaction of Environment and Behavior, P. J. Rentfrow (Editor)

altruism critically depends on (a) the recipient of the altruistic act, whether it is targeted toward kin (Hamilton, 1964) or reciprocating strangers (Trivers, 1985), and (b) the biological significance of the helpful act (i.e., whether it is an everyday favor vs. a lifesaving move; Burnstein, Crandall, & Kitayama, 1994). Although people everywhere may be equipped with the same social psychological heuristics that make various forms of human altruism possible (Burnstein et al., 1994; Cosmides & Tooby, 1992), the geographic-level data examined later in this chapter indicate that the rate of actual helping behavior for stranger-to-stranger everyday favors varies greatly from city to city and is profoundly affected by local conditions such as economic well-being, cultural patterns, and other factors yet to be identified. Indeed, the coevolution of culture and psyche suggests that the mental mechanisms that afford altruism (and conditional boundaries of helping others) are themselves dynamically shaped through interactions between previous generations of humans (see Adams & Markus, 2004).

MUTUAL CONSTITUTION THEORY OF CULTURE

Cultural psychologists have converged on the notion that culture and psyche are mutually linked in a dialectical relationship (Shweder, 1990). The *mutual constitution theory of culture* emphasizes the reciprocal interaction of the person in producing, reproducing, and modifying cultural worlds and simultaneously being influenced and actively interacting with the environmental settings in which one is embedded. Contrary to viewing culture as a monolithic force influencing passive recipients, the mutual constitution theory represents culture as patterns.

The *patterns view of culture*, as eloquently detailed by Adams and Markus (2004), implies that individuals create culturally afforded intentional worlds filled with meaning:

> Culture consists of explicit and implicit patterns of historically derived and selected ideas and their embodiment in institutions, practices, and artifacts; cultural patterns may, on one hand, be considered as products of action, and on the other as conditioning elements of further action. (p. 341)

Through the construction of one's environment (e.g., conversations with others, creation of artifacts such as architecture, news, entertainment), individuals are constantly shaping and being conditioned by the environments in which they are embedded. In other words, environments are culturally constructed, and individuals reproduce, reject, or modify those environments, thereby either reinforcing or changing the cultural patterns.

AUTOMATICITY AND PRIMING

Insight into how these dynamics operate may be seen in two concepts that are currently receiving a great deal of attention in social–cognitive psychology: automaticity and priming. A wealth of research demonstrates that unconsciously activated norms, stereotypes, goals, and emotions influence subsequent behavior, thoughts, and perceptions (Bargh, 1997, 2006). This is certainly the case for the behavior of helpfulness; it has been shown that everyday environmental cues can elicit helping behaviors outside of the conscious awareness of the helper. For example, Guéguen, Jacob, and Charles-Sire (2011) manipulated the shape of a donation box to resemble a heart (or control shape) and received more donations in the heart box, presumably due to priming the concept of love. Other research has shown that priming helping-related words (Macrae & Johnston, 1998), friendship (Fitzsimons & Bargh, 2003), prosocial model roles such as superheroes (Nelson & Norton, 2005), nonconscious mimicry during a social interaction (van Baaren, Holland, Kawakami, & van Knippenberg, 2004), and images of two figures facing one another in an affiliative pose (Over & Carpenter, 2009) lead to subsequent helping behaviors.

Normative patterns and environmental aspects (e.g., population density) are also embedded in cultural spaces. For example, viewing another person helping suggests a social norm (or pattern) leading to a greater likelihood that the viewer will also help (Cialdini, 2007). In this respect, cultural patterns of helping are afforded to individuals when viewing others within the culture performing helping behaviors. Observers in these environments are more likely to help others because they are unconsciously primed to help by viewing the helping behavior. Although environments can prime helping, the presence of others in one's space can also inhibit prosocial behaviors. Latané and Darley (1970) showed how the presence of others in one's physical environment, or even priming the perception that other people are present (Garcia, Weaver, Moskowitz, & Darley, 2002), can inhibit helping behaviors. Later research showed that the extent to which people feel that others are evaluating them moderates the inhibition of helping. In situations in which people believe they are under public scrutiny, priming the perception of others increases helping behaviors (Garcia, Weaver, Darley, & Spence, 2009).

OTHER FACTORS

Beyond the immediate environmental influences, researchers can also examine distal factors (e.g., macroenvironmental aspects) that may influence geographic variations in helping (Oishi & Graham, 2010). It is important to note that the relationship between macroenvironment, culture, and mind are all interconnected and mutually constituted. In the following section, we review a program of research conducted by the second author and his colleagues that demonstrates the richness of these relationships in a particular domain of everyday social behavior—the relative frequency of helping strangers in different cities. Underlying this research is the notion that cities are environmental settings that are filled with cultural patterns, and, therefore, differences between cities highlight differences in cultural patterns toward helping others.

This is not to say that cultural patterns are determined by arbitrary national boundaries or group memberships per se. Rather, we argue that the preponderance of cultural patterns, immediate environment (e.g., population density), and macroenvironmental factors (e.g., economic system) in a particular geographic area influence the norms for helping people in those settings. In other words, geographic differences may provide us with a window on the workings of culture.

We now turn to a description of studies that we believe demonstrate the value of a geographic approach toward examining the relationship between environmental factors and helping behavior. These studies have focused on two major questions: First, are there differences in helpfulness toward strangers between cities in different countries and regions? Second, are there characteristics of these communities—demographic, social, environmental and economic conditions—that predict these differences?

HELPING IN 23 CITIES AROUND THE WORLD

R. V. Levine, Norenzayan, and Philbrick (2001) assessed helping behavior and pace of life in 23 cities around the world and examined the relationship of these differences to multiple environmental and macroenvironmental factors. Students traveling abroad (mostly traveling home for summer vacation) served as experimenters to collect data in the downtown areas during business hours on clear summer days. The cities included Amsterdam (the Netherlands), Bangkok (Thailand), Bucharest (Romania), Budapest (Hungary), Calcutta (India), Copenhagen (Denmark), Kuala Lumpur (Malaysia), Lilongwe (Malawi), Madrid (Spain), Mexico City (Mexico), New York City (United States), Prague (Czech Republic), Rio de Janeiro (Brazil), Rome (Italy), San Jose (Costa Rica), San Salvador (El Salvador), Shanghai (China), Singapore (Singapore), Sofia (Bulgaria), Stockholm (Sweden), Taipei (Taiwan), Tel Aviv (Israel), and Vienna (Austria). See Figure 12.1 for a map of data collection sites.

Participants were individuals in these cities who were over the age of 18 and not visibly physically disabled or unable to help (e.g., carrying packages).

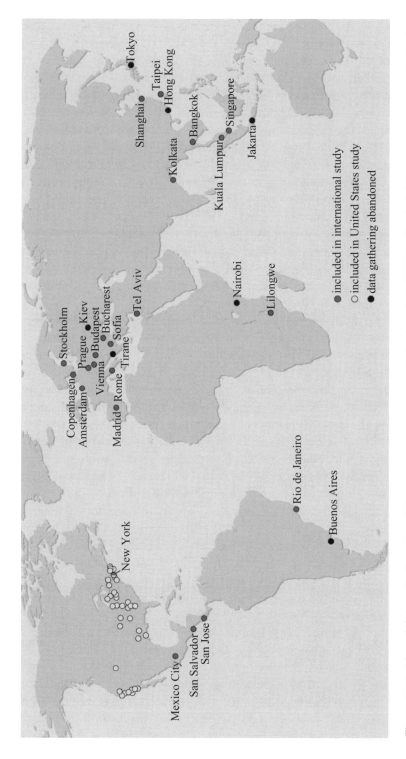

Figure 12.1. Map of data collection sites. Cities in grey were assessed in Levine et al. (2001), cities in light grey were were assessed in Levine et al. (1994), and cities in black were omitted due to issues with data collection. From "The Kindness of Strangers," by R. Levine, 2003, *American Scientist, 91*, p. 228. Copyright 2003 by Sigma Xi, The Scientific Research Society. Reprinted with permission.

Three measures of helping were assessed. First, experimenters measured the proportion of passersby in each city who retrieved an "accidentally" dropped pen. Specifically, the experimenter walked at a moderate pace, reached into his or her pocket, and "accidentally" dropped a pen 10 to 15 feet in front of solitary pedestrians walking in the opposite direction (*dropped pen measure*). Participants were coded as helpful if they notified the experimenter that he or she had dropped the pen. In a second measure of helping, experimenters wore a large leg brace outside their clothing and dropped a stack of magazines within 20 feet of an oncoming pedestrian. Helpfulness was recorded if the participant offered to pick up the magazines for the experimenter who was displaying difficulty in reaching to retrieve the magazines (*hurt leg measure*). As a third measure of helping, experimenters acted the role of a blind person seeking help crossing the street. They wore dark glasses, carried white canes (both props provided by a local agency providing support to blind people), and acted visually impaired while waiting at crosswalks containing traffic signals. Helping was shown when fellow pedestrians informed the experimenter when it was safe to cross the street (*blind person measure*).

Four community variables were examined in relation to the helping behaviors described previously. First, experimenters looked at a measure of the pace of life in each city: the amount of time the average pedestrian took to walk 60 feet during main business hours in main downtown areas in each city. Second, using the United Nations *Demographic Yearbook* (United Nations, Department of Economic and Social Development, 1996), population size of the city was assessed for each metropolitan area. Third, economic well-being as experienced by the average citizen in terms of how much the average income is capable of purchasing goods (purchasing power parity) was adopted from the World Bank (1996). Last, six cross-cultural psychologists rated each country on perceived individualism–collectivism using Triandis's (1996) definition (for more information about the measures, see R. V. Levine et al., 2001).

The results indeed showed differing degrees of helping between the cities (see Figure 12.2). Analysis of the community characteristics showed that the cities' pace of life (i.e., walking speed) was positively correlated with ratings of individualism and purchasing power but was unrelated to overall helping (indexed by the three helping measures). The correlations with pace of life support prior research in 31 international cities (R. V. Levine & Norenzayan, 1999) showing walking speed to be positively related to colder climates, greater purchasing power, and greater individualism (i.e., cities with faster walking speeds are related to stronger economic productivity and more individualism). Purchasing power was correlated with greater individualism. Of the four community variables, purchasing power was the best predictor of overall helping behavior, showing a moderately strong negative relationship.

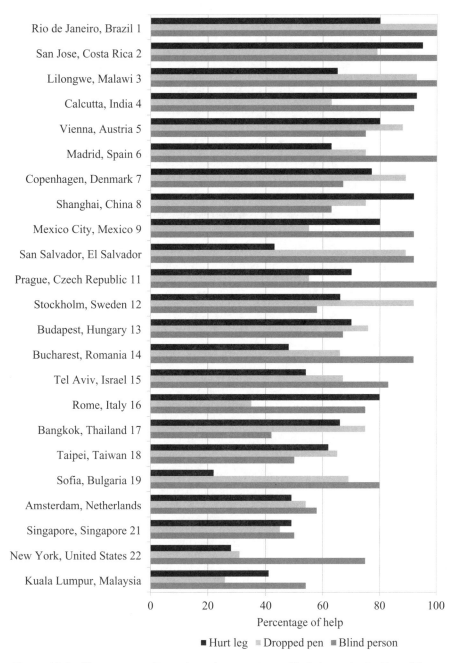

Figure 12.2. City, country, city rank, and percentage of help in each city. From "The Kindness of Strangers," by R. Levine, 2003, *American Scientist, 91,* p. 231. Copyright 2003 by Sigma Xi, The Scientific Research Society. Reprinted with permission.

A possible explanation is that individuals in cities with low purchasing power are relying on traditional value systems characterized by helping others in need.

These analyses led to further explanatory hypotheses. One interesting finding that emerged in the study was the general helpfulness of cities in Latin America (in Brazil, Costa Rica, El Salvador, and Mexico). All of the nations put a high value on the notion of *simpatia*. *Simpatia* is suggested to be a cultural norm characterized by values of minimization of conflict, respect and understanding of others, and social harmony (Markus & Lin, 1999). Consistent with the implied normative behavior, this cultural belief appears to be a strong predictor of helpfulness in this 23-city study.

Although this was not a major focus of the study, the researchers also examined gender differences in relation to helping the male experimenter on the dropped pen and hurt leg helping measures. Past research has suggested that men are more likely to help strangers than are women (see Eagly, 2009). The results showed no gender differences in helping. This result matches subsequent research showing few gender differences in helping for the dropped pen measure, regardless of whether the experimenter was male or female (Reysen & Ganz, 2006). Although men may be more likely to help others (especially women in need), consistent with the masculine gender role, the measures used by R. V. Levine et al. (2001) appear to be relatively gender neutral. A possible difference between the present research and prior studies on helping in realistic situations is the lack of threat or involvement related to helping (i.e., notifying another person she or he had dropped a pen) in the commonplace everyday situations used by the researchers.

Knafo, Schwartz, and Levine (2009) also reanalyzed the data, including survey data reflecting cultural embeddedness from 21 countries in the sample. Embeddedness is a suggested cultural pattern characterized by valuing ingroup goals above personal goals, traditional order, and obedience to the ingroup while rejecting outgroup members. Using the Schwartz Value Survey (Schwartz, 1992), the dimensions of social order, respect for tradition, security, and obedience were combined to form an index of embeddedness for responses from participants in each of the 21 countries. Consistent with findings from the original study, gross domestic product per capita was strongly negatively related to helping. However, cultural embeddedness was also a unique predictor of helping. Greater self-reported embeddedness from participants in the countries predicted less helping as assessed by R. V. Levine and colleagues (2001). The authors suggested that embeddedness is related to helping ingroup members (i.e., close friends and family) but not perceived outgroup members (i.e., strangers).

The results of the 23-city study and Knafo et al.'s (2009) follow-up provide an interesting link between economic purchasing power and two cultural characteristics (*simpatia*, embeddedness) in predicting helping behavior in different places. Thus, both cultural norms and larger economic indicators were strongly related to whether individuals embedded in culturally diverse cities were willing to help a stranger in everyday settings.

HELPING IN CITIES ACROSS THE UNITED STATES

An accompanying series of studies looked at geocultural differences in helping within a single nation. Cultural patterns can shift from neighborhood to neighborhood, just as helping patterns can change from city to city or region to region. To examine helping across cities in differing regions and cities of differing sizes, R. V. Levine, Martinez, Brase, and Sorenson (1994) assessed helping behaviors in 36 cities in the United States. The cities were located in the northeast (Boston, MA; Buffalo, NY; New York City, NY; Patterson, NJ; Providence, RI; Philadelphia, PA; Rochester, NY; Springfield, MA; Worcester, MA), north central (Canton, OH; Chicago, IL; Columbus, OH; Detroit, MI; Lansing, MI; Indianapolis, IN; Kansas City, MO; St. Louis, MO; Youngstown, OH), southern (Atlanta, GA; Chattanooga, TN; Dallas, TX; Houston, TX; Knoxville, TN; Louisville, KY; Memphis, TN; Nashville, TN; Shreveport, LA), and western (Bakersfield, CA; Fresno, CA; Los Angeles, CA; Sacramento, CA; Salt Lake City, UT; San Diego, CA; San Francisco, CA; San Jose, CA; Santa Barbara, CA) regions of the United States. Furthermore, within each region three cities contained populations that can be considered relatively small (350,000–600,000), medium (950,000–1,450,000), or large (2,000,000) in size.

Along with the three helping measures described earlier (dropped pen, hurt leg, blind person), R. V. Levine and colleagues (1994) used three additional helping indices. First, experimenters approached pedestrians with a quarter in an outstretched hand and asked politely whether the participant had change for a quarter (*change measure*). Participants were marked as helpful if they stopped and reached to check their pocket for change. Second, the experimenters placed "lost" letters on cars in city shopping areas with the note "I found this next to your car" (*lost letter measure*). The number of lost letters mailed to the researchers assessed the frequency of helping. Last, the researchers included the per capita contributions to the United Way of America (1991) for each city as a measure of helping behavior. Community variables included population size, population density (per square mile), per capita income, unemployment rate, cost of living, quality of life index (Boyer & Savageau, 1989), violent and property crime rates, environmental stress index (combination of measures including air, water, and sewage quality, toxic releases, and population change), and pace of life (a combination of walking speed, work speed, talking speed, and concern for clock time, assessed by R. V. Levine, Lynch, Miyake, & Lucia, 1989).

The results showed differing degrees of helping between the cities (see Figure 12.3). Significant regional differences were found, with southern and northern central cities showing greater overall helping compared with northeastern and western cities. Correlation analyses revealed population density (partialling out population size) and cost of living (partialling out population density) were negatively associated with overall helping. Population density and cost of living were also the strongest predictors of helping. The results were consistent with the international cities findings (R. V. Levine et al., 2001); people in cities where individuals had greater purchasing power were less likely to help others in need. The cities assessed were diverse with respect to population size. However, population size was less important in predicting helping than population density.

Purchasing power of individuals embedded in these city settings was negatively associated with helping both across cities and regions. Southerners are stereotypically characterized as friendly (Jost, Burgess, & Mosso, 2001), and the field data supported this cultural pattern. As with the international cities findings, both culturally normative patterns (southerners as helpful), a macroenvironmental factor (cost of living), and an environment factor (population density) were interconnected with helping behaviors of individuals embedded in those settings.

CHANGES OVER TIME

These rankings of places provide information on a number of levels. Taken individually, they provide tangible information for study of the quality of the helping environment in individual cities both within and across countries. In addition, however, these objective social indicators can be compared over time to mark trends in urban life in various locations. As cultural patterns are dynamically reproduced and modified to change over time, so too may the helping patterns observed in cities examined in the prior study. To examine possible change over time and its relationship to changes in environmental factors, roughly 12 years after R. V. Levine et al.'s (1994) study, R. V. Levine, Reysen, and Ganz (2008) revisited 24 of the 36 U.S. cities in the original study to replicate a portion of helping and pace-of-life measurements.

The cities were located in the northeast (Boston, MA; New York City, NY; Providence, RI; Rochester, NY; Springfield, MA; Worcester, MA), north central (Chicago, IL; Detroit, MI; Indianapolis, IN; Kansas City, MO; Lansing, MI; Youngstown, OH), southern (Atlanta, GA; Chattanooga, TN; Dallas,

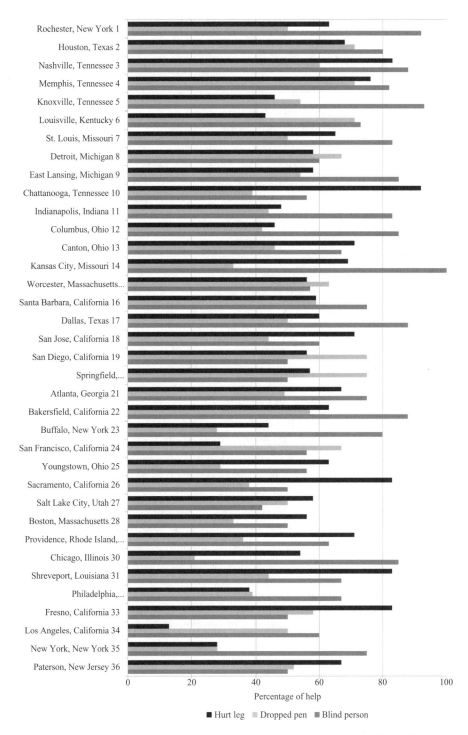

Rochester, New York 1
Houston, Texas 2
Nashville, Tennessee 3
Memphis, Tennessee 4
Knoxville, Tennessee 5
Louisville, Kentucky 6
St. Louis, Missouri 7
Detroit, Michigan 8
East Lansing, Michigan 9
Chattanooga, Tennessee 10
Indianapolis, Indiana 11
Columbus, Ohio 12
Canton, Ohio 13
Kansas City, Missouri 14
Worcester, Massachusetts...
Santa Barbara, California 16
Dallas, Texas 17
San Jose, California 18
San Diego, California 19
Springfield,...
Atlanta, Georgia 21
Bakersfield, California 22
Buffalo, New York 23
San Francisco, California 24
Youngstown, Ohio 25
Sacramento, California 26
Salt Lake City, Utah 27
Boston, Massachusetts 28
Providence, Rhode Island,...
Chicago, Illinois 30
Shreveport, Louisiana 31
Philadelphia,...
Fresno, California 33
Los Angeles, California 34
New York, New York 35
Paterson, New Jersey 36

0   20   40   60   80   100

Percentage of help

■ Hurt leg   ▨ Dropped pen   ■ Blind person

Figure 12.3. City, state, city rank, and percentage of help in each city. From "The Kindness of Strangers," by R. Levine, 2003, *American Scientist, 91,* p. 230. Copyright 2003 by Sigma Xi, The Scientific Research Society. Reprinted with permission.

TX; Knoxville, TN; Louisville, KY; Nashville, TN), and western (Bakersfield, CA; Fresno, CA; Los Angeles, CA; Sacramento, CA; San Francisco, CA; San Jose, CA) regions of the United States.

Helping was assessed with dropped pen, hurt leg, and asking for change measures (described earlier). Community variables included changes in population size, population density, average purchasing power, poverty rate, violent and property crime rate, and pace of life (walking speed). The rate of helping remained relatively similar across the two assessments, indicating little change in the helping patterns of the cities assessed. Increases in population size and poverty were related to less helping, whereas increases in purchasing power and crime were related to greater helping. We revisited the original data set to conduct further analyses.

We first conducted an analysis of variance using region as an independent variable, overall helping in the second assessment (because helping frequently was relatively unchanged we used the 2005 helping assessment) as the dependent variable, and change in population size between measurement times as a covariate. Helping behaviors differed significantly by region of the country, $F(3, 19) = 4.12$, $p = .021$, $\eta_p^2 = .39$. Post hoc analyses (using a Sidak correction for multiple comparisons) showed that participants in southern cities ($M = 1.75$, $SD = 1.82$) were significantly more helpful than participants in western cities ($M = -1.22$, $SD = 2.30$), marginally significantly more helpful than participants in northeastern cities ($M = -0.62$, $SD = 2.71$), and nonsignificantly different from participants in Northern Central cities ($M = 0.09$, $SD = 2.21$). Thus, the pattern of regional differences matched those found in the R. V. Levine et al. (1994) results when the change in population size of cities is taken into account.

Next, we conducted partial correlations controlling for the experimenters coding of region of country (i.e., south, west, northern central, and northeastern regions) and the size of the city (i.e., small, medium, large). Overall helping was significantly related to change in population density ($r = -.53$, $p = .020$), change in rates of poverty ($r = -.70$, $p = .001$), and change in overall crime rates ($r = .56$, $p = .013$). By controlling for the experimenters' codings (region and city size), the associations between helping and purchasing power and population size fell to nonsignificant levels. The results support the prior U.S. cross-city examination (R. V. Levine et al., 1994), with population density more strongly related to helping than population size.

Overall, the results across time suggested that the patterns of helping behavior in the assessed cities remained unchanged. Indeed, each of the three helping indices was significantly correlated with the equivalent measures 12 years after the initial observation. As found previously, there were regional differences that coincided with anecdotal reports of the southern and middle regions of the United States being more helpful than eastern or western regions. In addition, the change in population density as negatively related to helping supports the prior 1994 study. The unexpected positive association between increase in crime and helping is difficult to interpret. Change in crime and poverty were strongly negatively associated ($r = -.70$, $p = .001$), such that greater poverty was related to less crime. Correlations partialling out poverty resulted in crime as nonsignificantly associated with helping, however when partialling out crime, poverty was still negatively significantly related to helping. In other words, the relationship of greater importance is between greater poverty and less helping. Although the prior studies showed that greater economic well-being was related to less helping at one point, the present results show that over 10 years the increase in poverty is related to lower everyday helping.

Although these studies are important in terms of examining real-world behaviors in everyday settings, a methodology rarely used in current social psychology (Cialdini, 2009; Oishi & Graham, 2010), the results do not provide either a full picture of causal relationships or complete explanatory power. Thus far we have focused on the environmental aspects that have an influence on helping behavior. It would be naive to suggest that all behavior is externally controlled or that individuals do not have agency within situations. In the following section, we review past research on the interaction between the person and the situation and describe new research examining the dynamic interactive effects of identity on helping across geographic spaces.

PERSON WITHIN ENVIRONMENTS

In their classic seminary school experiment, Darley and Batson (1973) showed that environmental influence (being rushed to give a speech) was a better predictor of helping than person variables (personality, speech related to a valued identity). However, there are number of variables within the person that may affect whether individuals help in any given situation, such as their current emotional state (Zemack-Rugar, Bettman, & Fitzsimons, 2007), salient social identity (M. Levine, Prosser, Evans, & Reicher, 2005), or the various other individual difference explanations for helping behavior: biological evolution (Buss, 2003), personality (Eisenberg et al., 2002), and attachment (Van Lange, Otten, De Bruin, & Joireman, 1997). For example, feeling sad is related to greater helping (Cialdini & Fultz, 1990) but only when the helping task is pleasant (Isen & Simmonds, 1978). However, for individuals prone to feeling guilty, priming guilt (vs. sadness) leads to greater time volunteered to complete an unpleasant helping task (Zemack-Rugar et al., 2007). Although the research regarding the cultural patterns within and between cities (R. V. Levine et al., 1994, 2001, 2008) and priming effects on helping show an environmental influence, whether a person helps is likely a dynamic interaction between the person and the environment, as suggested by Kurt Lewin (1946): Behavior (B) is a function (F) of the person (P) and his or her environment (E), B = F (P, E).

Researchers using a social identity perspective (Reicher, Spears, & Haslam, 2010; Tajfel & Turner, 1979; Turner, Hogg, Oakes, Reicher, & Wetherell, 1987) have begun to focus on the effect of identity on helping (e.g., M. Levine et al., 2005). When a particular group membership is salient, the more strongly one identifies with the group, the greater depersonalization and self-stereotyping occur in line with the group's content—norms, beliefs, values, attitudes, behaviors (Turner et al., 1987), emotions (Reysen & Branscombe, 2008), and even personality (Jenkins, Reysen, & Katzarska-Miller, 2012). Consistent with the mutual constitution theory of culture, group members dynamically construct the content of the group, which in turn affects the self-concepts of those in the group (Postmes, Baray, Haslam, Morton, & Swaab, 2006). Because group memberships are often associated with, or are reciprocally influenced by, geographic locations, they may produce differences in normative behavior across these geographic locations.

Social identity researchers consistently show helping behaviors directed toward ingroup, but not outgroup, members (Saucier, Miller, & Doucet, 2005). Across the three studies conducted by R. V. Levine and colleagues (1994, 2001, 2008), the lowest frequency of helping was often found in New York City (15.4% on dropped pen measure in R. V. Levine et al., 2008). Reysen, Levine, and Ganz (2005) examined whether group membership would change New Yorkers' helping on the dropped pen measure by manipulating the shirt worn by the experimenter (Republican, Democrat, or no symbol). Participants helped significantly more when the experimenter wore the Democrat (57.7%) symbol compared with no symbol, whereas the control and Republican (36%) shirts did not result in significant differences in helping. Given that the majority of New Yorkers (66%) are registered Democrats (New York State Board of Elections, 2005), the results suggest that salience of ingroup membership can significantly influence helping, even in one of the most unhelpful cities.

Group memberships are influenced by the geographic location in which individuals are embedded. Just as different geographically disparate cities showed varying degrees of helping (R. V. Levine et al., 1994, 2001, 2008), cultural patterns in these settings could influence the degree to which individuals identify with certain groups. In a recent cross-national study (United States, Bulgaria, and India), Katzarska-Miller, Reysen, Kamble, and Vithoji (2012) examined the relationship between identification with global citizens and endorsement of intergroup helping. Participants sampled in America reported lower global citizenship identification than participants sampled in the other two countries. Supporting the notion that group memberships are influenced by the cultural spaces in which individuals are embedded, participant ratings of the extent their normative environment valued the identity mediated the comparison between cultural settings (United States vs. Bulgaria, United States vs. India) and identification with the group category—global citizen. Furthermore, identification with the group mediated the relationship between comparison of the cultural spaces and endorsed intergroup helping. In line with prior theorizing (e.g., Oxfam, 1997) and research finding the content of global citizenship identity to include helping outgroup members (Reysen & Katzarska-Miller, 2012), Katzarska-Miller and colleagues showed the influence of cultural space on identification with a group and desire to help others, even outside of one's ingroup.

Together, social identity perspective and mutual constitution theory can provide a useful integrated framework to researchers examining geographic influences of behavior. Although mutual constitution theory of culture does not constrain the cultural patterns of reciprocal influence of culture and mind within any specific group (and rightly so), once a group label is consensually shared (e.g., American, San Franciscan), social identity phenomena are likely to be found. Resolving the disconnect between mutual constitution theory and social identity perspective is a fruitful avenue for greater integration because the formation and maintenance of identity content is highly interconnected with cultural patterns in which individuals are embedded.

CONCLUSION: A PSYCHOLOGY OF PLACES

Cities are imbued with culturally constructed meanings, symbols, normative patterns, identities, and macroenvironmental factors that influence and are constantly reproduced and modified by individuals that inhabit these everyday environments. Research conducted by R. V. Levine and colleagues (1994, 2001, 2008) has highlighted the larger social–economic factors (purchasing power, poverty), characteristic cultural patterns (*simpatia*, southern regions of the United States), and immediate environmental settings (population density) that vary between cities internationally and regionally and affect helping behaviors in natural settings. Individuals influence and are influenced by everyday interaction with the environments they inhabit.

These geographic-level findings have something to offer to the evolutionary analysis of altruism, as mentioned at the beginning of this chapter. It would be interesting to examine in future research the extent of cultural variability of other types of helping behavior. It stands to reason, for example, that more cross-cultural similarity in helping rates (or in helping intentions) would emerge in situations having strong evolutionary significance, such as when the helping act is targeted at a close relative whose life is at stake (Burnstein et al., 1994).

In this chapter, we have made the assumption that places, like people, have their own "personalities." Anselm Strauss (1976) wrote that "the entire complex of urban life can be thought of as a person rather than a distinctive place, and the city can be endowed with a personality of its own" (p. 14). Places are marked by their own cultures and subcultures—each with their unique set of temporal fingerprints. Some places are friendlier than others. We have long known that they feel that way, and the studies by R. V. Levine and others (1994, 2001, 2008) have demonstrated that this feeling has empirical backing. There is variation within these cultures, but, overall, a stranger appears to be more likely to receive help in some places than in others.

The degree of variation in a culture may be viewed as a telling characteristic in itself. In Japan, for example, conformity is considered a virtue. A well-accepted Japanese saying is, "The nail that sticks up is quickly hammered down." As a result, there is considerably greater public uniformity in Japan than within an individualistic culture such as the United States, where "the squeaky wheel gets the grease." The extent of cultural tightness represents a significant difference between these two countries.

There are dangers in making generalizations about the characteristics of places, particularly when they are directed at the collective "personalities" of their people. The notion of applying a single set of characteristics to an entire population, or to any group for that matter, makes for sloppy thinking. The fact is that individuals in any setting differ greatly. Assigning global labels to the people of a particular city or country is overstereotyping and, as such, is potentially destructive. But although it may be careless to overgeneralize about the people from a single place, it would be naive to deny the existence of significant, overall differences between places and the cultural patterns displayed by inhabitants.

Herein lies the usefulness of integrating social identity perspective and mutual constitution theory of culture. People dynamically construct, reproduce, and change the cultural patterns flowing within cities (and groups). Following the patterns view, places contain a multitude of factors that are historically selected (and shaped and modified over time), embedded within the institutions and practices of people (e.g., everyday actions, products produced), and shaped and reciprocally shape individuals in which they are situated. Once a label is attached to those places (either by those within the group or by outgroup members), the place's characteristics are reified (in place and time), leading to essentializing, homogenizing, and stereotyping in line with a social identity perspective. *Essentializing* is viewing a group of people (e.g., New Yorkers) as sharing an essence (e.g., rudeness). The answer to why people help resides in the interaction between person and environment, both of which are influenced by culture. Focusing solely on either person or environmental factors ignores the essential complexity of human behavior and the unseen influence prior generations of humans have on people today.

REFERENCES

Adams, G., & Markus, H. R. (2004). Toward a conception of culture suitable for a social psychology of culture. In M. Schaller & C. S. Crandall (Eds.), *The psychological foundations of culture* (pp. 335–360). Mahwah, NJ: Erlbaum.

Bargh, J. A. (1997). The automaticity of everyday life. In R. S. Wyer, Jr., (Ed.), *The automaticity of everyday life: Advances in social cognition* (Vol. 10, pp. 1–61). Mahwah, NJ: Erlbaum.

Bargh, J. A. (2006). What have we been priming all these years? On the development, mechanisms, and ecology of nonconscious social behavior. *European Journal of Social Psychology, 36*, 147–168. doi:10.1002/ejsp.336

Boyer, R., & Savageau, D. (1989). *Places rated almanac.* New York, NY: Prentice Hall.

Burnstein, E., Crandall, E., & Kitayama, E. (1994). Some neo-Darwinian decision rules for altruism: Weighing cues for inclusive fitness as a function of the biological importance of the decision. *Journal of Personality and Social Psychology, 67*, 773–789. doi:10.1037/0022-3514.67.5.773

Buss, D. (2003). *Evolutionary psychology: The new science of the mind.* Boston, MA: Allyn & Bacon.

Cialdini, R. B. (2007). Descriptive social norms as underappreciated sources of social control. *Psychometrika, 72*, 263–268. doi:10.1007/s11336-006-1560-6

Cialdini, R. B. (2009). We have to break up. *Perspectives on Psychological Science, 4*, 5–6. doi:10.1111/j.1745-6924.2009.01091.x

Cialdini, R. B., & Fultz, J. (1990). Interpreting the negative mood-helping literature via "mega" analysis: A contrary view. *Psychological Bulletin, 107*, 210–214. doi:10.1037/0033-2909.107.2.210

Cosmides, L., & Tooby, J. (1992). Cognitive adaptations for social exchange. In J. H. Barkow, L. Cosmides, & J. Tooby, J. (Eds.), *The adapted mind* (pp. 163–228). New York, NY: Oxford University Press.

Darley, J. M., & Batson, C. D. (1973). "From Jerusalem to Jericho": A study of situational and dispositional variables in helping behavior. *Journal of Personality and Social Psychology, 27*, 100–108. doi:10.1037/h0034449

Eagly, A. H. (2009). The his and hers of prosocial behavior: An examination of the social psychology of gender. *American Psychologist, 64*, 644–658. doi:10.1037/0003-066X.64.8.644

Eisenberg, N., Guthrie, I. K., Cumberland, A., Murphy, B. C., Shepard, S. A., Zhou, Q., & Carlo, G. (2002). Prosocial development in early adulthood: A longitudinal study. *Journal of Personality and Social Psychology, 82,* 993–1006. doi:10.1037/0022-3514.82.6.993

Fitzsimons, G. M., & Bargh, J. A. (2003). Thinking of you: Nonconscious pursuit of interpersonal goals associated with relationship partners. *Journal of Personality and Social Psychology, 84,* 148–164. doi:10.1037/0022-3514.84.1.148

Garcia, S. M., Weaver, K., Darley, J. M., & Spence, B. T. (2009). Dual effects of implicit bystanders: Inhibiting vs. facilitating helping behavior. *Journal of Consumer Psychology, 19,* 215–224. doi:10.1016/j.jcps.2009.02.013

Garcia, S. M., Weaver, K., Moskowitz, G. B., & Darley, J. M. (2002). Crowded minds: The implicit bystander effect. *Journal of Personality and Social Psychology, 83,* 843–853. doi:10.1037/0022-3514.83.4.843

Guéguen, N., Jacob, C., & Charles-Sire, V. (2011). Helping with all your heart: The effect of cardioids cue on compliance to a request for humanitarian aid. *Social Marketing Quarterly, 17,* 2–11. doi:10.1080/15245004.2011.620683

Hamilton, W. D. (1964). The genetical evolution of social behavior, Parts I and II. *Journal of Theoretical Biology, 7,* 1–16. doi:10.1016/0022-5193(64)90038-4

Isen, A. M., & Simmonds, S. F. (1978). The effect of feeling good on a helping task that is incompatible with good mood. *Social Psychology, 41,* 346–349. doi:10.2307/3033588

Jenkins, S., Reysen, S., & Katzarska-Miller, I. (2012). Ingroup identification and personality. *Journal of Interpersonal Relations, Intergroup Relations and Identity, 5,* 9–16.

Jost, J. T., Burgess, D., & Mosso, C. O. (2001). Conflicts of legitimation among self, group and system: The integrative potential of system justification theory. In J. T. Jost & B. Major (Eds.), *The psychology of legitimacy: Emerging perspectives on ideology, justice, and intergroup relations* (pp. 363–388). New York, NY: Cambridge University Press.

Katzarska-Miller, I., Reysen, S., Kamble, S. V., & Vithoji, N. (2012). Cross-national differences in global citizenship: Comparison of Bulgaria, India, and the United States. *Journal of Globalization Studies, 3,* 166–183.

Knafo, A., Schwartz, S. H., & Levine, R. V. (2009). Helping strangers is lower in embedded cultures. *Journal of Cross-Cultural Psychology, 40,* 875–879. doi:10.1177/0022022109339211

Latané, B., & Darley, J. M. (1970). *The unresponsive bystander: Why doesn't he help?* New York, NY: Appleton-Century-Crofts.

Levine, M., Prosser, A., Evans, D., & Reicher, S. (2005). Identity and emergency intervention: How social group membership and inclusiveness of group boundaries shape helping behavior. *Personality and Social Psychology Bulletin, 31,* 443–453. doi:10.1177/0146167204271651

Levine, R. (2003). The kindness of strangers. *American Scientist, 91,* 226–233. doi:10.1511/2003.3.226

Levine, R. V., Lynch, K., Miyake, K., & Lucia, M. (1989). The type A city: Coronary heart disease and the pace of life. *Journal of Behavioral Medicine, 12,* 509–524. doi:10.1007/BF00844822

Levine, R. V., Martinez, T. S., Brase, G., & Sorenson, K. (1994). Helping in 36 U.S. cities. *Journal of Personality and Social Psychology, 67*, 69–82. doi:10.1037/0022-3514.67.1.69

Levine, R. V., & Norenzayan, A. (1999). The pace of life in 31 countries. *Journal of Cross-Cultural Psychology, 30*, 178–205. doi:10.1177/0022022199030002003

Levine, R. V., Norenzayan, A., & Philbrick, K. (2001). Cross-cultural differences in helping strangers. *Journal of Cross-Cultural Psychology, 32*, 543–560. doi:10.1177/0022022101032005002

Levine, R. V., Reysen, S., & Ganz, E. (2008). The kindness of strangers revisited: A comparison of 24 US cities. *Social Indicators Research, 85*, 461–481. doi:10.1007/s11205-007-9091-9

Lewin, K. (1946). Behavior and development as a function of the total situation. In L. Carmichael (Ed.), *Manual of child psychology* (pp. 791–844). New York, NY: Wiley. doi:10.1037/10756-016

Macrae, C. N., & Johnston, L. (1998). Help, I need somebody: Automatic action and inaction. *Social Cognition, 16*, 400–417. doi:10.1521/soco.1998.16.4.400

Markus, H. R., & Lin, L. R. (1999). Conflictways: Cultural diversity in the meanings and practices of conflict. In D. A. Prentice & D. R. Miller (Eds.), *Cultural divides: Understanding and overcoming group conflict* (pp. 302–333). New York, NY: Russell Sage Foundation.

Nelson, L. D., & Norton, M. I. (2005). From student to superhero: Situational primes shape future helping. *Journal of Experimental Social Psychology, 41*, 423–430. doi:10.1016/j.jesp.2004.08.003

New York State Board of Elections. (2005, April 1). *County enrollment totals.* Retrieved from http://www.elections.ny.gov/NYSBOE/enrollment/county/county_apr05.pdf

Oishi, S., & Graham, J. (2010). Social ecology: Lost and found in psychological science. *Perspectives on Psychological Science, 5*, 356–377. doi:10.1177/1745691610374588

Over, H., & Carpenter, M. (2009). Eighteen-month-old infants show increased helping following priming with affiliation. *Psychological Science, 20*, 1189–1193. doi:10.1111/j.1467-9280.2009.02419.x

Oxfam. (1997). *A curriculum for global citizenship.* Oxford, England: Author.

Postmes, T., Baray, G., Haslam, S. A., Morton, T. A., & Swaab, R. I. (2006). The dynamics of personal and social identity formation. In T. Postmes & J. Jetten (Eds.), *Individuality and the group: Advances in social identity* (pp. 215–236). London, England: Sage. doi:10.4135/9781446211946.n12

Reicher, S., Spears, R., & Haslam, S. A. (2010). The social identity approach in social psychology. In M. S. Wetherell & C. T. Mohanty (Eds.), *Sage identities handbook* (pp. 45–62). London, England: Sage. doi:10.4135/9781446200889.n4

Reysen, S., & Branscombe, N. R. (2008). Belief in collective emotions as conforming to the group. *Social Influence, 3*, 171–188. doi:10.1080/15534510802247438

Reysen, S., & Ganz, E. (2006). Gender differences in helping in six U.S. cities. *North American Journal of Psychology, 8*, 63–67.

Reysen, S., & Katzarska-Miller, I. (2012). A model of global citizenship: Antecedents and outcomes. *International Journal of Psychology.* doi:10.1080/00207594.2012.701749

Reysen, S., Levine, R. V., & Ganz, E. (2005). *The association between the display of group membership and helping behavior.* Unpublished manuscript, Department of Psychology, California State University, Fresno.

Saucier, D. A., Miller, C. T., & Doucet, N. (2005). Differences in helping whites and blacks: A meta-analysis. *Personality and Social Psychology Review, 9*, 2–16. doi:10.1207/s15327957pspr0901_1

Schwartz, S. H. (1992). Universals in the content and structure of values: Theoretical advances and empirical tests in 20 countries. *Advances in Experimental Social Psychology, 25*, 1–65. doi:10.1016/S0065-2601(08)60281-6

Shweder, R. A. (1990). Cultural Psychology—What is it? In J. Stigler, R. Shweder, & G. Herdt (Eds.), *Cultural psychology: Essays on comparative human development* (pp. 1–44). Cambridge, England: Cambridge University Press. doi:10.1017/CBO9781139173728.002

Strauss, A. L. (1976). *Images of the American city.* New Brunswick, NJ: Transaction Books.

Tajfel, H., & Turner, J. C. (1979). An integrative theory of intergroup conflict. In W. Austin & S. Worchel (Eds.), *The social psychology of intergroup relations* (pp. 33–47). Monterey, CA: Brooks/Cole.

Triandis, H. (1996). The psychological measurement of cultural syndromes. *American Psychologist, 51*, 407–415. doi:10.1037/0003-066X.51.4.407

Trivers, R. (1985). *Social evolution.* Menlo Park, CA: Benjamin Cummings.

Turner, J. C., Hogg, M. A., Oakes, P. J., Reicher, S. D., & Wetherell, M. (1987). *Rediscovering the social group: A self-categorization theory.* Oxford, England: Blackwell.

United Nations, Department of Economic and Social Development. (1996). *Demographic yearbook 1994.* New York, NY: Author.

United Way of America. (1991). *International directory 1991.* Alexandria, VA: Author.

van Baaren, R. B., Holland, R. W., Kawakami, K., & van Knippenberg, A. (2004). Mimicry and prosocial behavior. *Psychological Science, 15*, 71–74. doi:10.1111/j.0963-7214.2004.01501012.x

Van Lange, P. A. M., Otten, W., De Bruin, E. M. N., & Joireman, J. A. (1997). Development of prosocial, individualistic, and competitive orientations: Theory and preliminary evidence. *Journal of Personality and Social Psychology, 73*, 733–746. doi:10.1037/0022-3514.73.4.733

World Bank. (1996). *The world bank atlas: 1996.* Washington, DC: Author.

Zemack-Rugar, Y., Bettman, J. R., & Fitzsimons, G. J. (2007). The effects of nonconsciously priming emotion concepts on behavior. *Journal of Personality and Social Psychology, 93*, 927–939. doi:10.1037/0022-3514.93.6.927

13

THE PSYCHOGEOGRAPHY OF CREATIVITY

RICHARD FLORIDA AND CHARLOTTA MELLANDER

The fields of psychology, sociology, and economics have been interconnected in various ways for some time. At least two Nobel Prize awards in economics—Herbert Simon's 1978 award for his work on the subjects of satisficing and bounded rationality and Daniel Kahneman's in 2002 for his work with Tversky on prospect theory—draw heavily from psychology. Save for the field of environmental psychology, the link between psychology and geography and regional science has been considerably sparser and unrealized.

But recent years have seen growing research at the intersection of psychology and geography. This growing body of research has focused on the geographic distribution and variation in creativity (Florida, 2002), long a key construct in psychology (e.g., Sternberg & Lubart, 1999); the geographic distribution and variation of personality (Rentfrow, Gosling, & Potter, 2008); and the geography and regional determinants of happiness or subjective well-being (e.g., Diener & Seligman, 2004; Rentfrow, Mellander, & Florida, 2009).

http://dx.doi.org/10.1037/14272-014
Geographical Psychology: Exploring the Interaction of Environment and Behavior, P. J. Rentfrow (Editor)

This chapter focuses on the rich vein of research that seeks to bring together insights from psychology, geography, and urban economics around the topic of creativity. We begin by tracing the literature on the geography of creativity and of the creative class. We then turn to the central role of place and location, as opposed to firms and other forms of organization, in organizing creativity. Next, we discuss the role of diversity and tolerance in the geography of creativity and in the process of urban and regional development. We then shift our focus to recent research on the geography of personality, paying particular attention to the role that geographic clusters of Openness to Experience have on regional economic and cultural development. The fifth section discusses recent research on the happiness of cities and the factors that contribute to local happiness and community satisfaction. We close by drawing out some key conclusions and themes based on the existing research in this area, while noting directions for future research at the intersection of psychology and geography.

THE GEOGRAPHY OF CREATIVITY AND THE CREATIVE CLASS

In their *Handbook of Creativity*, Sternberg and Lubart (1999) noted, "If one wanted to select the best novelist, artist, entrepreneur, or even chief executive officer, one would most likely want someone who is creative" (p. 9). Creativity has long been the forte of psychologists, but recently economists, sociologists, geographers, and social scientists have begun to focus on and explore the value that creativity brings to economic growth; creativity is increasingly being viewed as a key economic and social resource. This is apparent in the works of many classic thinkers in economics and geography, as well as in the emerging literatures on creative cities, industries, organizations, and the creative class.

Creativity is the one thing that distinguishes humans from other species. Long ago, Adam Smith declared human capital, or creativity, as the additional fourth factor of production, suggesting, "The greatest improvement in the productive powers of labour, and the greater part of the skill, dexterity, and judgment with which it is anywhere directed, or applied, seem to have been the effects of the division of labour" (Smith, 1776/2000, Book 1, p. 7). Although he is remembered more for his labor theory of value and working class exploitation, Karl Marx also noted the importance of creativity in the *Grundrisse*:

> Nature builds no machines, no locomotives, railways, electric telegraphs, self-acting mules, etc. These are products of human industry; natural material transformed into organs of the human will over nature, they are organs of the human brain, created by the human hand; the power of knowledge objectified. (as quoted in Shuklian, 1995)

Joseph Schumpeter (1942) called attention to the process of *creative destruction*, whereby entrepreneurs creating new businesses shape periods of creative destruction, which in turn disrupt industries, society, and the economy. The economic historian, Joel Mokyr (1990) concluded,

> Economists and historians alike realize that there is a deep difference between *homo economicus* and *homo creativus*. One makes the most of what nature permits him to have; the other rebels against nature's dictates. Technological creativity, like all creativity, is an act of rebellion. (p. 175)

Technological creativity is a key driver of economic growth. Robert Solow (1956) documented the role of technology in the process of economic growth and development. In Paul Romer's (1986) theory of endogenous growth, economic growth stems from the accumulation of knowledge and ideas, highlighting the role of human creativity as central to this process. Romer (1993) noted,

> We produce goods by rearranging physical objects, but so do other animals, often with remarkable precision Where people excel as economic animals is in their ability to produce ideas, not just physical goods. An ant will go through its life without ever coming up with even a slightly different idea about how to gather food. But people are almost incapable of this kind of rote adherence to instruction. We are incurable experimenters and problem solvers. (p. 70)

Florida's (2002) *creative class theory* proposes three branches or classes of the workforce: the creative class, working class, and service class. Whereas Marx (1906) and other classical economists emphasized physical labor, or the ability of humans to transform nature and build products, creative class theory focuses on workers who work with their minds and creative capabilities. Florida identified three types of mutually dependent creativity that bind this class together: technological creativity (innovation), economic creativity (entrepreneurship), and artistic or cultural creativity. The creative class consists of two key subgroups: (a) the supercreative core who work in computer and mathematical occupations; architecture and engineering; the life, physical, and social sciences; education, training, and library positions; arts and design; and entertainment, sports, and media and (b) the creative professionals who work in management, business and financial operations, legal positions, health care, technical occupations, and high-end sales and sales management.

THE CREATIVE CITY

The history of human creativity and of human progress is intimately intertwined with that of cities. The *Epic of Gilgamesh*—perhaps the oldest known work of literature—closes with an awed description of the walls of the city of Uruk. Plato's *Republic*—which envisioned an ideal city—was a product of the cultural and intellectual flowering of the earthly city of Athens, as well as a broadside against its politics. Dante, Petrarch, Boccaccio, Brunelleschi, da Vinci, and Michelangelo all were born in or near the city of Florence. Great thinkers, artists, and entrepreneurs rarely come out of nowhere. Creative people cluster and thrive in places that attract other creative people and provide an environment that fosters and supports creative effort. That environment is provided by cities. Cities have long functioned as critical containers and mobilizers of creativity, attracting creative people from the surrounding countryside while providing the structures, scenes, and ecosystems that undergird and support creative efforts.

With the rise of technology and globalization, many assumed the end of geography, the death of distance, the decline of place, and the flattening of the world (Friedman, 2005). However, the flip side of globalization is the increasing concentration of creativity and other economic assets in cities and surrounding metro regions.

Recent years have seen increasing recognition of the city as a core social and economic organizing unit of work and society. In 2007, the percentage of the population living in urban areas surpassed 50% (UNFPA, 2007). This led *The Economist* ("The World Goes to Town," 2007) to coin the term *Homo urbanus* to describe the increasing importance of cities, declaring,

> Whether you think the human story begins in a garden in Mesopotamia known as Eden, or more prosaically on the savannahs of present-day east Africa, it is clear that *Homo sapiens* did not start life as an urban creature. Man's habitat at the outset was dominated by the need to find food, and hunting and foraging were rural pursuits. (para. 1)

But today, the story concludes, "Wisely or not, *Homo sapiens* has become *Homo urbanus*" (para. 1). If industrial production was organized in and around firms, knowledge-based or creative production is organized in cities.

Å. E. Andersson, a leading Swedish urban economist, provided a historical analysis of the relationship between creativity and cities. Examining the cities of Athens, Renaissance Florence, Enlightenment London, and fin de siècle Vienna, he argued,

> In the course of the past 2,500 years, a small number of relatively large cities have functioned as hotbeds of revolutionary creativity. These cities attracted a disproportionate share of migrants with creative inclinations, and they also facilitated the growth of creativity among those already present. Such cities were both used as arenas for presenting findings from elsewhere and as fertile locations for developing new ideas in collaboration with other creative people. (Andersson, 2011, p. 39)

Simply put, "creative people need creative cities" (Andersson, 2011, p. 14). In *Cities in Civilization*, Hall (1966) argued for the role of elite world cities in reshaping the geographic hierarchy of urban areas.

The groundbreaking work of Jane Jacobs provided a basic theory of the economic function of cities in economic development (1961, 1969). Jacobs focused on the capacity of cities to organize and mobilize human capabilities as the motor force of economic progress. She criticized the focus in conventional economics on Adam Smith's notion of a division of labor in firms. For Jacobs, deepening the division of labor resulted in greater efficiency, but it was insufficient to explain the rise of new ideas and the creation of new work. That requires innovation, and according to Jacobs, innovations require the constant combination and recombination of human capabilities that take place in cities. Such dynamism also requires not just density and concentration but also human and economic diversity, which again is a defining trait of cities. In *The Economy of Cities* (1969), Jacobs argued,

> The diversity, of whatever kind, that is generated by cities rests on the fact that in cities so many people are so close together, and among them contain so many different tastes, skills, needs, supplies, and bees in their bonnets. (as quoted by Florida, 2008, pp. 58–59)

The Nobel Prize–winning economist Robert Lucas later formalized Jacobs's emphasis on the clustering of creative people as the fundamental driver of economic growth. In his landmark essay, "On the Mechanics of Economic Development," Lucas (1988) argued that the productivity effects of human capital—or "Jane Jacobs externalities"—were the single most driving force in economic development.

> If we postulate only the usual list of economic forces, cities should fly apart. The theory of production contains nothing to hold a city together. A city is simply a collection of factors of production—capital, people and land—and land is always far cheaper outside cities than inside. . . . It seems to me that the "force" we need to postulate to account for the central role of cities in economic life is of exactly the same character as the "external human capital." . . . What can people be paying Manhattan or downtown Chicago rents for, if not for being near other people? Lucas (pp. 38–39)

Inherent in these arguments is the vital notion that creative and innovative processes are driven by people and organized in cities, as opposed to firms.

A great deal of empirical research confirms this perspective. Glaeser (1998) found that the exceptional productivity and innovation that result from clusters is driven by proximity to shared talent pools and human capital, rather than the clustering of firms. Similarly, Glaeser and Resseger (2010) found that urban density facilitates the spread of knowledge and ideas that in turn makes workers more skilled and entrepreneurs more productive. In a separate study, Glaeser, Kolko, and Saiz (2001) also found that the factors that best attract skilled labor to cities are those related to consumption rather than production, arguing that cities that have a diversity of goods and services are more appealing than cities that do not. In particular, it was found that higher-amenity cities attract more skilled labor and grow faster.

Florida (2002) identified the characteristics of places that attract highly skilled individuals. Building on research by Rosen (1979) and Roback (1982) on migration across regions, Florida's (2002) research demonstrated that in addition to the human capital externalities, productivity, and innovation-enhancing functions of places, cities also provide a key forum for consumption preferences of skilled individuals. Clark, Lloyd, Wong, and Jain (2002) observed that creative people are drawn to amenities and that amenities are not just add-ons but also part of the mix that underpins geographic variation in creativity, innovation, and wealth. This line of research suggests that people and places matter more than the economic role of businesses and firms.

Density also plays a role. In his 2011 book, *Triumph of the City*, Glaeser made a powerful case for density, suggesting that cities require considerably more of it. However, the question of density and creativity is more nuanced. Jacobs long ago called attention to the limits of density of the sort found in skyscraper districts that can function as vertical suburbs. For density to be effective, the key is human interaction, combination, and recombination.

A study by Gordon and Ikeda (2011) contrasted two types of density: *crude density* and *Jane Jacobs density*. The first type of density is associated with exceedingly tall buildings that can stifle the flow of information because they lack dynamism and pedestrian scale. In contrast, Jane Jacobs density harnesses the power of mixed-use development that allows for authentic and meaningful interactions to naturally occur. Density itself, Gordon and Ikeda noted, will not generate innovation, new firm formation, or economic development:

> If it could, county prisons or the streets around Yankee Stadium as fans crowd into and out of games would be economically diverse and dynamic places—they are not. The former are not dynamic for obvious reasons while the latter lacks because it fails to provide the foundation for dynamic long-term growth, although it may sustain businesses such as baseball cap and hot dog sales. (p. 438)

Too much density can stifle the exchange and flow of information and ideas, just as too little does. It is only when density goes hand in hand with walkability, pedestrian scale, and the like, that it can yield real cultural and economic benefits.

TOLERANCE, OPENNESS, AND DIVERSITY

In *Rise of the Creative Class*, Florida (2002) called attention to the role of tolerance, openness, and diversity as key factors in economic growth. Tolerance is closely related, as we will see, to the psychological construct of Openness. *Tolerance* is the third T in Florida's 3Ts model of economic growth, the other two being *technology* and *talent*. Although technology and talent are both long agreed on ingredients for economic prosperity, it is the pivotal role of tolerance in spurring economic growth that has garnered much attention. Although economists acknowledge the role of low barriers to entry for firms, Florida focuses on the role of low entry barriers for people to settle in locations. Places where newcomers are welcomed and accepted into myriad social, economic, and cultural arrangements are the places that gain an edge in mobilizing and attracting human creativity. All else being equal, they are likely to attract and retain the sorts of creative actors who power innovation and growth.

Florida (2002) argued that throughout the history of the United States, openness to entrepreneurial newcomers led to the tradition of immigrants being overrepresented among America's leading entrepreneurs since the days of the steel magnate Andrew Carnegie. Smart, talented people, whether in the form of human capital or creative class, are attracted to open and tolerant places where ideas will be accepted and can float freely between individuals. As Becker (1957) noted, these characteristics signal a labor market based on meritocracy that gives all individuals the opportunity to succeed and flourish. Jacobs (1961, 1969), too, noted that open and diverse places attract people of different backgrounds; this is linked to creativity and innovation, and ultimately, economic growth. Moreover, these urban areas not only attract creative people but also serve to stimulate their creativity.

Dean Keith Simonton (2011), a leading student of the psychology of creativity, argued that cities play a formative role in "creative development," which is facilitated through exposure to creative role models during young adulthood and through the "cultural heterogeneity" found in urban centers, whereby diverse and exciting environments provide the stimulus necessary for the formation of new and creative ideas. These are characteristics that are hard to come by in rural settings, which by and large lack the diversity and electricity of urban areas.

THE GEOGRAPHY OF PERSONALITY

This brings us to the connection between tolerance, openness, and personality. The past decade has seen rising interest in the geography of personality. Recently, Rentfrow et al. (2008) undertook a comprehensive geographic analysis of statewide differences in the Big Five personality traits. Their results indicated that people who were high in Openness to Experience were not only highly mobile but also clustered in certain areas that met their desire for the cultural diversity, vast social settings, and experiences found in states with large cities. It was found that although this was not done by design, clustering by personality trait was clearly evident as certain regions took on the personality traits associated with them.

More recently, Rentfrow (2011) focused on the distribution of personality across American cities. Again, the geographic clustering of personality was clear: Regions such as San Francisco, New York City, and Los Angeles have the nation's largest concentration of people high in Openness to Experience, with Detroit, Cleveland, and Pittsburgh showing the smallest concentrations.

Florida (2008) examined the relation between innovation, human capital, economic growth, and personality factors, finding that Openness to Experience was positively associated with the proportion of the population who were in the creative class, who were college graduates, and who were artistic and cultural bohemians, and even more so with concentrations of foreign-born residents, high-tech industries, and innovation, whereas it was negatively associated with concentrations of the working class. These findings converge with recent research on "character strengths." Specifically, Park and Peterson (2010) examined the relationship between character strengths and urban economic and political outcomes such as rates of firm formation or voting patterns. Using data from a sample of nearly 50,000 individuals across 50 cities, they distinguished between *head strengths*, which are intellectual and self-oriented, and *heart strengths*, which are emotional and interpersonal. The results indicated that character strengths were associated with various urban outcomes. For example, cities high on head strengths had high levels of creativity and innovation and also had more ballots cast for liberal politicians, whereas cities bigger in heart strengths were more conservative.

The findings from this research reinforce the vital contribution of psychology, in addition to economic and social factors, in understanding the causes of innovation and economic development. Although the creative class measure seeks to build on the use of human capital in measuring economic capabilities, psychological theory and research provides a valuable perspective on the traits and motives that influence individual creativity and foster geographic creativity and innovation. The recent research in geographical psychology makes the case that psychological factors are not just characteristics of individuals that influence their thoughts, feelings, and behaviors but also that these individual characteristics are geographically clustered across countries and are, at least for Openness and creativity, concentrated in large metropolitan cities. Understanding the dynamic relations between individuals and the places in which they live is central to developing a complete understanding of regional, social, and economic outcomes.

THE HAPPINESS OF CITIES

Happiness, or subjective well-being, has been the subject of considerable attention over the past couple of decades in economics and psychology. The work done in this area has significantly informed our understanding of the economic, social, and psychological factors that influence happiness. In 2009, the International Commission on the Measurement of Economic Performance and Social Progress acknowledged the need for better measures of economic growth and development (Stiglitz, Sen, & Fitoussi, 2009). "What you measure affects what you do," noted Stiglitz at the release of the commission's report. "If we have the wrong metrics, we will strive for the wrong things" (OECD, 2011). In particular, it was found that additional measures of social and economic well-being are necessary to measure progress, both economically and socially. Factors such as socioeconomic development, sustainable development, social inclusion, and public health were all cited as elements of well-being that must be considered as we lay the foundations for sustainable, long-term prosperity. Stiglitz et al. (2009) have joined a growing number of scholars who over the past decade have called for broader and less materialistic measures of social and economic well-being.

Early studies found that, at the national level, happiness was not simply a function of rising incomes. The famous *Easterlin paradox* (Easterlin, 1974) described the fact that although rich people are much happier than poor people, rich societies are only a little happier than poor societies, and countries as a whole do not get happier when they get richer. Other studies, notably by economists Stevenson and Wolfers (2008), have found a continuing connection between income and happiness.

Psychological research concerned with cross-national differences in well-being has found that people are happier in wealthier, democratic nations than in poorer, undemocratic nations (Diener, Oishi, & Lucas, 2003; Steel & Ones, 2002; Stevenson & Wolfers, 2008; Veenhoven, 1993). For a more nuanced perspective on national differences in well-being, Mellander, Florida, and Rentfrow (2011) examined the relationships between postindustrialism, class composition, and happiness across nations and found that class plays a role in high-income countries over and above that of income. Although this body of research has provided useful insights into the psychological, societal, and cultural correlates of well-being at the individual and national levels of analysis, it has failed to consider the ways in which well-being varies within countries.

Recently, Florida, Mellander, and Rentfrow (2011) used data from the Gallup organization to examine the factors that shape happiness across cities and metropolitan areas. The study, which considered the effects of income, home ownership, commuting, age, human capital, unemployment, and other factors, found that human capital and the creative class were positively associated with happiness, even after controlling for income, whereas happiness was negatively associated with the concentration of working class. These findings converge with national level results and suggest that the social demographics of cities contribute to individuals' life satisfaction.

Citywide differences in happiness could be the result of social and environmental forces, but it is also conceivable that people seek out places they believe might make them happy. Indeed, an individual's choice of location affects their happiness and subjective well-being as well. Gilbert (2006) noted that "most of us make at least three important decisions in our lives: where to live, what to do, and with whom to do it" (p. 235). Most happiness research until recently focused on the last two factors, but recent research has begun to probe the effects of place on happiness. For example, Florida (2008) examined Gallup data and found that place or location is the third leg in the triangle alongside work and social relationships. When people were asked to rate their happiness about aspects of life such as work, personal life, finances, and place on a 1 (*not at all happy*) to 5 (*extremely happy*) scale, place scored 3.63, ahead of finances (3.46), and just after personal life (4.08) and work (3.98). Furthermore, place, together with job satisfaction, accounted for a quarter of the total variance in overall life satisfaction, whereas income accounted for only 1.2% of the variance.

How and why do individuals choose where to live? Tiebout (1956) famously posed this as an economic tradeoff between individuals' preferences for services, public goods, and amenities versus how much they are willing to pay in taxes. Studies have shown that most choices are not rational (e.g., Kahneman, 2003; Simon, 1957). Recent research has added a psychological dimension to individual location choice. Mellander et al. (2011) distilled the factors that influence happiness at the community level by asking the question "Why do some people stay in locations while others move?" Rather than focusing on why people leave a location, the researchers focused on what influences people's decisions to stay in a neighborhood. Their research examined the interplay of economic factors, psychological or aesthetic factors, and individual-levels factors on the decision to stay in a community. They found that two psychological factors—beauty and community aesthetic appeal, and the ability to meet new people—were the most important factors in determining happiness with an area. These factors were more important than were traditional economic factors, such as individual income or education, or community-level factors, such as jobs, crime rates, and housing costs.

In a related line of research that focused explicitly on the role of beauty or aesthetics on individuals' satisfaction with their communities, Florida et al. (2011) found that, along with the ability to meet and make friends and the quality of public schools, beauty is significantly associated with community satisfaction, even after statistically controlling for personal characteristics, job markets, and the regional economy. The study found that beauty is a stronger explanatory variable for levels of community satisfaction than other factors such as job opportunities, housing markets, and high-quality public services. These findings raise the question of whether community satisfaction might resemble a Maslow-like process whereby individuals' satisfaction increases as communities meet different levels of higher order needs.

CONCLUSION

This chapter has examined the growing body of research that has drawn from psychology, economics, and geography to better understand the spatial distribution and economic consequences of human creativity. This work points the way for a variety of fruitful research streams. One line of inquiry that strikes us as particularly intriguing concerns the notion of energy— anyone who studies or simply lives in communities and cities is struck by the differences in their underlying energy or their "hustle and bustle." People often say that a city has energy or that the energy in the community is infectious. But we lack effective ways to measure or understand what is meant by *energy*. A potentially fruitful line of research would explore the concept of city energy to determine its various forms, how it can be measured, and what, if any, relations it has to the psychology of city residents.

Several years ago, one of us (see Florida, 2008) broached this subject at a conference with leading psychologists Martin E. P. Seligman and Mihaly Csikszentmihalyi. Seligman zeroed in on the centrality of the construct of energy to economic and social life. He noted,

> Energy is a concept that cuts across biology, physics, and chemistry, and is evident in everything from brain scans to heart rate monitors. The human body is an energy system, and indeed life itself is based on energy processes, insofar as living things must constantly consume and burn energy. (Florida, 2008, p. 193)

Moreover, "a good day," he pointed out, "starts with high energy, positive feelings, and an excited mood. Bad days are marked by low energy and the sluggish, discouraged, and overwhelmed feeling that it brings" (Florida, 2008, p. 193). Csikszentmihalyi added that if you want to identify places with energy, particularly high-level creative energy, look for concentrations of people who exhibit high levels of curiosity (Florida, 2008). It seems to us that a particularly fruitful line of inquiry would be devoted to how places and communities both select for and activate human energy.

In conclusion, the work emerging in this promising new research area has shown that psychological factors play a key role in explaining geographic and urban phenomena. Psychological factors, like economic and social ones, have distinctive geographic dimensions and affect geographic outcomes. The field of geographical psychology offers considerable promise along multiple lines of inquiry. This research is still in its infancy, and there are considerable opportunities for future research on this topic and the intersection of these fields.

REFERENCES

Andersson, Å. E. (2011). Creative people need creative cities. In D. E. Andersson, Å. E. Andersson, & C. Mellander (Eds.), *Handbook of creative cities* (pp. 14–55). Cheltenham, England: Edward Elgar.

Becker, G. (1957). *The economics of discrimination.* Chicago, IL: Chicago University Press.

Clark, T. N., Lloyd, R., Wong, K. K., & Jain, P. (2002). Amenities drive urban growth. *Journal of Urban Affairs, 24,* 493–515. doi:10.1111/1467-9906.00134

Diener, E., Oishi, S., & Lucas, R. E. (2003). Personality, culture, and subjective well-being: Emotional and cognitive evaluations of life. *Annual Review of Psychology, 54,* 403–425. doi:10.1146/annurev.psych.54.101601.145056

Diener, E., & Seligman, M. E. P. (2004). Beyond money: Toward an economy of well-being. *Psychological Science in the Public Interest, 5,* 1–31. doi:10.1111/j.0963-7214.2004.00501001.x

Easterlin, R. A. (1974). Does economic growth improve the human lot? Some empirical evidence. In P. A. David & M. W. Reder (Eds.), *Nations and households in economic growth: Essays in honor of Moses Abramowitz* (pp. 89–125). New York, NY: Academic Press.

Florida, R. (2002). *The rise of the creative class.* New York, NY: Basic Books.

Florida, R. (2008). *Who's your city? How the creative economy is making where to live the most important decision of your life.* New York, NY: Random House.

Florida, R., Mellander, C., & Rentfrow, P. J. (2011). The happiness of cities. *Regional Studies,* 1–15. doi:10.1080/00343404.2011.589830

Friedman, T. (2005). *The world is flat.* New York, NY: Farrar, Straus & Giroux.

Gilbert, D. (2006). *Stumbling on happiness.* New York, NY: Knopf.

Glaeser, E. L. (1998). Are cities dying? *The Journal of Economic Perspectives, 12,* 139–160. doi:10.1257/jep.12.2.139

Glaeser, E. L. (2011). *Triumph of the city*. New York, NY: Penguin.

Glaeser, E. L., Kolko, J., & Saiz, A. (2001). Consumer city. *Journal of Economic Geography, 1*, 27–50.

Glaeser, E. L., & Resseger, M. G. (2010). The complementarity between cities and skills. *Journal of Regional Science, 50*, 221–244. doi:10.1111/j.1467-9787.2009.00635.x

Gordon, P., & Ikeda, S. (2011). Does density matter? In D. E. Andersson, Å. E. Andersson, & C. Mellander (Eds.), *Handbook of creative cities* (pp. 435–455). Cheltenham, England: Edward Elgar.

Hall, P. (1966). *The world cities*. London, England: Weidenfeld & Nicholson.

Jacobs, J. (1961). *The death and life of great American cities*. New York, NY: Random House.

Jacobs, J. (1969). *The economies of cities*. New York, NY: Random House.

Kahneman, D. (2003). Maps of bounded rationality: Psychology for behavioral economics. *The American Economic Review, 93*, 1449–1475. doi:10.1257/000282803322655392

Lucas, R. (1988). On the mechanics of economic development. *Journal of Monetary Economics, 22*, 3–42. doi:10.1016/0304-3932(88)90168-7

Marx, K. (1906). *Capital*. New York, NY: Modern Library.

Mellander, C., Florida, R., & Rentfrow, J. (2011). The creative class, post-industrialism and the happiness of nations. *Cambridge Journal of Regions, Economy and Society, 5*(1), 3–13. doi:10.1093/cjres/rsr006

Mokyr, J. (1990). *The lever of riches*. New York, NY: Oxford University Press.

OECD. [oecden]. (2011, October 19). *Joseph Stiglitz talks about going beyond GDP* [Video file]. Retrieved from http://www.youtube.com/watch?v=G4d_-zaJXuA

Park, N., & Peterson, C. (2010). Does it matter where we live? The urban psychology of character strength. *American Psychologist, 65*, 535–547. doi:10.1037/a0019621

Rentfrow, P. J. (2011). The open city. In D. E. Andersson, Å. E., Andersson, & C. Mellander (Eds.), *Handbook of creative cities* (pp. 117–127). Cheltenham, England: Edward Elgar.

Rentfrow, P. J., Gosling, S. D., & Potter, J. (2008). A theory of the emergence, persistence, and expression of regional variation in basic traits. *Perspectives on Psychological Science, 3*, 339–369.

Rentfrow, R., Mellander, C., & Florida, R. (2009). Happy states of America: A state-level analysis of psychological, economic, and social well-being. *Journal of Research in Personality, 43*, 1073–1082. doi:10.1016/j.jrp.2009.08.005

Roback, J. (1982). Wages, rents, and the quality of life. *Journal of Political Economy, 90*, 1257–1278. doi:10.1086/261120

Romer, P. M. (1986). Increasing returns and long-run growth. *Journal of Political Economy, 90*, 1002–1037. doi:10.1086/261420

Romer, P. M. (1993, September 11). Ideas and things. *The Economist, 328*(7828), 70.

Rosen, S. (1979). Wage-based indexes of urban quality of life. In P. Mieszkowski & M. Straszheim (Eds.), *Current issues in urban economics* (pp. 74–104). Baltimore, MD: Johns Hopkins University Press.

Schumpeter, J. A. (1942). *Capitalism, socialism and democracy.* New York, NY: Harper & Row.

Shuklian, S. (1995). Marx, Dewey, and the instrumentalist approach to political economy. *Journal of Economic Issues, 29,* 781–806.

Simon, H. (1957). *Models of man.* New York, NY: Wiley.

Simonton, D. (2011). Big-C creativity in the big city. In D. E. Andersson, Å. E. Andersson, & C. Mellander (Eds.), *Handbook of creative cities* (pp. 72–84). Cheltenham, England: Edward Elgar.

Smith, A. (2000). *The wealth of nations.* New York, NY: Random House. (Original work published 1776)

Solow, R. (1956). A contribution to the theory of economic growth. *Quarterly Journal of Economics, 70,* 65–94. doi:10.2307/1884513

Steel, P., & Ones, D. S. (2002). Personality and happiness: A national-level analysis. *Journal of Personality and Social Psychology, 83,* 767–781. doi:10.1037/0022-3514.83.3.767

Sternberg, R. J., & Lubart, T. I. (1999). The concept of creativity: Prospects and paradigms. In R. J. Sternberg, *Handbook of creativity* (pp. 3–15). New York, NY: Cambridge University Press.

Stevenson, B., & Wolfers, J. (2008, Spring). *Economic growth and subjective well-being: Reassessing the Easterlin Paradox* (NBER Working Paper 14282). Cambridge, MA: National Bureau of Economic Research. Retrieved from http://www.nber.org/papers/w14282.pdf?new_window=1

Stiglitz, J. E., Sen, A., & Fitoussi, J.-P. (2009). *Report by the Commission on the Measurement of Economic Performance and Social Progress.* Paris, France: Commission on the Measurement of Economic Performance and Social Progress.

Tiebout, C. M. (1956). A pure theory of local expenditures. *Journal of Political Economy, 64,* 416–424. doi:10.1086/257839

UNFPA (2007). *State of world population 2007.* Retrieved from http://www.unfpa.org/public/publications/pid/408

Veenhoven, R. (1993). *Happiness in nations: Subjective appreciation of life in 56 nations 1946–1992.* Rotterdam, Netherlands: Risbo.

The World Goes to Town. (2007, May 3). *The Economist.* Retrieved from http://www.economist.com/node/9070726

14

PLACES, PRODUCTS, AND PEOPLE "MAKE EACH OTHER UP": CULTURE CYCLES OF SELF AND WELL-BEING

ALYSSA S. FU, VICTORIA C. PLAUT, JODI R. TREADWAY,
AND HAZEL ROSE MARKUS

The run-up to the second largest initial public offering in U.S. history ($16 billion) gave a front row view to culture in action. When Facebook founder Mark Zuckerberg arrived on Wall Street sporting his signature gray hoodie, he provoked a clash, not of national or ethnic cultures or even generational cultures but of regional cultures. The buttoned-downed investors of the Northeast accused Zuckerberg of immaturity and failing to respect tradition. In the West, tech bloggers jumped to Zuckerberg's defense, praising his independent-minded loyalty to the free and informal culture of Silicon Valley.

Although regions of the United States share many significant characteristics, a journey from one region to another can bring about significant friction—from the inchoate feeling that something is not quite right to strong reprisals about the folly of donning a sweatshirt while representing one's billion dollar company (Sengupta, 2012). In this chapter, we examine how such

http://dx.doi.org/10.1037/14272-015
Geographical Psychology: Exploring the Interaction of Environment and Behavior, P. J. Rentfrow (Editor)

culture clashes may stem from a mismatch in understandings about how to be a person and how to behave appropriately (e.g., what to wear) that are deeply rooted in place—in historically shaped regional and local environments.

As people live their lives, they interact with cultural products and practices of particular places (e.g., informal Western sweatshirts vs. formal Northeastern suits) that reflect key cultural ideas and values (e.g., Western independence vs. Northeastern tradition). Thus, through exposure to these products and practices, these places shape people's psychological tendencies. At the same time, in creating and enacting products and practices, people sustain and recreate these places. We call this process the *culture cycle*.

In this chapter, we first analyze how four U.S. regions (West, Northeast, Midwest, South) each produces their own culture cycle, and we then consider how place intersects with both race and class (Latinos in the Southwest, Asians in the Pacific region, Blacks in industrial northern cities, and rural Appalachians). We organize each analysis around a geographic unit and its associated historically shaped ideas and values, a set of products and practices that residents of that place create and come into frequent contact with (e.g., promotional material for universities, websites, personal ads), and residents' psychological tendencies related to self and well-being.

THE CULTURE CYCLE

The United States is rooted in individualistic values that emphasize independence, and indeed across regions, people in the United States often reveal similar independent tendencies whether assessed implicitly or explicitly (Kitayama, Conway, Pietromonaco, Park, & Plaut, 2010). The prevalence of independence across the United States stems from a shared ideological foundation and history, shared economic and political structures, national media, and a national culture of individualism, independence, personal control, and responsibility (e.g., Bellah, Madsen, Sullivan, Swidler, & Tipton, 1985). Yet the United States also encompasses a great deal of regional diversity—in ways of being (self) and being well (well-being) that are tied to specific histories and practices.

In this chapter, we take the perspective that understanding how region shapes psychological tendencies requires examining the culture cycle that characterizes each region. In other words, we need to understand how people—their psychological tendencies (e.g., how they think and feel)—and their worlds—pervasive historically-derived ideas, norms, practices, and products (e.g., media, law, daily routines)—mutually constitute each other or, in the words of anthropologist and cultural psychologist Richard Shweder (2003), "make each other up" (p. 33; see also Markus & Conner, 2013; Plaut, Markus,

Treadway, & Fu, 2012). A comparison of regional culture cycles involves an examination of three components of the cycle: (a) *place*, or a locality with specific ideas, values, and history that set its cycle in motion; (b) *products*, or the norms, practices, and products that propel the cycle; and (c) *people*, or embodiment of the cycle in self and well-being.

Place

Even within the same country, places can vary widely in their ecology and history (e.g., economic, political, social, demographic). Local or regional ecologies and histories produce specific, sometimes subtle and implicit, cultural understandings of how to be a self and how to be well (Plaut et al., 2012). Thus, although we should see a shared national ideal of becoming an independent individual among regions in the United States, we should also find that self and well-being take on regionally specific forms, because local ideas and practices differ in how they represent and achieve this ideal (Rentfrow, Gosling, & Potter, 2008; Vandello & Cohen, 1999).

Products

To fully understand people's psychological tendencies, it is useful to examine the products and practices that make up their context. These products and practices not only reflect the psychological tendencies of the residents of a place but also continually reinforce them. For example, several studies comparing national or regional cultures have shown that products such as books, ads, and websites, which are widespread and used on a daily basis, mirror psychological tendencies (e.g., Kim & Markus, 1999; Lun, Mesquita, & Smith, 2011; Tsai, 2007). In fact, according to Morling and Lamoreaux (2008), not only do cultural products reflect American-context individualism and Asian-context collectivism but they also show cultural differences more strongly compared with analyses of psychological measures. Tsai (2007) also found that cultural differences in how people ideally want to feel manifest in the products they produce (e.g., religious texts, children's books) and in their behavior and preferences for certain activities (e.g., recreational activities). For example, European Americans create products featuring broad, excited smiles and prefer high intensity activities such as hiking, reflecting their preference for high arousal positive affect and feeling excited. East Asians, in contrast, create products featuring closed, calm smiles and prefer low intensity activities such as meditation, reflecting their preference for low arousal positive affect and feeling calm. Similarly, although Americans share many cultural products and practices, we should also find that cultural practices and products reflect regionally specific ideas and values.

People

People who reside in different regions with different products indeed differ in their psychological tendencies. An examination of personality differences among people from different U.S. regions revealed that 30% of personality differences among individuals could be attributed to their geographical origin (Krug & Kulhavy, 1973), and in a more recent survey of half a million Americans, Rentfrow et al. (2008) found state-level patterns in Big Five personality factors. Studies have also revealed significant regional differences in other types of psychological tendencies—for example, in self-description (Plaut, Markus, & Lachman, 2002), in the form that well-being takes (Plaut et al., 2002, 2012), in endorsement of independent values (Kitayama et al., 2010), and in endorsement of violence (Cohen & Nisbett, 1994). Thus, although Americans share some psychological tendencies, they also differ widely across regions in certain aspects of self and well-being.

Reflecting the dynamic nature of the culture cycle, people create products that reflect their understandings of how to be and how to be well, and in turn, exposure to and engagement with these products reinforce their understandings of self and well-being. In this way, the local and regional cultures reflect historically specific ideas, products, and psychological tendencies. The embodiment of self in products—and hence in place—is a process that typically goes unnoticed. The culture cycle therefore often operates outside of conscious awareness, rendering daily ideas, practices, and psychological tendencies as seemingly natural and right.

PLACE, PRODUCTS, AND PEOPLE IN FOUR REGIONS

In this section, we compare the culture cycles of four regions in the United States: West, Northeast, Midwest, and South. Wee defined these regions in terms of the regional scheme set forth by the U.S. Census Bureau (2000; see Figure 14.1 for map of regions).[1] In each of these regions, we examine the pervasive ideas and values that put each one's culture cycle in motion (*place*); the norms, products, and practices that keep the cycle in motion (*products*); and the reflection of these ideas and products in self and well-being (*people*). For the purpose of highlighting some of the distinguishing features in these regional culture cycles, we have labeled the Western culture cycle as *new and free*, the Northeastern culture cycle as *old and established*, the Midwestern culture cycle as *friendly and average*, and the Southern culture cycle as *honor and community*. We determined these characterizations

---

[1] We did not include Hawaii and Alaska because of their different histories and locations.

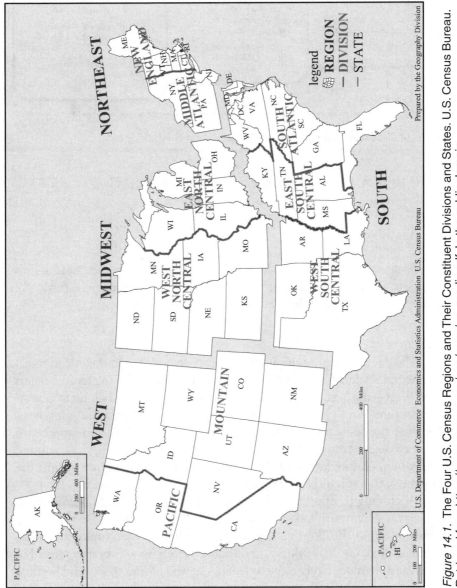

Figure 14.1. The Four U.S. Census Regions and Their Constituent Divisions and States. U.S. Census Bureau. Retrieved from https://www.census.gov/geo/www/us_regdiv.pdf. In the public domain.

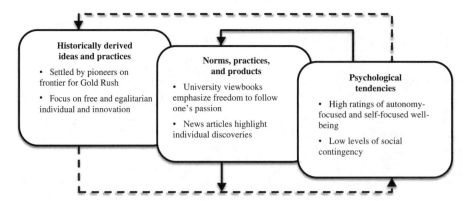

Figure 14.2. Western Culture Cycle—Emphasis on New and Free.

on the basis of a sampling of the past literature (e.g., Plaut et al., 2002; Rentfrow et al., 2008; Vandello & Cohen, 1999).

The West: New and Free

As shown in Figure 14.2, the West's culture cycle is characterized as new and free to capture the region's emphasis on doing one's own thing, innovation, egalitarianism, and the individual as a free, unencumbered agent.

Place

The development of the West by European and Anglo-American transcontinental settlers occurred much later than in other U.S. regions.[2] Settlers of the West—the home of the Gold Rush—left their homes behind to change their fortunes and pursue the promise of achieving riches and greatness. Moreover, the desire for freedom required mastering new, harsh environments, which created a frontier region resident who was, as described by cultural geographer Zelinsky (1973/1992), a "resourceful, isolated fighter against the wilderness, triumphantly carving out his own autonomous barony" (p. 42).

According to Triandis, Bontempo, Villareal, Asai, and Lucca (1988), settling the Mountain West frontier played an important role in promoting individualism in the West and in the United States. Developing this idea, Kitayama et al. (2006) hypothesized that settlers who voluntarily moved to the West were more likely to be independent and autonomous, and because they encountered the West's barren environment and harsh climate, they developed psychological tendencies such as self-promotion and self-reliance

---

[2]Of course, the West and other regions already had other inhabitants, including Native Americans, Mexicans, and immigrants and colonizers from other places.

to ensure their survival and ability to protect themselves and their property. As settlers came together to develop a new community in the West, they built into the region ideas, institutions, and daily practices and routines that reflected and reinforced being free and doing their own thing. For example, the economic systems in the West at the time, such as cattle ranching and animal herding, mirrored the values of new and free and promoted individualism (Vandello & Cohen, 1999). Today, as home to major technology centers such as Silicon Valley, the economic systems in the West continue to embody values of freedom and independence.

Products

An examination of products in the West reveals the historically pervasive ideas and values of new and free, being autonomous from others, and pushing boundaries. For example, the viewbook from Stanford University (2009) conveys the prominent California university's commitment to providing a place where "the wind of freedom blows" (p. 1) and students have "the freedom to be themselves: innovative, creative, unconstrained by any predetermined look or affect" (p. 22; Plaut et al., 2012). Newspapers and websites examined by Plaut et al. (2012) also revealed the West's attention to innovation and being a unique individual. Over a period of 6 weeks, over one third of article headlines in the *San Francisco Chronicle* (significantly more than the *Boston Globe*) focused on the new, unique, and creative—including pushing the boundaries of discovery. Moreover, two thirds or greater of San Francisco venture capital firm websites made reference to individuals (as opposed to groups), to new and creative themes of changing and transforming industries and being pioneers, and to encouraging egalitarian working relationships with their portfolio companies (significantly more than Boston-area firms). Analyses of health care websites revealed similar patterns: Approximately one quarter or more of medical center websites in San Francisco focused on individual empowerment, alternative medicine, or themes of the new, unique, and creative.

Daily practices in the West also represent values of being free and unique. For example, parents in the West were more likely than those in other regions to give their children names that were less likely to be popular at that time, such as Ryker or Willow (Varnum & Kitayama, 2011). By giving their children names that were less likely to be shared with others, parents in the West convey their desire to bestow on their children a unique and personal identity.

People

Psychological tendencies of people in the West also reflect and promote the new and free values of individualism. People in the West (as well as in the Northeast) were more likely to report higher Openness compared with people in the Midwest and South (Rentfrow et al., 2008), and in a survey on health and well-being, people in the Mountain West showed a greater focus on autonomy and self (Plaut et al., 2002). Furthermore, although their ratings of their social well-being tended to be high, they were less likely to rate themselves as high on positive relations with others or civic obligation. Similarly, San Franciscans revealed selves that were less contingent on norms and relationships (Plaut et al., 2012). Westerners were also less likely to be religious, more likely to be self-employed, and more likely to live alone and to drive alone (Vandello & Cohen, 1999).

The Northeast: Old and Established

As shown in Figure 14.3, the Northeast's culture cycle is characterized by *old and established* to capture the region's emphasis on experience, hierarchical control, avoiding constraints, and well-being that is contingent on factors such as relationship and status (e.g., Plaut et al., 2002).

Place

The oldest establishments and institutions in the United States began in the Northeast. For example, Boston produced the country's first public school and first college. Pennsylvania was the birthplace of the nation's first hospital and first commercial bank. The Northeast served as the site of Puritan settlement and the birthplace of the American Revolution and scaffolded the adoption of the Declaration of Independence and the first U.S. government. Thus, freedom and independence from imposed constraints is the foundational theme in this region. Establishment, family, and community

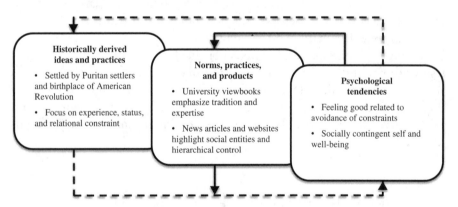

Figure 14.3. Northeast Culture Cycle—Emphasis on Old and Established.

ties are also prominent in the region (and sometimes serve as constraints), and so other important cultural themes in the Northeast include attention to the status and relationships of individuals and focus on the embeddedness or tightness of the norms in the region (Plaut et al., 2012).

Products

Products in the Northeast tend to reflect values of old and established—specifically, attention to community and status in the form of expertise and prestige. For example, the viewbook from Harvard College (2008) begins by expressing its "tradition of excellence . . . since its founding in 1636" (p. 4). As the nation's oldest college and "what many consider America's finest university" (p. 5) students "benefit directly from the university's eminence as a national and international crossroads" (p. 16). Yale's (2012) viewbook also emphasizes themes of tradition, achievement, and community, describing Yale as a place of "tradition, a company of scholars, a society of friends" (p. 9) where students are a "part of all the scholars and students who have trod paths of learning across her campus, of their ideals and accomplishments, and of their lives and times" (p. 72).

Newspapers and venture capital websites from Boston also have been shown to reflect the prevalent values of status through expertise and attention to ties to the community in the Northeast (Plaut et al., 2012). In a series of content analyses, the *Boston Globe* and Boston area venture capital websites were more likely to mention social entities (e.g., domestic and international communities, companies) compared with the *San Francisco Chronicle* and San Francisco websites. In addition, over half of Boston area venture capital firm websites (significantly more than San Francisco) emphasized companies' status and hierarchical control over their portfolio companies, conveying that with their knowledge and expertise, they had the ability to ensure the success of their investments. Health care websites also followed this pattern, with one quarter to half of web sites mentioning establishment and experience or the number of employees in the organization.

People

Although psychological tendencies in the West often emphasize explicit independent values such as individualism and anti-power more so than in the Northeast (Kitayama et al., 2010), perhaps reflecting their history as the birthplace of the American Revolution (against imperial constraint), Northeasterners' well-being is characterized by a greater attention to the constraints that they contend with on a daily basis and their attempts to avoid them (Plaut et al., 2002, 2012). People in the Northeast (as well as the Southeast) generally rate themselves highest in Neuroticism compared with other regions and low in Conscientiousness (Rentfrow et al., 2008), though they also tended to focus on good relations with others, reflecting their embeddedness in social relationships and attention to their relationships with others and community (Plaut et al., 2002).

The Midwest: Friendly and Average

As shown in Figure 14.4, the Midwest's culture cycle is characterized as *friendly and average* to capture the region's emphasis on being middle-of-the-road, stable and responsible, and satisfied with the self, and on promoting good relations with others.

Place

Whereas well-known people and events characterize the histories of the West, Northeast, and South (e.g., Gold Rush, Founding Fathers, Civil War), the history of the Midwest tends to revolve around local events and communities (Ryden, 1999). As described by Ryden (1999), other regions build grand monuments to memorialize defining aspects of their regional histories, whereas the Midwest emphasizes its local community accomplishments by, for example, posting athletic and academic awards of students from the local high school.

The landscape of the Midwest mirrors its values of stability: It is flat and relatively unchanging. Historically, the fertile and less populated terrain of the Midwest has suited it to agriculture. As the nation's "breadbasket" and All-American heartland, the Midwest accounts for almost three quarters of U.S. grain (particularly corn) production and approximately 60% of U.S. agricultural exports (Baird, Bittner, Gollnik, & Gardner, 2011). Moreover,

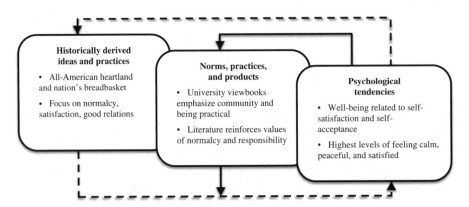

Figure 14.4. Midwest Culture Cycle—Emphasis on Friendly and Average.

the agricultural economy of the Midwest consists of an interconnected web of small and large cities focused on farming and development within the region rather than on external expansion (Page & Walker, 1991). The Midwest is also home to the three major automobile companies in the United States (General Motors, Ford, and Chrysler), which like farming, embody ideals of hard work and responsibility.

Products

Products in the Midwest generally represent the values of being friendly and average, as well as being practical and down-to-earth. The University of Chicago's (2012) viewbook describes its students as "smart, funny, down-to-earth—the kind of people who become friends for life" (p. 9), and Northwestern's (2012) viewbook describes its students as having "an idealism grounded in reality and a great sense of responsibility" (p. 29). Community and care are also prevalent themes in the viewbooks of Midwestern universities. For example, University of Chicago describes its residence housing as a place that "integrates faculty, staff, upperclass resident assistants, and a cadre of 50 to 100 students who live together, learn together, laugh together, and care for one another" (p. 17).

Literary representations of the Midwest also often emphasize its values of self-acceptance and normalcy. According to Jane Smiley, an American novelist who grew up in Missouri,

> In the Midwest, we say to ourselves, 'Gee, I got this; I got that' and 'Wow, they didn't have to give me anything' and I guess there is a group of people in the country, whether they are Midwesterners or middle class, or whatever their background is, whose parents tell them all their lives, "Just be happy you got anything." (as quoted in Pearlman, 1994, p. 102)

Historian Andrew Cayton (2001) described how characters in stories about the Midwest often come to terms with their normalcy, such as the Iowa farmwife in *The Bridges of Madison County* by Robert James Waller who escapes her quiet life for a few days of romantic excitement with a visiting photographer but eventually comes to her senses and returns to the "well-worn patterns of duty and responsibility" (p. 143).

Media and politics often take advantage of the prevalence of the "median" American in the Midwest by applying the "Will it play in Peoria?" test to new products and ideas. For example, companies send newly developed products first to the Midwest—specifically, Peoria, Illinois—before launching to the nation. Presidential hopefuls are also sure to stop there, believing that if products or people succeed in Peoria, they will succeed nationally.

People

Well-being and self in the Midwest also reflect the prevalent values of *friendly and average*. In the Midwest, people are seen as "tolerant, friendly, open, generous, and respectful of others and their opinions" (Madison, 1988, p. 109) and value being stable and rooted, having a sense of permanence, and accepting themselves as they are. In the Midwest, people are more likely to accept their life and conditions. In fact, Plaut et al. (2002) showed that people in the Midwest, compared with those in other regions, tended to report the lowest ratings of autonomy and personal growth and highest ratings of self-acceptance and self-satisfaction, as well as the highest levels of feeling calm, peaceful, and satisfied; they also rated themselves as high on family obligation. They were also more likely to rate high in Agreeableness and Conscientiousness compared with other regions and low in Openness and lowest in Neuroticism (Rentfrow et al., 2008).

The South: Honor and Community

As shown in Figure 14.5, the South's culture cycle is characterized by *honor and community* to capture the region's emphasis on strong regional identification, protection of one's reputation and property, and one's status and role in relationships and hierarchies.

Place

The South is frequently thought of as the home of charm, grace, and southern hospitality. Regional identification is strong in the South (Grantham, 1994), and there is an emphasis on remembering and honoring the past, particularly the Civil War. Church life also tends to play a prominent role in the

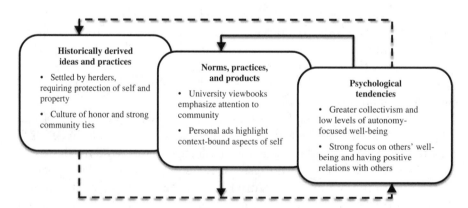

Figure 14.5. South Culture Cycle—Emphasis on a Culture of Honor and Collectivism.

South, which contributes to the cultivation of strong ties to the community through meetings and organizations (Markus & Conner, 2013; Vandello & Cohen, 1999).

The South is also characterized by its focus on honor. According to Cohen and Nisbett (1994) a "culture of honor" in the South was fostered in part by its economic history. The first settlers to the South often made their livelihood through herding (Fischer, 1989), which requires open spaces for the animals and greater attention to protecting oneself and property. Because of this, herding cultures—and the South—have been related to violence that is specifically in response to loss of honor and slights to one's reputation and property (Cohen & Nisbett, 1994; Cohen, Nisbett, Bowdle, & Schwarz, 1996). In the South, defending one's honor represents an intertwining of protecting one's reputation and family with showing that one is not easy to push around even in the face of the slightest insult (Cohen & Nisbett, 1994).

The legacy of slavery in the South also served to sanction the use of violence to control one's property or slaves (Cohen, 1996). For example, laws in the South at the time of slavery and organizations such as the Ku Klux Klan allowed for the use of violence through beatings and whippings to keep slaves in the control of White slave owners, (Cohen, 1996). By some accounts, slavery also contributed to collectivism in the South by supporting an agricultural, plantation-based economy (Vandello & Cohen, 1999).

Products

Products in the South often emphasize protecting one's self and honor. For example, in the South (as in the West), self-defense laws are more likely to sanction deadly force, and gun control laws are more lenient (Cohen & Vandello, 1998). In fact, in a field experiment, Cohen and Vandello (1998) found that when they provided college newspapers across the country with a fact sheet about crime, newspapers in the South (and West) were more likely to write stories that justified the actions of the perpetrators and deemphasized aggravating circumstances to the crime.

Products in the South also emphasize collectivism and communities. For example, Vanderbilt University's viewbook represents itself as a place where students are connected to and gain experience from the real world, specifically that they can "learn and grow inside the classroom and outside the classroom" (Vanderbilt University Creative Services, 2011, p. 2). At Vanderbilt, "caring" is one of its core values and students "are dedicated to supporting one another within our community. We make a lifelong commitment to channeling service, knowledge, and experience toward the betterment of humanity" (Vanderbilt University Creative Services, 2011, p. 13). Other products such as personal ads in the South also have been shown to draw attention to how people are embedded within a context (Lun et al.,

2011). Specifically, when people in the South write personal ads, they tend to describe aspects of themselves that are more contextualized and less controllable, such as race, religion, or age, compared with people in the Northeast who tend to describe themselves as context-free and made up of abstract traits and attributes (e.g., "confident"; Lun et al., 2011).

People

People in the South are more likely to focus on the well-being of others and having positive relations with others, and they tend to report high levels of social responsibility and low levels of autonomy-focused well-being (Plaut et al., 2002). According to Vandello and Cohen (1999), people in the Deep South are also more likely to engage in collectivistic behaviors such as living with others, carpooling, and having greater affiliation with religious communities. Southern psychological tendencies also reflect attention to honor. For example, Southern White males have been found to show heightened aggression when insulted (Cohen et al., 1996), and Whites in "honor states," which are particularly prevalent in the South and West, show more risk-taking, manifested in elevated accidental death rates (Barnes, Brown, & Tamborski, 2012).

INTERSECTIONS OF REGION WITH RACE AND CLASS

An analysis of regional culture cycles requires attention to how these cycles intersect with race and class. In this section, we describe four such intersections: the Latino Southwest, Asian Pacific, Black industrial northern cities, and rural Appalachia. Although people from these racial groups certainly reside in regions other than the ones listed here, we focus on these regions because of their historical significance for each of these groups.

Regional culture cycles take on different forms as they interact with the racialized or class-based culture cycles of particular groups in those regions. Psychological studies of region, however, have yet to examine how race and class matter across regions. Given our focus on how places, products, and people make each other up, we think it is important to draw attention to how historically derived ideas and practices associated with race and class interact with those of region.

The Latino Southwest

Place

Latinos in the Southwest region are exposed to the culture cycle of being free and independent, but they also contend with a racialized culture cycle that encompasses ideas, products, and practices that cast them as "perpetual invaders" and "illegal" immigrants. Yet, "Latinos" have been in the United States since the 16th century. Together with Spaniards, Mexican Indians in the late 16th century explored the geographical area that is now known as the Southwest. Spain and then Mexico occupied this territory until 1848, when the Mexican–American War ended with the ceding of Mexico's northern territories to the United States. Under the Treaty of Guadalupe Hidalgo, tens of thousands of Mexicans living in this territory became U.S. citizens. Many of these residents were subsequently disenfranchised of rights and property despite their legal claim to land and citizenship (Massey, 2009). Moreover, when Whites began to move to the Southwest in greater numbers in the mid-19th century, they adopted established Latino cultural practices and lifestyles (Paul, 1988). Today Latino Americans make up a large proportion of the population of many of the major cities in the Southwest—for example, Phoenix (41%), Tucson (42%), Las Vegas (32%), Denver (32%), and Albuquerque (47%; U.S. Census Bureau, 2010). Despite Latinos' significant presence and long history in the United States, their characterization as "illegal" and unwanted immigrants persists.

Products

In the media, Latino Americans and undocumented immigrants are often portrayed as illegal and a threat to the country's general prosperity and social development (Chavez, 2008). These representations can take on a dehumanizing form. For example, newspaper articles often depict Latinos as "invading soldiers" or "tidal waves" of illegal immigrants (Santa Ana, 2002). U.S. federal and state laws and policies have helped to institutionalize the idea of Latinos as illegal (regardless of their actual legal status) by questioning their status as valid U.S. citizens and residents. In 1954, the Immigration and Naturalization Service apprehended over one million "Mexican-looking" people during Operation Wetback. Today, Latinos comprise 93% of individuals arrested through the government's Secure Communities program but comprise only 77% of the undocumented population; a sizeable number of those detained are U.S. citizens (Kohli, Markowitz, & Chavez, 2011). In 2010, Arizona passed a law expressly to encourage "attrition through enforcement" (S. 1070, 2010, § 1) and requiring law enforcement officials to check the immigration status of those they suspected might be in the country without authorization. Arizona also passed another law (H.R. 2281, 2010)—originally aimed at Tucson's high school Mexican American Studies program—banning ethnic studies classes at every grade level (see Fryberg et al., 2012, for role of media in the delegitimization of immigrants).

People

Despite the presence of well-established communities of Mexican Americans in the United States, overall Latinos are represented as immigrants and illegal. Jiménez (2010) has theorized that one reason this perception of Latinos exists is because of the constant immigration of Mexicans into the United States. Research suggests that these representations of Latinos as illegal and "invading" (Santa Ana, 2002) may reinforce negative racial attitudes toward Latinos. For example, when asked which ethnic group is associated with rodents, people often answer that it is Latinos (Marshall & Eberhardt, 2011). In fact implicit and explicit racial associations of Latinos have been found to undergird negative attitudes toward Latinos and immigration policy (see Plaut, Tecle, & Feddersen, 2013).

Representations of Latinos undoubtedly also affect their own psychological experiences. Legal and social realities have created a hostile environment for both documented and undocumented Latinos. Research by Dovidio, Gluszek, John, Ditlmann, and Lagunes (2010) has suggested that signals of ethnic difference (e.g., accents) play a role in lowering sense of belonging and increasing feelings of being an outsider in Latinos. Studies conducted in southern California and Texas have suggested that Latino immigrants encounter many challenges and fear deportation, which contributes to acculturative stress (Arbona et al., 2010; Padilla, Cervantes, Maldonado, & Garcia, 1988). Undocumented college students facing concerns over their status in the United States often avoid situations that risk revealing their undocumented status, such as going to the hospital, finding jobs, or engaging in close contact with others (Dozier, 1993). Lack of belonging and avoidance of certain situations will not necessarily diminish with President Obama's 2012 Deferred Action for Childhood Arrivals (see http://www.dhs.gov/deferred-action-childhood-arrivals). At least one state (Arizona) has retaliated by denying these youth state benefits such as driver's licenses. Moreover, one study conducted in Texas suggested that Latino immigrants report fears of deportation regardless of legal status (Arbona et al., 2010).

The Asian Pacific

Place

Asians in the Pacific region are exposed to the culture cycle of being new and free, but they also contend with a racialized culture cycle that encompasses ideas, products, and practices that portray them as "perpetual foreigners." Asian immigrants (particularly Chinese and Japanese) traveled to America in the late 19th century to work in the gold mines and later on the transcontinental railroad. Practically from the start, they were cast as inassimilable perpetual foreigners. They were stereotyped as bearers of disease and of vices such as gambling or opium use. They worked for low wages, which caused friction with competing labor groups, who eventually "drove out" thousands of Asian residents, most of them Chinese, from their jobs and homes (Pfaelzer, 2007). Asian workers began to group together in enclaves that became Chinatowns and Japantowns, and many struggled to find work, leading them to open restaurants and laundry businesses, which were a few of the only options available to them at the time (Takaki, 1993).

Products

In the late 19th century, the small but increasing immigration of Asian groups fed a growing fear that Asians would take over the United States. In response to this perceived threat, the United States passed several laws such as the Asian Exclusion Act and the Chinese Exclusion Act. Angel Island, the Pacific entry point for immigration became a processing center for Asian immigrants, and many were turned away from entering the United States. These acts effectively stopped the growth of the Asian population in the United States, and they remained in place until the 1940s.

The courts also served to reinforce the perpetual foreigner stereotype and legalize discrimination against Asian Americans. In 1922, Takao Ozawa, a Japanese man who was considered ineligible for naturalization because of his Asian origin, attempted to have Japanese classified as White. The case was brought before the Supreme Court, which ruled that Japanese were not white and that Ozawa could not be naturalized as a U.S. citizen, maintaining the racial boundaries between Whites and Asians (Chang, 2001). Twenty years later during World War II, President Franklin D. Roosevelt, fearing that Japan had spies in the United States, authorized thousands of Japanese and Japanese American citizens to be sent to internment camps along the Pacific Coast. Italian and German Americans did not face the same consequences, though their countries of origin were also enemies in the war.

People

Asian Americans are aware of the perception that they are seen as perpetual foreigners, "not American," and "unable to speak English." When faced with the threat of identity denial or that others do not see them as part of a group with which they identify—being American—Asian Americans respond by asserting their American identity (Cheryan & Monin, 2005). For example, one line of research showed that if asked, "Do you speak English?" Asian American students at Pacific region universities asserted their "American" cultural knowledge (e.g., TV shows), reported engaging in more "American" practices (e.g., sports, music), and showed more preference for less healthy,

"American" foods than those whose American identity was not questioned (Cheryan & Monin, 2005; Guendelman, Cheryan, & Monin, 2011).

Black Industrial Northern Cities

Place

Blacks in industrial northern cities are exposed to the culture cycle of being old and established, but they also contend with a racialized culture cycle that encompasses ideas, products, and practices that include racial discrimination and segregation. In the early part of the 20th century, approximately 6 million African Americans left the South, many of them bound for cities in the North. Between 1910 and 1920, for example, Detroit's Black population grew from 5,000 to 40,800, Cleveland's from 8,400 to 34,400, Chicago's from 44,000 to 109,400, and New York's from 91,700 to 152,400 (Takaki, 1993). This Great Migration drew African Americans who imagined safer, more prosperous, and less oppressed lives than those they had experienced in the South. But despite some greater access to jobs, especially during a wartime labor shortage, African American communities in northern cities experienced persistent racialized poverty. According to Thomas Sugrue's (2005) account of race and class in Detroit, changes in the labor market such as the loss of jobs during deindustrialization, workplace discrimination against Blacks, and segregation abetted by White anti-Black mobilization (e.g., from government subsidies to suburban-bound Whites, to real estate agent racist steering, to violent attackers of black homeowners) all contributed to an urban crisis.

Products

Geographically anchored interpersonal and institutional practices have contributed to the continued inability of Black families to gain status and wealth. For example, systematic paired-testing studies have repeatedly found discrimination against Black home-seekers by housing agents (e.g., Yinger, 1986). In addition to these daily interpersonal practices, housing discrimination also occurs at an institutional level. For example, lenders often engaged in *redlining*, or drawing lines around certain geographical areas, and denying or offering lower value mortgages to families in those areas. Though the Fair Housing Act of 1968 and other regulations made many of these practices illegal, the consequences of systemic discrimination had already solidified a culture cycle that maintains residential segregation by race, hindering Black families' ability to accumulate wealth for future generations (Lang & Nakamura, 1993).

More recently, the foreclosure crisis has disproportionately affected Black families. Rugh and Massey (2010) argued that racial discrimination occurred at every stage in the series of events leading to the foreclosure crisis, from obtaining a loan to foreclosure on one's house. Through historical practices of steering, redlining, and loan discrimination, neighborhoods became increasingly segregated, which facilitated unequal lending to families in different neighborhoods (Engel & McCoy, 2007) as well as an increase in subprime mortgages offered to Black families (Been, Ellen, & Madar, 2009). When the housing bubble burst, the foreclosure rate was particularly pronounced in Black neighborhoods (Schuetz, Been, & Ellen, 2008).

People

Institutional and daily practices of discrimination clearly affect African Americans' wealth accumulation. They also affect other aspects of lived experience, including psychological tendencies. Although they are able to draw on many positive aspects of their identity, African Americans must also contend with negative representations of their group. In research that originated with observations of African American students' experiences at the University of Michigan, Claude Steele and his colleagues have shown that African Americans often suffer academically when under the threat of confirming a negative stereotype about their group (e.g., Steele & Aronson, 1995). Other research conducted in Detroit has shown that African American students who feel more positive about their ethnic identity and experience themselves as connected to their family and community find it easier to generate possible selves related to academic achievement than those who are more oriented toward individualism or being separated from one's community (Oyserman, Gant, & Ager, 1995).

James Jones (2003) proposed a model called *time, rhythm, improvisation, orality, and spirituality* (TRIOS), which describes other psychological tendencies African Americans have created to cope with systematic and sustained racism and discrimination. TRIOS refers to several important and valued African American cultural ideas and practices that Jones suggested African Americans developed to tie themselves to their African origins and to claim positive aspects of their identity in response to the racism they have experienced in the United States.

Rural Appalachia

Place

Those who live in the Appalachian Mountains are exposed to the culture cycle of honor and community, but they also contend with a class-based culture cycle that encompasses ideas, products, and practices that include economic exploitation and a nearly exclusive focus on family as the basis of social organization.

Appalachia is both a geographical and cultural region. Geographically, the Appalachian Mountains reach from Canada to the Gulf of Mexico, and various subcultures can be found at any point along the chain. The most commonly recognized and most concentrated Appalachian culture is that of Central Appalachia, which encompasses eastern Kentucky and Tennessee, western Virginia and North Carolina, and the entire state of West Virginia. This region represents the highest and most rugged stretches of the Appalachians and was the longest isolated from other parts of the country.

Until large coal companies began to arrive in the mid 1800s, Appalachian natives lived by subsistence farming. Plots of the family land were divided equally among children; as families added adjoining tracts, they would eventually occupy entire valleys, mountaintops, or hollows. Parents, children, and siblings often lived in sight of each other. This practice continued as the economy shifted from family farms to coal mining, and entire families moved to the company towns. Therefore, families became the central focus of identity for Appalachian natives, though at times the focus on family prevalent in Appalachia could be so intense as to be limiting, even debilitating, regardless of the family's functionality. Close-knit families tend to stay physically close together, even at the risk of losing economic opportunities, and those in fractious, dysfunctional families can become consumed by interpersonal drama to the exclusion of all else (Keefe, 1998). Social networks, businesses, politics, and religion all centered on family and community allegiances, which became even more important as "flatlanders" began to filter into the region. These visitors could be coal magnates, government agents, missionaries, or educational institutions, but they were all considered outsiders by the natives (Halperin, 1990).

Products

Appalachian cultural products often reflect two intertwined concerns: economic exploitation and family as ingroup. Early Appalachian natives passed down and embellished old folk songs and tales from their predominately English, Scottish–Irish, and German ancestors; ballads and stories such as "Lord Daniel" and "Pretty Saro" spread the themes of clan feuds, betrayal, and the necessity of leaving loved ones to seek one's fortune. As the hard life of the company miner became the norm, and especially once the unions and the labor movement began to fight with the companies in the 1920s and 1930s, the products likewise adapted. Miners and their wives, such as Sarah Ogan Gunning and Florence Reece, adapted old songs and wrote new ones to reflect their actual living conditions and experiences during the skirmishes between the mine operators and those miners who were trying to organize. For example, Florence Reece wrote "Which Side Are You On?" the night she and her children were terrorized in their home by mine-hired "thugs" who were looking for her organizer husband. Sarah Ogan Gunning referenced the deaths of her husband and child in her songs such as "Dreadful Memories" and "I Hate the Capitalist System," which broadcast the state of Appalachian natives to a larger audience. Through this music, Appalachians express their rage and despair over the struggle between families and impersonal institutions and thereby gain some measure of agency against the wealthy outsiders.

People

People in Appalachia also tend to show the focus on family in their psychological tendencies. Collectivism is higher in this region than for the rest of the United States, as it is in many high-poverty and rural areas (Vandello & Cohen, 1999). Natives are far more likely to interact with their families than non-Appalachian natives (Treadway, Plaut, Gore, & Wilburn, 2013) and are more likely to benefit from collectivism. For example, Native Appalachian college students who are higher in collectivism have been shown to have better academic outcomes than non-Appalachian natives who are high in collectivism (Gore, Wilburn, Treadway, & Plaut, 2011).

CONCLUSION

Despite the frequent casting of the United States as a homogeneous, independent culture, as we have shown here, independence in different regions across the country takes considerably different forms: from the West with its values of *new and free*, to the Northeast with its values of *old and established*, to the Midwest with its values of *friendly and average*, and to the South with its values of *honor and community*. Each region has developed its own distinct culture cycle, which is made up of different histories and ecologies (place); norms, products, and practices (products); and psychological tendencies (people) that make each other up. Therefore, when conducting an analysis of cultural differences in self and well-being, regional variation should be considered in addition to national variation.

Moreover, as we have described using examples of Latinos in the Southwest, Asians in the Pacific West, Blacks in industrial northern cities, and rural Appalachians, the experiences of different ethnic, racial, or cultural groups also vary depending on the group's history in a region. For example, being Latino in the Southwest—unlike being White in the Southwest—occurs in a context not only of "new and free" but also of "illegal immigrant." Therefore, just as region should be taken into account when evaluating or comparing national cultures, race and class should be considered when conducting an analysis by region. In addition, though we did not present this analysis, we expect that the experiences of being Latino, Asian, Black, or poor vary by region. Therefore, regional influences should be considered when analyzing race and class.

Given the pervasive influence of context on self and well-being, cultural clashes naturally occur as people move from one place to another whether they cross national or regional lines. Mark Zuckerberg, representing his region's emphasis on new and free in the West, came up against the Wall Street investors who bristled at his lack of regard for their old and established ways in the Northeast. These individual present-day reactions—rather than being superficial—are deeply tied to the histories, products, practices, and people that characterize their respective regions. Understanding these dissimilar actions and reactions requires understanding how each region's culture cycle is made up of different, mutually constituting places, products, and people.

REFERENCES

Arbona, C., Olvera, N., Rodriguez, N., Hagan, J., Linares, A., & Wiesner, M. (2010). Acculturative stress among documented and undocumented Latino immigrants in the United States. *Hispanic Journal of Behavioral Sciences, 32,* 362–384. doi:10.1177/0739986310373210

Baird, T., Bittner, J., Gollnik, R., & Gardner, S. (2011). *Understanding the consequences of the Panama Canal Expansion on Midwest grain and agricultural exports.* Madison, WI: National Center for Freight & Infrastructure Research & Education.

Barnes, C. D., Brown, R. P., & Tamborski, M. (2012). Living dangerously: Culture of honor, risk-taking, and the nonrandomness of "accidental" deaths. *Social Psychological and Personality Science, 3*(1), 100–107. doi:10.1177/1948550611410440

Been, V., Ellen, I., & Madar, J. (2009). The high cost of segregation: Exploring racial disparities in high-cost lending. *The Fordham Urban Law Journal, 36,* 361–393.

Bellah, R. N., Madsen, R., Sullivan, W. M., Swidler, A., & Tipton, S. M. (1985). *Habits of the heart: Individualism and commitment in American life.* Berkeley, CA: University of California Press.

Cayton, A. R. L. (2001). The anti-region: Place and identity in the history of the American Midwest. In A. R. L. Cayton & S. E. Gray (Eds.), *The American Midwest: Essays on regional history* (pp. 140–159). Bloomington, IN: Indiana University Press.

Chang, G. H. (2001). *Asian Americans and politics: Perspectives, experiences, prospects.* Washington, DC: Woodrow Wilson Center Press.

Chavez, L. R. (2008). *The Latino threat: Constructing immigrants, citizens, and the nation.* Stanford, CA: Stanford University Press.

Cheryan, S., & Monin, B. (2005). "Where are you really from?" Asian Americans and identity denial. *Journal of Personality and Social Psychology, 89,* 717–730. doi:10.1037/0022-3514.89.5.717

Cohen, D. (1996). Law, social policy, and violence: The impact of regional cultures. *Journal of Personality and Social Psychology, 70,* 961–978. doi:10.1037/0022-3514.70.5.961

Cohen, D., & Nisbett, R. E. (1994). Self-protection and the culture of honor: Explaining Southern violence. *Personality and Social Psychology Bulletin, 20,* 551–567. doi:10.1177/0146167294205012

Cohen, D., Nisbett, R. E., Bowdle, B. F., & Schwarz, N. (1996). Insult, aggression, and the southern culture of honor: An "experimental ethnography". *Journal of Personality and Social Psychology, 70,* 945–960. doi:10.1037/0022-3514.70.5.945

Cohen, D., & Vandello, J. A. (1998). Meanings of violence. *The Journal of Legal Studies, 27,* 567–584. doi:10.1086/468035

Dovidio, J. F., Gluszek, A., John, M.-S., Ditlmann, R., & Lagunes, P. (2010). Understanding bias toward Latinos: Discrimination, dimensions of difference, and experience of exclusion. *Journal of Social Issues, 66*(1), 59–78. doi:10.1111/j.1540-4560.2009.01633.x

Dozier, S. B. (1993). Emotional concerns of undocumented and out-of-status foreign students. *Communication Review, 13,* 29–33.

Engel, K. C., & McCoy, P. A. (2007). Turning a blind eye: Wall Street finance of predatory lending. *Fordham Law Review, 75,* 2039–2103.

Fair Housing Act of 1968, 42 U.S.C.A. §§ 3601–3631 (1968).

Fischer, D. H. (1989). *Albion's seed: Four British folkways in America.* New York, NY: Oxford University Press.

Fryberg, S. A., Stephens, N. M., Covarrubias, R., Markus, H. R., Carter, E. D., Laiduc, G. A., & Salido, A. J. (2012). How the media frames the immigration debate: The critical role of location and politics. *Analyses of Social Issues and Public Policy, 12,* 96–112. doi:10.1111/j.1530-2415.2011.01259.x

Gore, J. S., Wilburn, K. R., Treadway, J., & Plaut, V. (2011). Regional collectivism in Appalachia and academic attitudes. *Cross-Cultural Research, 45,* 376–398. doi:10.1177/1069397111403396

Grantham, D. W. (1994). *The South in modern America.* New York, NY: HarperCollins.

Guendelman, M. D., Cheryan, S., & Monin, B. (2011). Fitting in but getting fat: Identity threat as an explanation for dietary decline among U.S. immigrant groups. *Psychological Science, 22,* 959–967. doi:10.1177/0956797611411585

Halperin, R. H. (1990). *The livelihood of kin: Making ends meet "The Kentucky Way".* Austin: University of Texas Press.

Harvard College. (2008). *Harvard viewbook.* Retrieved from http://admissions.college.harvard.edu

H.R. 2281, 49th Leg., 2d Reg. Sess. (Ariz. 2010) http://www.azleg.gov/legtext/49leg/2r/bills/hb2281s.pdf

Jiménez, T. R. (2010). *Replenished ethnicity: Mexican Americans, immigration, and identity.* Berkeley, CA: University of California Press.

Jones, J. M. (2003). TRIOS: A psychological theory of the African legacy in American culture. *Journal of Social Issues, 59*(1), 217–242. doi:10.1111/1540-4560.t01-1-00014

Keefe, S. E. (1998). Appalachian Americans: The formation of "reluctant ethnics." In G. R. Campbell (Ed.), *Many Americas: Critical perspectives on race, racism, and ethnicity* (pp. 129–153). Dubuque, IA: Kendall/Hunt.

Kim, H., & Markus, H. R. (1999). Deviance or uniqueness, harmony or conformity? A cultural analysis. *Journal of Personality and Social Psychology, 77*, 785–800. doi:10.1037/0022-3514.77.4.785

Kitayama, S., Conway, L. G., III, Pietromonaco, P. R., Park, H., & Plaut, V. C. (2010). Ethos of independence across regions in the United States: The production–adoption model of cultural change. *American Psychologist, 65*, 559–574. doi:10.1037/a0020277

Kitayama, S., Ishii, K., Imada, T., Takemura, K., & Ramaswamy, J. (2006). Voluntary settlement and the spirit of independence: Evidence from Japan's "Northern Frontier." *Journal of Personality and Social Psychology, 91*, 369–384. doi:10.1037/0022-3514.91.3.369

Kohli, A., Markowitz, P. L., & Chavez, L. (2011). *Secure communities by the numbers: An analysis of demographics and due process* (Research Report). Retrieved from the Chief Justice Earl Warren Institute on Law and Social Policy website: http://www.law.berkeley.edu/files/Secure_Communities_by_the_Numbers.pdf

Krug, S. E., & Kulhavy, R. W. (1973). Personality differences across regions of the United States. *The Journal of Social Psychology, 91*(1), 73–79. doi:10.1080/00224545.1973.9922648

Lang, W. W., & Nakamura, L. I. (1993). A model of redlining. *Journal of Urban Economics, 33*, 223–234. doi:10.1006/juec.1993.1014

Lun, J., Mesquita, B., & Smith, B. (2011). Self- and other-presentational styles in the Southern and Northern United States: An analysis of personal ads. *European Journal of Social Psychology, 41*, 435–445. doi:10.1002/ejsp.804

Madison, J. H. (1988). *Heartland: Comparative histories of the Midwestern states*. Bloomington, IN: Indiana University Press.

Markus, H. R., & Conner, A. C. (2013). *Clash! Eight cultural conflicts that makes us who we are*. New York, NY: Hudson Street Press.

Marshall, S. M., & Eberhardt, J. L. (2011, January) *The function of animal associations: Latinos as rats and anti-immigrant sentiment*. Paper presented at the meeting of the Society for Personality and Social Psychology, San Antonio, TX.

Massey, D. S. (2009). Racial formation in theory and practice: The case of Mexicans in the United States. *Race and Social Problems, 1*(1), 12–26. doi:10.1007/s12552-009-9005-3

Morling, B., & Lamoreaux, M. (2008). Measuring culture outside the head: A meta-analysis of individualism–collectivism in cultural products. *Personality and Social Psychology Review, 12*, 199–221. doi:10.1177/1088868308318260

Northwestern University. (2012). *Northwestern University viewbook*. Retrieved from http://www.ugadm.northwesterns.edu

Oyserman, D., Gant, L., & Ager, J. (1995). A socially contextualized model of African American identity: Possible selves and school persistence. *Journal of Personality and Social Psychology, 69,* 1216. doi:10.1037/0022-3514.69.6.1216

Padilla, A. M., Cervantes, R. C., Maldonado, M., & Garcia, R. E. (1988). Coping responses to psychosocial stress among Mexican and Central American immigrants. *Journal of Community Psychology, 16,* 418–427. doi:10.1002/1520-6629(198810)16:4<418::AID-JCOP2290160407>3.0.CO;2-R

Page, B., & Walker, R. (1991). From settlement to Fordism: The agro-industrial revolution in the American Midwest. *Economic Geography, 67,* 281–315. doi:10.2307/143975

Paul, R. W. (1988). *The Far West and Great Plains in transition.* New York, NY: Harper & Row.

Pearlman, M. (1994). *Listen to their voices: Twenty interviews with women who write.* Amherst, MA: University of Massachusetts Press.

Pfaelzer, J. (2007). *Driven out: The forgotten war against Chinese Americans.* New York, NY: Random House.

Plaut, V. C., Markus, H. R., & Lachman, M. E. (2002). Place matters: Consensual features and regional variation in American well-being and self. *Journal of Personality and Social Psychology, 83,* 160. doi:10.1037/0022-3514.83.1.160

Plaut, V. C., Markus, H. R., Treadway, J. R., & Fu, A. S. (2012). The cultural construction of self and well-being: A tale of two cities. *Personality and Social Psychology Bulletin, 38,* 1644–1658. doi:10.1177/0146167212458125

Plaut, V. C., Tecle, A., & Feddersen, M. (2013). A sociocultural analysis of U.S. immigration law and psychology. In E. Tartakovsky (Ed.), *Immigration: Policies, challenges and impact* (pp. 73–96). Hauppauge, NY: NOVA Science.

Rentfrow, P. J., Gosling, S. D., & Potter, J. (2008). A theory of the emergence, persistence, and expression of geographic variation in psychological characteristics. *Perspectives on Psychological Science, 3,* 339–369. doi:10.1111/j.1745-6924.2008.00084.x

Rugh, J. S., & Massey, D. S. (2010). Racial segregation and the American foreclosure crisis. *American Sociological Review, 75,* 629–651. doi:10.1177/0003122410380868

Ryden, K. C. (1999). Writing the Midwest: History, literature, and regional identity. *Geographical Review, 89,* 511–532. doi:10.2307/216100

S. 1070, 49th Leg., 2d Reg. Sess. (Ariz. 2010), http://www.azleg.gov/legtext/49leg/2r/bills/sb1070s.pdf

Santa Ana, O. (2002). *Brown tide rising: Metaphors of Latinos in contemporary American public discourse.* Austin, TX: University of Texas Press.

Schuetz, J., Been, V., & Ellen, I. G. (2008). Neighborhood effects of concentrated mortgage foreclosures. *Journal of Housing Economics, 17,* 306–319. doi:10.1016/j.jhe.2008.09.004

Sengupta, S. (2012, May 11). Why is everyone focused on Zuckerberg's hoodie? *The New York Times*. Retrieved from http://bits.blogs.nytimes.com/?s=why+is+everyone+focused+on+zuckerberg%27s+hood

Shweder, R. (2003). *Why do men barbecue? Recipes for cultural psychology*. Cambridge, MA: Harvard University Press.

Stanford University. (2009). *Stanford viewbook*. Retrieved from http://www.stanford.edu/dept/uga/site/publications/

Steele, C. M., & Aronson, J. (1995). Stereotype threat and the intellectual test performance of African Americans. *Journal of Personality and Social Psychology, 69*, 797–811. doi:10.1037/0022-3514.69.5.797

Sugrue, T. J. (2005). The origins of the urban crisis: Race and inequality in postwar Detroit. Princeton, NJ: Princeton University Press.

Takaki, R. T. (1993). *A different mirror: A history of multicultural America*. New York, NY: Back Bay Books/Little, Brown.

Treadway, J. R., Plaut, V. C., Gore, J. S., & Wilburn, K. R. (2013). *Climbing mountains in the mountains: Cultural models of success among Kentucky Appalachian college students*. Unpublished manuscript.

Triandis, H. C., Bontempo, R., Villareal, M. J., Asai, M., & Lucca, N. (1988). Individualism and collectivism: Cross-cultural perspectives on self-ingroup relationships. *Journal of Personality and Social Psychology, 54*, 323. doi:10.1037/0022-3514.54.2.323

Tsai, J. L. (2007). Ideal affect: Cultural causes and behavioral consequences. *Perspectives on Psychological Science, 2*, 242–259. doi:10.1111/j.1745-6916.2007.00043.x

University of Chicago. (2012). *University of Chicago viewbook*. Retrieved from http://collegeadmissions.uchicago.edu

U.S. Census Bureau. (2000). Census regions and divisions of the United States [Demographic map]. Retrieved from https://www.census.gov/geo/www/us_regdiv.pdf

U.S. Census Bureau. (2010). *State & county quickfacts*. Retrieved from http://quickfacts.census.gov/qfd/states/04/0477000.html

Vandello, J. A., & Cohen, D. (1999). Patterns of individualism and collectivism across the United States. *Journal of Personality and Social Psychology, 77*, 279–292. doi:10.1037/0022-3514.77.2.279

Vanderbilt University Creative Services. (2011). *Vanderbilt University viewbook*. Nashville, TN: Author.

Varnum, M. E. W., & Kitayama, S. (2011). What's in a name? Popular names are less common on frontiers. *Psychological Science, 22*, 176–183. doi:10.1177/0956797610395396

Yale College. (2012). *Yale viewbook*. Retrieved from http://admissions.yale.edu

Yinger, J. (1986). Measuring racial discrimination with fair housing audits: Caught in the act. *The American Economic Review, 76*, 881–893.

Zelinsky, W. (1992). *The cultural geography of the United States*. Englewood Cliffs, NJ: Prentice Hall. (Original work published 1973)

15

THE TYNESIDE NEIGHBORHOODS PROJECT: INVESTIGATING THE PSYCHOLOGICAL GEOGRAPHY OF ONE BRITISH CITY

DANIEL NETTLE AND AGATHE COLLÉONY

Don't think but look!
—Ludwig Wittgenstein, *Philosophical Investigations*

Modern Western societies are characterized by a quite remarkable degree of internal heterogeneity in terms of vitally consequential behaviors. This fact is often forgotten in cross-cultural studies that compare a sample from one or more Western countries with samples from other kinds of society. The key pattern that pervades Western societies is the *socioeconomic gradient*. There are marked gradients by socioeconomic position in behavioral variables as diverse as smoking (Kleinschmidt, Hills, & Elliott, 1995), physical exercise (Pampel, Krueger, & Denney, 2010), diet (Drewnowski & Specter, 2004), marital behavior (Nettle, 2010), civic participation (Schoon & Cheng, 2011), breast-feeding (Nettle, 2010), parental investment (Lawson & Mace, 2009), violence (Shaw, Tunstall, & Dorling, 2005), conduct disorder (Boden, Fergusson, & Horwood, 2010), and anxiety and depression (Najman et al., 2010). Many of these gradients are so extreme that the contrast between the most affluent sector of the population and the most deprived

http://dx.doi.org/10.1037/14272-016
Geographical Psychology: Exploring the Interaction of Environment and Behavior, P. J. Rentfrow (Editor)

is much greater than the average difference between, say, a Western European country and a country in sub-Saharan Africa; this is true, for example, for age at first childbearing (Nettle, 2011a), marital behavior (Nettle, 2010), and exposure to violence (Shaw et al., 2005).

There is increasing appreciation that socioeconomic gradients are not just a matter of individual-level socioeconomic parameters. In all cities in the developed world, individuals with similar socioeconomic characteristics tend to be spatially assorted. Moreover, the aggregate socioeconomic characteristics of neighbors have effects on people's behavioral and health outcomes beyond the effects of their personal characteristics. In epidemiology, these are called *ecological, area,* or *neighborhood* effects (Sampson, Morenoff, & Gannon-Rowley, 2002). The consequence of the combination of spatial assortment and neighborhood effects is that behavior in contemporary Western cities has a definite geographical dimension. We are all familiar with the experience of walking in an unfamiliar city and becoming aware after a few blocks that something has changed: Suddenly, people are doing different kinds of things, as evident both from the direct observation of their behavior and the inferences one can draw from the physical state of the environment. Such subtle differences are evocative and exert powerful and immediate influences on people's social decision making (Keizer, Lindenberg, & Steg, 2008; O'Brien & Wilson, 2011).

We have been studying social gradients in behavior in England for some time.[1] As is typical of many studies in this field, we had made use of various large, representative cohorts of people who had been (often repeatedly) surveyed using mainly self-report instruments to gain some insight into their behaviors (e.g., Nettle, 2008; Nettle, Coall, & Dickins, 2011). Some of these studies had an explicit geographical dimension. For example, one study used the level of socioeconomic deprivation of the census neighborhood in which the respondent resided as a predictor variable for age at motherhood, paternal and grandmaternal behavior, breast-feeding, and interaction with infants, finding striking socioeconomic gradients in most cases (Nettle, 2010). However, when we decided to address social gradients in social behavior in particular, we began to be concerned about sole reliance on large-scale survey studies.

Certain obvious methodological criticisms can be made. Surveys rely on formal invitation and voluntary participation, and the rate of volunteering is generally much lower in deprived than affluent areas. Thus, whereas in affluent areas we may document a nearly complete spectrum of the population, in deprived areas we may document only a volunteer-minded minority whom

---

[1]For simplicity, we use the first-person plural pronoun throughout this chapter, although some of the work we describe was carried out by Nettle prior to collaborating with Colléony.

the researchers have successfully been able to contact, which itself excludes certain whole categories of people. Survey questions may also be interpreted differently by different groups of people. In particular, people answer many self-report scale items by judging themselves relative to those in the immediately surrounding population, producing averages that are remarkably similar across population groups when there could be vast differences in their actual experience. Moreover, social desirability considerations may lead people to underreport certain types of behavior and experience, a phenomenon that is likely to affect the populations of deprived areas, where more nonnormative and stigmatized behaviors are assumed to occur, more strongly than it affects the populations of affluent areas.

These points are obvious and have been made many times before, but there are other concerns that are more nebulous and harder to articulate. In essence, they come down to the following: By virtue of the availability of survey data, one could publish papers on the behavior of people in deprived communities without ever going to visit any and without any real appreciation of what actually happens there. This is important not just because direct experience hones the intuitions of the researcher, which it does, but also because conventional surveys tend to give us little insight into the psychological mechanisms leading to socioeconomic gradients in attitudes or behaviors: What is it about being there that makes one feel or want to act this way? This is a question for which one's own reactions as an observer are themselves a kind of pilot data because every child is an observer in his own community and we can only see what he sees by going where he goes.

We came to feel that there was a paucity of research in this area based on direct measurement of spontaneously occurring behavior. Our concerns about the most common methodologies, both qualitative and quantitative, had been well summed up many years earlier by the pioneer of urban observational research, William H. Whyte. Writing of the literature available to him when he began his work on behavior in the streets of U.S. cities, Whyte (1988) said:

> Some of the studies were illuminating. Taken together, however, they suffered one deficiency: the research was vicarious; it was once or twice removed from the ultimate reality being studied. That reality was people in everyday situations. That is what we studied. (p. 5)

Of course, there was plenty of precedent for observational research on naturally occurring behavior. Social psychology had had a strong tradition of this kind, which had died away dramatically (Baumeister, Vohs, & Funder, 2007), and there were relevant traditions in anthropology and human ethology, but they were seldom invoked in British social research.

Whyte had, 40 years ago, applied to the National Geographic Society for a research grant to observe people on the streets of New York City, arguing that they had supported observational studies of "far-off peoples" but never the systematic observation of behavior closer to home. With rather a similar feeling in mind, we embarked on the Tyneside Neighborhoods Project.

The goal of the project is to map the psychological geography of this one remarkable English city, with a special focus on social behaviors. It was inspired to some degree by an established neighborhood project in Binghamton, New York (Wilson, O'Brien, & Sesma, 2009). However, the Tyneside version was to be distinguished by using multiple methodologies, with a particular emphasis placed on the direct observation of naturally occurring behavior. The goal was not just to describe differences in outlook between denizens of different neighborhoods but also to try to elucidate the psychological mechanisms by which any such differences arose. By the end of 2011, the Tyneside Neighborhoods Project had amassed a large amount of data of various kinds.

This chapter presents key aspects of those data, focusing on social behavior. Some of the data have been published elsewhere, in articles on particular topics (Nettle, 2011b, 2012; Nettle & Cockerill, 2010; Nettle, Colléony, & Cockerill, 2011), but several of the analyses presented here are new; the data from different sources have not previously been brought together in one place, and we present here a broader overview with a fuller discussion of the possible meaning of the patterns we observed.

STUDY CONTEXT

Tyneside (the collective name for the towns and cities that line the River Tyne) is a conurbation of around 900,000 inhabitants situated in the northeast of England. It was an early-industrializing and historically prosperous area; by the time of the English Civil War in 1642, 450,000 tons of coal had been exported annually from the Tyne, making London economically dependent on the Tyne trade. Later growth of the area was on the basis of shipbuilding and other heavy industries. These traditional sources of employment began to decline after the World War II, a decline that became a collapse after the 1970s. Other types of economic activity, such as service industries, science, and education, have grown in their place, and parts of the city have become affluent in recent years. However, this growth has been spatially uneven, leading to the current marked disparity in economic level between neighborhoods. Tyneside contains several neighborhoods that are above the national average for affluence and, within a few miles, others that are in the poorest 1% of all English census tracts (see Nettle & Cockerill, 2010; Nettle, Colléony, & Cockerill, 2011, for more details).

Most of the Tyneside neighborhoods (outside of Newcastle city center) are architecturally similar, and indeed, many were built at similar times. The variation in affluence at the time of their development was modest; and relative neighborhood affluence in the 19th century is not a uniformly good predictor of relative affluence today (Robinson, 2005). Industrial decline hit certain neighborhoods particularly hard, especially those along the riverside to the west and east of Newcastle city center. These neighborhoods have since experienced a decades-long pattern of high unemployment, economic deprivation, and physical dilapidation, accompanied by demographic loss. The population of Newcastle's West End, for example, has declined by around one third over the last few decades (Robinson, 2005). This is an unusual situation for a modern city in a densely populated country. The West End contains many disused houses and, since recent large-scale demolitions, a considerable amount of land that is simply empty. Despite a number of regeneration initiatives, indicators relating to employment, health, crime, teenage pregnancy, and other factors remain strikingly poorer than in other neighborhoods.

The simplest technique for mapping Tyneside neighborhoods is to use the *index of multiple deprivation* (IMD). This is a government-created measure at the neighborhood level (available either for the census tract, representing about 1,500 people, or the electoral ward, representing about 10,000) that amalgamates the level of socioeconomic deprivation along several dimensions into a single arbitrary index. Low values represent low levels of deprivation, with the most affluent neighborhoods in England scoring close to zero, and higher values represent higher deprivation, with the most deprived areas scoring 50 or more.

PRELIMINARY SELF-REPORT SURVEY

In a first attempt to take a snapshot of the psychological geography of the city, we (with the assistance of Maria Cockerill) surveyed the social attitudes of over one thousand young people (ages 9–14) from eight different large Tyneside neighborhoods representing the full spectrum of IMD (for a full account of methods, see Nettle & Cockerill, 2010). We found significant neighborhood differences in many variables. As IMD increased, liking for the neighborhood, trust in others, and positiveness about one's personal future all decreased (see Figure 15.1). The effect of neighborhood IMD was in each case significant by multilevel regression. Some of the effects, particularly those involving social trust, get stronger with age: For children of 9 to 11 years, there was only a slight gradient in social trust. By 13 to 15 years, social trust was just as high as at the younger ages in the most affluent neighborhoods, whereas in the more deprived neighborhoods, it dramatically collapsed (see Figure 15.2). Thus, the self-report evidence suggested that there are substantial differences

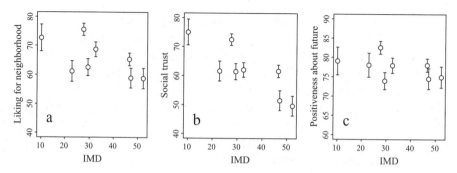

Figure 15.1. Results from a survey of 1,046 young people (ages 9–15 years) in eight large Tyneside neighborhoods. By Index of Multiple Deprivation (IMD) of the neighborhood are plotted (a) mean liking for the neighborhood, (b) mean trust in others in general, and (c) mean positiveness about one's personal future. Age group and sex are controlled for, and bars represent +/- one standard error. The relationship with IMD is significant by multilevel regression in each case.

in people's experience of daily life according to the level of deprivation of the neighborhood in which they live. With these findings in mind, we planned our first observational study.

OBSERVATIONAL STUDIES

Direct observational research is time intensive, and so for feasibility we decided to focus initially on just two neighborhoods at contrasting ends of the local IMD spectrum. Following extensive preliminary research, we alighted

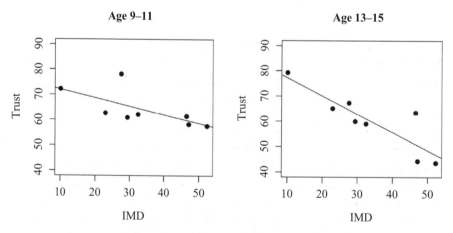

Figure 15.2. Neighborhood mean social trust by Index of Multiple Deprivation, for 9- to 11-year-olds only ($n = 409$) and 13- to 15-year-olds only ($n = 246$). IMD = Index of Multiple Deprivation.

on two neighborhoods (henceforth, A and B) that were remarkably similar in terms of layout (main shopping street and perpendicular residential streets), density (low-rise housing with park), distance from the city center (about three miles), population size (3,098 vs. 3,223 at last census), age structure (median age 37.0 vs. 34.5), and ethnic composition (92% of residents born in the United Kingdom for both neighborhoods). However, on the IMD, Neighborhood A, with a score of 8.74, is one of the more affluent nationally and the most affluent in Tyneside, whereas Neighborhood B scored 76.43, putting it in the handful of most deprived neighborhoods in the whole country. The two neighborhoods are only around four miles apart.

Methods

We spent considerable time in each neighborhood just walking and watching. This may appear uncontrolled, even aimless, but simple observation is an essential stage in good behavioral research. With practice, Nettle found that by wearing a digital voice recorder and using a system of numerical codes, he could easily record, for every social group passed, the number of men, women, children (taken to be 16 or younger, sexes not distinguished), and babes-in-arms and which of them, if any, were crying, smoking, drinking alcohol, dropping litter on the ground, or running. In addition, it was possible to note all instances of police patrols passing (in cars or on foot) and front doors being open. The voice record could then be transcribed to a database on return from the field.

To achieve meaningful comparison, it was essential to match observations between the two neighborhoods in terms of time of day, day of the week, and ideally, weather. To do this, we constructed a sampling grid whereby, over a 3-month period, every minute of 1 composite day (9 a.m.–9 p.m.) would be sampled in both neighborhoods. We divided the day into 24 half-hour slots, which were completed in random order but with the time slot completed in the second neighborhood as soon as possible after it had been completed in the first (median delay 1 day, maximum 4 days). The order of sampling of the two neighborhoods for a given time slot was randomized, and there were no neighborhood differences in the frequencies of sampling on the different weekdays. Temperature and weather were recorded and did not differ overall between the two neighborhoods.

In each time slot, we spent the first 10 minutes completing a transect of the main shopping street. For the remaining 20 minutes, we followed a pseudorandom, variable route around the residential streets. We observed only persons who were in the street or in yard areas visible to the street. Thus, in accordance with ethical norms for observational research, behavior was only recorded in settings where people would reasonably believe their behavior to be publicly visible anyway. These were generally busy city streets, and the observation and recording elicited no comments or reactions. This data set yielded observations of 12,641 individuals in 7,896 social groups. Although we have used parts of it elsewhere to test specific predictions (Nettle, 2011b, 2012), here we present it more descriptively, simply as a slice of social life in the two locations.

Results

Use of the Streets

Figure 15.3 shows the total number of adults and children observed in each time slice for the main streets and residential streets. The main streets were used in similar ways in the two neighborhoods. Use of the residential streets, however, differed by neighborhood. In Neighborhood B, there were more adults on the residential streets overall (rate ratio [RR] = 1.31, $\chi^2 = 60.16$, $p < .05$), and this was particularly true after 6:30 p.m. (RR = 1.46, $\chi^2 = 27.46$, $p < .05$). Adults in Neighborhood A came home in the afternoon and went inside

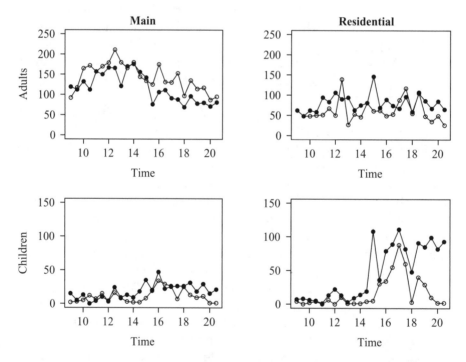

Figure 15.3. Numbers of adults and children observed. Adults and children in the residential streets of the two neighborhoods described in the text observed for 30-minute time slots through the day. Open circles represent Neighborhood A and filled circles Neighborhood B.

their houses. By contrast, Neighborhood B adults lingered on the streets, often socializing. This picture was reinforced by the prevalence of "street drinking," consumption of alcohol in street groups, which was common in Neighborhood B (38 observations), usually occurring in sizable social groups (M = 2.66 adults), and almost unobserved in Neighborhood A (one observation). Similarly, front doors were much more likely to be open in Neighborhood B (275 occurrences) than Neighborhood A (61 occurrences; RR = 4.51, χ^2 = 136.30, $p < .05$).

Thus, the immediate impression was that life is more social and extends into the spaces between houses more in Neighborhood B, and the use of the streets by the children amply confirmed this view. In Neighborhood A, children came home and went inside, whereas in Neighborhood B, they left school at the end of the compulsory school day and could be seen in numbers on the streets until the end of recording at 9 p.m. (children on the streets after 5 p.m., Neighborhood A: 327, Neighborhood B: 882, RR = 2.70, χ^2 = 254.78, $p < .05$).

Social Groups

Social groups differed in size between the two neighborhoods (means: A, 1.43; B, 1.79; Mann-Whitney $U = 9.07*10^6$, $p < .05$). This remains true when adult-only groups are considered (means: A, 1.29; B, 1.49, Mann-Whitney $U = 6.28*10^6$, $p < .05$). Closer inspection of the data showed that the effect is driven entirely by adults in Neighborhood B being significantly less likely to be alone (i.e., to be the sole adult of the group). In Neighborhood A, 80.7% of adult groups were just one adult versus 70.4% in neighborhood B (χ^2 = 106.11, $p < .05$). This finding cannot be driven by fewer adults in Neighborhood B residing alone; in fact, the census tells us that the opposite is true: Many more adults resided alone in Neighborhood B than Neighborhood A, and the proportion of households with children that were headed by a sole adult approached half in Neighborhood B. Thus, despite more often living on their own, the adults of Neighborhood B more often frequented the streets with others, others who must in many cases have come from different households.

The greater sociality in Neighborhood B is confirmed by examining the composition of social groups containing adults and children. Children were more likely to be on the street with no adults in Neighborhood B (see Figure 15.4a; 35.6% of groups of children in Neighborhood B vs. 25.4% in neighborhood A; χ^2 = 18.24, $p < 0.05$), but when they were with adults, they were with more adults: M = 1.58 (SD = 0.91) versus M = 1.27 (SD = 0.67, Mann-Whitney $U = 54706$, $p < .05$). This was driven by a relative paucity of children with just a lone female and a relative excess of children accompanied by multiple adult females or by some combination of more than two adults (see Figure 15.4b). Thus, even in their child care, the adults of Neighborhood B took a more social approach than those in Neighborhood A, with women teaming up with other women to go about their lives.

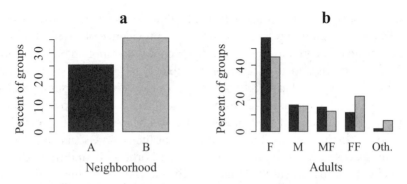

Figure 15.4. (a) Proportion of groups of children unaccompanied by any adult for the two neighborhoods; (b) the adults present in groups containing adults and children. Dark bars represent Neighborhood A and light bars Neighborhood B. M = males; F = females.

Antisocial Behavior and Policing

We have seen that the denizens of Neighborhood B spent more time in their streets than those of Neighborhood A and did more socializing in them. One might imagine this would mean that they would be more inclined to take care of them. Spending more time using a space might lead to greater personal identification with it. More social partners on the streets means more informal enforcement of social norms and thus might reduce the need for formal police enforcement of prosocial behavior in these spaces. To assess this, we recorded all instances of (a) antisocial behavior (people breaking, burning, or placing graffiti on public structures), (b) people dropping litter on the street, and (c) police patrols passing.

There were only six instances of antisocial behavior. Although these broke down as one in Neighborhood A and five in Neighborhood B, the number is too small for statistical analysis. Littering was much more frequent in Neighborhood B than A (25 vs. four observations, or one every 29 minutes vs. one every 180 minutes; Fisher's exact test, $p = .005$). For police patrols, we observed four in Neighborhood A and 23 in Neighborhood B, or one every 180 minutes versus one every 31 minutes (Fisher's exact test, $p = .009$). Thus, despite people spending more social time in the streets, being less likely to be alone, and the residential streets often being busier, there was more antisocial behavior and less care taken of the public space in Neighborhood B than was true of A and, relatedly, much greater need for formal police enforcement. This was borne out by an analysis of local crime data, which revealed the crime rate of Neighborhood B to be around twice that of Neighborhood A (Nettle, Colléony, & Cockerill, 2011).

Summary

Direct observation of public behavior showed that the form of social life differed significantly between these two neighborhoods of the same city. The differences spanned use of the public space, group size and composition, drinking, littering, and many other parameters not discussed here, such as crying by children, physical activity, and smoking (Nettle, 2011b, 2012). The neighborhood differences are, however, somewhat contradictory. Neighborhood B featured greater public socializing, more open doors, and less likelihood of adults being on their own, which seems to imply that there must be more social ties that cross households. This implies, in essence, stronger social cohesion in Neighborhood B, a characterization that has often been given to communities of low socioeconomic position (Piff, Kraus, Cote, Cheng, & Keltner, 2010). However, the analysis of littering and policing suggests that the strength of cohesion may be lower in Neighborhood B than in A. Moreover, our self-report data suggested that social trust, an index of social cohesion if there ever was one, was low in deprived areas of Tyneside. Thus, in the next stage of the research, we decided to use additional behavioral assays to investigate social cohesion and connectedness in Neighborhoods A and B.

ALTERNATIVE ASSAYS OF BEHAVIOR

The next series of studies used alternative methodologies to elicit information about people's social relationships and motivations in the two neighborhoods. These studies have been reported in more detail elsewhere (Nettle, Colléony, & Cockerill, 2011), but key results are summarized here. The following sections describe a survey of personal social networks completed by a sample of residents and a version of the Dictator Game played by the same individuals. The subsequent section describes a series of additional field experiments looking at help given to strangers.

Social Networks

Methods

We used electoral lists and wrote to residents of both neighborhoods, inviting them to respond to a survey concerning their social networks. The survey repeated our question about social trust of people in the neighborhood (*trust*) and in addition asked respondents to rate the extent to which they knew their neighbors (*know neighbors*) and had good friends locally (*friends locally*). We also asked people to list all those individuals they had contacted in the past 2 weeks for social reasons and all those individuals they could turn to if there was a problem. We counted the responses to arrive at the *social contacts* and *social support* variables, respectively.

The greater street sociality, the reduced likelihood of being alone in Neighborhood B, the street drinking, and the open front doors, would all lead us to predict greater knowledge of neighbors and more social contacts and friends locally in Neighborhood B than Neighborhood A, though our previous self-report data suggested that social trust might not necessarily go in the same direction.

Results

We received 124 responses to the survey (74 from Neighborhood A, constituting a return rate of 43.5%, 50 from Neighborhood B, a significantly lower return rate of 21.7%). All of the variables of interest here, namely, trust, know neighbors, friends locally, social contacts, and social support, were significantly correlated with one another (r's 0.3–0.7) and unrelated to time spent living in the neighborhood. All five produced significant neighborhood differences and all in the same direction (see Figure 15.5; Cohen's d ranges from 0.36–1.80, so the effects are from medium to large by conventional criteria). Thus, contrary to some indications from the observational data, people

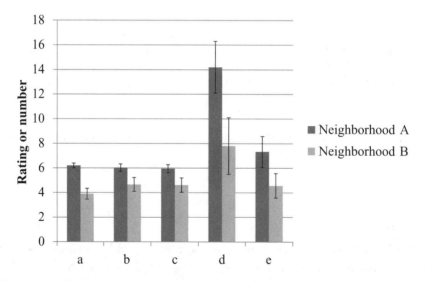

Figure 15.5. Self-reported survey responses. a = social trust; b = knowledge of neighbors; c = feeling of having friends locally; d = number of social contacts; e = number of people to whom one could turn across the two neighborhoods. Items (a) to (c) are on a 7-point Likert scale, whereas (d) and (e) are actual numbers. Bars represent means and error bars 95% confidence intervals. All neighborhood differences are significant according to t-tests.

living in Neighborhood B (compared with those living in A) felt socially isolated, had relatively few people they contacted socially or felt they could turn to, and perceived that they did not know their neighbors.

Dictator Game

Methods

In recent years, experimental economic games have become popular as assays for studying social motivations. These are standardized artificial scenarios in which the respondent has to propose or respond to a division of a sum of money between him- or herself and an unknown stranger. The simplest of these is the Dictator Game (DG), in which participants decide unilaterally how much of a pot of money they will keep and how much they will leave to another unseen player (Forsythe, Horowitz, Savin, & Sefton, 1994).

There are differences between populations in DG play (Henrich et al., 2005); moreover, DG offers are sensitive to such factors as social observation or interaction between players, suggesting it is a sensitive assay of motivation to invest socially in others (Haley & Fessler, 2005). We implemented a simple version of the DG attached to our social network survey described earlier. The respondent was offered £10 as a thank you for their participation, to be delivered in cash to their houses. However, the payment form asked them to indicate how much they would like to receive personally and how much they would like us to deliver to someone else. There were three between-subjects conditions. In the *unknown recipient* condition, the money would be delivered to another address in the neighborhood randomly chosen by us (and not known to the respondent). In the *friend* condition, the respondent gave us the name and address of a friend to deliver the balance to. Moreover, in this condition, the amount passed to the friend would be doubled. Finally, in the *charity* condition, the balance would be delivered to a well-known city charity and again doubled.

One obvious problem with the DG method is that a few pounds might have different values for the residents of the two neighborhoods, leading to different decisions for reasons that are not interesting. Set against this, researchers have examined the impact of changing the absolute size of the monetary stake in DGs and have found that it makes no discernible difference, even up to quite large sums of money (Carpenter, Verhoogen, & Burks, 2005; Forsythe et al., 1994). This suggests that the dilemma taps into some kind of social cognition or norm that is not strongly sensitive to the magnitude of the financial gain. Moreover, by doubling any amount shared in the friend condition, we created a potential financial incentive to share. A respondent could name a nearby friend and transfer the whole £10 to him or her. The friend would then receive £20. If this were shared equally between respondent and friend, the recipient would have earned the friend £10 at absolutely no cost to him- or herself. Indeed, if it were shared £15/£5 between respondent and friend, both would be better off than under any other scenario, and only the experimenter would have lost out. Thus, collective action actually became more attractive in the friend condition because the value to the participant of a few extra pounds increased, as long as he or she had a good friend nearby who he or she could trust to take collective action. Thus, we expected that the respondents in Neighborhood B might donate less in the unknown recipient and charity conditions but more in the friend condition, compared with respondents from Neighborhood A.

Results

There were significant effects of condition on DG allocation to other, $F(2,112) = 7.86, p < .05, \eta^2 = 0.12$, due to generosity being significantly higher in the charity condition than in unknown recipient (Tukey test, mean difference 3.11, $p < .05$) or friend (Tukey test, mean difference 3.30, $p < .05$) conditions, though unknown recipient and friend did not differ from one another (Tukey test, mean difference 0.19, *ns*). There was also a significant neighborhood effect, $F(1,112) = 31.58, p < .05, \eta^2 = 0.22$ (see Figure 15.6).

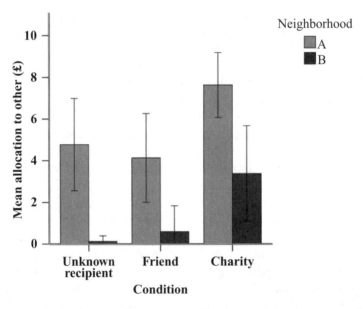

Figure 15.6. Mean allocation of money in the dictator game. Mean allocation to the other party (from a possible £10) in a Dictator Game played from home, where the recipient is unknown, a nominated friend, or a local charity and by which neighborhood the respondent resides. Error bars represent 95% confidence intervals.

The Condition × Neighborhood interaction was not significant, $F(2,112) = 0.19$, ns. The mean allocation across all conditions was £5.55 ($SD = £4.74$) in Neighborhood A and £1.35 ($SD = £3.15$) in Neighborhood B. This is a large difference; in fact, it is a larger difference than the largest difference observed in a recent cross-cultural study that compared 15 populations as diverse as U.S. citizens and African hunter-gatherers (Henrich, 2006). Thus, respondents from Neighborhood B transferred much less money to others across all three conditions than respondents from Neighborhood A. There was no hint at all of the possibly expected Condition × Neighborhood interaction; even when taking collective action with a friend could lead to financial advantage for both parties, residents of Neighborhood B were unlikely to want to initiate it.

Field Experiments

Methods

Finally, we drew on a long-standing tradition from the social psychology of prosocial behavior (Levine, Martinez, Brase, & Sorenson, 1994; Pearce & Amato, 1980) to compare helpfulness toward strangers in the two locations. Our assays included the *lost letter* (Merritt & Fowler, 1948; Milgram, Mann, & Harter, 1965), where stamped, addressed envelopes are left on the street, and the outcome variable is the number mailed in by persons unknown. We dropped 22 letters in each neighborhood over 3 months, matching the distances from a mailbox across the two neighborhoods. We also used a *dropped object* paradigm (Levine et al., 1994), wherein research assistants (24 different ones but balanced across neighborhoods) walked in the street and dropped a small personal item (e.g., keys, glove, pen) at 10 meters from an oncoming lone pedestrian, seeming not to notice. The target was classed as helping if he or she picked up the object or drew the research assistant's attention to it. Sixty objects were dropped in each neighborhood in total. Using the same research assistants, we tried *asking for directions*, where we approached a lone pedestrian and asked for directions to a nearby hospital. People were classified as helping if they gave detailed instructions on how to get there. There were 30 trials in each neighborhood. Finally, we asked people to *make change*: The same research assistants approached a different pedestrian and asked for help to make change from a 50p or 20p coin. People were classed as helping if they checked in their wallets or pockets. There were again 30 trials in each neighborhood.

Results

Of the four field experiments reported here, only the lost letter showed a significant neighborhood difference (see Figure 15.7). The difference for lost

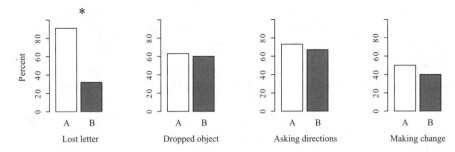

Figure 15.7. Results of field experiments in Neighborhoods A and B. The figure shows percentage of lost letters returned, proportion of people dropping an object who are helped, proportion of people asking directions who receive help, and proportion of people trying to make change who are helped. * = significant difference using Fisher's Exact Test.

letters was large, with 20 of 22 letters returned from Neighborhood A and seven of 22 from Neighborhood B (Fisher's exact test, $p = .0001$). For the other three experiments, though, behavior was remarkably similar in the two neighborhoods, with people in both places being scored as helpful about half the time.

Summary

The additional assays of social behavior again revealed a host of neighborhood differences, which again contained many results that apparently contradicted each other and also contradicted aspects of the direct behavioral observations. People in Neighborhood B were less inclined to feel that they had friends in the neighborhood, and when asked through the DG to make a social investment in someone else living nearby, were much less inclined to do so, even if it was a friend they had named. They felt they could trust others in the nearby area much less than those in Neighborhood A did. Yet we know from this work that people in Neighborhood B are less likely to be alone on the streets, do more public socializing, and have their front doors open more often. They were also much less likely to help a stranger by mailing in a letter but just as likely to help a stranger who accosted them face-to-face. In the next section of this chapter, we return to what sense we can make of these confusing observations.

DISCUSSION

Perhaps the first and most striking generalization to arise from the Tyneside Neighborhoods Project so far is simply that neighborhood matters: Using a series of assays briefly described here, we found that people's social behavior differs significantly between neighborhoods of the same city far more often than it does not differ, even though the city is architecturally and ethnically fairly homogenous. The differences are so large that were Neighborhoods A and B two exotic ethnic groups, we would doubtless take the data as evidence of a cultural difference in social system. As already mentioned, the difference in DG play between these two neighborhoods is as large as any cross-cultural difference that has ever been reported.

Intracultural diversity is an important and underappreciated phenomenon. How many cross-cultural researchers have sampled one site from each of several ethnic groups, observed different behavior, and reported their findings within the framework of ethnically based cultural differences? What is much more rarely done is to sample multiple sites from the same ethnic group. Doing this may reveal differences that are every bit as important (Gurven, Zanolini, & Schniter, 2008; Lamba & Mace, 2011). This speaks to the great importance of fine-grained local ecological, spatial, and demographic factors in influencing social behavior. It also reminds us of the need for caution in generalizing about social behavior from the samples of university students who constitute the majority of research participants in contemporary social psychology (Peterson, 2001).

As for the content of the neighborhood differences, the results suggest that no unidimensional categorization, such as people in deprived neighborhoods being more social overall than those in affluent neighborhoods, will be possible. A more defensible generalization would be that social attachments in the affluent neighborhood are in some sense thin but secure. The *thin* part draws on established sociological terminology (e.g., Lancee, 2010) to refer to ties with diverse others that may not necessarily involve extensive time together or physical adjacency. The *secure* part is a nod to attachment theory (Hazan & Shaver, 1987) and describes relationships in which each party is comfortable becoming vulnerable to the other's potential future behavior. Thus, individuals in Neighborhood A, though actually spending more public time alone, reported that they trusted others more, had more others they could turn to, and were happy to make social investments in others in the DG, whether they knew them or not.

The sociality of Neighborhood B, by contrast, might be described as thick but insecure. People's front doors were open, they spent more of their day with others, and they were more likely to socialize in the public space immediately surrounding their houses. However, they reported profound concern about the future behavior of others, as indexed by low trust and a perception of low social support, and were extremely unwilling to open up a social investment, whether with someone they know or not, in the DG. However, when they were accosted by a research assistant and thus had no choice as to whether to engage in a social interaction, they were just as helpful as the residents of Neighborhood A.

These differences in sociality can be broadly interpreted in behavioral–ecological terms. In Neighborhood A, people had sufficient resources to draw on that they could buffer any small loss arising from the behavior of others. Moreover, they were sufficiently materially secure that they could afford to take a long-term perspective in decisions about adherence to social expectations. This made them reliable interaction partners who, by not needing each other, can, paradoxically, interact without anxiety. In Neighborhood B, by contrast, many people were at the margin of economic survival, and their immediate futures were profoundly uncertain. This had the effect, on the one hand, of meaning that they may have relied more heavily on their social affiliations to provide informal services that they could not afford to obtain through the formal market (child care is an obvious example). On the other hand, it may mean that the others on whom they depended heavily were sufficiently close to the threshold of impulsive desperation that their future behavior was quite unpredictable. This makes for social relationships that are intensive but anxiety provoking; the relatively high rates of interpersonal violence in Neighborhood B (5.67 times the rate in Neighborhood A; see Nettle, Colléony, & Cockerill, 2011) speak to this. Interestingly, recent research has shown that people coming from deprived communities may show increased empathic accuracy (Kraus, Côté, & Keltner, 2010) and increased detection of angry faces in particular (Gianaros et al., 2008). This may reflect social behavior being more unpredictable in their lives and correctly reading social interactions as more critical to their well-being.

Having demonstrated these differences between neighborhoods, our research is now turning toward understanding the mechanisms producing social behavior. There is the issue of selection versus causation. Does living in Neighborhood B cause people to behave a certain way, or is it that people with certain dispositions end up living there (or failing to leave in a time of declining population)? Only longitudinal data using personality and dispositional measures are likely to answer this question.

A related issue is how trait-like the variation is. Note that even if the effects of neighborhood are due to causation rather than selection, they could still become ingrained so that people who grow up there stably show the characteristics even if they subsequently move somewhere different. Alternatively, the differences might be entirely state-like in that if the neighborhood context could be altered, people's behavior would rapidly follow suit.

A key question in adjudicating this issue is whether people moving into or leaving Neighborhood B rapidly adopt the attitudes and behaviors of the people who now surround them. There is some evidence to suggest that, surprisingly, this kind of change can occur almost instantaneously. The urban environment is dense in cues to the social state and behavior of the people in it (Keizer et al., 2008; O'Brien & Wilson, 2011), and thus, locally appropriate social attitudes and cognitive strategies may appear almost immediately in response to being in a neighborhood, seeing litter, seeing broken windows, and so forth. If this is the case, it would be an example of what has been termed *evoked culture*— apparent cultural differences which are in fact driven by universal psychological responses to chronic environmental cues (Nettle, 2009). We hope to test these possibilities in the next phases of the Tyneside Neighborhoods Project.

REFERENCES

Baumeister, R. F., Vohs, K. D., & Funder, D. C. (2007). Psychology as the science of self-reports and finger movements: Whatever happened to actual behavior? *Perspectives on Psychological Science, 2,* 396–403. doi:10.1111/j.1745-6916.2007.00051.x

Boden, J. M., Fergusson, D. M., & Horwood, L. J. (2010). Risk factors for conduct disorder and oppositional/defiant disorder: Evidence from a New Zealand birth cohort. *Journal of the American Academy of Child & Adolescent Psychiatry, 49,* 1125–1133. doi:10.1097/00004583-201011000-00006

Carpenter, J., Verhoogen, E., & Burks, S. (2005). The effect of stakes in distribution experiments. *Economics Letters, 86,* 393–398. doi:10.1016/j.econlet.2004.08.007

Drewnowski, A., & Specter, S. E. (2004). Poverty and obesity: The role of energy density and energy costs. *The American Journal of Clinical Nutrition, 79*(1), 6–16.

Forsythe, R., Horowitz, J. L., Savin, N. E., & Sefton, M. (1994). Fairness in simple bargaining experiments. *Games and Economic Behavior, 6,* 347–369. doi:10.1006/game.1994.1021

Gianaros, P. J., Horenstein, J. A., Hariri, A. R., Sheu, L. K., Manuck, S. B., Matthews, K. A., & Cohen, S. (2008). Potential neural embedding of parental social standing. *Social Cognitive and Affective Neuroscience, 3,* 91–96. doi:10.1093/scan/nsn003

Gurven, M., Zanolini, A., & Schniter, E. (2008). Culture sometimes matters: Intracultural variation in pro-social behavior among Tsimane Amerindians. *Journal of Economic Behavior & Organization, 67,* 587–607. doi:10.1016/j.jebo.2007.09.005

Haley, K. J., & Fessler, D. M. T. (2005). Nobody's watching? Subtle cues affect generosity in an anonymous economic game. *Evolution and Human Behavior, 26,* 245–256. doi:10.1016/j.evolhumbehav.2005.01.002

Hazan, C., & Shaver, P. (1987). Romantic love conceptualized as an attachment process. *Journal of Personality and Social Psychology, 52,* 511–524. doi:10.1037/0022-3514.52.3.511

Henrich, J. (2006, April 7). Cooperation, punishment, and the evolution of human institutions. *Science, 312*(5770), 60–61. doi:10.1126/science.1126398

Henrich, J., Boyd, R., Bowles, S., Camerer, C., Fehr, E., Gintis, H., . . . Tracer, D. (2005). "Economic man" in cross-cultural perspective: Behavioral experiments in 15 small-scale societies. *Behavioral and Brain Sciences, 28*, 795–815. doi:10.1017/S0140525X05000142

Keizer, K., Lindenberg, S., & Steg, L. (2008, November 20). The spreading of disorder. *Science, 322*(5908), 1681–1685. doi:10.1126/science.1161405

Kleinschmidt, I., Hills, M., & Elliott, P. (1995). Smoking behaviour can be predicted by neighbourhood deprivation measures. *Journal of Epidemiology and Community Health, 49*, S72–S77. doi:10.1136/jech.49.Suppl_2.S72

Kraus, M. W., Côté, S., & Keltner, D. (2010). Social class, contextualism, and empathic accuracy. *Psychological Science, 21*, 1716–1723. doi:10.1177/0956797610387613

Lamba, S., & Mace, R. (2011). Demography and ecology drive variation cooperation across human populations. *Proceedings of the National Academy of Sciences of the United States of America, 108*, 14426–14430. doi:10.1073/pnas.1105186108

Lancee, B. (2010). The economic returns of immigrants' bonding and bridging social capital: The case of the Netherlands. *The International Migration Review, 44*(1), 202–226. doi:10.1111/j.1747-7379.2009.00803.x

Lawson, D. W., & Mace, R. (2009). Trade-offs in modern parenting: A longitudinal study of sibling competition for parental care. *Evolution and Human Behavior, 30*, 170–183. doi:10.1016/j.evolhumbehav.2008.12.001

Levine, R. V., Martinez, T. S., Brase, G., & Sorenson, K. (1994). Helping in 36 United States cities. *Journal of Personality and Social Psychology, 67*, 69–82. doi:10.1037/0022-3514.67.1.69

Merritt, C. B., & Fowler, R. B. (1948). The pecuniary honesty of the public at large. *The Journal of Abnormal and Social Psychology, 43*, 90–93. doi:10.1037/h0061846

Milgram, S., Mann, L., & Harter, S. (1965). The lost letter technique: A tool of social research. *Public Opinion Quarterly, 29*, 437–438. doi:10.1086/267344

Najman, J. M., Hayatbakhsh, M. R., Clavarino, A., Bor, W., O'Callaghan, M. J., & Williams, G. M. (2010). Family poverty over the early life course and recurrent adolescent and young adult anxiety and depression: A longitudinal study. *American Journal of Public Health, 100*, 1719–1723. doi:10.2105/AJPH.2009.180943

Nettle, D. (2008). Why do some dads get more involved than others? Evidence from a large British cohort. *Evolution and Human Behavior, 29*, 416–423. doi:10.1016/j.evolhumbehav.2008.06.002

Nettle, D. (2009). Beyond nature versus culture: Cultural variation as an evolved characteristic. *The Journal of the Royal Anthropological Institute, 15*, 223–240. doi:10.1111/j.1467-9655.2009.01561.x

Nettle, D. (2010). Dying young and living fast: Variation in life history across English neighborhoods. *Behavioral Ecology, 21*, 387–395. doi:10.1093/beheco/arp202

Nettle, D. (2011a). Flexibility in reproductive timing in human females: Integrating ultimate and proximate explanations. *Philosophical Transactions of the Royal Society of London: Series B. Biological Sciences, 366*, 357–365. doi:10.1098/rstb.2010.0073

Nettle, D. (2011b). Large differences in publicly visible health behaviours across two neighbourhoods of the same city. *PLoS ONE, 6*(6), e21051. doi:10.1371/journal.pone.0021051

Nettle, D. (2012). Behaviour of parents and children in two contrasting urban neighbourhoods: An observational study. *Journal of Ethology, 30,* 109–116. doi:10.1007/s10164-011-0303-z

Nettle, D., Coall, D. A., & Dickins, T. E. (2011). Early-life conditions and age at first pregnancy in British women. *Proceedings of the Royal Society: B. Biological Sciences, 278,* 1721–1727. doi:10.1098/rspb.2010.1726

Nettle, D., & Cockerill, M. (2010). Development of social variation in reproductive schedules: A study from an English urban area. *PLoS ONE, 5,* e12690. doi:10.1371/journal.pone.0012690

Nettle, D., Colléony, A., & Cockerill, M. (2011). Variation in cooperative behavior within a single city. *PLoS ONE, 6,* e26922. doi:10.1371/journal.pone.0026922

O'Brien, D. T., & Wilson, D. S. (2011). Community perception: The ability to assess the safety of unfamiliar neighborhoods and respond adaptively. *Journal of Personality and Social Psychology, 100,* 606–620. doi:10.1037/a0022803

Pampel, F. C., Krueger, P. M., & Denney, J. T. (2010). Socioeconomic disparities in health behaviors. *Annual Review of Sociology, 36,* 349–370.

Pearce, P. L., & Amato, P. R. (1980). A taxonomy of helping: A multidimensional scaling analysis. *Social Psychology Quarterly, 43,* 363–371. doi:10.2307/3033956

Peterson, R. A. (2001). On the use of college students in social science research: Insights from a second-order meta-analysis. *Journal of Consumer Research, 28,* 450–461. doi:10.1086/323732

Piff, P. K., Kraus, M. W., Cote, S., Cheng, B. H., & Keltner, D. (2010). Having less, giving more: The influence of social class on prosocial behavior. *Journal of Personality and Social Psychology, 99,* 771–784. doi:10.1037/a0020092

Robinson, F. (2005). Regenerating the West End of Newcastle: What went wrong? *Northern Economic Review, 36,* 15–42.

Sampson, R. J., Morenoff, J. D., & Gannon-Rowley, T. (2002). Assessing "neighborhood effects": Social processes and new directions in research. *Annual Review of Sociology, 28,* 443–478. doi:10.1146/annurev.soc.28.110601.141114

Schoon, I., & Cheng, H. (2011). Determinants of political trust: A lifetime learning model. *Developmental Psychology, 47,* 619–631. doi:10.1037/a0021817

Shaw, M., Tunstall, H., & Dorling, D. (2005). Increasing inequalities in risk of murder in Britain: Trends in the demographic and spatial distribution of murder, 1981–2000. *Health & Place, 11*(1), 45–54. doi:10.1016/j.healthplace.2004.01.003

Whyte, W. H. (1988). *City: Rediscovering the center.* Philadelphia: University of Pennsylvania Press.

Wilson, D. S., O'Brien, D. T., & Sesma, A. (2009). Human prosociality from an evolutionary perspective: Variation and correlations at a city-wide scale. *Evolution and Human Behavior, 30,* 190–200. doi:10.1016/j.evolhumbehav.2008.12.002

INDEX

Authoritarian governments, 64
Automaticity, of helping behavior, 243
Autonomy (in West culture cycle),
    280–282
Avery, M. L., 99
Azerbaijan, collectivism in, 25

Baker, W. E., 33
Bakersfield, California, 251
Baltimore, Maryland, 183
Bangkok, Thailand, 245, 247
Barbaranelli, C., 143
Bardi, A., 198, 208
Batson, C. D., 253
Beauty, community satisfaction and, 270
Becker, G., 267
Behavior. *See also* Helping behavior
    antisocial, 310
    and geography, 4–5, 115–116
    laws about homosexual behaviors, 147
    prosocial, 60, 62–63
Behavioral assays (Tyneside Neighbor-
    hoods Project), 311–316
Behavioral flexibility, 99
Behavioral immune system, 52–53
Behavioral Risk Factor Surveillance
    System (BRFSS), 170, 171
Behavioral syndromes, 102–104
Belonging, feelings of, 290
Between-habitat movements, 91. *See also*
    Dispersal
BFI. *See* Big Five Inventory
BHPS (British Household Panel Survey),
    75–80
Bible Belt, 208, 210
Big Cities Health Inventory, 183
Big Five Inventory (BFI), 120, 121, 144,
    146, 153. *See also specific facets*
Big Five personality traits, 116–117.
    See also specific traits
    in British Household Panel Survey, 76
    conservatism and, 142–155
    dimensions of, 142
    geographic clustering of, 268
    and happiness in mobile states,
        231–233
    measures of, 146, 153
    and Midwest culture cycle, 286
    and migration behavior, 77–79

in nonhuman animals, 105
and Northeast culture cycle, 283–284
and pathogen prevalence, 57–60
and reasons for moving, 80, 81
regional patterns in, 278
statewide differences in, 120–129
theory of geographic variation in, 144
Binding moral values, 63–64
Binghamton, New York, 304
Biotic niche construction, 27
Biro, P. A., 98
Black industrial northern cities, culture
    cycle of, 292–293
Blind person measure, 246
Boccaccio, Giovanni, 264
Bohemian index, 123
Boldness. *See* Shyness–boldness (in
    nonhuman animals)
Bontempo, R., 280
Boomsma, D. I., 84
Boston, Massachusetts, 282, 283
    character strengths in, 187
    helping behavior in, 251
    suicide rate in, 183
Boston Globe, 283
Botswana, Extraversion in, 51
Bottom-up perspective, on personality
    and social indicators, 130–131
Bowler, D. E., 93, 95
Brase, G., 249–251, 315
Brazil
    helping behavior in, 245, 247, 248
    residential mobility in, 236
Breakwell, G. M., 153
Brett, J. M., 221
BRFSS (Behavioral Risk Factor Surveil-
    lance System), 170, 171
The Bridges of Madison County (Waller),
    285
British Household Panel Survey
    (BHPS), 75–80
Brunelleschi, Filippo, 264
Bucharest, Romania, 245, 247
Budapest, Hungary, 245, 247
Buffalo, New York, 251
Bulgaria
    collectivism in, 25
    Extraversion in, 51
    helping behavior in, 245, 247
    intergroup helping in, 254–255

Bureau of Labor Statistics, 123
Bush, George W., 122
Buss, D. M., 55
Butler, J. C., 143

Calcutta, India, 245, 247
California
    character strengths in, 187
    culture cycle in, 281, 282
    helping behavior in, 251
    individualism in, 46, 47
Calogero, R. M., 198
Campbell W. K., 198
Canada, personal concerns in, 200
Canton, Ohio, 251
Capital, social, 119, 122, 127, 128
Cárcaba, A., 182–183
Carnegie, Andrew, 267
Carney, D. R., 140, 143
Cayton, Andrew, 285
CBS News, 146
Centers for Disease Control and Preven-
    tion (CDC), 121, 163, 170
Central America, 118. *See also specific*
    cities and countries
Central Appalachia, 294
Central region, personality traits in,
    124
Change measure, 249, 315–316
Character strengths, 185–189, 268
Charles-Sire, V., 243
Chattanooga, Tennessee, 251
Chicago, Illinois
    helping behavior in, 251
    residential mobility in, 224–225
Chicago Cubs, 224–225
Children
    likelihood of having, 83
    residential mobility and well-being
        of, 226–228
    residential moves by, 221
    in social groups, 309, 310
    use of streets by, 308, 309
China
    climato–economic covariation of
        collectivism in, 26
    helping behavior in, 245, 247
    residential mobility in, 236
Chinese Exclusion Act, 291
Chung, C. K., 199, 200

Cities. *See also* Psychology of cities
    creativity in, 263–266
    happiness in, 269–271
    helping behavior in, 244–253
    quality-of-life differences in, 182–183
    socioeconomic gradients in, 301–302
    tolerance, Openness, and diversity
        in, 267, 268
    as units of analysis, 180–181
Cities in Civilization (Hall), 264
City energy, 271–272
Civic participation, 122
Civil War, 286
Clark, T. N., 266
Class, U.S. culture cycles and, 288–295
Cleveland, Ohio, 184
Climate
    helping behavior and, 246
    precipitational, 20
    psychosocial, 153
Climate change, 98
Climatic demands
    and ingroup love/outgroup hate,
        22–26
    measuring, 19–20
Climato–economic theory of culture,
    15–27
    and collectivism, 18–27
    demands axiom, 16
    demands–resources effects in, 17–18
    needs axiom, 16
    resources axiom, 17
Cockerill, Maria, 305
Cohen, A. B., 189
Cohen, D., 43, 287, 288
Cohesion, social, 95, 173, 311
Collective good, 31–32
Collectivism
    analyzing natural language for trends
        in, 198
    climato–economic impact on, 18–27
    in culture cycles, 287, 295
    defined, 32, 33
    and individualism, 32–34
    measures of, 21–22
    and pathogen prevalence, 60–61
    and residential mobility, 234–235
Collectivists, 15, 25
College students, residential mobility of,
    220–221
Colonization, 99, 106

Culture. *See also* Climato–economic theory of culture; National culture
    defined, 34
    effect of physical environment on, 39–46
    evoked, 319
    individualism/collectivism in, 32
    mutual constitution theory of, 242, 254–257
    patterns view of, 242
    regional, 34–36, 46–47
Culture clashes, regional, 275–276, 296
Culture cycles (United States), 275–296
    Asian Pacific, 290–292
    Black industrial northern cities, 292–293
    components of, 276–278
    and culture clashes, 275–276, 296
    defined, 276
    Latino Southwest, 288–290
    Midwest, 284–286
    Northeast, 282–284
    people in, 278
    place in, 277
    products in, 277
    and race/class, 288–295
    regional, 278–288
    rural Appalachia, 293–295
    South, 286–288
    West, 280–282
Culturomics, 198
Cyprinids, migration by, 102

Dallas, Texas, 251
Daly, M. C., 183, 184
Dante Alighieri, 264
Danziger, K., 179–180
Darley, J. M., 243, 253
Data Archive, 147
Dave Leip's Atlas of U.S. Presidential Elections, 122
Da Vinci, Leonardo, 264
Death penalty, 147, 154
Death Penalty Information Center, 147
Death rate, 148, 166, 174
Death sentences, number of, 147
Decision making, about moving, 270
Declaration of Independence, 282
Decomposable effects, psychological investigation of, 180

Deductive approaches to assessing personal concerns, 198–199
Deep South (U.S. region)
    culture cycle of, 288
    personal concerns in, 208
    personality traits in, 124
Deferred Action for Childhood Arrivals, 290
De Groot, C., 83
Demands (in climato–economic theory of culture), 17–18
Demands axiom, 16
Democracy, 37
Democratic voting preference, 144–145
Demographic factors
    and conservatism, 150, 151
    in subjective well-being, 166, 173–174
Demographic Yearbook (United Nations), 246
Deportation, fear of, 290
Depression (BFI facet)
    discriminant correlations for, 124
    geographic distribution of, 124, 126
    social indicators correlated with, 127, 128
    social influence on, 129
Depressive symptoms, residential mobility and, 73
Desire to move (migration stage), 71. *See also* Migration desires
Detroit, Michigan, 292
    happiness rating for, 184, 229
    helping behavior in, 251
    mobile communities in, 229
Devereux, J. D., 153
Dictator Game (DG), 313–315
Dictatorship, 38
Differential migration, 102
Dingemanse, N. J., 94
Direct measurement of socioeconomic gradients, 303
Disclosure crisis, 292–293
Discriminant validity, of state-level BFI analysis, 123–124
Discrimination, 290–293
Disease. *See also* Pathogen prevalence
    parasitic disease burden, 21–23, 25
    and physical attractiveness in mate selection, 54–55

Dispersal, 91, 93–97
  by humans vs. nonhuman animals, 105
  and pace of life, 103
  and sociability, 105
Dispositional Openness, 59
Ditlmann, R., 290
Diversity, creativity and, 267
Dopamine D4 receptor, 105
Dovidio, J. F., 290
"Dreadful Memories" (Gunning), 294
Dropped object measure, 246, 315, 316
Durkheim, Emile, 183, 236

East Asia. *See also specific cities and
    countries*
  cultural differences in products of, 277
  quality of life in, 182
East Coast region, personal concerns
    in, 208
Easterlin paradox, 269
Eastern Europe. *See also specific cities and
    countries*
  personality traits in, 118
  residential mobility in, 84
East Lansing, Michigan, 251
Eberhard, J. R., 99
Ecological effects
  on behavioral syndromes, 104
  on personality, 129–130
  of socioeconomic gradients, 302
Ecological fallacy, 190
Ecological invasion, 91, 97–99, 103
Economic conservatism
  defined, 141
  individual-level analysis of Big Five
    and, 142, 143
  measures of, 145, 148, 154
  state-level analysis of Big Five and,
    145–155
Economic conservatism composite, 148
Economic creativity, 263
Economic development, character
    strength and, 268–269
Economic factors in subjective well-
    being, 162, 166, 172–173
Economic geography, 4
Economic growth
  cities' function in, 265
  and happiness, 269
  3Ts model of, 267

The Economy of Cities (Jacobs), 265
Education level
  and happiness, 230
  and residential mobility, 231
  and subjective well-being, 173, 175
Einarsen, S., 37n3
Elovainio, M., 73, 220
El Paso, Texas, 187
Emergent markets, residential mobility
    in, 236
Emotions (as personal concern)
  regional variations in, 208
  social indicators and, 205
  state-level variations in, 205, 209–210
  words associated with, 203
Empathic accuracy, 318
Energy, in cities, 271–272
England. *see* United Kingdom
Entrepreneurship, 188
Environmental factors. *See also* Physical
    environment
  in dispersal, 95
  in helping behavior, 244
  and personality traits, 115
Environmental psychology, 4–5
Epic of Gilgamesh, 263
Erikson, R. S., 146, 147, 154
Essentializing, 256–257
Establishment (in Northeast culture
    cycle), 282–284
Ethnocentrism, 60, 63
Europe, 118. *See also specific cities and
    countries*
European Americans, 226–227, 277
Eusocial (term), 104
Evangelical Protestantism, 147
Evoked culture, 319
Expectation to move (migration stage),
    71
  and Conscientiousness, 82
  and personality, 76–77
  realization of, 78–79
  and residential mobility, 74–75
Experience (in Northeast culture cycle),
    282, 283
Explicit expressions of individualism,
    33–34
Exploration tendency
  defined, 89–90
  and dispersal, 94, 97

Meaning extraction method (MEM), 199–211
Mehlman, P. T., 94
Mehrabian, A., 143
Mellander, C., 269, 270
MEM (meaning extraction method), 199–211
Memphis, Tennessee, 251
Mental health, happiness and, 228
Mesa, Arizona, 187
Mexican–American War, 289
Mexico
    helping behavior in, 245, 247, 248
    personal concerns in, 200
Mexico City, Mexico, 245, 247, 248
Miami, Florida
    character strengths of, 187
    residential mobility in, 224
Michel, J. B., 198
Michelangelo, 264
Mid-Atlantic region, personality traits in, 118, 124
Midlife in U.S. (MIDUS), 73, 74, 221, 226
Midwest (U.S. region)
    culture cycle of, 279, 284–286
    personal concerns in, 208
    personality traits in, 118, 124
    religiousness in, 185
Migration (human). See also Migration desires
    and life course, 85
    and pace of life, 103
    partial, 101
    selective, 73, 129
    stages of, 71–72
Migration (nonhuman animals), 91, 100–102
Migration desires, 71–85
    in British Household Panel Survey, 75–80
    and future directions for psycho-demography research, 83–85
    migration decisions vs., 80–83
    and personality traits, 72–74, 80–83
    and residential mobility, 74–75
Migration syndromes, 100, 101
Miller, C. T., 254–255
Minneapolis–St. Paul area, Minnesota, 224

Mobile communities, 220n2, 222
    conditional group identification in, 224–225
    happiness in, 228–229
    helping behavior in, 225
Mobility, residential. See Residential mobility
Mokyr, Joel, 263
Mole rats, dispersal by, 94
Mondak, J. J., 140–141, 143
Monetary resources
    and ingroup love/outgroup hate, 22–26
    measurement of, 20
Moral values, 63–64
Morling, B., 277
Morocco, collectivism in, 25
Motivation for social investment, 313–315
Mountain bluebirds, invasion by, 99
Mountainous terrain
    in frontier areas, 40–43
    and individualism/legal freedom, 44–46
Mountain region, personality traits in, 118, 124
Mountain West, culture cycle of, 280, 282
Movers (residential)
    identification of, with groups, 223
    self-concepts of, 222–223
    well-being of childhood, 226–228
Moving. See Residential mobility
Mullen, B., 198
Murray, D. R., 58
Murray, G., 72
Murrow, Edward R., 201
Music, of rural Appalachia, 294–295
Mutual constitution theory of culture, 242, 254–257

Narratives, about personal concerns, 196–197
Narrative therapy techniques, 197
Nashville, Tennessee, 251
National analyses. see Cross-national analyses
National culture
    helping behavior in, 256–257
    individualism in, 223–224

National culture, *continued*
    pathogen prevalence and changes in,
        65–66
    in personal concerns, 200
    and principle of triangulation, 36
    regional vs., 34–35, 46–47
    in residential mobility studies,
        234–235
National Geographic Society, 304
National Institute of Mental Health, 228
National Public Radio, 201
National Survey of Children's Health,
    122
Natural experiments, on residential
    mobility, 220–221
Natural language processing, 197–198
Needs axiom, 16
Neighborhood effects
    on social behavior, 316–319
    of socioeconomic gradients, 302
Neighborhood mobility, 228. *See also*
    Mobile communities
Neighborhood satisfaction, 74
Nepotism, 21
Netherlands, mobility in, 84
Nettle, D., 302, 307
Neuroticism, 117
    and conservatism, 143–145, 150–153
    and culture cycles, 283, 286
    and migration behavior, 77, 78, 80–82
    and migration probability, 78, 79, 82
    and pathogen prevalence, 59
    and personal concerns, 209
    and residential mobility, 73–74
    social indicators correlated with,
        119, 127, 128
    in United States, 118, 119, 124
    and well-being in mobile states,
        231–233
Nevada
    residential mobility in, 235
    suicide rate in, 183
New England, personality traits in, 118,
    124
New Hampshire, 33
Newness (in West culture cycle),
    280–282
New York City
    helping behavior in, 245, 247, 251
    observational studies in, 304

New York State
    helping behavior in, 245, 247, 251
    observational studies in, 304
    residential mobility in, 235
New York Times, 146
Ngram Viewer (Google books), 198
Nisbett, R. E., 287
Non-English speaking residents,
        proportion of
    and social tolerance, 123
    and subjective well-being, 174
Nonhuman animals
    behavioral immune system of, 52
    personality traits of. *See* Personality
        traits [nonhuman animal]
    spatial ecology of. *See* Spatial ecol-
        ogy [in nonhuman animals]
Nordic countries, 84, 182
Norenzayan, A., 244–248
Normalcy (in Midwest culture cycle),
    284–286
Norms, 153, 243
North Central (U.S. region)
    helping behavior in, 249, 250, 252
    personal concerns in, 208
    personality traits in, 124
Northeast (U.S. region)
    culture cycle of, 279, 282–284
    helping behavior in, 249, 250, 252
    personal concerns in, 208
    personality traits in, 118, 119, 124
Northwestern University, 285
Norway, leadership in, 37n3
Novelty seeking, 83
Nutritional flexibility, 100

Oakland, California, 187
Obama, Barack, 139, 188, 209, 290
Obedience, 62
Observational studies (Tyneside Neigh-
    borhoods Project), 306–311
Occupation, subjective well-being and,
    173
Oishi, S., 224–227, 234
Oklahoma City, Oklahoma, 187
Oldness (in Northeast culture cycle),
    282–284
Omaha, Nebraska, 187
Openness to Experience, 117, 142
    in cities, 268
    and conservatism, 143–145, 150–153

and creativity, 267
and culture cycles, 282, 286
ecological influence on, 130
and migration behavior, 77, 78, 80,
    81, 129
and pathogen prevalence, 59–60
and personal concerns, 209
and reasons for moving, 80, 81
and residential mobility, 73, 220, 221
social indicators correlated with,
    119, 127, 128
in United States, 118, 119, 124
Operation Wetback, 289
Opportunity costs, with dispersal, 96–97
Order (BFI facet)
    discriminant correlations for, 124
    geographic distribution of, 124, 125
    social indicators correlated with,
        127, 128
The Organization Man (Whyte), 226
Oswald, A. J., 163–169, 183
Outgroup hate
    and climatic demands, 22–24
    in collectivist cultures, 18–27
    measures of, 21–22
    and monetary resources, 22–24
    and parasitic disease burden, 22, 23
Outgroup members
    helping behaviors toward, 248, 254
    pathogen/disease transmission by,
        21, 60
Ozawa, Takao, 291

Pace of life
    behavioral syndrome related to,
        102–103
    and helping behavior in cities, 246,
        249–250
Pacific region, personality traits in, 118
Pacific Research Institute, 148
Page, S., 147
Palearctic passerine species, feeding
    behavior of, 100
Parasite–stress theory, 18, 21
Parasitic disease burden
    and climate, 22
    and ingroup love/outgroup hate, 22,
        23, 25
    measurement of, 21
Park, N., 268

Partial migration, 101
Pathogen prevalence, 51–66
    binding moral values and, 63–64
    conformity pressure and, 61–62
    Extraversion and, 58–59
    future research, directions for, 65–66
    geographic variation in psychology
        and, 53–64
    individualistic/collectivistic values
        and, 60–61
    Openness and, 59–60
    political ideology and, 64
    sociosexual attitudes and, 56–57
    strength of family ties and, 62–63
    xenophobia/ethnocentrism and, 63
Pathogens, behavioral immune system
    and, 52–53
Patterns view of culture, 242
Patterson, New Jersey, 251
Pennebaker, J. W., 199, 200
Pennsylvania, 251, 282
People (in U.S. culture cycles), 278
    Asian Pacific, 291–292
    Black industrial northern cities, 293
    Latino Southwest, 290
    Midwest, 286
    Northeast, 283–284
    rural Appalachia, 295
    South, 288
    West, 281–282
Peoria, Illinois, 285
Perpetual foreigners, Asian immigrants
    as, 290–292
Perry, Rick, 46
Personal concerns, 195–211
    analyzing natural language to assess,
        197–201
    deductive approaches to assessing,
        198–199
    defined, 195, 196
    future research, directions for, 211
    meaning extraction method for
        assessing, 199–201
    narratives about, 196–197
    newspaper searches in assessments
        of, 198–199
    regional and state-level differences
        in, 204–210
    and "This I Believe" project,
        201–211

Personality traits (human). *See also* Big
     Five personality traits
  conformity pressure and, 62
  and creativity, 267–269
  cross-national differences in,
       116–118
  and ecological influence, 129–130
  and migration decisions, 80–83
  and migration desires, 72–74, 80–83
  and personal concerns, 209
  regional differences in, 72–73,
       118–120, 124, 278
  and selective migration, 129
  social indicators and, 120–131
  and social influence, 129
  and subjective well-being, 169
  and well-being in mobile states,
       229–234
Personality traits (nonhuman animal)
  and behavioral syndromes, 102–104
  categories of, 89–90
  and dispersal, 93–97
  and invasion/range expansion, 97–99
  and migration, 100–102
  and spatial ecology in humans/
       animals, 104–106
  and within-habitat movements,
       92–93
Peterson, C., 268
Peterson, S. A., 143, 153
Petrarch, Francesco, 264
Philadelphia, Pennsylvania, 251
Philbrick, K., 244–248
Phoenix, Arizona, 224
Physical attractiveness, in mate
     selection, 54–55
Physical environment. *See also* Environ-
     mental factors
  and culture, 39–46
  and individualism, 39–46
Physical fitness, character strength and,
     188–189
Physical geography, in cultural psychol-
     ogy, 4
Place (in U.S. culture cycles), 277
  Asian Pacific, 290–291
  Black industrial northern cities, 292
  Latino Southwest, 288–289
  Midwest, 284, 285
  Northeast, 282–283

rural Appalachia, 293–294
  South, 286, 287
  West, 280–281
Place utility, 75
Plato, 263
Plaut, V. C., 118, 281, 283, 286
Policing, 310
Political conservatism
  individual-level analysis of Big Five
       and, 142, 143
  measures of, 122–123, 145, 146, 153
  social/economic and, 141
  state-level analysis of Big Five and,
       127–128, 144–155
Political conservatism composite, 146
Political freedom, 38–39
Political geography, 4
Political ideology
  and conservatism, 140–142
  and helping behavior, 254
  and pathogen prevalence, 64
Political orientation
  and character strength, 188
  and personal concerns, 209
  and personality traits, 119
  state and regional differences in,
       139–140
Political structures, individualism and,
     37–39
Poor neighborhoods, happiness and
     mobility in, 228–229
Population density
  and creativity, 266
  and dispersal by nonhuman animals,
       95
  in frontier areas, 42–43
  and helping behavior in cities, 250,
       252, 253
  and pace of life, 104
  and subjective well-being, 174
Population size
  and helping behavior in cities, 252
  and subjective well-being, 174
Positiveness about personal future, 305,
     306
Post, J. R., 98
Posthuma, D., 84
Potter, J., 119, 144
Poverty rate, helping behavior and,
     252, 253

Power of the situation, 241
Practices, in culture cycles, 277
Prague, Czech Republic, 245, 247
Precipitational climate, 20
Predation risk, 96, 101–102
Predators, personality and response to, 92–93
Presidential election results, 123, 146, 209
Presocial (term), 104
Primary appraisals of livability, 17–18
Priming, of helping behavior, 243
Principle of triangulation, 36–37
Productivity
    in cities, 265–266
    creative, 118
Products (in U.S. culture cycles), 277
    Asian Pacific, 291
    Black industrial northern cities, 292–293
    Latino Southwest, 289
    Midwest, 285
    Northeast, 283
    rural Appalachia, 294–295
    South, 287–288
    West, 281
Property values, 172–173
Prosocial behavior, 60, 62–63
Providence, Rhode Island, 251
Provincial differences in quality of life, 182–183
Proximal effects, 180
Psychodemography, 83–85
Psychological geography, 180
Psychology of cities, 179–190
    character strengths in United States, 185–189
    and cities as units of analysis, 180–181
    future research, directions for, 189–190
    quality of life in Spain, 182–183
    suicide rates in United States, 183–184
Psychosocial climate, 153
Public health initiatives, 65
Public policy, well-being as basis for, 169–170
Purchasing power, helping behavior and, 246, 248–250
Putnam, R. D., 122

Quality of life
    measures of, 165, 166, 168–169
    in Spain, 182–183
    and well-being, 162
Questionnaires, personal concerns on, 196–197

Race, culture cycles and, 288–295
Ramírez-Esparza, N., 200
Randall, J., 228
Range expansion, 97–99
Réale, D., 89, 102–103
Redlining, 292
Reece, Florence, 294
Regional analyses (United States)
    character strength, 185
    culture cycles, 278–288
    helping behavior in cities, 249–253
    individualism, 35–47, 224–225
    personal concerns, 204–211
    personality, 72–73, 118–120, 124, 278
    political orientation, 139–140
    subjective well-being, 169–174
Regional analyses (worldwide)
    conformity pressure, 61–62
    Extraversion, 58–59
    Openness to Experience, 59–60
    pathogen prevalence, 56
    and personality in Australia and Italy, 72–73
    and quality of life in Spain, 182–183
    subjective well-being, 170
Regional culture
    and individualism, 35–36
    national vs., 34–35, 46–47
Reliability, of state-level BFI analysis, 123–124
Religion (as personal concern)
    regional variations in, 208
    social indicators and, 205
    state-level variation in, 207, 210
    words associated with, 203
Religion, conservatism and, 154
Religious fundamentalism, 147
Religiousness, 185
Ren, X., 26
Rentfrow, P. J., 119, 120, 144, 145, 153, 155, 164–166, 172–174, 190, 268, 269, 270, 278
Republic (Plato), 263

ABOUT THE EDITOR

Peter J. Rentfrow, PhD, bounced around the United States, from Louisiana to Texas to New York to Massachusetts, and somehow landed in England, where he is currently a university senior lecturer (associate professor) in the Department of Psychology at the University of Cambridge and a Fellow of Fitzwilliam College. His research concerns Person × Environment interactions and focuses on the ways in which personality is expressed in everything from people's preferences for music to the places in which they live. Dr. Rentfrow's research on these topics has appeared in several of the most prestigious journals in psychology—including *American Psychologist*, the *Journal of Personality*, the *Journal of Personality and Social Psychology*, *Personality and Social Psychology Bulletin*, *Perspectives on Psychological Science*, and *Psychological Science*. He is committed to educating the public about psychological research and does so by giving lectures and designing online interactive psychology surveys, most recently the BBC's Big Personality Test.